■ **DEDICATED TO MURIEL COOPER** I believe that Muriel had wings. We met. I was 29, she was 38. We last laughed and planned together on the day before she was to die. I was 59, she was 68. I knew her for 30 years. ■ On my first meeting, I felt those wings as they wrapped around me like a mother hen. I was sharp-edged, arrogant, coming to the MIT Press trying to get my ideas published and she walked me through door after door that I couldn't myself navigate or open. ■ I next saw the wings as they created a wind and showed me the wind of change. She introduced me to Nicholas and the notion of dreams of finding your way through information—a different kind of navigation. ■ The next wings I saw her wear were the wings of a peace dove, as she—red eyed and passionate—struggled to get McCullins' book *Is Anyone Taking Any Notice?* published— that poignant book about the Vietnam War, and death. ■ She wore wings on her many cartographic exercises: Flying on airplane wings, flying in space, over maps, over information. Watching as the aerial perspective changed with clouds re-focusing her vision of a man-created reality. ■ The wings of triumph and aura of discovery were all around Muriel at the TED5 Conference. She worked with David Small for three days to assemble together the premiere of a presentation which she—hesitantly at first and then with noticeable joy—showed to the extraordinary audience of that Conference. It changed forever the visual paradigm of information for all who saw the presentation. As I came on the stage—holding back the tears of joy that come when you've seen something absolutely magnificent, I said "Muriel, I believe we've all had dreams of flying and here you've allowed us to make those dreams a reality as we were flying through information." ■ It was a real time display of heavenly navigation. Later, here at the Media Lab, she once again went through the presentation with Bill Mitchell and myself as bookends—the three of us talking to Nicholas' class. ■ And then, three months later, having re-titled the presentation *Flying Through Information*, she showed the video-tape to the Alliance Graphique Internationale (AGI), in Cambridge, England. Henry Steiner, who is from Hong Kong, and president of AGI, had seen it at TED, Bob Greenberg and I spoke with her of what was going to happen next and what the dreams of flying through information released in each of us. For me it was the ability to control one's personal understanding. ■ That was the day before she died. ■ I do believe Muriel has wings. They are wings that will encourage her students to be more of themselves, that will allow the people seeing her epiphianic and empowering information structure to dream of understanding. ■ She was an architect of information. ■ She now has the wings that a few get at death. ■ She'll be in the waking dreams of those who were touched by the wind from her feathers of change and discovery. *Richard Saul Wurman, September 1994*

Miguel,

Is it my imagination or could the cover information be better architected? Anyway, I have every confidence that you're the man to solve it.

Here's to a talent, a leader, and a friend.

Happy Holidays.

Matt.

I was going to write my thesis on how great it is having you on our team but this stinkin' info architect took up all the whole space →

←

Anyway—I can never thank you enough for your spirit, your ideas + the overall great work that you bring to Poppe. You are a gem among men (or is that a MAN among the hmung.) Regardless... here goes...

THANK YOU!!

—JOHN

RICHARD SAUL WURMAN

INFORMATION ARCHITECTS

PETER BRADFORD *EDITOR*

B. MARTIN PEDERSEN *AND* RICHARD SAUL WURMAN *PUBLISHERS*

GRAPHIS INC.

NEW YORK, NEW YORK USA

GRAPHIS PUBLICATIONS

GRAPHIS, THE INTERNATIONAL BI-MONTHLY JOURNAL OF VISUAL COMMUNICATION

GRAPHIS SHOPPING BAG, AN INTERNATIONAL COLLECTION OF SHOPPING BAG DESIGN

GRAPHIS MUSIC CD, AN INTERNATIONAL COLLECTION OF CD DESIGN

GRAPHIS BOOK DESIGN, AN INTERNATIONAL COLLECTION OF BOOK DESIGN

GRAPHIS DESIGN, THE INTERNATIONAL ANNUAL OF DESIGN AND ILLUSTRATION

GRAPHIS ADVERTISING, THE INTERNATIONAL ANNUAL OF ADVERTISING

GRAPHIS BROCHURES, A COMPILATION OF BROCHURE DESIGN

GRAPHIS PHOTO, THE INTERNATIONAL ANNUAL OF PHOTOGRAPHY

GRAPHIS ALTERNATIVE PHOTOGRAPHY, THE INTERNATIONAL ANNUAL OF ALTERNATIVE PHOTOGRAPHY

GRAPHIS NUDES, A COLLECTION OF CAREFULLY SELECTED SOPHISTICATED IMAGES

GRAPHIS POSTER, THE INTERNATIONAL ANNUAL OF POSTER ART

GRAPHIS PACKAGING, AN INTERNATIONAL COMPILATION OF PACKAGING DESIGN

GRAPHIS LETTERHEAD, AN INTERNATIONAL COMPILATION OF LETTERHEAD DESIGN

GRAPHIS DIAGRAM, THE GRAPHIC VISUALIZATION OF ABSTRACT, TECHNICAL AND STATISTICAL FACTS AND FUNCTIONS

GRAPHIS LOGO, AN INTERNATIONAL COMPILATION OF LOGOS

GRAPHIS EPHEMERA, AN INTERNATIONAL COLLECTION OF PROMOTIONAL ART

GRAPHIS PUBLICATION, AN INTERNATIONAL SURVEY OF THE BEST IN MAGAZINE DESIGN

GRAPHIS ANNUAL REPORTS, AN INTERNATIONAL COMPILATION OF THE BEST DESIGNED ANNUAL REPORTS

GRAPHIS CORPORATE IDENTITY, AN INTERNATIONAL COMPILATION OF THE BEST IN CORPORATE IDENTITY DESIGN

GRAPHIS TYPOGRAPHY, AN INTERNATIONAL COMPILATION OF THE BEST IN TYPOGRAPHIC DESIGN

GRAPHIS PUBLIKATIONEN

GRAPHIS, DIE INTERNATIONALE ZWEIMONATSZEITSCHRIFT DER VISUELLEN KOMMUNIKATION

GRAPHIS SHOPPING BAG, TRAGTASCHEN-DESIGN IM INTERNATIONALEN ÜBERBLICK

GRAPHIS MUSIC CD, CD-DESIGN IM INTERNATIONALEN ÜBERBLICK

GRAPHIS BOOKS, BUCHGESTALTUNG IM INTERNATIONALEN ÜBERBLICK

GRAPHIS DESIGN, DAS INTERNATIONALE JAHRBUCH ÜBER DESIGN UND ILLUSTRATION

GRAPHIS ADVERTISING, DAS INTERNATIONALE JAHRBUCH DER WERBUNG

GRAPHIS BROCHURES, BROSCHÜRENDESIGN IM INTERNATIONAL ÜBERBLICK

GRAPHIS PHOTO, DAS INTERNATIONALE JAHRBUCH DER PHOTOGRAPHIE

GRAPHIS ALTERNATIVE PHOTOGRAPHY, DAS INTERNATIONALE JAHRBUCH ÜBER ALTERNATIVE PHOTOGRAPHIE

GRAPHIS NUDES, EINE SAMMLUNG SORGFÄLTIG AUSGEWÄHLTER AKTPHOTOGRAPHIE

GRAPHIS POSTER, DAS INTERNATIONALE JAHRBUCH DER PLAKATKUNST

GRAPHIS PACKAGING, EIN INTERNATIONALER ÜBERBLICK ÜBER DIE PACKUNGSGESTALTUNG

GRAPHIS LETTERHEAD, EIN INTERNATIONALER ÜBERBLICK ÜBER BRIEFPAPIERGESTALTUNG

GRAPHIS DIAGRAM, DIE GRAPHISCHE DARSTELLUNG ABSTRAKTER TECHNISCHER UND STATISTISCHER DATEN UND FAKTEN

GRAPHIS LOGO, EINE INTERNATIONALE AUSWAHL VON FIRMEN-LOGOS

GRAPHIS EPHEMERA, EINE INTERNATIONALE SAMMLUNG GRAPHISCHER DOKUMENTE DES TÄGLICHEN LEBENS

GRAPHIS MAGAZINDESIGN, EINE INTERNATIONALE ZUSAMMENSTELLUNG DES BESTEN ZEITSCHRIFTEN-DESIGNS

GRAPHIS ANNUAL REPORTS, EIN INTERNATIONALER ÜBERBLICK ÜBER DIE GESTALTUNG VON JAHRESBERICHTEN

GRAPHIS CORPORATE IDENTITY, EINE INTERNATIONALE AUSWAHL DES BESTEN CORPORATE IDENTITY DESIGNS

GRAPHIS TYPOGRAPHY, EINE INTERNATIONALE ZUSAMMENSTELLUNG DES BESTEN TYPOGRAPHIE DESIGN

PUBLICATIONS GRAPHIS

GRAPHIS, LA REVUE BIMESTRIELLE INTERNATIONALE DE LA COMMUNICATION VISUELLE

GRAPHIS SHOPPING BAG, UNE COMPILATION INTERNATIONALE SUR LE DESIGN DES SACS À COMMISSIONS

GRAPHIS MUSIC CD, UNE COMPILATION INTERNATIONALE SUR LE DESIGN DES CD

GRAPHIS BOOKS, UNE COMPILATION INTERNATIONALE SUR LE DESIGN DES LIVRES

GRAPHIS DESIGN, LE RÉPERTOIRE INTERNATIONAL DE LA COMMUNICATION VISUELLE

GRAPHIS ADVERTISING, LE RÉPERTOIRE INTERNATIONAL DE LA PUBLICITÉ

GRAPHIS BROCHURES, UNE COMPILATION INTERNATIONALE SUR LE DESIGN DES BROCHURES

GRAPHIS PHOTO, LE RÉPERTOIRE INTERNATIONAL DE LA PHOTOGRAPHIE

GRAPHIS ALTERNATIVE PHOTOGRAPHY, LE RÉPERTOIRE INTERNATIONAL DE LA PHOTOGRAPHIE ALTERNATIVE

GRAPHIS NUDES, UN FLORILÈGE DE LA PHOTOGRAPHIE DE NUS

GRAPHIS POSTER, LE RÉPERTOIRE INTERNATIONAL DE L'AFFICHE

GRAPHIS PACKAGING, LE RÉPERTOIRE INTERNATIONAL DE LA CRÉATION D'EMBALLAGES

GRAPHIS LETTERHEAD, LE RÉPERTOIRE INTERNATIONAL DU DESIGN DE PAPIER À LETTRES

GRAPHIS DIAGRAM, LE RÉPERTOIRE GRAPHIQUE DE FAITS ET DONNÉES ABSTRAITS, TECHNIQUES ET STATISTIQUES

GRAPHIS LOGO, LE RÉPERTOIRE INTERNATIONAL DU LOGO

GRAPHIS EPHEMERA, LE GRAPHISME – UN ÉTAT D'ESPRIT AU QUOTIDIEN

GRAPHIS PUBLICATION, LE RÉPERTOIRE INTERNATIONAL DU DESIGN DE PÉRIODIQUES

GRAPHIS ANNUAL REPORTS, PANORAMA INTERNATIONAL DU MEILLEUR DESIGN DE RAPPORTS ANNUELS D'ENTREPRISES

GRAPHIS CORPORATE IDENTITY, PANORAMA INTERNATIONAL DU MEILLEUR DESIGN D'IDENTITÉ CORPORATE

GRAPHIS TYPOGRAPHY, LE RÉPERTOIRE INTERNATIONAL DU MEILLEUR DESIGN DE TYPOGRAPHIE

ISBN 1-888001-38-0
© COPYRIGHT UNDER UNIVERSAL COPYRIGHT CONVENTION
COPYRIGHT © 1997 BY GRAPHIS INC., 141 LEXINGTON AVENUE NEW YORK, NY10016 USA
JACKET AND BOOK DESIGN COPYRIGHT © 1996, 1997 BY PEDERSEN DESIGN
141 LEXINGTON AVENUE, NEW YORK, NY10016 USA
LIBRARY OF CONGRESS CATALOG CARD NUMBER. 97-71230

PRINTED IN CHINA THROUGH PALACE PRESS INTERNATIONAL

■ This is a book about explaining. Using over 100 examples of information design, the book reveals the heart of a good explanation, showing that inside every one, beneath every clever application of technology and style, lies a disciplined process of logic and common sense. A worthy thought process is the only constant on these pages. ■ In 1976, Richard Saul Wurman was chairman of the national convention of the American Institute of Architects and for its theme he created *The Architecture of Information*. So was the seed planted. The term aptly described the methodology of books he published himself, just as it does the work gathered here. Two years ago the publisher of the world's finest books about design, B. Martin Pedersen of *Graphis*, agreed to publish *Information Architects*. In doing so, he has legitimized the book's title, the emerging science of information design, and the unique body of its skills all at once. ■ From the relatively small world of information architects, Wurman chose 20 sources of illustrations, diagrams, publications, electronic programs, and exhibits. Requests were sent for products and descriptions—"please include extended and I mean *extended* captions." We were obliged with detailed, almost treatise-length texts and a lot more work than could possibly fit in one volume. The source-profiles were arranged in (very fuzzy) categorical order, illustrations were selected and sized to be large and legible, and captions were written to knit the thought processes together. ■ Problems soon arose: how to explain the explaining. Format stories and page architectures could be diagrammed, that was easy. But how could we picture the complex, invisible structures of stories in the interactive computer programs? Well, Krzysztof Lenk knew: he provided the first clear diagram I have seen of electronic content (right), and then agreed to draw his own *Encyclopædia Africana* in the same manner (pages 190–195). He spent a lot of time with us and helped develop what we call the Z diagram: a frozen view of hidden content and routes of content access. We

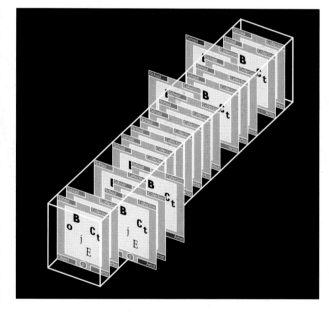

THE Z DIAGRAM To explain interactive electronic programs, this book uses a spatial diagram of content sequences and navigation routes. It descends from Krzysztof Lenk's logic for a "slide tray" context for organizing the collections of the Seattle Art Museum.

sent a sketch of it to contributors of interactive programs and every one adopted the technique—in most cases spending many hours regurgitating projects in its format. But then, everyone in this book has been generous with time; relentlessly we have asked for more of this, or more of that, and we have been richly rewarded. ■ The results can be viewed as a mosaic of artful intellect. But as one might expect, the book is also a mosaic of motives, both professional and personal, standing shoulder-to-shoulder throughout. Beneath the whole however, is a common thread of searching curiosity. Now, if a science begins with inquiry as they say, and grows with consensus as they also say, will our next book discuss our shared discoveries and coordinated vocabularies?

CONTENTS: THE INFORMATION ARCHITECTS

■ **THIS BOOK,** *Information Architects*, is intended to honor professionals in our industry whose quest or design philosophy is to take complex information and convey it to a target audience as simply as possible. In other words, to communicate efficiently. ■ Richard Saul Wurman has a passion for clarity and precision in the interchange of information. His renowned *Access* guides attest to this. He has challenged the design industry for years, labeling many designers as mere decorators or stylists. The practitioners presented in this book, on the other hand, have been chosen by Richard because they have aspired to the directive for clarity and precision in their work. ■ When the portfolios and manuscripts arrived, I decided, at Richard's suggestion, to work with Peter Bradford in designing and producing this book. The unexpected gift we got in the process was that not only did Peter design the book, he also edited all the text material for consistency. This was time-consuming and also reflective of Peter, in that when he takes a job, he does so with his whole soul. I laud and compliment Richard and Peter for their ideas and caring for this book. ■ *B. Martin Pedersen, Publisher and Creative Director, Graphis Press Corp.*

■ **CREDITS** *Information Architects* was created by Richard Saul Wurman, and co-published with B. Martin Pedersen of Graphis Press Corp. It was edited, captioned, and designed by Peter Bradford and Danielle Whiteson, production was managed by Jane Rosch, and it was printed by Palace Press International. ■ Photographs on page 7: Richard Saul Wurman by Reven T.C. Wurman; 8: David Macaulay by The Bristol Workshops; 9: Richard A. Curtis by Barbara Ries, *USA TODAY*, John Grimwade by Grant Delin; 11: Leslie Smolan by Rodney Smith; 13: David Small by Suguru Ishizaki, Clement Mok by Doug Menuez.

■ **OPPOSITE** Alexander Tsiaras uses advanced photographic techniques to enter the human body and computer techniques to enhance what he finds. Whether he looks into his own head, travels deep inside the lung, or follows a child's operation, his science is eloquent (see page 224).

■ **RICHARD SAUL WURMAN,** FAIA, describes his 30 years of confrontations with unreasonably disorganized information and shows a series of publications that he created to do something about it. He explains his application of simple logic to the comparing of cities, buildings, and urban statistics, and the mapping of content in disparate subjects like careers, city environments, surgical processes, telephone books, atlases, and corporate chronologies. ■ Richard trained in architecture at the University of Pennsylvania, where he earned his graduate degree in 1959. During the next 13 years of partnership prac-

20

tice in Philadelphia, he began producing a series of architecturally oriented books on building comparisons, city analyses, and Louis Kahn. He has been awarded several grants from the National Endowment for the Arts and a Guggenheim Fellowship. In 1981, he founded Access Press in Los Angeles, and produced his revolutionary *Access Guides* to clarify the understanding of American and foreign cities, sports events, and other complex subjects like financial investing, and medical tests and procedures. ■ In 1987 he formed The Understanding Business in San Francisco to continue "making things understandable" with new formats for telephone books, road atlases, airline guides, and many others. In 1990, he wrote *Information Anxiety,* the bestselling book dedicated to our adjustment to the information age. The book represents an overview of his motivating principles, and was followed by *Follow the Yellow Brick Road.* In 1991, he sold both companies. ■ In parallel, as part of the same commitment, he is the founder, chairman, and creative director of the TED Conferences on Technology Entertainment Design. Now in its tenth year, TED represents the new coalition of energies that "information" now requires. ■ Address: Box 186, Newport, RI 02840. Telephone (401) 848–2299, Fax (401) 848–2599, E-mail: rsw@ted.com Web site URL: http://www.ted.com

■ **ERIK SPIEKERMANN** of MetaDesign in Berlin explains his designing of one of information's essential building blocks, a clear and flexible typeface. From its rejection in his publications program for the German Post Office, his type design migrated through digitizing software to commercial success as a family of independently marketed fonts. Also, as the designer of the new diagram for Berlin's transportation system, he traces the evolution of the system from the 1960s, through its division in the days of the Berlin Wall, to its reorganization as a coordinated system today. ■ Insatiable curiosity, and a strong de-

38

sire to find out why things look the way they do, are given by Erik as motivations for experimenting with his first printing press at the age of twelve, for studying art history at university, designing typefaces, writing books about typography, and for his travels around the world as a typographic evangelist. After seven years in London, Erik returned to Berlin in 1979 and founded MetaDesign. Now Germany's largest design firm with more than 80 designers, MetaDesign opened an office in San Francisco in 1992, and a studio in London in 1995. ■ He has written many articles about type and, with his considerable reputation as an international authority on typeface design, he travels frequently to judge design competitions and is a member of many professional associations in Europe and the United States. He claims that designing complex information systems is his hobby. Adobe Press published his book *Stop Stealing Sheep & Find Out How Type Works* in 1993. Two of his most recent typeface designs, FF Meta and ITC Officina, have become very popular among designers, especially in the United States; FF Meta has been described as the "Helvetica for the Nineties." ■ Address: MetaDesign plus GmbH, Bergmannstraße 102, D–10961 Berlin. Telephone (030) 69 57 92–00, Fax (030) 69 57 92–22. E-mail: 100347.767

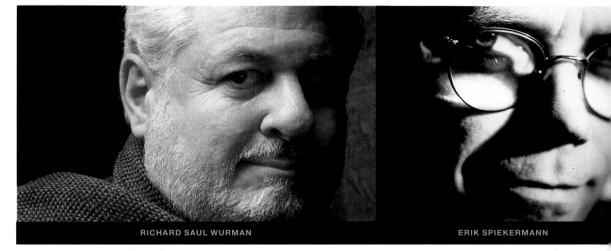

RICHARD SAUL WURMAN

ERIK SPIEKERMANN

■ **DAVID MACAULAY** uses his early sketches and book mock-ups to explain the unique points-of-view he finds to represent complex subjects. In *Underground* he places himself beneath the street to show what's happening there, in *The Amazing Brain* he traces the nerve routes of images entering the brain. In both, he reveals his subject by simply walking into it. ■ David is the author and illustrator of many internationally acclaimed and bestselling books about architecture. David was 11 when his family moved from **46** England to the United States. His fascination with simple technology and the way things worked, to-

■ **PETER BRADFORD** of the Cement Boat Company in New York City questions the validity of conventional information methods. He describes his search for essential understandings in nutrition and calories, plate tectonics, literary plot diagrams, dictionaries, and (with David Kelley) animated encyclopedias. He proposes new formats for them all and new visual techniques to link bodies of knowledge. ■ Peter is a designer of information, instruction, and identification materials. Since founding his firm in 1964, he has **62** created many communication program strategies and products for corporations, institutions, and pub-

■ **MARIA GIUDICE** and **LYNNE STILES** are partners of YO in San Francisco. In a series of visual guides from Agfa, the complex subject of electronic pre-press production was divided into discrete topics. Maria and Lynne describe the process of organizing the text, format, and diagrams of the guides. In a project for Peachpit Press, they also describe their rationale in solving a new kind of information problem: the electronic promotion of a company and its products on the interactive, world-wide Internet. ■ Maria **76** is a well-known calligrapher and information designer. Lynne studied architecture at the University of

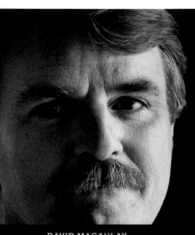   

DAVID MACAULAY   PETER BRADFORD   MARIA GIUDICE   LYNNE STILES

gether with his love of model-making and drawing, led him to study architecture at Rhode Island School of Design. After a fifth year in RISD's Honors Program in Rome, he received his degree in 1969 and spent the next four years designing interiors, teaching high school art, and tinkering with the idea of making books. ■ One result of his book tinkering was an idea about a gargoyle beauty pageant set in Medieval France. Brimming with confidence, he ventured to Houghton-Mifflin in Boston with his sketches. They seemed much more impressed with the cathedrals behind the gargoyles than with the gargoyles themselves, and soon David was off to France to work on his first book *Cathedral*. He also built a Roman city (*City*, published in 1974), erected monuments to the pharaohs (*Pyramid*, 1975), built a Medieval fortress (*Castle*, 1977), and dismantled the Empire State Building (*Unbuilding*, 1980). ■ David is best known for *The Way Things Work* (1988), a book about the hows and whys of almost everything that functions. His most recent book *Ship* tells two stories: the discovering of the remains of an early 16th century Spanish caravel in the Caribbean and the constructing of a new one. ■ Address: 146 Water Street, Warren, RI 02885. Telephone (401) 247–2560, Fax (401) 245–8930.

lishers in America and abroad. For ten years, he designed all communications for Urban America Inc. and the national American Institute of Architects, both in Washington. He has produced projects for CBS Inc., Hitachi of Japan, Random House, the Ford Foundation, and the USIA, along with over 30 monographs of master photography for Aperture Inc. ■ He was creative director of a complete elementary basal reading textbook program for Xerox Corporation's Ginn and Company. He has designed math, science, and spelling programs for Ginn, Holt, and Random House. Recently, he has designed computer strategies and new knowledge representations for printed and electronic encyclopedias and dictionaries. ■ This work, together with his other books, posters, magazine formats, films, diagram essays, and illustrations have won the company more than 300 design awards, and a place in the permanent collections at the Library of Congress and the Cooper-Hewitt Museum. In 1978, he produced *Chair*, his first independent book venture, and in 1982, he co-founded Wingspan Inc. to develop educational software. He created Cement Boat in 1990 to initiate, develop, and write book and animation projects, including *True Blue and The Figures of Speech* and *The Furniture Design of Nicos Zographos*. ■ Address: Cement Boat Company, 928 Broadway, New York, NY 10010. Telephone (212) 982–2090, Fax (212) 982–2092.

North Carolina. The two met at the The Understanding Business in San Francisco where they both managed editions of *USAtlas* and helped develop the *Pacific Bell Smart Yellow Pages*. They founded YO in 1991. ■ Their speciality is start-to finish implementation of projects, assembling hand-picked teams of writers, illustrators, and production artists to realize a publication. Says Giudice, "We like to collaborate with our clients and with our creative teams to select the information that's really needed and how best to present it." Stiles adds, "We always feel that we need to thoroughly understand the material ourselves before we are able to communicate it. We put ourselves in the place of the reader or end user of the material." YO's project list includes books for Addison-Wesley, HarperCollins, Peachpit Press, and IDG Books, as well as projects for Apple Computer, *Publish* magazine, Agfa, Gray Line Tours, and RIDES for Bay Area Commuters. ■ Address: YO, 852 Folsom Street, San Francisco, CA 94107. Telephone (415) 357–4880, Fax (415) 357–4884. E-mail: YO@applelink.apple.com

■ **BRUCE ROBERTSON** of The Diagram Group in London. As connoisseurs of brevity and simplicity, The Diagram Group has been developing models of clear information for almost 30 years. In a few well chosen words, Bruce describes the Group's techniques of information compression and diagrammatic style in publications including the Collins Gem reference series (with its 660-page encyclopedia "the size of a pack of fags"), the book *Handtools of Arts and Crafts*, the book *Woman's Body* (shown in its Japanese Braille edition), and the much imitated *Rules of the Game*. ■ Bruce trained at the Sunderland Art College where

84

■ **RICHARD CURTIS** traces the evolution of the *USA TODAY* Weather Page and its format architecture over a period of 13 years. As the newspaper's current managing editor of graphics and photography, he directed the development of the page, along with its popular diagramming techniques. He expresses the journalistic foundation of the graphics and explains their application to other kinds of story features, both brief and full-page. He also shows and describes one of the successful publications derived from the graphics, *The Weather Book*. ■ A member of *USA TODAY*'s founding editorial staff in 1982, Richard is also

92

■ **JOHN GRIMWADE** explains the creating of dimensional "walking" maps in articles and publications for *Condé Nast Traveler*. He simplifies the understanding of the art and architecture in the Ottoman Empire's Topkapi Palace and, in the magazine's series of sixty-minute guides, does the same with the Vatican Museum. Then in quick changes of pace, he explains the diagramming of boat and plane connections in an article about the Caribbean, the year-long, 500-mile circular route of the Wildebeest migration in Africa, and the structural refitting of the QE2 luxury liner. ■ John has designed diagrammatic illus-

102

BRUCE ROBERTSON   RICHARD CURTIS   JOHN GRIMWADE

he obtained an Honours Degree in Drawing, and later at the Royal College of Art where he won the James Knott Drawing Prize. ■ In 1967, he co-founded his studio Diagram Visual Information (The Diagram Group) to produce a large body of diagrammatic publications and visual displays of information for the international publishing market. Bruce and The Diagram Group are acknowledged as leading creators of information charts and diagrams. Countless designers and artists have trained at the studio, some of whom arrived with little formal training. Bruce has always preferred to nurture raw talent rather than "unteach the half-trained." He has also lectured many times at the Chelsea School of Art, the Slade, St. Martin's, and the London College of Art. ■ Address: Diagram Visual Information Ltd., 195 Kentish Town Road, London, NW5 8SY. Telephone (0171) 482–3633, Fax (0171) 482–4932.

an independent publications design consultant. He has practiced, lectured, and consulted on publication graphics for many years, twice winning the annual *American Journalism Review* award for the best designed newspaper. ■ Richard is a graduate of the School of Design at North Carolina State University and a member of the board of directors of that school's foundation. In 1992, he was Hearst Visiting Professional in graphics and design at the University of North Carolina, and in 1993, he was named a School of Design distinguished alumnus. He has lectured at many professional meetings and universities throughout the United States and Europe, and is an adjunct member of the University of Maryland, School of Journalism. ■ He is co-founder and past president of the Society of Newspaper Design, and was founder and editor of the Society's quarterly journal, *Design*. He is also co-founder of the Freedom Forum's annual flying shortcourse in photojournalism in Eastern Europe. ■ Richard is co-editor of *Portraits of the USA*, a photography book, editor and designer of *USA TODAY's The Weather Book* and *The USA TODAY Weather Almanac*, and designer and editor of The Freedom Forum's 1994 book, *Death by Cheeseburger: High School Journalism in the 1990s and Beyond*. ■ Address: *USA TODAY*, 1000 Wilson Boulevard, Arlington, VA 22229. Telephone (703) 276–3415, Fax (703) 276–6583.

trations since receiving his degree from the Canterbury College of Art in the United Kingdom. After illustrating for *The Sunday Times*, and serving as Head of Graphics for *The Times* in London, he was appointed the Graphics Art Director for *Condé Nast Traveler* in New York City where his clear diagramming has become a popular trademark of the magazine. The graphics-driven information section, *Traveler's File*, won a National Magazine Award in 1989. His work has also appeared in numerous other major magazines and books. In 1995, a portfolio of work for *Condé Nast Traveler* won a gold medal at the Malofiej World Infographic Awards. ■ Address: *Condé Nast Traveler*, 360 Madison Avenue, New York, NY 10017. Telephone (212) 880–2319, Fax: (212) 880–2190. E-mail: grimwade@cntraveler.com

■ **DAVE MERRILL** discusses his determination to avoid the tedium of business oriented graphics in his illustrations for *US News and World Report*. In a story about production line techniques titled The Manufacturing Revolution, he shows a parallel dimensional diagram of old and new techniques and describes his use of common symbols to represent ideas within the graphics. Then he tells a story about the failure of graphics at the Pentagon, describes his experience with trying to improve them, and shows an illustration from the magazine that tracks another political event: the diversion of aid money from the U.S. by

■ **NIGEL HOLMES** made large contributions at *Time* magazine to the popularity of graphics in consumer newsmagazines. He describes the process of making illustrations for *Time*, showing the step-by-step process of developing a visual representation of the fraudulent practices at The Bank of Credit and Commerce. Then, in a reference to his many lectures about picturing information, he shows how a simple line can dramatize a simple issue: the quantity of toothpaste used in one day in the United States. He also describes the series of posters he created for the *Time Education Program*, which includes *En-*

■ **JOEL KATZ** of Joel Katz design associates in Philadelphia discusses the visual metaphors he used to explain the complexities of biotechnology in his Star Wars illustrations for Centocor. For a poster announcing a Paediatric Nephrology Association symposium, he describes another kind of information departure: a more logical design of diagrams to monitor the health of kidneys in newborn infants. He also discusses area maps for the marketing of development sites in Philadelphia, more convenient road construction maps for the Pennsylvania Department of Transportation, and his own interpretive maps

DAVE MERRILL   NIGEL HOLMES   JOEL KATZ   KEN CARBONE

Iraq to purchase military weapons. Finally, he describes his embarrassing overconfidence in a symbolic representation of military commitments by the United States around the world. ■ After earning degrees in Government and Art from the University of Virginia, Dave began drawing political cartoons for the *Washington Business Review*. Later, as a designer and infographic specialist at *US News and World Report*, he pioneered the implementing of computer systems to produce four-color desktop illustrations for newsmagazine stories. ■ Dave has also consulted and produced graphics for *National Geographic* and *National Geographic Traveler* magazines, as well as for *New Republic*, *National Review*, and *Changing Times*. He has produced corporate graphics for companies like Mobil, taught the use of computer graphics software, and won design awards from the U.S. National Exhibit for the International Cartographic Association, and from the *Print* magazine Regional Design Competition. ■ Address: 11686 Stockbridge Lane, Reston, VA 22094. Telephone (703) 481–1776.

dangered Cultures, *The World's Largest Rivers and Highest Mountains*, and *The Earth and the Solar System*. ■ After graduating from the Royal College of Art, Nigel worked in London until 1978, when he moved to New York City to design information graphics for *Time* magazine. Since then he has designed maps, charts, and diagrams for most major American publications. Nigel has lectured all over the United States, and in Europe, India, Japan, and Brazil. He has also written four books about diagrammatic language: *Designer's Guide to Creating Maps and Charts* (1984), *Designing Pictorial Symbols* (1985), *Pictorial Maps* (1991), and *The Best in Diagrammatic Graphics* (1993). ■ Address: 544 Riverside Avenue, Westport, CT 06880. Telephone (203) 226–2313, Fax (203) 222–9545. E-mail: nigelholme@aol.com

or icons of historic cities. ■ Joel graduated BA Scholar of the House with Exceptional Distinction from Yale College, and holds BFA and MFA degrees from the Yale School of Art's graphic design program. He has taught at Yale, Rhode Island School of Design, and the Philadelphia College of Art, and is the co-author of two publications, *Aspen Visible* and *The Nature of Recreation*, both published by MIT Press. ■ Joel writes and lectures widely on his special interest and expertise in the visualization of complex cartographic, process, financial, and statistical information. His articles have appeared in *Messages*, the *AIGA Journal of Graphics*, and *Visible Language*. He has spoken at Siggraph and numerous universities and professional design organizations. His diagrammatic work has been featured in *Graphis Diagram 1*, *The Best in Diagrammatic Graphics* (by Nigel Holmes), *Diagram Graphics* (by Fumihiko Nishioka), and *ID* magazine. He was made an honorary life member of the International Paediatric Nephrology Association in 1980 for his development of better graphic notation for visualizing the function of infant kidneys. ■ Address: Joel Katz design associates, 1616 Walnut Street, Suite 1919, Philadelphia, PA 19103–5313. Telephone (215) 985–4747, Fax (215) 985–4748. E-mail: Mapfarm@aol.com

■ **KEN CARBONE** and **LESLIE SMOLAN** of Carbone Smolan in New York City show wayfinding signage systems designed for the Louvre in Paris and the World Bank headquarters building in Washington D.C. Their design program for Putnam Investments, based on an assessment of its marketing practices and needs, resulted in a reorganization of the company itself and the manner in which it sold its products. ■ Since Ken and Leslie began working together in 1977, they have emphasized the creating of innovative design solutions that are intelligent, memorable, and distinctive. They have target-

142

■ **RALPH APPELBAUM** of Ralph Appelbaum Associates Inc. in New York City, designed the new mammal halls at the American Museum of Natural History. He describes the Museum's rationale for developing a new exhibit about evolutionary history, and the use of an evolutionary diagram as its organizing principle and circulation path. ■ Ralph has had extensive involvement for over twenty years in every facet of museum exhibit design. After graduating from Pratt Institute with a bachelor of industrial design degree, he was a designer in the Peace Corps. He became design advisor to Southern Peru

150

■ **NANCYE GREEN, MICHAEL DONOVAN, MARJORIE LEVIN, SUSAN BERMAN** and **SUSAN MYERS** of Donovan and Green in New York City explain the firm's process of documenting and displaying data in the Reagan Presidential Library, the documenting of a company in two interactive programs for 3M, and the documenting of pharmaceutical research for F. Hoffmann-LaRoche. ■ After earning degrees in Political Science and Environmental Design, Nancye co-founded her firm in 1974. She has developed and managed communications programs, environmental design projects, and

162

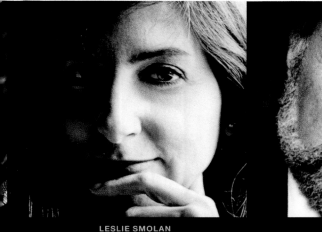

LESLIE SMOLAN

RALPH APPELBAUM

MARJORIE LEVIN SUSAN BERMAN NANCYE GREEN
SUSAN MYERS MICHAEL DONOVAN

ed diverse projects that use the full range of their talents. Knowing that great design comes from great ideas, their approach has always been driven by strong concepts. This has attracted an impressive clientele including major corporations, some of the world's great cultural institutions, and many entrepreneurial enterprises. Carbone Smolan Associates searches for the creative opportunities in its projects, and builds partnerships with clients to achieve appropriate results. It excels in work that requires dramatically simple solutions to complex problems, always trying to maintain a successful balance between aesthetics and function. ■ The firm's design ranges from branding and corporate communications programs, to extensive signage and wayfinding systems, large publishing programs, special books, exhibitions, product development, and merchandising. Its clients are diverse, including the Museum of Modern Art, Tiffany & Co., The Disney Company, McGraw-Hill, Sotheby's, and Steuben. ■ Address: Carbone Smolan Associates, 22 West 19th Street, New York, NY 10011. Telephone (212) 807–0011, Fax: (212) 807-0870. E-mail: 102625.333@compuserve.com

for the United States Agency for International Development, and later the director of the New York Task Force of Project Earning Power. This nationwide effort to create products made by handicapped labor was sponsored by the Department of Labor, the Department of Health, Education and Welfare, and the Industrial Designers Society of America . ■ At Robert P. Gersin Associates from 1970 to 1975, Ralph designed exhibit, product, and environmental projects. In 1975, he joined Raymond Loewy International and became vice president of exhibits and museum environments. He founded Ralph Appelbaum Associates in 1987 to bring interdisciplinary design services to museums and nonprofit institutions, beginning with several NEH-sponsored projects now recognized as influential examples of interpretive exhibition design. ■ The recipient of many design awards, Ralph has taught for 15 years on the under-graduate and graduate levels at Pratt Institute and at New York University, where he is assistant professor of museum studies. He has lectured at national and international conferences on a wide variety of museum design issues. Ralph currently directs RAA's undertakings while retaining a daily involvement in selected commissions. ■ Address: Ralph Appelbaum Associates Inc., 133 Spring Street, New York, NY 10012. Telephone (212) 334-8200, Fax (212) 334-6214. E-mail: muzdzign@cnct.com

complex exhibitions, as well as consulting widely on communication management. ■ Michael earned degrees in environmental design and taught the subject for many years. He has created and directed many corporate identity programs, as well as permanent exhibitions on a variety of topics ranging from volcanoes to the history of Hollywood and, most recently, the design of furniture. ■ Marjorie trained in design, was Design Director at Knoll International, and joined Donovan and Green after nine years of independent practice. She has broad experience in all areas of graphic design and marketing communications. ■ Susan Berman is a registered architect whose design work has included new buildings, interiors, exhibitions, and architectural signage. Presently, she directs the firm's design and management staffs for all its three-dimensional design projects. ■ Susan Myers has 17 years of administrative and managerial experience in the fields of design and communication, public relations, and travel and leisure. Her work at Donovan and Green has involved the developing of advertising and marketing campaigns for clients in a wide range of industries. ■ Address: Donovan and Green, 71 Fifth Avenue, New York, NY 10003. Telephone (212) 989–4050, Fax (212) 989-1453. E-mail: ngreen@dongrn.com

■ **DON MOYER** of Agnew Moyer Smith in Pittsburgh explains the developing of new product guides for the Steelcase furniture company. He describes the division of content into two companion guides, and the organization of content in each one. He shows the consistent drawing standards that allow the clustering and assembling of products on both printed pages and interactive computer screens. He also describes the clustering of zoological content in "morsels" of text on large panels illustrating a Tropical Rain Forest at the Pittsburgh Zoo.

■ Don is a graphic designer and writer who enjoys working

■ **NATHAN SHEDROFF** of vivid studios in San Francisco explains the function and flexibility of his multimedia CD-ROM product created from the educational program *Voices of the 30s*. He describes the interactive architecture that transformed the historical material, and the activities and manipulations it provides for users. He also discusses the organization and format design of *Demystifying Multimedia*, a book about creating a variety of interactive projects. ■ Nathan has been an information and interface designer for over six years. He worked with Richard Saul Wurman as a senior designer at The Under-

■ **KRZYSZTOF LENK** and **PAUL KAHN** of Dynamic Diagrams in Providence describe the evolution of two kinds of interactive multimedia programs: *Encyclopædia Africana* has many interlinked chapters and uses a global database, *The Mongolian Felt Tent* has sequential chapters and uses a linear database. They also explain the graphics used to represent a software language tool and the diagram used to help a buyer place and assemble the components of an IBM computer. ■ Krzysztof studied graphic design at Poland's Academy of Fine Arts and earned his MFA degree in 1961. He practiced and taught

DON MOYER   NATHAN SHEDROFF   KRZYSZTOF LENK   PAUL KAHN

on thorny communication problems. While a student at the Philadelphia College of Art, Don first met Richard Saul Wurman and became intrigued by his enthusiasm for making information clear. After graduation, Don worked in Wurman's Philadelphia office, at Burton Kramer Associates in Toronto, then returned to earn his MFA degree in graphic design at Yale University. ■ Don and his wife Karen jointly coordinated the AIGA's Symbol Signs project for the U.S. Department of Transportation. In 1976, Don joined the Westinghouse Corporate Design Center in Pittsburgh where he met Reed Agnew and Grant Smith. Four years later, they founded their communication planning and design firm. ■ With a team of 25, AMS now concentrates on projects in publishing, corporate identity, packaging, interface design, and exhibits for clients in this country and abroad. Don's work has been published in *Graphis Diagrams* and *Graphis Ephemera*, and has received many awards from the Society of Typographic Arts and the American Institute of Graphic Arts. For recreation, he draws creatures that look like a mix of Beatrix Potter, Albrecht Dürer, and a Biology 101 textbook. ■ Address: Agnew Moyer Smith Inc., 503 Martindale Street, Pittsburgh, PA 15212. Telephone (412) 322–6333, Fax: (412) 322–6350. E-mail: ams322@aol.com

standing Business, helping to design the Pacific Bell *Smart Yellow Pages* and the book *Information Anxiety*. Since co-founding vivid in 1990, Nathan has supervised the development of new interaction paradigms for digital reference tools, online worlds, and productivity software. He is currently Creative Director at vivid. ■ He received an Honorable Mention in the 1987 Unisys Industrial Design Competition, and was nominated for a Chrysler Innovation in Design Award in 1994. Nathan has spoken at international conferences in Helsinki and Tampere, Finland and at Stanford University, and lectures at San Francisco State University. He earned a Bachelor of Science degree in Transportation Design from the Art Center College of Design in Pasadena, is a co-author of *Understanding Computers*, and has participated in publishing over 20 other print and electronic titles including *Danny Goodman's Macintosh Handbook*. ■ His clients include Hands On Technology, Softbank, Inc., ETAK, Apple Computer, Paramount New Media, The University of Calgary, Pioneer, VECTA, and TED Conferences, and is a member of ACM, SIGCHI, SIGLINK and BayCHI. Nathan is now coding information viruses in his spare time for widespread release. ■ Address: vivid Studios, Suite 200, Box 7, San Francisco, CA 94107. Telephone (415) 512–7200, Fax (415) 512–7202. E-mail: nathan@vivid.com Web site URL: http://www.vivid.com

in Europe until 1982 when he was appointed professor of graphic design at the Rhode Island School of Design. His work and teaching concentrates on information design and appropriate uses of computer screens, and has been widely published in both national and international design magazines. Krzysztof is a partner and design director at Dynamic Diagrams, a consulting company concentrating on interface design for both print and electronic media. ■ Paul has trained in literature and typography, and has worked with many electronic publishing systems since 1977. At Brown University's IRIS, he served as project manager and director to develop educational hypertext applications. He is an experienced designer of hypermedia publications in many software systems, and with his partner Krzysztof presents seminars on the visual aspects of the computer environment. ■ Project team members at Dynamic Diagrams include Magdalena Kasman, Elaine Froehlich, John Matthew Skidgel, David Durand, and John Shepherd. Clients of the firm include Harvard University, IBM, Interleaf, Silicon Graphics, Sun Microsystems, and Simens Nixdorf. ■ Address: Dynamic Diagrams, 12 Bassett Street, Providence, RI 02903. Telephone (401) 331–2014, Fax (401) 331–2015. E-mail: lenk@DynamicDiagrams.com Paul_Kahn@DynamicDiagrams.com Web site URL: http://www.DynamicDiagrams.com

■ **MURIEL R. COOPER** and **DAVID SMALL** of MIT's Visible Language Workshop in Cambridge propose computer environments to display and clarify complex data. Shown are information structures that describe the school itself, investment analyses, public services in the Cambridge area, various ways to view the news, and different ways to look at a video conferencing system. ■ Muriel founded the Visible Language Workshop with Ron MacNeil in 1975. She coordinated its overall plan to investigate the inter-

202 sections of visual communication, design research, and artificial intelligence. Her own

■ **CLEMENT MOK** of CMd in San Francisco explains his use of interactive multimedia to advance and manage different kinds of information, including the design of products at Herman Miller, pharmaceutical information for the Mayo Clinic, the visual identity for the Microsoft Network, and school reference information for College View. ■ Clement started his career in New York where he developed print, on-air broadcast graphics, and three-dimensional design projects for Rockefeller Center, Republic National Bank, and CBS.

212 Clement spent five years as the Creative Director at Apple Computer, where he was in-

■ **ALEXANDER TSIARAS** in New York City discusses his use of different scanning methods and computer enhancements of the scans to study the human body. He applies his methods to views of his own body, a cranial operation on a young girl, and a trip into the lining of the human lung. He articulates the aesthetics he finds in science and his success in "revealing body landscapes that defy the imagination." ■ After studying art history and film at Amherst College, Alexander began producing his extraordinary photograph-

224 ic essays for *Life* magazine in 1980. For these stories he developed and adapted endo-

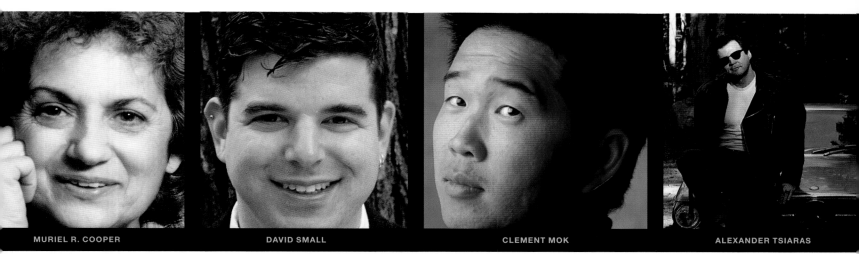

MURIEL R. COOPER   DAVID SMALL   CLEMENT MOK   ALEXANDER TSIARAS

research concerns were the qualitative graphic filtering of information in a dynamic, interactive, and expressive multimedia environment, the relationship of traditional design knowledge to electronic media, and the evolution of a new graphics vocabulary to delineate synthesized static and dynamic characteristics. ■ An active and progressive designer, educator, and researcher until her death in 1994, she produced over 500 books, many of which have earned special recognition. The second AIGA Design Leadership Award was awarded to MIT for the design excellence of the MIT Press, Design Services, and the VLW—all of which were founded and directed by Muriel. ■ David received his Bachelor's degree from MIT's Cognitive Science department in 1987 and his Master's degree from the Media Laboratory in 1990 where he was Muriel's student. He creates and teaches information design for high-resolution displays, develops research software, and has published a watercolor simulation written on the Media Lab's Connection Machine II. Many of his images have appeared in *Scientific American* and the *IMB Systems Journal*. ■ Address: Massachusetts Institute of Technology, Visible Language Workshop, 20 Ames Street, Cambridge, MA 02139, Room E15–443. Telephone (617) 253–4416, Fax (617) 258–6264. E-mail: dsmall@media.mit.edu Web site URL: http://www.media.mit.edu/~dsmall

volved in projects including the launch of the Macintosh and HyperCard. During those years, he defined and developed many graphics standards that are closely associated with Apple's corporate image. ■ Clement formed Clement Mok designs, Inc. to integrate the emerging computer technologies with all aspects of his design. As Creative Director of CMd, Clement spends much of his time making new products, new concepts, and new models understandable in a variety of media including print, video, computer-based multimedia, environmental design, and event marketing. Recently he founded CMCD, a separate digital publishing company to dedicate resources to developing titles for the information market. ■ Clement's work has been published internationally and has received hundreds of awards from professional organizations and publications. His designs have also been exhibited in museums and galleries in Europe and the Far East. He has served on the National Board of Directors for the AIGA and was featured in *ID* magazine's Top 40 issue. ■ Address: Clement Mok designs, Inc., 600 Townsend Street, San Francisco, CA 94103. Telephone (415) 703–9900, Fax (415) 703–9901. E-mail: clement@cmdesigns. com Web site URL: http://www.cmdesigns.com.\

scopic lenses to record some of the first photographs of human egg fertilization and the development of the fetus from three weeks old to just before birth. For this work he won the World Press Photo Award, the Missouri School of Journalism Award, and numerous art directors club awards. In 1984, he produced and photographed the Least Invasive Surgery story for *Life* magazine, and in 1988, The Smallest Human Heart Transplant story which was published in many magazines and purchased by Disney for a film. ■ Alexander has created stories for many other national and international publications including *New York Times Magazine*, *London Times Magazine*, *GEO*, and *Smithsonian*. In 1992, he began working with three-dimensional volume rendering software to produce his first *Anatomical Travelogue* which was published as a book, a special issue of *Life* magazine, and produced as a documentary film. ■ Alexander is now producing two educational CD-ROM programs for Time-Warner, two books, and eight half-hour documentaries on the subject of the human body and reproduction. A book of his paintings, sculptures, design, and digitally generated artwork will be published simultaneously with an exhibit of his work at the Museum of Modern Art. ■ Address: 225 West 80 Street, Apt. 3D, New York, NY 10024–7004. Telephone (212) 874–4562, Fax: (212) 874–1943. E-mail: 70353.1330@compuserve.com

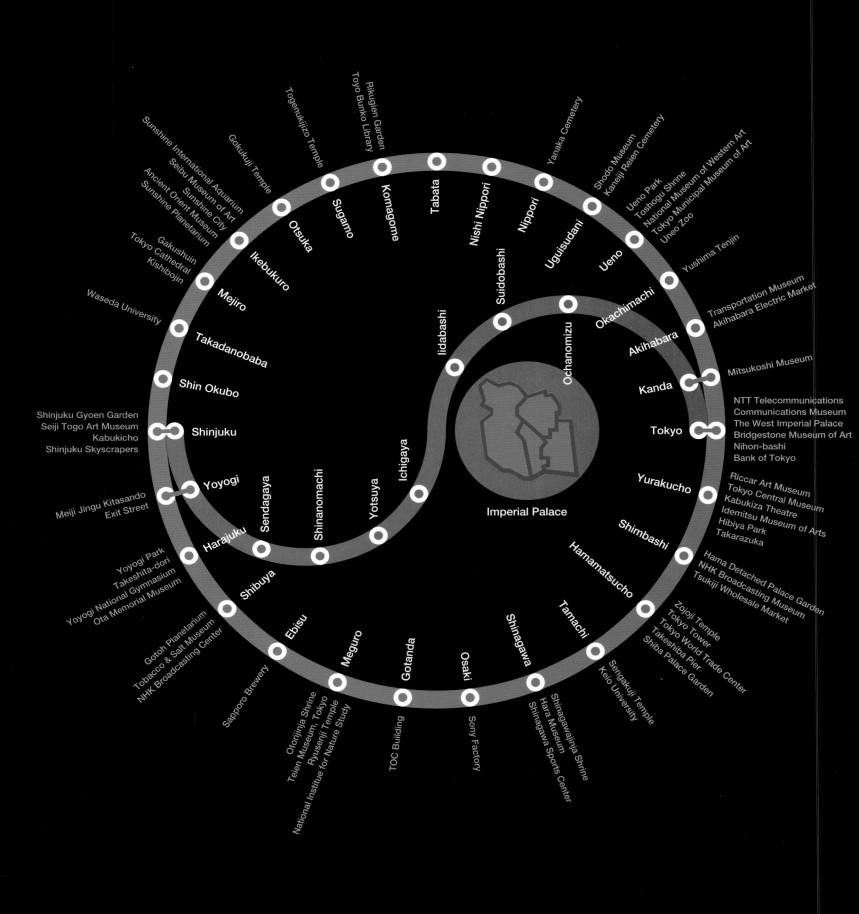

Rikugien Garden
Toyo Bunko Library

Togenukijizo Temple

Gokukuji Temple

Sunshine International Aquarium
Seibu Museum of Art
Ancient Orient Museum
Sunshine City
Sunshine Planetarium

Gakushuin
Tokyo Cathedral
Kishibojin

Waseda University

Shinjuku Gyoen Garden
Seiji Togo Art Museum
Kabukicho
Shinjuku Skyscrapers

Meiji Jingu Kitasando
Exit Street

Yoyogi Park
Takeshita-dori
Yoyogi National Gymnasium
Ota Memorial Museum

Gotoh Planetarium
Tobacco & Salt Museum
NHK Broadcasting Center

Sapporo Brewery

Otorijinja Shrine
Teien Museum, Tokyo
Ryusenji Temple
National Institue for Nature Study

Yanaka Cemetery

Shodo Museum
Kaneiji Reien Cemetery

Ueno Park
Toshogu Shrine
National Museum of Western Art
Tokyo Municipal Museum of Art
Uneo Zoo

Yushima Tenjin

Transportation Museum
Akihabara Electric Market

Mitsukoshi Museum

NTT Telecommunications
Communications Museum
The West Imperial Palace
Bridgestone Museum of Art
Nihon-bashi
Bank of Tokyo

Riccar Art Museum
Tokyo Central Museum
Kabukiza Theatre
Idemitsu Museum of Arts
Hibiya Park
Takarazuka

Hama Detached Palace Garden
NHK Broadcasting Museum
Tsukiji Wholesale Market

Zojoji Temple
Tokyo Tower
Tokyo World Trade Center
Takeshiba Pier
Shiba Palace Garden

Sengakuji Temple
Keio University

Shinagawajinja Shrine
Hara Museum
Shinagawa Sports Center

Sony Factory

TOC Building

Otsuka
Ikebukuro
Sugamo
Komagome
Tabata
Nishi Nippori
Nippori
Uguisudani
Ueno
Mejiro
Takadanobaba
Shin Okubo
Suidobashi
Okachimachi
Ochanomizu
Akihabara
Kanda
Iidabashi
Shinjuku
Tokyo
Yoyogi
Ichigaya
Sendagaya
Shinanomachi
Yotsuya
Yurakucho
Shimbashi
Harajuku
Hamamatsucho
Shibuya
Ebisu
Meguro
Gotanda
Osaki
Shinagawa
Tamachi

Imperial Palace

There is a tsunami of data that is crashing onto the beaches of the civilized world. This is a tidal wave of unrelated, growing data formed in bits and bytes, coming in an unorganized, uncontrolled, incoherent cacophony of foam. It's filled with flotsam and jetsam. It's filled with the sticks and bones and shells of inanimate and animate life. None of it is easily related, none of it comes with any organizational methodology. ■ As it washes up on our beaches, we see people in suits and ties skipping along the shoreline, men and women in fine shirts and blouses dressed for business. We see graphic designers and government officials, all getting their shoes wet and slowly submerging in the dense trough of stuff. Their trousers and slacks soaked, they walk stupidly into the water, smiling—a false smile of confidence and control. The tsunami is a wall of data—data produced at greater and greater speed, greater and greater amounts to store in memory, amounts that double, it seems, with each sunset. On tape, on disks, on paper, sent by streams of light. Faster, more and more and more. ■ Some of these people go back to their desks where, folded back and forth like accordions, are gobs of paper printouts of this stuff. They nod their heads and say "Yes, this is important, this is good stuff. The person sitting next to me, sitting in the next office down the aisle, they understand it, so I will smile, making believe I understand it too." ■ These same people read the newspaper, thinking they understand the issues of the day, whether it's the Savings and Loan crisis, the health-care crisis, Bosnia-Hercegovina, or taxes, or insurance. They nod their heads, knee-jerking to key words in headlines, but unable to tell anybody else, including themselves, the essence of any issue. ■ All day, from morning at home, to workday lunches, to dinner at night, out loud or to themselves, they "uh-huh, uh-huh, uh-huh" making believe they understand a reference to a name, a reference to a fact, the references to knowledge that supposedly make the world coherent. They "uh-huh" some friend, some teacher, a boss, a peer when a book or movie or magazine article, or piece of machinery, or software, or hardware is discussed. They "uh-huh" everybody because they were taught when they were young that it is not good to look stupid, that it is not good to say "I don't know," it is not good to ask questions, not good to focus on failure. Instead, the rewards come from acknowledging or answering everything with "I know." ■ You're supposed to look smart in our society. You are supposed to gain expertise and to sell it as the means of moving ahead in your career. You are supposed to focus on what you know how to do, and then do it better and better. You're supposed to revel in some niche of ability. That is where the rewards are supposed to come from.

■ Of course, when you sell your expertise—and what I mean by sell is to move ahead

MAKING THE COMPLEX CLEAR The *Tokyo Access* guide shows the railway line encircling the city. The route looks quite abstract when compared with a map of its real path. But, it clarifies the fact that the route is essentially a circle around the city, making it easier to understand and remember. The actual route is pear-shaped, with a bump at the bottom twisting to the right. Since you can't get on and off the train between stops, it doesn't matter what twists the train route takes. What does matter is the essential path and the sequence of stops, with reference to a familiar place—the Imperial Palace. *Access* guides are shown on page 28.

in a corporation, or sell an idea to a publisher, or sell an ability to a client—when you sell your expertise, by definition, you're selling from a limited repertoire. However, when you sell your ignorance to move ahead, when you sell your desire to learn about something, when you sell your desire to create and explore and navigate paths to knowledge, when you sell your *curiosity*—you sell from a bucket with an infinitely deep bottom that represents an unlimited repertoire. And, you sell in a way that's not intimidating, in a way that joins the explanation to the fascination that comes with understanding. ■ How opposite is our life from what we have been taught. Our educational system is based on the memorization of things we're not interested in, bulimically spewed out on a paper called a test, and then forgotten. We learn to use our short-term memory rather than long-term memory. Many of our interests are shunted aside. The teenagers' interest in music and cars and sports are looked on as second-rate themes for their lives instead of embraced as connections to all knowledge and wisdom. The car connects to the history of transportation, to our road systems, to our cities and our highways. It connects to the balance of payments and economics around the world. To steel and iron, and steel construction, and plastics and design. It connects to physics and mathematics and chemistry. It connects to foreign languages and culture. To medicine and governmental policy. And, all the things the car connects to connect to everything else. So do sports. And so does entertainment, which connects to technologies of all sorts, to design and hardware and software and information. Information is everything. We are what we read. ■ Well, let's talk about design. Unfortunately, design, which used to be a perfectly good word, means to make something look better for most people. A company invents or develops some new piece of electronic hardware. When it is finished it calls in a designer to wrap it up in a nice package. Then the company gets an engineer who understands how it works to write the instruction booklet. He suffers from the disease of familiarity, and so few customers really learn how to use the product. The designer picks the typefaces in that booklet and (maybe) puts a cover on it. The designer is not involved in the use, organization, or understanding of the instructions, except tangentially to make it easy to read. The designer is called in to make a magazine article look better, or an illustrator is asked to make a picture look arresting, or a photographer is asked to take an interesting view of an author or a subject. Nowhere are any of these designers used in the fundamental sense of creating meaning or understanding. ■ That's why I've chosen to call myself an Information Architect. I don't mean a bricks and mortar architect. I mean architect as used in the words *architect of foreign policy*. I mean architect as in the creating of systemic, structural, and orderly principles to make something work—the thoughtful making of either artifact, or idea, or policy that informs because it is clear. I use the word information in its truest sense. Most of the word information contains the word *inform,* so I call things information only if they inform me, not if they are just collections of data, of stuff. ■ If I throw 140,000 words on the floor and connect those words with a sentence or two, we wouldn't call that a dictionary. A dictionary, or an encyclopedia, or many of the collections of data in our world, are based on being able to find something. The ability to find something goes hand-in-hand with how well it's organized. We choose to organize the dictionary alphabetically, and for most of us, most of the time, that's a useful organizing principle. ■ In fact, the alphabet is the only organizing principle that we actually have to learn. Because the alphabet was not given to us by God. Alphabets change with languages; in Russia it is different, in Japan different again. For us, the alphabet is a learned order of 26 letters. The 26 letters have no functional sequence, but have proved useful in the evolution of our literate society. It really works quite well and it is one of our acceptable ways of organizing information. Now we could organize dictionary words by groups. All words that have to do with climate or weather could be together, all words that have to do with automobiles or speed or traffic could be together, all words about health and well-being could be lumped in a group. Therefore, great groups of these words could have one or another category as their organizing principle. In turn, the categories could be organized alphabetically, with words about automobiles in that category in the beginning under the "A's," and words about animals and zoology under "A" and "Z." ■ Some things are best organized by where they are. The thousands of roads and sites and towns and bodies of water are best organized by location on a map. We want to be able to find those places that are immediately around us as we look on a map. We certainly don't want to drive across France alphabetically. We don't want the United States in an atlas organized with Alabama first, and Alaska next, and Washington last, because we don't drive that way. That's not how we find where we're going, or how we find something. ■ As I looked into the organization of information, I realized that there were only five ways to do it. They can be remembered by the acronym LATCH: L) by location, A) by alphabet, T) organized by time (many museum shows are organized by timeline; the famous Charlie Eames *Franklin and Jefferson* timeline of those two great men was probably one of the best ever devised), C) by category (as I've alluded to; it's the way department stores are organized), and H) by hierarchy, from the largest to the smallest of something, from the reddest to the lightest red, from the densest to the least dense, and so on. The primary choice of which way you organize something is made by deciding how you want it to be found. ■ These are all examples of information architecture; the building of information structures that allow others to understand. But, the structures of information go well beyond basic organization. Many principles of clarity can be employed. For example, you only understand something new relative to something you already understand, whether visually, verbally, or numerically. Something will have an understandable size if it is related to the size of something you know. This is easy to see when viewing a photograph of a building that seems to have no human scale. Or visiting a painting and being surprised by its size, because all the reproductions of it are not relative to a human being. Scale always relates to us. ■ For most things (not everything) in our everyday life, scale is based on a relationship to a human being. When things that are vastly large, beyond comparison to a person, or very small, they have to be understood relative to something else and the task becomes difficult. Small things can be shown beside the head of a pin (if we can see them), vast things like those that have to do with astronomy and the solar system tend to lie beyond our visceral comprehension. ■ Well, why am I going into the organization of information in such detail? Just to show that thoughtful structuring of information is an essential skill that a graphic designer, information architect, or information designer needs to have in his or her repertoire. There is not a single school of design in the United States that has a degree program called *Understanding.* True, a problem is given out here and there to learn how to do pretty charts and pretty graphs and pretty maps. There's an occasional faculty member who goes into the subject more thoughtfully. But, as a fundamental discipline it is missing. And yet, there is quite simply an explosion of work to be done in this arena nationally and internationally. In 1962, now more than 30 years ago, I produced my first book with plans of 50 cities in the world, all the same scale. Nobody had done that before. Five years later I did an atlas, again with all maps and legends and statistical analysis in the same scales, the same weighting of information. But, even now in 1996, these are not the ways that people use when they print masses of information about cities, statistics, corporate information, guide books, maps, sports, medicine or finance. The list is endless. It has been 30 years now that I have been lecturing about this oncoming wave of greater and greater amounts of data, and the need to establish school courses and degrees to manage it—the architecture of information. ■ In 1976, I chaired the AIA national convention with a theme called *The Architecture of Information.* Now we leap ahead to the information superhighway of 1996, when information has become national policy. When it fills the front sections and most of the business pages of the newspaper. When it graces the entertainment sections of most of our magazines—when *Time* and *Newsweek* devote special issues to it. And, when the most popular of the new magazines *Wired* focuses on leading-edge issues in what is now referred to as the Information Age. ■ Well, it's not the age that has been addressed by designers. Because of their access to computers, like everybody else, designers do make prettier pie-charts, now in 256 or in millions of colors, now in three dimensions, now exploding apart in wedges, floating in space, with shadows on some strange ethereal background. Each of these decisions has made the information less understandable. But apparently they are applauded by other graphic designers and by clients who don't seem to care about understanding, or are convinced that jazz and beauty and design as they know it—making things prettier—is the wave of the future. Confetti with shadows was brought to us by designers 20 years ago, and it is still around us. We continue to flatter the makers of these things and invite them to speak at our major design invocations like Aspen and others. They are followed by students around the country whose main claim to fame is to make type unintelligible, to break it up in abominations of understanding. ■ And yet, through this field of black volcanic ash has come a group of people, small in number, deep in passion, called Information Architects, who have begun to ply their trade, make themselves visible, and develop a body of work on paper, in electronic interfaces, and in some extraordinary exhibitions. These people will be the wave of the future. The broken type will self-destruct and be nary a footnote of the 1990s. In the 21st century, the floating confetti and its shadows will blow away along with all the exploded pie charts. The field of Information Architecture will soon be the degree-giving focus of choice at most of our "design" schools.

MAKING THE COMPLEX CLEAR AGAIN The *Medical Access* guide used a system of layered schematics to show the workings of the human body. Again, the near-abstract clarified essentials within an extraordinarily complex structure. Designed by Richard Saul Wurman and drawn by Michael Everitt, the layers of bone structures and organs were separated or combined to explain tests and 32 surgical procedures. *Medical Access* is shown on page 29.

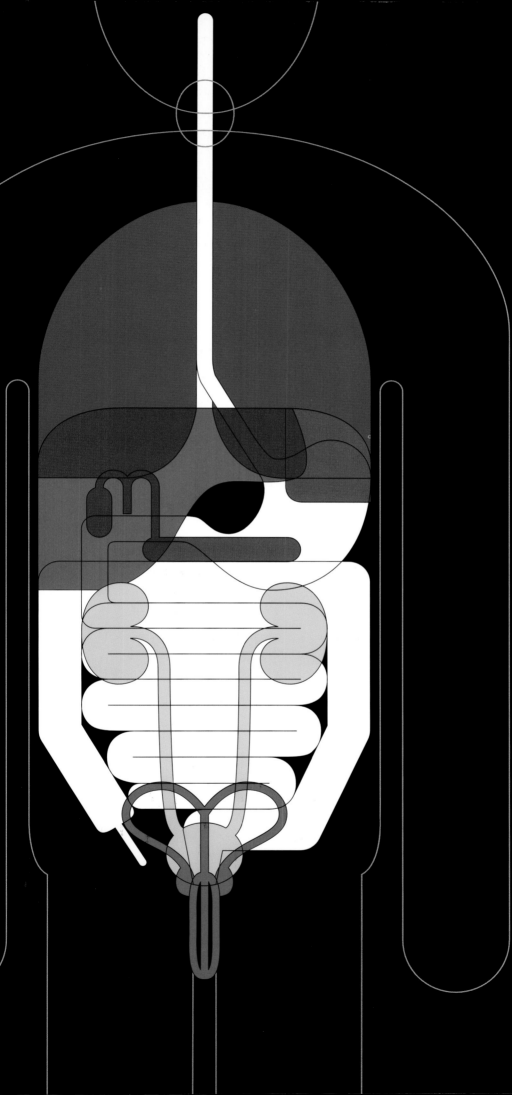

FIRST STORY In 1962, an arrogant northerner, 26 years old, wet behind the ears, in his first teaching job, finds himself talking to a group of architecture students in Raleigh, North Carolina, some of whom take pride in never having been "above the Mason-Dixon line." So, parallel with teaching second-year architecture, I decided to acquaint them with the rest of the world. This was brought about one day when I commented on Alvar Aalto and Helsinki and two of the students said "What's a Helsinki?" ■ I drew up a list of 50 cities, had them choose out of a hat, and said "find me a plan of your city and we'll make little clay models out of kindergarten clay, white plasticine, of each of the cities. And for the convenience of it all, so that we could talk to each other, we'll make all the models the same

COMPARING SCALE In the book *Cities: Comparisons of Form and Scale*, photographs of 50 same-scale clay models of contemporary and ancient cities like New York's Manhattan island (opposite) and Babylon (below) revealed surprising size relationships.

scale." ■ What a surprise! The book I did, based on this short problem, was called *Cities: Comparisons of Form and Scale*,

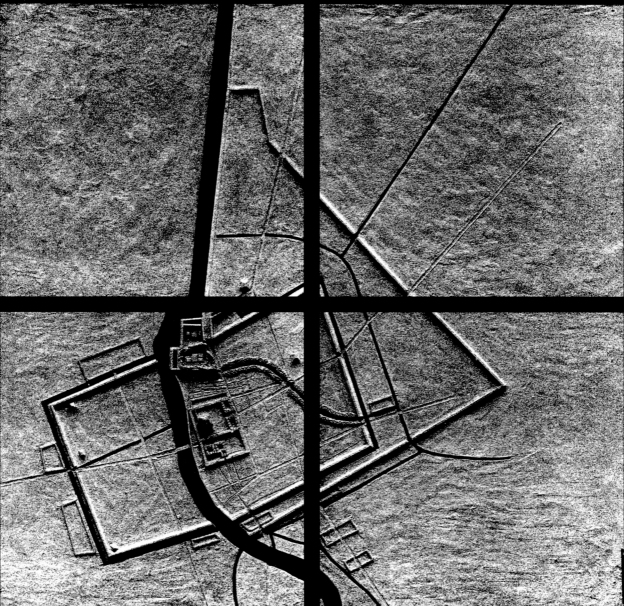

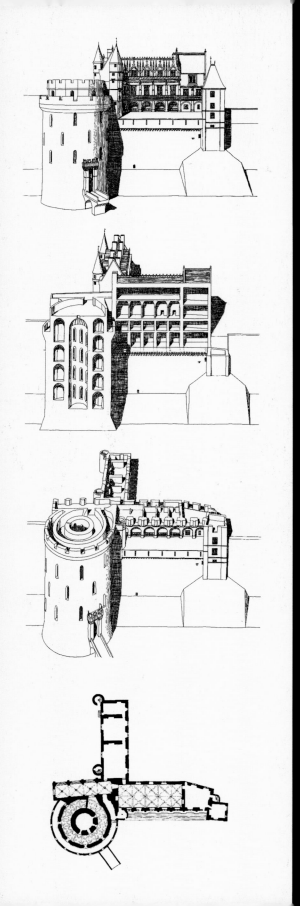
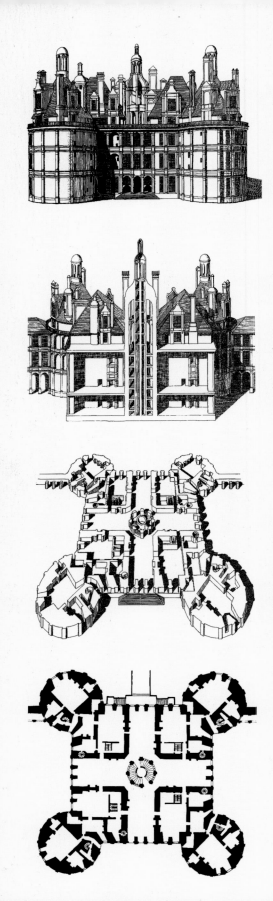

was certainly a surprise to me and, judging by the response of others, a welcome surprise to magazines and schools around the world. It was my first taste of the power of word-of-mouth. We printed 1200 copies and they were gone in six weeks. It appeared on the cover of a Norwegian architectural magazine, the frontispiece of *Architecture d'Aujourd-hui*, and a 10-year permanent exhibit at the Yale School of Architecture. ■ What a revelation to see together the relative sizes of Philadelphia, Versailles, Washington, Paris , Rome, and Beijing (Peking at the time). Thus Wurman's First Law: You only understand something new relative to something you already understand. ■ This

COMPARING SIZE AND STATISTICS A consistent sequence of elevation, section, perspective and plan was drawn at the same scale for each of 30 notable houses in the book *Various Dwellings Described in a Comparative Manner* (opposite). In the *Urban Atlas*, a similar, but symbolic discipline compared the statistics of cities, like personal income density in Detroit and New York (below), and residential population density in New York (following two pages).

was followed shortly after (in 1964) by a book called *Various Dwellings Described in a Comparative Manner*. It showed 30 houses in a style freely borrowed from Steen Eiler Rasmussen, which helps you

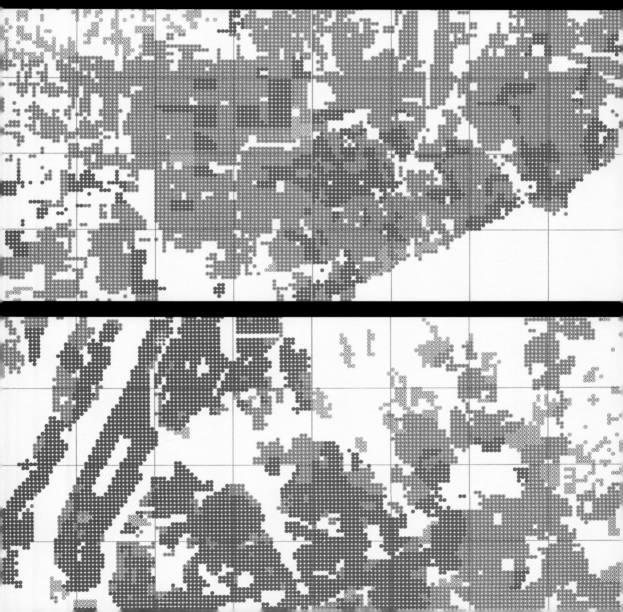

Linear/Nonlinear

You're probably pretty confident that you know the size of a football field, especially if you play the game or watch it on television. You're used to measuring it in your mind by the kind of activity that takes place on it, and by seeing all of it used at once. But did you know that if the area of a football field were a bicycle path five feet wide, it could wind along a river, cut through a wood, or parallel a street for over two miles!

This example demonstrates that the shape of recreational space is just as important as its size. Just as there are activities that have to take place in defined areas—rectangles, squares, or circles—there are other activities that are linear in nature, such as walking, bicycling, horseback riding, and canoeing. While it's true that you could take a walk across a football field or canoe across

a lake, neither of these activities is as well suited to those sites as to a long, winding space.

Knowing the potential of variously shaped areas can help you maximize their recreational possibilities. And knowing the shape requirements and alternatives of different recreational activities makes it easier for you to understand the potential of recreational spaces. Nonlinear spaces are often created by the intersection or deviation of linear systems, and usually surrounded, bisected, or connected by them as well.

The photographs below, from ground level and from above, show some of the huge variety of linear and nonlinear spaces, and how they fit together. If we learn to open our eyes to all the funny-shaped, left-over spaces around us—especially places like streets, sidewalks, vacant lots and rooftops—we might find solutions to a lot of our recreational needs near at hand.

Bicycling
The first two-wheeled bicycle was designed in Paris in 1690 by M. de Sivrac but proved rather unsatisfactory because it lacked pedals. Other efforts followed but it wasn't until 1821 that Louis Gompertz of England invented a gear-type rope system which became the basic bicycle chain.

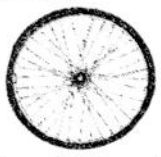

Nonlinear

The strip picture at the right is a slice of New York City's Central Park, seen from above, with south at the left, north at the right. It is a combination of an engraving of the park in 1870 and a recent aerial photograph. The changes that can be seen is the replacement of the Old Reservoir by ball-fields. Some of the changes that cannot be seen are: an addition of acres of space for buildings, services, and parking between 1900 and 1966; a tripling of paved walks and drives in the same

time; the enclosure of 30 acres for special activities; and the reduction of open meadow between 1900 and 1966 from 55 to 16 acres. The area of city north of the park is included to demonstrate that linear and nonlinear spaces are a characteristic of nearly every environment.

Linear

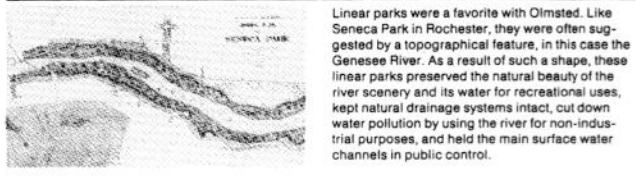

Linear parks were a favorite with Olmsted. Like Seneca Park in Rochester, they were often suggested by a topographical feature, in this case the Genesee River. As a result of such a shape, these linear parks preserved the natural beauty of the river scenery and its water for recreational uses, kept natural drainage systems intact, cut down water pollution by using the river for non-industrial purposes, and held the main surface water channels in public control.

Baseball
Baseball, the American derivative of the English games of cricket and rounders, was first developed in this country around 1900. Napleased versions of the so-called "Town Ball Game" grew up in Boston, New York, and Philadelphia between 1820 and 1833. The rules were standardized in 1842 and the first baseball club was formed in 1845.

30   31

Flat/Sloped

Cliffs, mountains, valleys, and rolling hills aren't just good to look at: they're good to use. If you live in a city (other than San Francisco and other hilly cities) and don't get much of a chance to wander over topographically interesting terrain, or if you strongly prefer games played on prepared flat surfaces, recreation to you is flat. But there are a great many interesting activities that can only be pursued on terrain that slopes: skiing, sledding, and

rolling down a hill, for example. There are also activities that can take place on several different kinds of topography, but which are made more enjoyable by stretching across a hill or two, such as hiking and golf.

The drawing below represents different topographies from absolutely vertical to absolutely horizontal, both above and below ground. At the left are different activities. Draw a line from each activity that needs a specific kind of topography to the appropriate terrain in the drawing. Then, in the column below at the right, write in the activities that can take place on a variety of topographies.

Bocce
Bocce originated in Italy and is considered one of the oldest sports. It can be played anywhere on a hard, level surface that measures 60 to 10 feet.

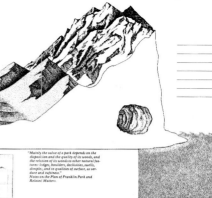

Skiing
The earliest ski edges were bones from large animals, strapped to the skis with leather thongs. The oldest pair of skis (approximately 5000 years old) was found in Sweden.

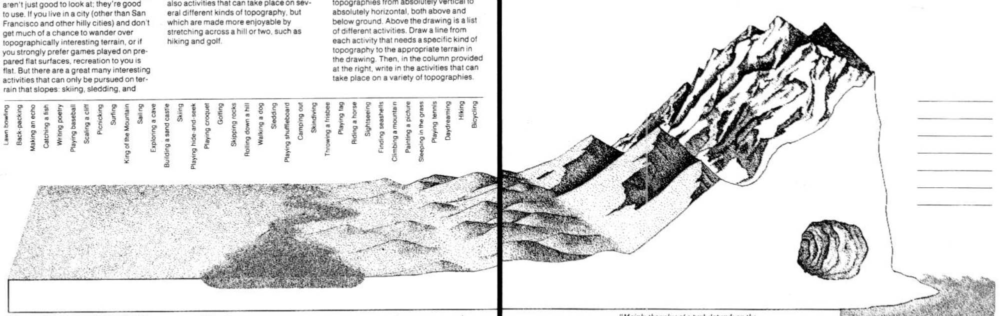

"It is a mistake to suppose that a considerable extent of nearly flat ground is inadmissible or undesirable in a great park, or that it must be overcome, at any cost, by vast artificial elevations and depressions, or by covering all the surface with trivial objects of interest." Chicago Park Report, 1871.

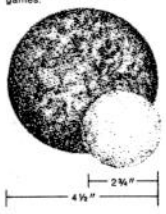

At right, profiles of Central Park south-to-north along Sixth and Seventh Avenues.

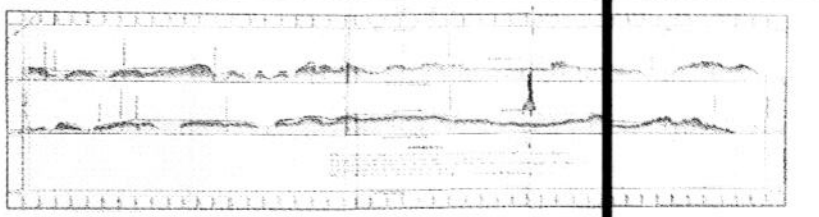

"Mainly the value of a park depends on the disposition and the quality of its woods, and the relation of its woods to other natural features: ledges, boulders, declivities, swells, dimples, and on qualities of surface, as verdure and turfiness." Notes on the Plan of Franklin Park and Related Matters.

32   33

10:30 am	11:00	11:30

On the left, Charlie selects wood for the form he is about to build. On a site as large as this one, materials are moved by laborers to be as close as possible to the work; however, as the work proceeds, material is picked up and moved on to the next location for the carpenters. On the right, after lunch, Charlie hammers, drills and inserts reinforcing rods through the form's walls.

11:30 am	12 noon	12:30 pm

After lunch Paul begins to finish a cabinet similar to the one he had been making in the morning. Cabinetmaking is a satisfying experience. Through the skillful use of planes, hand sanders and a power sander, Paul turns a piece of wood into an object to admire.

12 noon	12:30 pm	1:00	1:30

On the left, Rick uses a power saw and finishes putting a header in the doorway. Rick removes old cork. On the right, they load some materials into their car and move to another job they are working on—a city house that is being converted to apartments. In the kitchen, new counters and cabinets are being installed. Rick attaches the sink to the counter top and then, having installed the counter top, checks the level.

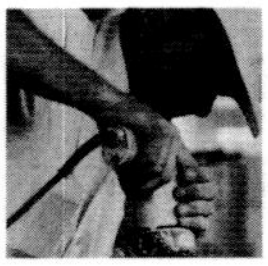

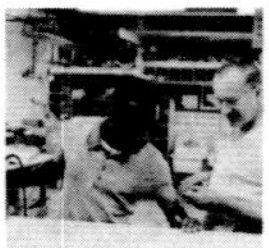

12:30 pm	1:00	1:30

---

12 noon	12:30 pm	1:00	1:30

1:00 pm	1:30	2:00	2:30

2:00 pm	2:30	3:00

After another check on the upper floor of this low-rise apartment construction, Nick works in his field office—checking records, reviewing schedules and, with the help of an automatic answering device, returning phone calls that have been received in his absence. On the right, a carpenter puts his signature on an account stating the number of pieces he has installed; this carpenter is paid on a per piece basis.

2:00 pm	2:30	3:00	3:30

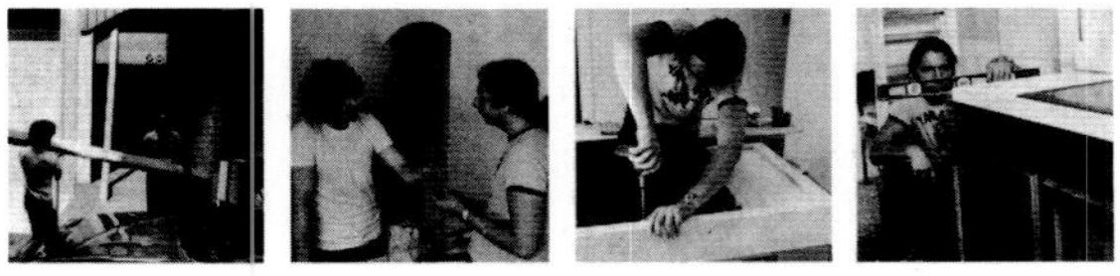

understand the plan, section and elevation of a group of notable dwellings in very short strokes. ■ **SECOND STORY** I met Edward Higbee when I was a special assistant to Governor Terry Sanford in Raleigh. I was then 27 years old. We struck up a friendship that led him to include me in a Twentieth-Century Grant two or three years later, which paid for travelling around the United States for a couple of months and visits to all the major cities. Packrat that I am, I came home with all the material—maps, graphs, charts—that I collected as we visited every city planning and urban design agency in each city. Those were heady times for urban design, the mid-60s, money poured out of Washington for urban renewal and the Federal bulldozer was in full flair. But, despite the money being given out left and right, I soon discovered while going through the materials, that no two cities in the United States drew their maps at the same scale, or used the same map legends, or even used the same methods of recording population statistics, the quality of housing, the levels of income—oh, the list was endless. There was no way anybody giving out money could understand why they were funding one city instead of another, which city needed more and which needed less, and where census data could help. There was simply no consistency within or between cities. It was a mess if anybody wanted to understand the pattern of problems in American cities, make some value judgments, and put money to good use. ■ Cut to 1966 and Washington University in St. Louis. Joe Passonneau, the marvelous Dean of Architecture at that school, and I began a project called *Urban Atlas*—the first comparative, statistical atlas of major American cities. Published in 1967 by the MIT Press, 3000 copies were printed and sold for $100 each—a really expensive price at that time—and it was soon a collector's item. No effect on the federal government. ■ Shortly after that, I started my first experiments with books and page navigation. The year was 1967, the book this time was called *The Nature of Recreation,* celebrating the work of the great landscape architect, Frederick Law Olmsted, shown at the National Gallery of Art, commissioned by Carter Brown. I developed the project with Joel Katz, who worked for me at the time, and used themes of continuity, hierarchy, parallel text, marginalia and connectivity. ■ **THIRD STORY** I developed a series of career guidebooks when I realized that, in the simplest sense, we all go to school for 12 years to figure out what to do on the day we graduate. Twelve years of schooling for that one day, and yet nothing we learn helps us understand the world of work and how to make that decision. The existing literature comes in 3 varieties: 1) A great dictionary of out-dated, single-page descriptions of 1000 careers that the counselor keeps behind the desk; 2) 300-page books in the library on each career—which tell you more than anybody wants to know; and 3) booklets from related sources

MAPPING CONTENT Dividing a subject into understandable parts can conquer its complexity. Especially if the parts are enhanced by the structure of the design. The work of Frederick Law Olmsted was used in *The Nature of Recreation* (opposite top) to explain our needs and use of recreation resources. Information was presented using themes of hierarchy, parallel text, and marginalia—all reflected in the design of the page. *The Yellow Pages Career Library* (opposite bottom) used hour-by-hour photographic timelines to show *A Day in the Life Of* a range of careers in separate books, like *Engineer*, *Cook*, *Architect*, and *Carpenter* (shown).

like *Nancy Nurse Writes on Nursing* from an insurance company, which tell you that each career is the best thing invented since Philadelphia Brand Cream Cheese. ■ I developed 12 of a projected series of 100 books called the *Yellow Pages Career Library,* with a visual essay called *A Day in the Life Of* in the center of each book. This was well before other Day in the Life Of concepts were introduced, and it shows the value of using time to explain things. ■

FOURTH STORY The year is 1980, I move into Los Angeles close to a state of unemployment, and in a full state of disorientation. Unable to find my way around, seeing that L.A. is about to celebrate its bicentennial, I decide to do my own guide book to access everything I want to know about the city for myself. The city's agencies and Atlantic Richfield are helpful, but I am completely unable to find a publisher or a distributor. Because of these failures I am backed into forming my own publishing company and selling the books out of the back of my car. After analyzing many guides, I realize that all I really want to know is where I am at any moment and what's around me. That simple-minded want leads to the or-

MAPPING CONTEXT The idea for a new kind of city guide was born in 1980 after moving to Los Angeles and feeling a "full state of disorientation." *LA Access* was organized primarily by location—a simple desire to know where one was and what was nearby. The guides had color-coded resource categories and unique styles. Guides for 30 cities have been produced, including (clockwise from map below) Hawaii, San Francisco, Tokyo, and Las Vegas

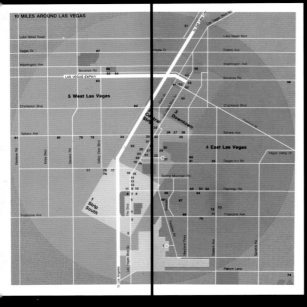

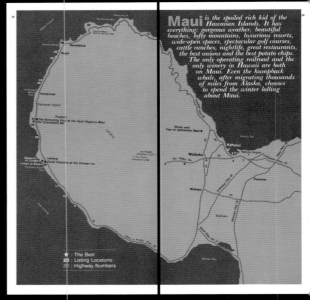

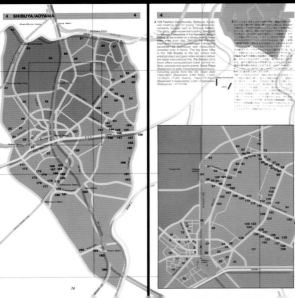

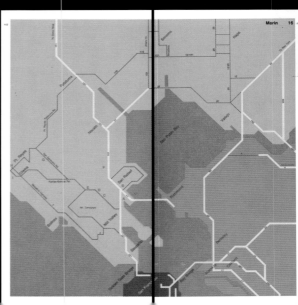

ganization of the book—primarily by location, with secondary organizations by category and hierarchy. The books are successful. *Access Guides* have now been published for about 30 cities. ■ **FIFTH STORY** I decide to explore different territory and, after developing a few guides on sports and the Olympics (3,500,000 sold), I initiated *Medical Access*, a book about diagnostic tests and surgical procedures. The underlying reason for doing this book was similar to my reasons for *LA Access*—I was going to have a physical, I couldn't find any literature to help dispel my anxiety or give me questions to ask my doctor, and every good medical illustration and photograph made me

MAPPING PROCESS The book *Medical Access* explains 32 common surgical procedures using a system of anatomical schematics on many layers (see page 19) drawn by Michael Everitt and applied by Lorraine Christiani. The nature, preparation, procedure, and recovery stages of each operation are described on one tightly structured page. The book also answers common questions, explains 120 diagnostic tests, and shows an operating room.

ill. The book consists of three sections: 1) diagnostic tests, 2) surgical procedures (done with Peter Bradford), and 3) questions and answers. The book is a success (1,250,000 sold). ■ **SIXTH STORY** I'm

---

TONSIL REMOVAL — TONSILLECTOMY

303,000	1-2½ hrs			
Frequency in 1982	Duration of Operation	30-90 minutes on your side in recovery room painkiller for postop pain upon waking from anesthesia	walking 6 hrs	sore throat several days strenuous activity 2 wks

Nature of problem.

A tonsillectomy is performed for these reasons when a patient is over 5 years old: a history of **4 or more documented tonsillitis attacks** a year; at least 2 throat cultures positive for **streptococcus bacteria;** severe recurrent **middle ear infection** (*otitis media*) with hearing loss. The adenoids are almost always removed (adenoidectomy), especially if they are very enlarged and block the rear of the nose.

Frequency. Of the tonsillectomies performed in 1982, 89 percent of the patients were under 15 years old.

Before admission to the hospital, you will have these tests and studies: **Complete blood count, Urinalysis, Blood clotting series** and **Chest x-ray.**

Adenoids, located at the back of the nose, above the tonsils, also help to protect children from respiratory infections. At about age 5, they begin to shrink and virtually disappear by puberty. If they become infected, antibiotics are usually effective. If unchecked, the infection can spread to the middle ear. Because the adenoids disappear with time, surgical removal is a last resort. But if the infection occurs in conjunction with tonsillitis, then a tonsilloadenoidectomy (T&A) may be performed.

Surgical preparation.

About an hour before surgery, you will receive a tranquilizer injection, change into a surgical gown, cap and socks, and if you are an adult or adolescent, the needle for an intravenous fluid line will be placed in the back of your hand. For a young child, this is delayed until after the anesthesia has been given in the operating room.

Anesthetic. General anesthetic is used for the procedure.

The tonsils, which are part of the immune (lymphatic) system, help protect children from respiratory infections. They are very small at birth, gradually reaching their full size by age 6 or 7. As a child grows older, the tonsils tend to shrink. However, the tonsils may become infected from a virus or bacteria causing them to become unusually large, and you may be able to see pus and white spots on them. This condition, tonsillitis, is often accompanied by fever, pain in the throat, tenderness in the neck and a cough; it is first treated with antibiotics. However, if a child has recurrent tonsillitis or the tonsils interfere with general health, breathing or hearing, your physician may advise removing the tonsils. This is only used as a last resort, contrary to the common myth that all children should have their tonsils removed.

Procedure.

1 You are placed on your back, with your head tilted slightly backward.

2 The **mucosa** (soft, moist tissue lining the throat) is opened to reveal the tonsil. The surgeon slowly dissects or teases the tonsil and its encasing tissue away from the **fossa** (muscle bed). Extensive cutting of the *mucosa* is carefully avoided.

3 The tonsil is now connected to the throat only at its base. A **snare** (a thin wire loop) is slowly tightened around the base, freeing the entire tonsil from the throat. This procedure is repeated for the second tonsil on the other side of the throat. The tonsils may be sent to the pathology laboratory for analysis.

labels: tonsil, mucosa, snare, fossa

Stages of recovery.

Immediately following your operation, you will be positioned on your side with your mouth pointing slightly downward. The foot of your bed will be raised a little above your head, to prevent blood and mucus from flowing downward into your lungs. This also helps in early detection of any bleeding. You will be in the recovery room for 30 to 90 minutes, while being closely watched for bleeding and any difficulty breathing.

As soon as you begin to wake from the anesthesia, you will be given a pain-killer by injection.

Your throat will be sore for several days and you will have difficulty swallowing. Ice cream is a welcome and favorite treatment.

Limitations. Strenuous activity should be avoided for a couple of weeks.

Drugs. You will be given an oral medicine for your throat pain.

Complications. Other than a sore throat and difficulty swallowing for the first few days after surgery, there are usually no complications.

PROSTATE — TRANSURETHRAL RESECTION OF THE PROSTATE (TURP)

258,000	1-1½ hrs			
Frequency in 1982	Duration of Operation	recovery room 1-2 hrs	walk 1st postop day	strenuous activity after 6 wks

Nature of problem.

In men, the prostate gland surrounds the upper part of the urethra as it leaves the bladder. If the gland becomes significantly enlarged, as it often does with age, it may squeeze the bladder outlet interfering with the flow of urine and eventually cause bladder and kidney infection and damage. In TURP, the procedure described here, an instrument is introduced through the urethra and a large portion of the gland is cut away. There is no abdominal incision. When the prostate is above a certain size or cancer is suspected, other surgical procedures (suprapubic, retropubic or perineal) may be used. These are more radical operations where an incision must be made, and a much higher incidence of impotence is associated with them. While TURP is not usually emergency surgery, it may be urgently required to prevent urinary retention and infection.

Frequency. Three-fourths of the men who received TURP in 1983 were age 65 or older.

Surgical preparation.

Before the decision to operate is made, you may undergo several tests including **Intravenous**

pyelography (IVP), Acid phosphatase (elevated in prostate cancer) and perhaps **Cystoscopy.** You will also have a group of routine presurgery tests that may include: **Complete blood count, Urinalysis, Urine culture, Electrolytes, Chest x-ray** and if you are over 40, an **EKG.** About an hour before surgery you are sedated by injection. An intravenous needle is inserted, usually in the back of your hand for later administration of IV fluids.

Anesthetic. Usually, a regional nerve block or spinal anesthesia is used.

Stages of recovery.

Limitations. You will be instructed to avoid all strenuous exercise for at least 6 weeks following surgery. Sexual activity can resume in about 4 to 6 weeks when bleeding has stopped and you feel comfortable.

Drugs. You will be given oral medication to control postoperative pain, perhaps antibiotics to prevent infection and stool softeners to reduce strain during bowel movements.

Complications. A 10 percent impotency rate has been reported after TURP; however, this may be due to the older age group involved.

Procedure.

1 A resectoscope is inserted into the urethra to visually establish certain landmarks of the bladder neck and prostate gland. The surgeon evaluates the size and shape of the gland by means of a manual rectal examination.

2 With a cutting instrument fitted into the resectoscope, the overgrowth on the prostate is gradually cut away. Specimens of tissue are sent to the pathology laboratory for analysis.

3 Fragments of tissue are flushed out through a resectoscope. A urinary catheter will be inserted following surgery to carry away urine.

labels: bladder, bladder neck, overgrowth of prostate gland, resectoscope, urethra, fragments of tissue, prostate gland

No nerves are severed in the operation that would affect potency. If you had good erections before surgery, you will probably continue to have good erections. After TURP, most patients experience **retrograde ejaculation.** Instead of flowing out of the penis, semen flows into the bladder during orgasm. You may notice the lack of ejaculate, but it is not painful and does not reduce the other feelings of climax. The semen is later eliminated in the urine. **Urinary infection** is another possible complication. It is treated with antibiotics.

Scar. With the TURP procedure, there is no scar because entry is through the urethra, without an incision.

A radical retropubic prostatectomy is a common operation used to remove a cancerous prostate. The incision, which is made in the lower abdomen, tends to injure a nerve bundle linked to erection function. Impotence may be as high as 80-85 percent after surgery. However, a new, nerve-sparing technique has recently been invented by Dr. Patrick Walsh of Johns Hopkins University. Preliminary studies show 60-80 percent of the men who undergo the procedure are able to have intercourse within 6 months of surgery.

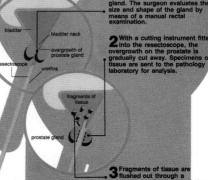

asked to re-design the Pacific Bell Yellow Pages. I realize the yellow pages, in their simplest form, are an exercise in finding something. And, the find-it process has broken down because of the proliferation of incoherent headings all arranged alphabetically. These being unchangeable, I developed the *Smart Yellow Pages* branding symbols, and a series of indices that help you find the headings based on categorical groupings. For instance, "Automobile" has hundreds of headings, 90% of which do not start with "Auto" but relate to it, like auto repairing, buying, selling, insuring, accidents, all sorts of parts, and so on. I ended up designing the first 80 pages of each of the 96 directories I did to show that you can find things by category. I also categorized by time (which places are open all the time, on holidays, or on weekends), by location (where places are on maps, so you can tell which gas station or restaurant is closest to where you are) as well as alphabetically. Each year 30,000,000 are printed. ■ **SEVENTH STORY** I move to New York City and I am told that to be a "player" I must have a house in the Hamptons. I buy

Just for Kids · A85

Everything for children organized by subjects, with specific listings and page numbers.

For more information turn to the following SMART Yellow Pages sections:

Community Access Pages
Places to Go
Parks & Recreation Areas
Calendar of Events

Subject Search Pages
Clothing & Personal
Care

Child Care

Baby Sitters	287
Camps	407
Child Care Centers	451
Child Care Centers Consultants	452
Parents Guidance Instruction	1367

Clothing

Boys' Clothing & Furnishings Retail	373
Children's & Infants' Garments Retail	453
Dancers' Supplies	609
Department Stores	660
Dresses-Retail	693
Girls' Wearing Apparel	904
Jeans	1044
Knit Goods-Retail	1065
Riding Apparel & Equipment	1677
Shoes-Orthopedic	1775
Shoes-Retail	1775
T-Shirts	1850
Western Apparel	2048

Hobbies

Art Goods-Retail	76
Art Instruction & Schools	76
Baseball Cards	317
Collectibles	504
Comic Books	507
Computers-Dealers	511
Computers-Software & Services	537
Craft Supplies-Retail	602
Hobby & Model Construction Supplies-Retail	961
Magazine Dealers	1146
Magazines-Back Number	1146
Miniature Items For Collectors	1202
Quilting Materials & Supplies	1659
Stamps For Collectors	1817
Telescopes	1881
Youth Organizations & Centers	2080

Toys

Bicycles	341
Doll Clothing & Accessories	678
Doll Houses & Accessories	678
Dolls-Repairing	678
Dolls-Retail	678
Five Cents To One Dollar Stores	613
Games & Game Supplies-Retail	886
Kites	1065
Magicians' Supplies	1146
Miniature Items For Collectors	1202
Novelties-Retail	1277
Playground Equipment	1499
Puppets	1659
Toys-Retail	1929
Video Games-Dealers	2008
Video Games-Renting & Leasing	2008
Video Games-Service & Repair	2008

Sports & Activities

Amusement Places	38
Baseball Batting Ranges	317
Baseball Clubs & Parks	317
Camping Equipment	407
Camps	407
Ceramic Instruction	447
Dancing Instruction	609
Gymnasiums	937
Gymnastics Instruction	938
Martial Arts Instruction	1169
Martial Arts Supplies & Equipment	1172
Playground Equipment	1499
Playgrounds & Parks	1499
Recreation Centers	1599
Sewing Instruction	1766
Skateboards & Equipment	1796
Skating Equipment & Supplies	1796
Skating Instruction	1796
Skating Rinks	1796
Soccer Clubs	1801
Sporting Goods-Dealers	1809
Surf Boards	1846
Swimming Instruction	1848
Swimming Pools-Public	1849
Tennis Instruction	1892
Trampoline Equipment & Supplies	1934

Places to Visit

Amusement Places	38
Arboretums	65
Museums	1265
Planetariums	1489
Playgrounds & Parks	1499
Zoological Gardens	2080

Infants

Baby Accessories-Retail	286
Baby Carriages & Strollers	287
Children's & Infants' Garments Retail	453
Diaper Service	663

Health Care

Clinics	489
Crisis Intervention Service	608
Dentists//Pediatrics	658
Marriage, Family & Child Counselors	1166
Parents Guidance Instruction	1357
Physicians & Surgeons, M.D.//Pediatric Allergy	1452
Physicians & Surgeons, M.D.// Pediatrics (Infants, Children & Adolescents)	1452
Physicians & Surgeons, M.D.// Pediatrics-Cardiology	1453
Physicians & Surgeons, M.D.// Psychiatry-Child	1467
Psychologists	1547
Social Service Organizations	1801

Education

Book Dealers-Retail	360
Book Dealers-Used & Rare	366
Encyclopedias	755
Libraries-Circulating & Rental	1086
Libraries-Public	1086
Reading Improvement Instruction	1571
School Supplies	1727
Schools-Academic-Pre-School & Kindergarten	1730
Schools-Academic-Secondary & Elementary	1732
Schools-Academic-Special Education	1738
Schools Information	1747
Tutoring	1975

Music

Music Instruction-Instrumental	1266
Music Instruction-Vocal	1267
Music Libraries	1267
Music-Sheet	1267
Musical Instrument Accessories	1267
Musical Instruments-Renting	1268
Musical Instruments-Repairing	1268
Musical Instruments-Retail	1268
Musical Instruments-Used	1272
Pianos	1467
Violins	2021

a terminally cute house and a car to get there. I buy the correct car, and I buy road atlases so I can use the car for other trips. But, despite the arrangement of the atlases, I
soon find that you do not drive across the United States alphabetically. So, in a continued act of indulgence, I decide to do my own road atlas. This becomes a Herculean
effort, stretching the capacities of the newly-released Photoshop program beyond its
limits. Still, I produced the *USAtlas* with the help of many, including Maria Giudice and
Lynne Stiles. The book has some features from earlier books and new ideas as well. I
put time and distance together with a 50-mile/80-kilometer page grid, each segment

MAPPING ACCESS Logically, one hunts for information in terms
of its nature, or topic, not its alphabetical listing. The *Smart Yellow Pages* for Pacific Bell were given topic indices marked with
symbols (opposite). The *USAtlas* has a similar logic. One travels
by car geographically, not aphabetically—adjacent states were
placed on adjacent pages or nearby (cover/contents map below).
Also, pages have driving time/distance grids (following two pages).

taking one hour to drive. I used the ideas
of marginalia from *The Nature of Recreation*, the varieties of trivia from the *Access*
guides, the large page numbers from *The
Smart Yellow Pages*, and the ideas of scale

*"Graphics wiz Richard Saul Wurman . . . has finally figured out a way to make
a nationwide road guide that's legible and well organized . . ."* Condé Nast Traveler

RICHARD SAUL WURMAN'S NEW ROAD ATLAS
USATLAS

ACCESS®PRESS

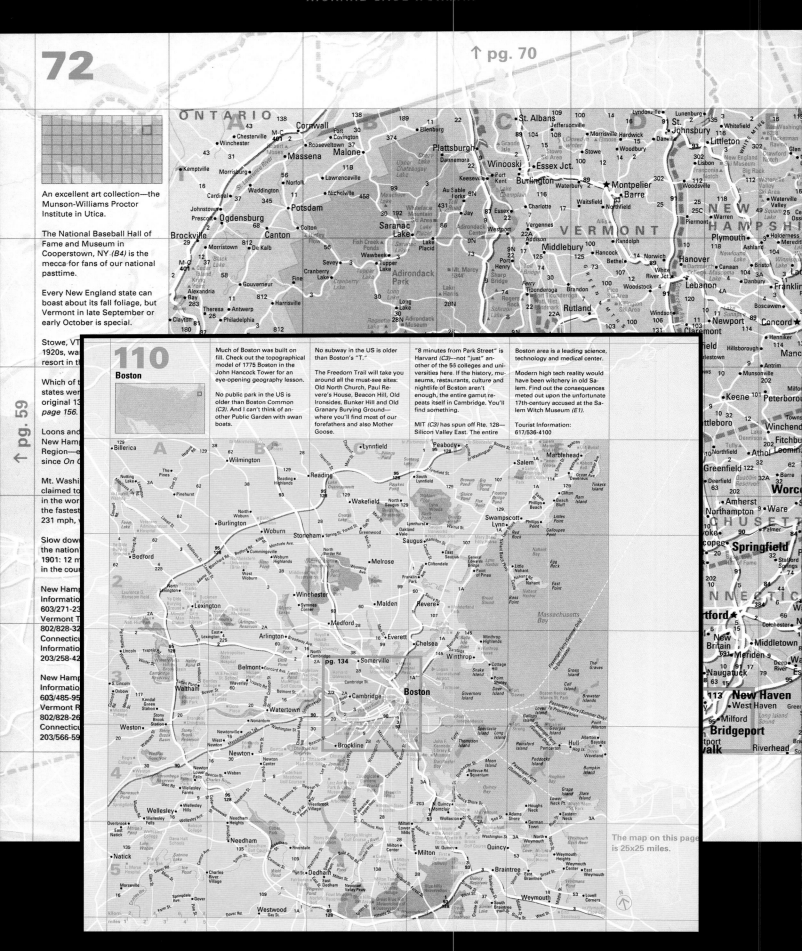

↑ pg. 70

An excellent art collection—the Munson-Williams Proctor Institute in Utica.

The National Baseball Hall of Fame and Museum in Cooperstown, NY *(B4)* is the mecca for fans of our national pasttime.

Every New England state can boast about its fall foliage, but Vermont in late September or early October is special.

Stowe, VT 1920s, was resort in th

Which of t states wer original 13 *page 156.*

Loons and New Hamp Region—e since *On C*

Mt. Washi claimed to in the wor the fastest 231 mph, v

Slow dow the nation 1901: 12 m in the cour

New Hamp Informatio 603/271-23 Vermont T 802/828-32 Connecticu Informatio 203/258-42

New Hamp Informatio 603/485-95 Vermont R 802/828-26 Connecticu 203/566-59

↑ pg. 59

110
Boston

Much of Boston was built on fill. Check out the topographical model of 1775 Boston in the John Hancock Tower for an eye-opening geography lesson.

No public park in the US is older than Boston Common *(C3)*. And I can't think of another Public Garden with swan boats.

No subway in the US is older than Boston's "T."

The Freedom Trail will take you around all the must-see sites: Old North Church, Paul Revere's House, Beacon Hill, Old Ironsides, Bunker Hill and Old Granary Burying Ground—where you'll find most of our forefathers and also Mother Goose.

"8 minutes from Park Street" is Harvard *(C3)*—not "just" another of the 53 colleges and universities here. If the history, seums, restaurants, culture and nightlife of Boston aren't enough, the entire gamut repeats itself in Cambridge. You'll find something.

MIT *(C3)* has spun off Rte. 128—Silicon Valley East. The entire

Boston area is a leading science, technology and medical center.

Modern high tech reality would have been witchery in old Salem. Find out the consequences meted out upon the unfortunate 17th-century accused at the Salem Witch Museum *(E1)*.

Tourist Information:
617/536-4100

The map on this page is 25x25 miles.

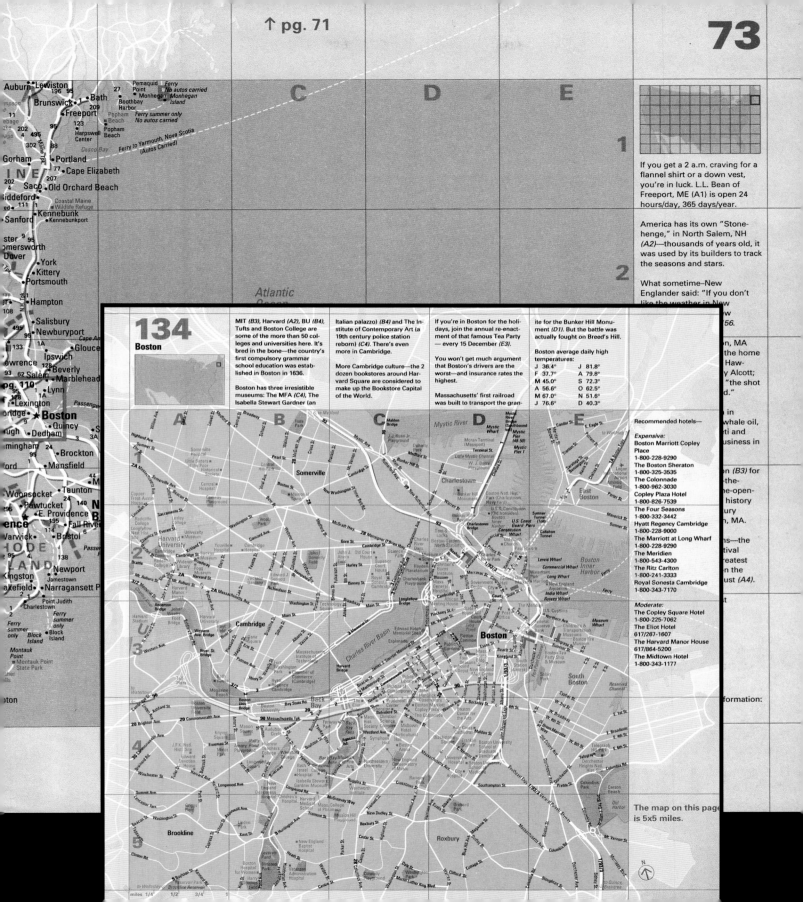

If you get a 2 a.m. craving for a flannel shirt or a down vest, you're in luck. L.L. Bean of Freeport, ME (A1) is open 24 hours/day, 365 days/year.

America has its own "Stonehenge," in North Salem, NH (A2)—thousands of years old, it was used by its builders to track the seasons and stars.

What sometime–New Englander said: "If you don't like the weather in New

134

Boston

MIT (B3), Harvard (A2), BU (B4), Tufts and Boston College are some of the more than 50 colleges and universities here. It's bred in the bone—the country's first compulsory grammar school education was established in Boston in 1636.

Boston has three irresistible museums: The MFA (C4), The Isabella Stewart Gardner (an Italian palazzo) (B4) and The Institute of Contemporary Art (a 19th century police station reborn) (C4). There's even more in Cambridge.

More Cambridge culture—the 2 dozen bookstores around Harvard Square are considered to make up the Bookstore Capital of the World.

If you're in Boston for the holidays, join the annual re-enactment of that famous Tea Party — every 15 December (E3).

You won't get much argument that Boston's drivers are the worst—and insurance rates the highest.

Massachusetts' first railroad was built to transport the gran-

ite for the Bunker Hill Monument (D1). But the battle was actually fought on Breed's Hill.

Boston average daily high temperatures:
J 36.4° J 81.8°
F 37.7° A 79.8°
M 45.0° S 72.3°
A 56.6° O 62.5°
M 67.0° N 51.6°
J 76.6° D 40.3°

Recommended hotels—

Expensive:
Boston Marriott Copley Place
1-800-228-9290
The Boston Sheraton
1-800-325-3535
The Colonnade
1-800-962-3030
Copley Plaza Hotel
1-800-826-7539
The Four Seasons
1-800-332-3442
Hyatt Regency Cambridge
1-800-228-9000
The Marriott at Long Wharf
1-800-228-9290
The Meridien
1-800-543-4300
The Ritz Carlton
1-800-241-3333
Royal Sonesta Cambridge
1-800-343-7170

Moderate:
The Copley Square Hotel
1-800-225-7062
The Eliot Hotel
617/267-1607
The Harvard Manor House
617/864-5200
The Midtown Hotel
1-800-343-1177

The map on this page is 5x5 miles.

Too many personal computer owners overlook the importance of a comfortable work area for their machines and themselves.

Ergonomics, the study of human interaction with work, should play a key role in setting up your work environment. Ignoring these issues can lead to muscular and skeletal health problems if you frequently spend many hours in front of a computer.

In particular, you should pay close attention to the height of the keyboard from the floor and the angle between your eyes and the video monitor. If typing at the keyboard is a major part of your work, then also investigate wrist supports to reduce the likelihood of contracting a repetitive strain injury.

Viewing Angle

Establishing the proper angle between your eyes and the video monitor can make the difference between headaches and painless computing. To impose the least stress on your eyes, the monitor should not be straight ahead (although this is difficult to avoid with 19" and 21" monitors). An angle of 5° to 15° from your eyes down to the center of the screen is considered comfortable for most computer users, especially if you must move your eyes constantly from copy source to keyboard to screen. Try to avoid frequent focus adjustments (i.e., the distance between your eyes and what you're looking at) by adding a document holder (a device that lets you set papers adjacent to the monitor).

If you are using a separate video monitor, a tilting swivel monitor stand is highly recommended. It allows for myriad adjustments to suit your mood or fatigue level, as well as allowing you to adjust the monitor for reduced glare. For more about video monitor safety, see page ➔ 37.

A compact Macintosh (like today's Classic model) takes up so little space on the desk that it is often convenient to place one or more peripherals (external hard disks, CD-ROM players, etc.) underneath the machine. The problem with this tower arrangement, however, is that the viewing angle may get uncomfortably high with too many items stacked below.

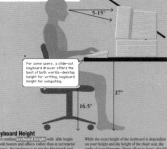

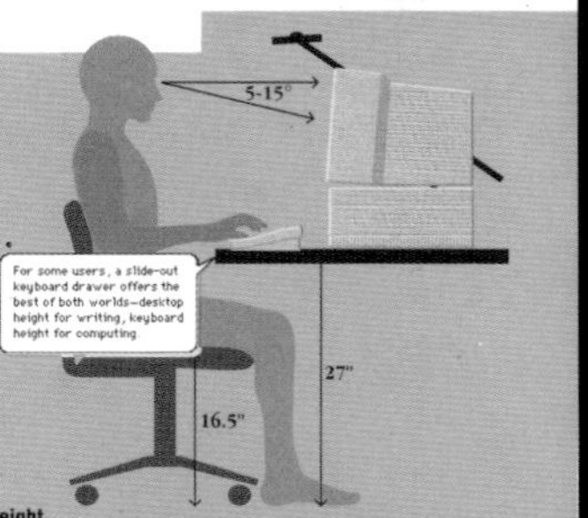
5-15°
For some users, a slide-out keyboard drawer offers the best of both worlds—desktop height for writing, keyboard height for computing.
27"
16.5"

Keyboard Height

Don't confuse keyboard height with able height. In both homes and offices (other than at secretarial stations), the tendency is to put the Macintosh and keyboard on the main desk surface. In the United States, a standard office desk surface is 29" from the floor. But for most people, a keyboard at that height is uncomfortable, and may be dangerous during extensive use. If you must use a standard, fixed-height table for your Macintosh, make sure the keyboard is either in a recessed keyboard tray or on a typewriter height desk (typically 27" high).

While the exact height of the keyboard is dependent on your height and the height of the chair seat, the angle of your forearms (from elbow to keys) should be about parallel with the floor. The chair should offer good lower back support, be very mobile, and allow your feet to touch the floor fully.

Repetitive Strain Injury

Only within the past few years have the potential health dangers of excessive computer keyboard typing been observed and studied. While not everything is understood at this point, it is clear that repetitive hand, wrist, and upper body motions—especially when some level of force is applied—can lead to painful injuries. This affects virtually every occupation that requires repetitive motions, from store clerks to assembly line workers. A common cause is straining tendons that can lead to inflammation and swelling, which starts squeezing on nerves.

Among the most common injuries are tendinitus, tenosynovitis, and carpal tunnel syndrome (CTS). As a group, these are called repetitive strain injuries (RSIs) or cumulative trauma disorders (CTDs).

No exact measure exists about how much keyboarding is too much, so be aware of these symptoms: pain, numbness, or tingling anywhere from your neck down to your fingers; inability to grasp objects; swelling. If you suspect a problem caused by intensive computing work, consult a physician experienced in RSIs.

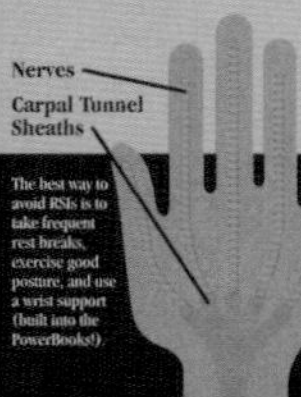
Nerves
Carpal Tunnel Sheaths

The best way to avoid RSIs is to take frequent rest breaks, exercise good posture, and use a wrist support (built into the PowerBooks!).

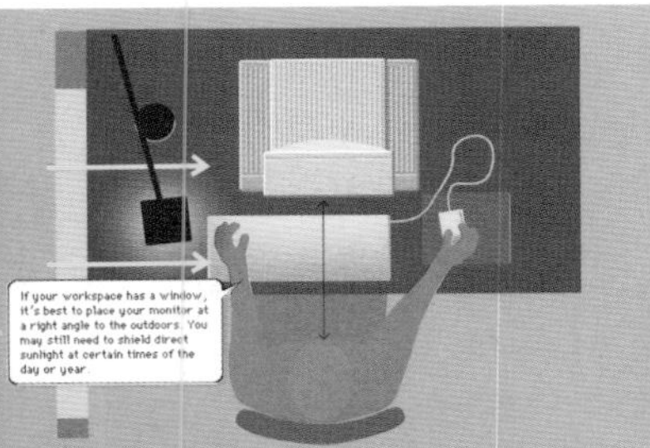
If your workspace has a window, it's best to place your monitor at a right angle to the outdoors. You may still need to shield direct sunlight at certain times of the day or year.

Lighting

In many circumstances lighting conditions are out of your control, especially in an office. Most overhead lighting glare (light reflecting off the screen, looking like hot spots) can be reduced with the help of a tilting monitor stand. Light from windows can be especially troublesome because the quantity and direction changes during the day. Direct sunlight on most video screens renders them useless, because the monitors can't deliver enough brightness to overcome the sun's light. If you are near a window, it is best to keep the window to one of your sides. This reduces glare (when the monitor faces the window) and the strong contrast between outside light and the monitor (when the monitor's back faces the window). Depending on your window's exposure and the time of year, you may still need to shield the monitor from the sun's rays during parts of the day.

Also, be sure to adjust the monitor brightness to fit the surrounding light ➔ 31, 35. During the day, the brightness may need to be turned up full blast. At night, in a darkened room, turn the brightness down to reduce the sharp contrast between surrounding darkness and the illuminated screen.

Breathing Room

No, not for you. For the Macintosh. As a piece of electronic equipment, all Macintoshes heat up while in use. The power supply generates heat. Some microchips on the circuit boards get hot. The hard disk motor gets warm.

Heat is a personal computer's worst natural enemy. The Macintosh's designers know that, and have devised various systems to prevent the Macintosh's innards from overheating. Key to those systems are ventilation holes, most of which you can't see because they're disguised by aesthetic cabinet designs. Most of the holes are located along the outside bottoms of the cabinets (to allow cool air to come in) and on the top (to allow the heated air to flow out). This kind of convection cooling is a critical part of your Macintosh's hardware. Keep at least a one-inch breathing zone around your Macintosh's sides. And if you see vents along the top of the machine or monitor, don't block them with other equipment, a notebook, or papers.

Some modular Macintosh system units (the Macintosh IIci for example) may be set on their sides while maintaining proper cooling—but use the special feet included. The Quadra 700 even encourages a vertical orientation. The largest Macintosh II models (e.g., Macintosh II, IIx, IIfx) should be placed on end only if they are used in cool environments and with stands designed to allow a free flow of air from the side nearest the floor.

Keep it Moving

Ergonomic studies of workers who spend their entire workdays at computer keyboards have discovered that it is important to allow for frequent adjustment of all the surfaces surrounding your workspace. That includes chair height, chair angle, keyboard height, and viewing angles. Office and computer supply companies offer self-contained carts that provide almost infinite adjustment of virtually every part of your workstation. In concert with a highly adjustable chair, these carts give each individual the most flexibility in creating a comfortable environment.

Mouse Pads

The mouse is an important element of the Macintosh, but few commercial computer desks take them into account (after all, a mouse is still optional on most IBM-style personal computers). The undersides of Macintosh mice have become more durable over time, but running them around a hard desk surface can wear them down after a couple of years. Moreover, many desk surfaces don't give the mouse ball good traction.

A mouse pad is a slice of rubber measuring about 6" by 8". Pads have various surfaces, such as plain rubber, cloth, and a slightly mottled plastic. Few mouse pads are available that don't have some advertising printed on them. That's actually good in a way, because it is often possible to get mouse pads for free from hardware and software manufacturers at Macintosh trade shows (you may have to sit through a formal demo of the product to qualify) or as a bonus when you buy goods at computer stores.

Importantly, a mouse pad reserves space on your desk for the mouse. If you leave too little space on your desk for the mouse, you may find the mouse rather inconvenient, since you'll constantly run out of surface to move the pointer where you need it (and then have to pick up the mouse and shift to the other side of the space to continue moving the pointer). Even if you don't use a mouse pad, try to reserve a 10 by 8-inch space for the mouse next to your keyboard (either on the right or left, depending on your mouse hand of preference).

Earthquake Proofing

You probably won't think about this until after you've lost a Macintosh or monitor to a tremor, but it's important for Macintosh owners in many parts of the world to prepare for an earthquake. In the experience of the October 1989 Loma Prieta earthquake (which rocked San Francisco, Silicon Valley, and Santa Cruz areas), many Macintosh users had their system units or monitors creep off the table as the buildings shook from side to side. Monitors, which typically rest on relatively slippery surfaces without rubber feet, were particularly vulnerable. One of the best defenses is to secure the system unit and monitor to the table. Then, even if the table does a waltz, the Macintosh will go with it.

1986

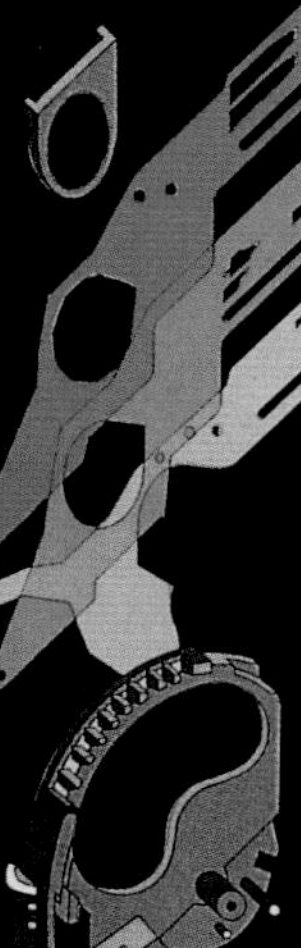

Polaroid
Polaroid

The Spectra camera debuts at Jordan Marsh in Boston, thirty-eight years after the Polaroid Land camera Model 95 was introduced.

Polaroid's Spectra System sets new standards of quality in instant photography and incorporates major innovations in film chemistry, optics, and electronics to produce a truer, brighter, and more saturated instant picture. The system is introduced in Europe at Photokina under the name Image System.

The final print is rectangular with an image area larger than 600 Series film.

The system is comprised of a computerized camera that focuses and controls exposure automatically; an instant color film that uses two imaging chemistries; a host of accessories, including a remote-control device; and Polaroid's laser print service, which provides computer-enhanced, laser-produced prints and enlargements. The camera's folding wedge shape mimics the natural position of a person's hands when framing a scene.

Optics: The Quintic Lens focusing system has a scale focusing length of 125 millimeters. The lens does not focus by moving toward or away from the film plane. Rather, the movable Quintic plate pivots laterally in front of the fixed Quintic element to a position determined by an electronic encoder. The unique shape of the moving Quintic plate allows the 10 areas of its surface used for focus positions to overlap each other in a continuous way so the Quintic plate does not have far to move. When the lens is in the correct focus position, the movable element is locked and the exposure is made. The entire mechanism has three elements: a highly corrected aspheric plastic meniscus main lens, a fixed Quintic element, and a moving Quintic plate. The viewfinder is also a sophisticated optical system: six precision plastic lenses and one prism with five aspheric surfaces, four mirrors to erect the image for right-side-up viewing, and a reflecting prism for viewing the data displays. Its front window has been placed close to the camera's picture-taking lens to minimize parallax when shooting subjects at close range.

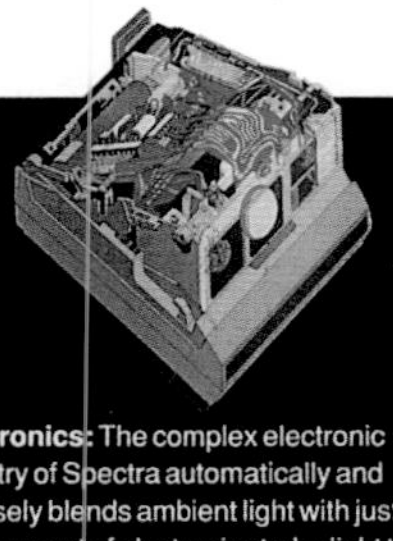

Electronics: The complex electronic circuitry of Spectra automatically and precisely blends ambient light with just the right amount of electronic strobe light to reduce harsh shadows and contrast.

Aperture follow-focus diminishes the aperture size to minimize the potential for overexposure when the camera is close to the subject. The photocell prevents excess strobe light from reaching the subject by signalling the strobe to shut off when the correct exposure is reached. The Spectra sonar transducer is 30% smaller than previous Polaroid sonar units. Spectra communicates with the photographer through a series of photographic status indicators, visible in the viewfinder once the shutter button is touched.

Corporation: On April 25 a federal appeals court in Washington, D.C., upholds a district court ruling that Eastman Kodak Company has violated patent rights held by Polaroid Corporation in its manufacture of instant cameras and film. On October 6 the US Supreme Court denies Kodak's petition for a *writ of certiorari* to review that decision.

Polaroid donates Model 4 and 8 video printers, instant films, and technical assistance to space agencies and universities around the world that join in a cooperative effort to study Halley's Comet.

Corporate Culture: The company complements its existing bonus plan with a new employee incentive compensation plan—the *First Dollar* bonus plan.

Sales: Two years after entering the field, Polaroid accounts for more than 10% of the US video cassette market.

Environment: Polaroid signs a consent order with the Massachusetts Department of Environmental Quality Engineering and completes the installation of equipment to achieve a 91% reduction in the emissions of volatile organic compounds from its film coating operations.

Subsidiaries: With the creation of MagMedia Limited, a diskette finishing and conversion firm, Polaroid becomes an integrated diskette manufacturer, capable of controlling the quality of its $5\frac{1}{4}$-inch diskettes from coating to finishing to packaging to distribution.

from the earliest of my publications. ■ **EIGHTH STORY** In 1994, I begin a new series of guides whose title is a single initial. The first one is *N*, standing for Newport (following two pages). It is a mini-version of the *USAtlas*, but with a grid of 10 minutes' walking time per page instead of one hour's driving time, of 250 miles. And, the entire book is annotated maps. The maps were drawn by John Grimwade and production was by Donovan and Green. ■ **NINTH STORY** I develop a series of publications with parallel texts again, picking up themes from *The Nature of Recreation* (which seems to have become a wellspring of ideas). I produced a book, organized by time, with three parallel texts called *Polaroid Access: Fifty Years*, which I did with Abbott Miller when he was in my employ. With Danny Goodman I produced *The Danny Goodman MacIntosh Handbook*. It used a series of parallel texts arranged hierarchically by instructional difficulty, and was done with Nathan Shedroff when he worked at my company, The Understanding Business. ■ **TENTH** and **LAST STORY** My shortest, most concise, and my simplest attempt to combine conversational text with sidebar marginalia can be seen in two serious volumes about information theory—*Information Anxiety* and *Follow The Yellow Brick Road*. ■ These 10 stories touch on some of the more than 60 books I've authored, designed, and published. Each one was inspired by something I didn't understand, whether it was diagnostic tests on my own body, finding my way around Tokyo, or the Olympics on TV, or understanding the city where I now live, Newport, Rhode Island. In all of them I have tried to embrace my ignorance by finding a phrase that captures a solution to pursue, like "I want to know where I am and what's around me," or "You don't travel alphabetically," or "Most Auto headings don't begin with *Auto*." My struggle has been to discover the road, the pattern that leads to memory. The junctures of road to road and path to path celebrate that connection. That connection is learning, and learning is remembering what you are interested in. The delight of trivia that touches on curiosity, which is the velcro of learning, makes me smile. The quality of my work depends especially on the many wonderful individuals who make my thoughts and ideas even better. ■ The ONE STORY, my largest story, is filling the empty bucket of ignorance with things I understand.

MAPPING HIERARCHIES Different kinds of parallel texts were organized in two books. Levels of computer expertise were separated in *Danny Goodman's Macintosh Handbook* (opposite top, diagram below). *Polaroid Access, 50 Years* shows a company's history in a timeline with three content bands: products, research and news (opposite, diagram bottom). The most recent guide, entirely made of annotated maps, is show on the following two pages.

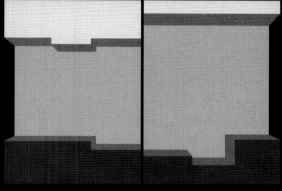

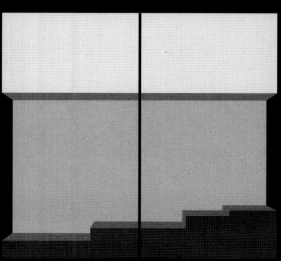

Forty Steps

CLIFF WALK

10 MINUTES WALKING

The Orchard

Ochre Point

SALVE REGINA UNIVERSITY

Ochre Court

Gatehouse

Vinland

THE BREAKERS

CLIFF WA

ayhouse

tehouse

NARRAGANSETT AVENUE

ANNANDALE ROAD

RUGGLES AVENUE

The *Newport* Guide

re Point

WEBSTER STREET

Richard Saul Wurman

CHRE POINT

● Landmarks

● Accommodations

● Restaurants

● Shopping

SALVE REGINA
UNIVERSITY

e Court

Vinland

Gatehouse

OCHRE POINT AVENUE

Wakehurst

ATM

LEROY AVENUE

SHEPARD AVENUE

❷ The Orchard *1871*
180 Narragansett Avenue

While everyone else was building resort cottages in derived English styles, career army officer, year-round resident, and then mayor, **Colonel George R. Fearing** sent to the continent to have a French architect deliver him measured drawings of a French château. The Orchard, with its academic symmetries and formal gardens, is the earliest Newport example of a complete translation of a continental model to newly-wealthy America. It was later owned by the **Cassatt** family of Philadelphia and by **Mrs. Harvey S. Firestone, Jr.** Private.

❸ Forty Steps
Sometime in the 1830s a doting father, **David Priestley Hall**, had the first Forty Steps constructed so his children could climb down the cliffs to the beach below and to a now much-eroded grotto called **Conrad's Cave**. The steps have been washed away and rebuilt many times since then—not always tallying up to 40 either. Over the years, they have acquired a romantic aura; lovers have courted here, suicides have leaped, fishermen have fished and countless tourists have climbed down and up. In the 1920s and 30s it was the favorite spot for servants from the estates to gather after hours. Often townspeople would join them. There, to the accordian tunes of crippled **Dick Sullivan**, they would dance in the summer evening. Not a few Newport marriages began at these nightly trysts. *RSW Recommends*

❹ Ochre Point *1882*
Narragansett at 40 steps

Built for real estate tycoon **Robert Goelet** by **McKim, Mead & White**, this villa is an important example of the Queen Anne shingle style of architecture they pioneered in the 1880s. Sketches of the opulent carved woodwork and ample interiors were widely published in the years after the house was built. Sometimes erroneously identified as *Southside*. Private.

Salve Regina University

An educational institution that's on the move, Salve Regina University has grown in the past 25 years from a small, sequestered women's college to a respected, independent Roman Catholic university with an enrollment of 2,200 women and men from all 50 states and 10 foreign countries. Chartered in 1934 by the Sisters of Mercy, the college acquired Ochre Court in 1947 and welcomed its first class of 58 students that fall. Today, led by its new president, Dr. M. Therese Antone, R.S.M., the university offers over 40 concentrations leading to associate and bachelor's degrees, master's degrees in 15 areas, and a doctoral program in the humanities. Through its location on the scenic Cliff Walk, through new construction, and especially through the acquisition of historic Gilded Age estate properties, Salve (SAL-VAY) has developed one of the loveliest campuses in the eastern United States.

❺ Ochre Court *1891*
Ochre Point Avenue

Built for New York real estate tycoon **Ogden Goelet**, this was the first of the Newport Beaux Arts palaces commissioned from **Richard Morris Hunt**. It is a rather grandiose limestone experiment in combining classical models with a French chateau. The interior is a soaring 3-story central hall of marble, mahogany and Mannerism, with balconies leading off into the upstairs rooms. In the post-World War II slump of 1947, Goelet's heirs left it to the **Sisters of Mercy** as a site for a college they had chartered, with what can only be faith, a full 13 years earlier. Somehow the unceasing bustle of college kids really warms up the classical formality of Ochre Court, which is now the administration building of **Salve Regina University**. Often used for concerts, conferences and public programs (as well as regular Sunday mass, open to the public), interested visitors are welcome to poke a nose in for a look around. Portions of the movie **True Lies** were filmed here in 1994.

FF META: TYPE FOR A PURPOSE In 1984, I persuaded the German Post Office (Bundespost) to commission an exclusive typeface for all their printed materials. We had started a comprehensive design program for the state-owned agency, which had been using a plethora of typefaces including dozens of dissimilar fonts from the "Helvetica" family. An exclusive typeface could end this chaos and give a coherent look to thousands of forms, brochures, advertisements and telephone books. ■ In 1985, we started the typeface, which was to meet clearly defined targets: 1) legible in small sizes, 2) neutral not fashionable design, 3) available on all systems, 4) available from all suppliers, 5) economical (space-saving), 6) available in several, clearly distinguishable weights, 7) unmistakable and characteristic, and 8) technologically up to date. ■ After careful analysis, we looked at existing typefaces as possible candidates for redesign and sketched some alternatives. We assessed what makes a typeface legible under certain conditions, and developed what still appears to be a coherent theory. Having presented this to the client, we drew two weights, regular and bold, which were then digitized at Linotype in Frank-

Hamburg
Helvetica   0.63

Hamburg
Frutiger   0.64

Hamburg
Gill   0.59

Hamburg
News Gothic   0.53

Hamburg
Syntax   0.60

Hamburg
Meta   0.60

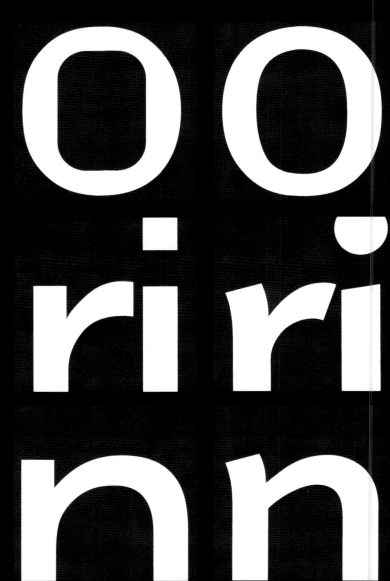

setting, the people in Bonn never believed the work could be done using hundreds of typesetters and printers across Germany. They continued to use Helvetica in all its variations, as they do today. ■ By 1988, desktop software could digitize type characters. We developed the typeface for use by our studio, MetaDesign, and so we named the font Meta. It took "real" type designers to finish it: Just van Rossum, our first resident type designer, and Lucas de Groot, who added new weights to the family. When we set a catalog for FontShop, a distributor of digital fonts, they liked it and persuaded me to license it. They released it as FF Meta and it quickly became a bestseller. FF Meta now has 18 weights and designers around the world use it for all sorts of projects, none as prosaic as the job that first prompted it.

REFINING ELEMENTS A typeface was designed for the German Post Office to set small-type texts . Various faces were studied, proper x-heights and shape contrasts were developed, then weights were added in a commercial version (below, left to right).

bauen

bauen

bauen

Hbauen 15

FF Meta plus Normal (with Caps, *Italic* & *Caps Italic*)
Handgloves 123 Handgloves 456
Handgloves 78 Handgloves 90
ABCDEFGHIJKLMNOPQRSTUVWXYZ
····> abcdefghijklmnopqrstuvwxyzß
<···· fi,ffi.1234567890 & 1234567890

FF Meta plus Book (with Caps, *Italic* & *Caps Italic*)
Handgloves 123 Handgloves 456
Handgloves 78 Handgloves 90
ABCDEFGHIJKLMNOPQRSTUVWXYZ
····> abcdefghijklmnopqrstuvwxyzß
<···· fi,ffi.1234567890 & 1234567890

FF Meta plus Medium (with Caps, *Italic* & *Caps Italic*)
Handgloves 123 Handgloves 456
Handgloves 78 Handgloves 90
ABCDEFGHIJKLMNOPQRSTUVWXYZ
····> abcdefghijklmnopqrstuvwxyzß
<···· fi,ffi.1234567890 & 1234567890

FF Meta plus Bold (with Caps, *Italic* & *Caps Italic*)
Handgloves 123 Handgloves 456
Handgloves 78 Handgloves 90
ABCDEFGHIJKLMNOPQRSTUVWXYZ
····> abcdefghijklmnopqrstuvwxyzß
<···· fi,ffi.1234567890 & 1234567890

■ **GUIDE TO A NEW CITY** When the Berlin Wall fell in November 1989, two parts of a city were reunited which had been apart for so long they had become unknown to each other. There had been few border crossings between East and West, and the Berliners didn't know their way around their own city anymore. ■ Public transport—railways, subways, trams, and buses—had and still has a large share of all traffic in Berlin. In the East, 80% of the people had to use it as their only alternative. Private cars were few and far between. While in the West the ratio was more like 40 to 60, public transportation still played a bigger role than would be thinkable in most American cities. ■ Passenger information plays an important part in making a transit system work. That was especially true in 1990, when Berlin's two transport corporations merged and suddenly had to cater to twice the passengers. Maps and signs had to be changed almost overnight. ■ The existing maps and diagrams of the two sides were quickly adapted, but proved inadequate. Stations were being renamed, dormant stations and old lines reopened, and the whole system was being rethought. The old production process with mechanical artwork just could not keep up with all the changes. ■ In 1991, MetaDesign was commissioned to redesign the combined transit diagram. It was to include suburban railroads, the city railroads (S-Bahn), and the underground railroads (U-Bahn). These were all operated by different authorities and had their own logos, signage systems, and line colors. The conditions for a redesign were less than ideal, but certainly presented a unique challenge. ■ While the colors were given, we did decide to modify an existing typeface to suit the task. The new diagram would have to be printed in a great variety of sizes, from pocket folders to billboards 3 meters (10 feet) wide. The symbols for the lines were also redesigned, following the traditional shapes—a green circle for the S-Bahn and a blue square for the U-Bahn—with line numbers in lozenges or rectangles that echoed those shapes. Logos, pictograms and arrows were incorporated in special fonts. Our aim was to enable the Berlin Transit Corporation

SEPARATING SYSTEMS The Berlin Wall divided the city into two halves, severed traffic links, and separated the transportation systems. The first diagram (below) shows what public transportation looked like in 1961 before the Wall was built. In the 1970s, the wall appears as a shaded line in the upper right of the diagram (bottom). East German systems were either eliminated or shown in black, and two Western lines ran below East Berlin with no stops.

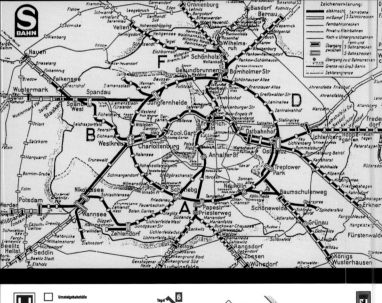

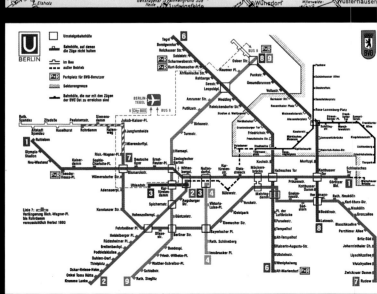

totype. ■ We designed the diagram on our Macintosh computers using Aldus Free-hand. It had a feature which proved invaluable: layers on which we could place each transit line. Alterations—which were frequent—could thus be carried out on the appropriate layer without upsetting other elements; 33 layers were necessary (including one for text which was changed every other day). ■ Hundreds of color laser printouts in A3 (roughly 11 x 17) size were made and sent to various departments for approval at every revision stage. After more than 400 hours, a final design was approved, data was output to high-resolution laser recorders, and final film for four-color offset printing in many different sizes was provided. ■ Since MetaDesign finished the project in 1992, new versions of the transit diagram have been produced every six months as new lines

have been opened. The rail system gets more complex all the time, but our design has allowed for continual change. It still provides clear and rapid visual access to public transportation in this changing city.

UNIFYING SYSTEMS MetaDesign was commissioned to completely redesign the diagram in 1991. It evolved from pencil sketches, to computer redrawings, to enumerable adjustments and alignments of the systems, to the fitting of type and identifying logo shapes (all below). The systems were "unified" on separate computer layers for easy, constant revisions (following two pages). The final diagram was printed in many sizes (see pages 44 and 45).

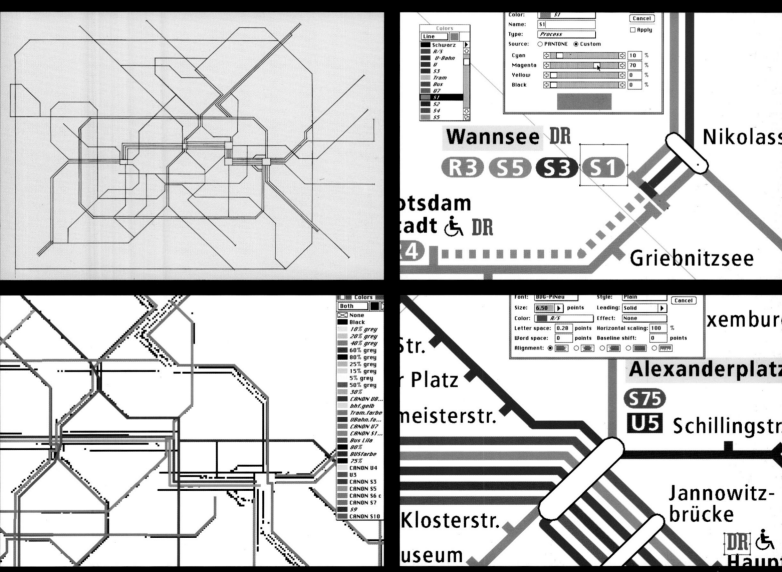

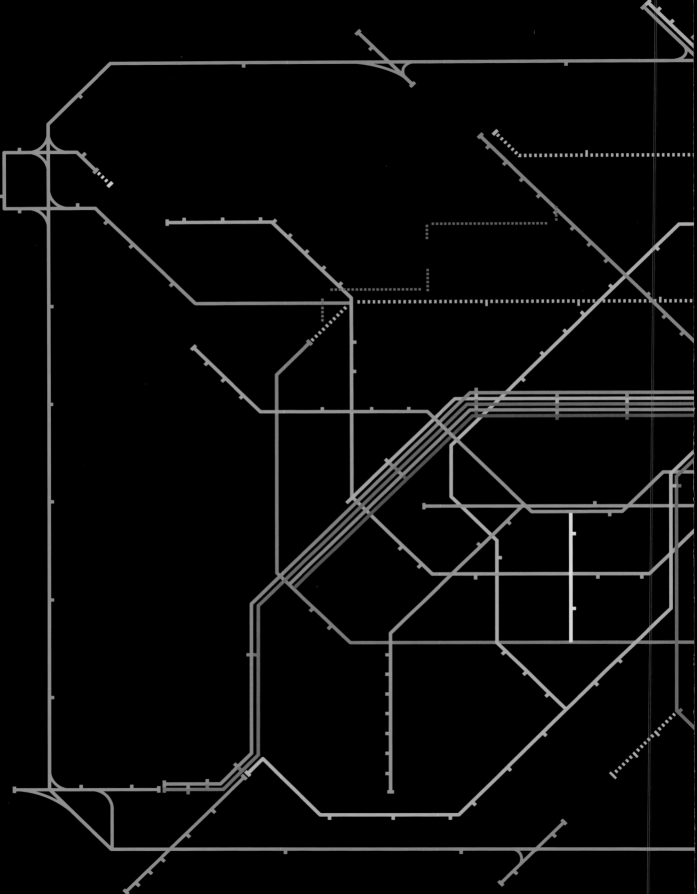

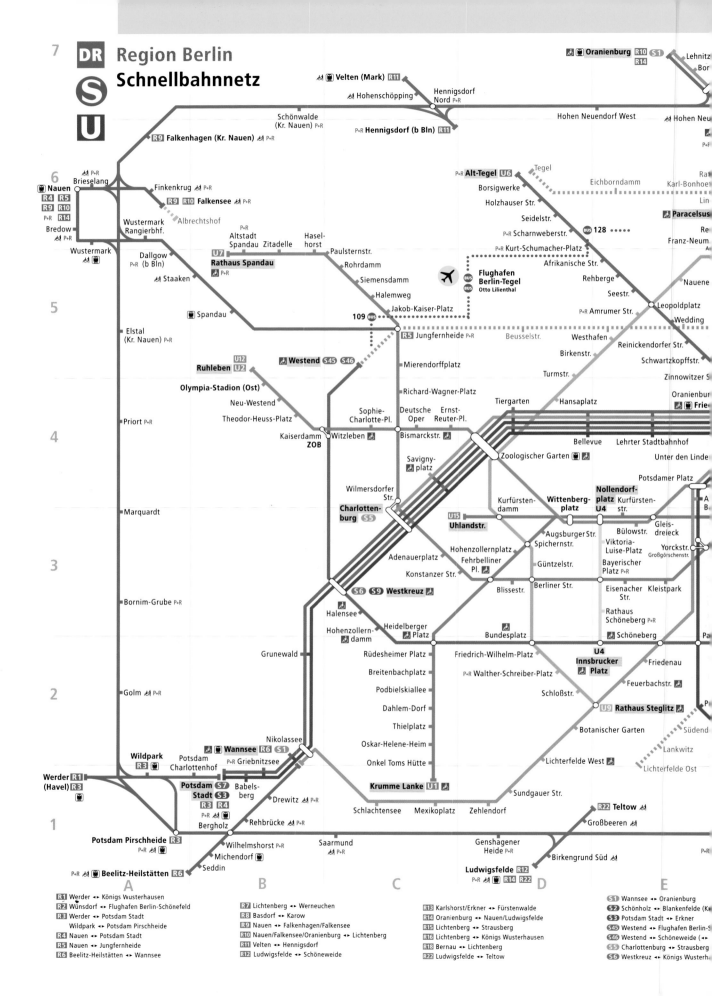

DR Region Berlin
S Schnellbahnnetz
U

7

Oranienburg R10 S1
R14

Velten (Mark) R11
Hohenschöpping
Hennigsdorf Nord P+R

Schönwalde (Kr. Nauen) P+R
Hohen Neuendorf West
Hohen Neu

6 Brieselang
R9 Falkenhagen (Kr. Nauen) P+R
Hennigsdorf (b Bln) R11
Alt-Tegel U6 Tegel
Eichborndamm
Karl-Bonhoef

Nauen
R4 R5
R9 R10
P+R R14
Bredow
Finkenkrug P+R
R9 R10 Falkensee P+R
Borsigwerke
Holzhauser Str.
Seidelstr.
P+R Scharnweberstr.
Paracelsus

Lin

Wustermark
Rangierbhf.
Albrechtshof
Altstadt Haselhorst
Spandau Zitadelle
Paulsternstr.
Kurt-Schumacher-Platz
BUS 128

Franz-Neum

Wustermark
Dallgow P+R (b Bln)
U7
Rathaus Spandau P+R
Rohrdamm
Afrikanische Str.
Rehberge

5
Staaken
Siemensdamm
Flughafen Berlin-Tegel Otto Lilienthal
BUS
BUS
Seestr.
Amrumer Str.
Leopoldplatz
Wedding

Spandau
Halemweg
Jakob-Kaiser-Platz
109 BUS
R5 Jungfernheide P+R
Beusselstr.
Westhafen
Reinickendorfer Str.
Schwartzkopffstr.
Zinnowitzer S

Elstal (Kr. Nauen) P+R
Ruhleben U12 U2
Westend S45 S46
Mierendorffplatz
Birkenstr.
Turmstr.
Oranienbur
Frie

4 Priort P+R
Olympia-Stadion (Ost)
Neu-Westend
Theodor-Heuss-Platz
Kaiserdamm ZOB
Witzleben
Sophie-Charlotte-Pl.
Deutsche Oper
Ernst-Reuter-Pl.
Bismarckstr.
Richard-Wagner-Platz
Tiergarten
Hansaplatz
Bellevue
Lehrter Stadtbahnhof
Unter den Linde
Zoologischer Garten
Savigny-platz

Marquardt
Wilmersdorfer Str.
Charlottenburg S5
Kurfürstendamm
Wittenberg-platz
Nollendorf-platz U4 Kurfürsten-str.
Potsdamer Platz
A
B

3
Adenauerplatz
Hohenzollernplatz
Uhlandstr.
U15
Augsburger Str.
Spichernstr.
Viktoria-Luise-Platz
Bülowstr.
Gleis-dreieck
Yorckstr. Großgörschenstr.

Bornim-Grube P+R
Fehrbelliner Pl.
Konstanzer Str.
S6 S9 Westkreuz
Halensee
Hohenzollern-damm
Heidelberger Platz
Blissestr.
Berliner Str.
Güntzelstr.
Bayerischer Platz P+R
Eisenacher Str.
Kleistpark
Rathaus Schöneberg P+R
Schöneberg

Grunewald
Rüdesheimer Platz
Bundesplatz
Friedrich-Wilhelm-Platz
U4 Innsbrucker Platz
Friedenau
Feuerbachstr.

2 Golm P+R
Breitenbachplatz
Podbielskiallee
Dahlem-Dorf
P+R Walther-Schreiber-Platz
Schloßstr.
U9 Rathaus Steglitz
Botanischer Garten
Südend
Lankwitz

Wildpark R3
Nikolassee
Thielplatz
Oskar-Helene-Heim
Onkel Toms Hütte
Lichterfelde West
Lichterfelde Ost

Potsdam Charlottenhof
Wannsee R6 S1
P+R Griebnitzsee
Krumme Lanke U1

Werder R1 (Havel) R3
Potsdam Stadt S7 S3
Babelsberg
R3 R4
Drewitz P+R
Schlachtensee
Mexikoplatz
Zehlendorf
Sundgauer Str.
R22 Teltow

1
Bergholz
Rehbrücke P+R
Großbeeren

Potsdam Pirschheide R3
P+R
Wilhelmshorst P+R
Saarmund
Genshagener Heide P+R
Birkengrund Süd

Michendorf
P+R Beelitz-Heilstätten R6
Seddin
Ludwigsfelde R12
P+R R14 R22

A   B   C   D   E

R1 Werder ↔ Königs Wusterhausen
R2 Wünsdorf ↔ Flughafen Berlin-Schönefeld
R3 Werder ↔ Potsdam Stadt · Wildpark ↔ Potsdam Pirschheide
R4 Nauen ↔ Potsdam Stadt
R5 Nauen ↔ Jungfernheide
R6 Beelitz-Heilstätten ↔ Wannsee

R7 Lichtenberg ↔ Werneuchen
R8 Basdorf ↔ Karow
R9 Nauen ↔ Falkenhagen/Falkensee
R10 Nauen/Falkensee/Oranienburg ↔ Lichtenberg
R11 Velten ↔ Hennigsdorf
R12 Ludwigsfelde ↔ Schöneweide

R13 Karlshorst/Erkner ↔ Fürstenwalde
R14 Oranienburg ↔ Nauen/Ludwigsfelde
R15 Lichtenberg ↔ Strausberg
R16 Lichtenberg ↔ Königs Wusterhausen
R18 Bernau ↔ Lichtenberg
R22 Ludwigsfelde ↔ Teltow

S1 Wannsee ↔ Oranienburg
S2 Schönholz ↔ Blankenfelde (K
S3 Potsdam Stadt ↔ Erkner
S45 Westend ↔ Flughafen Berlin-S
S46 Westend ↔ Schöneweide ↔
S5 Charlottenburg ↔ Strausberg
S6 Westkreuz ↔ Königs Wusterh

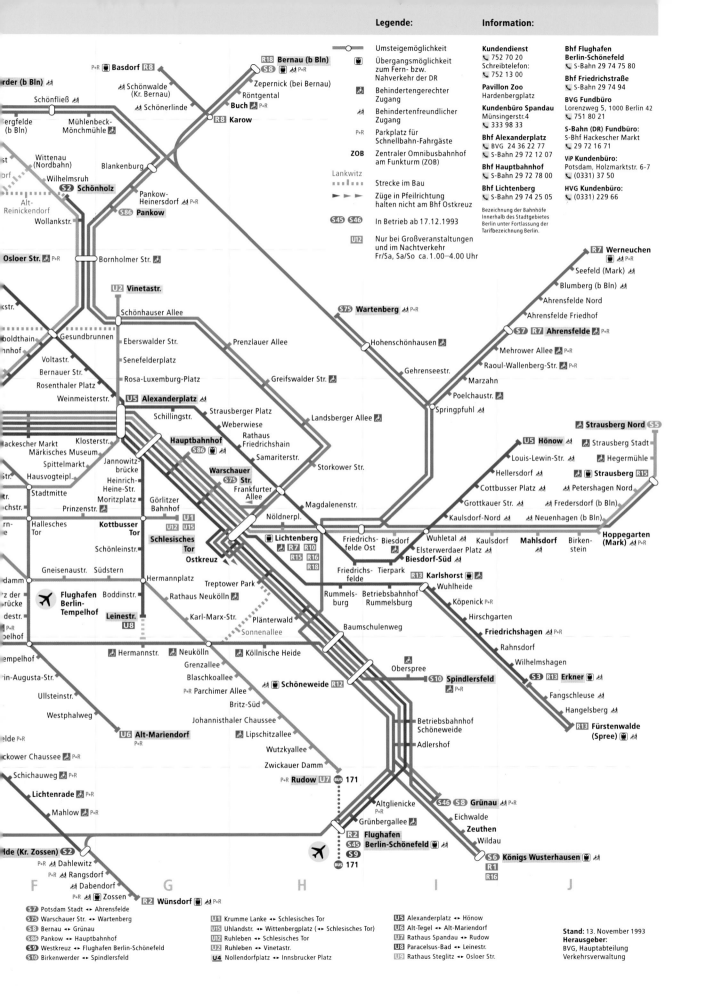

Legende:

○—○ Umsteigemöglichkeit

○—○ Übergangsmöglichkeit zum Fern- bzw. Nahverkehr der DR

♿ Behindertengerechter Zugang

♿ Behindertenfreundlicher Zugang

P+R Parkplatz für Schnellbahn-Fahrgäste

ZOB Zentraler Omnibusbahnhof am Funkturm (ZOB)

Lankwitz Strecke im Bau

►►► Züge in Pfeilrichtung halten nicht am Bhf Ostkreuz

S45 S46 In Betrieb ab 17.12.1993

U12 Nur bei Großveranstaltungen und im Nachtverkehr Fr/Sa, Sa/So ca. 1.00–4.00 Uhr

Information:

Kundendienst
📞 752 70 20
Schreibtelefon:
📞 752 13 00

Pavillon Zoo
Hardenbergplatz

Kundenbüro Spandau
Münsingerstr.4
📞 333 98 33

Bhf Alexanderplatz
📞 BVG 24 36 22 77
📞 S-Bahn 29 72 12 07

Bhf Hauptbahnhof
📞 S-Bahn 29 72 78 00

Bhf Lichtenberg
📞 S-Bahn 29 74 25 05

Bhf Flughafen Berlin-Schönefeld
📞 S-Bahn 29 74 75 80

Bhf Friedrichstraße
📞 S-Bahn 29 74 94

BVG Fundbüro
Lorenzweg 5, 1000 Berlin 42
📞 751 80 21

S-Bahn (DR) Fundbüro:
S-Bhf Hackescher Markt
📞 29 72 16 71

ViP Kundenbüro:
Potsdam, Holzmarktstr. 6-7
📞 (0331) 37 50

HVG Kundenbüro:
📞 (0331) 229 66

Bezeichnung der Bahnhöfe innerhalb des Stadtgebietes Berlin unter Fortlassung der Tarifbezeichnung Berlin.

Stand: 13. November 1993
Herausgeber:
BVG, Hauptabteilung
Verkehrsverwaltung

S7 Potsdam Stadt ↔ Ahrensfelde
S75 Warschauer Str. ↔ Wartenberg
S8 Bernau ↔ Grünau
S86 Pankow ↔ Hauptbahnhof
S9 Westkreuz ↔ Flughafen Berlin-Schönefeld
S10 Birkenwerder ↔ Spindlersfeld

U1 Krumme Lanke ↔ Schlesisches Tor
U15 Uhlandstr. ↔ Wittenbergplatz (↔ Schlesisches Tor)
U12 Ruhleben ↔ Schlesisches Tor
U2 Ruhleben ↔ Vinetastr.
U4 Nollendorfplatz ↔ Innsbrucker Platz

U5 Alexanderplatz ↔ Hönow
U6 Alt-Tegel ↔ Alt-Mariendorf
U7 Rathaus Spandau ↔ Rudow
U8 Paracelsus-Bad ↔ Leinestr.
U9 Rathaus Steglitz ↔ Osloer Str.

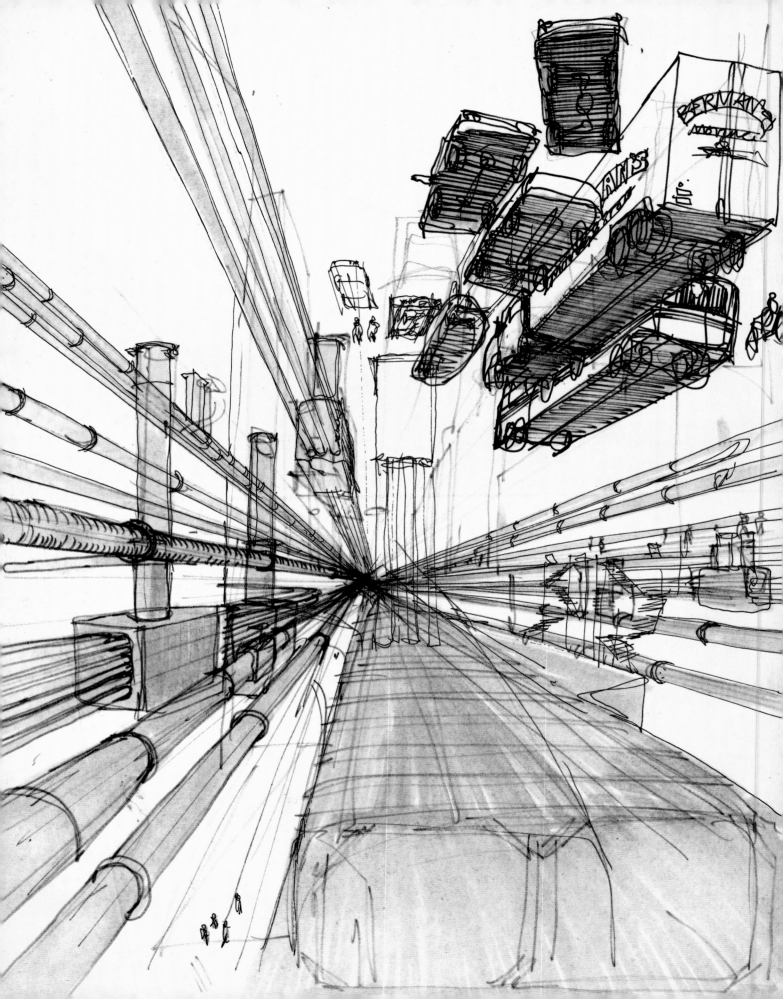

UNDERGROUND One day, while having lunch with my editor, the conversation turned to things below the ground. I don't remember how, but I don't think it had anything to do with the food. In any event, my curiosity was piqued and the idea for a new book born. Honest. ■ I had learned from my earlier books that one way of really getting information across is to involve people with it as directly as possible. You don't put them on the other side of the street from a building under construction if you want them to understand the construction process. At least not all the time. Depending on precisely what you're trying to show, you put them in or above or below the building as it's being built. From the beginning, my intent with *Underground* was to take the reader below ground and show them what it looks like, rather than simply tell them. ■ In order to get some sense of what this might mean, and to begin to familiarize myself with the subject matter, I made a few sketches of views from below street level showing both pipes and traffic, and views from bedrock showing different kinds of foundations. I knew a close-up of a wooden pile foundation would be a dramatic image if I could just draw it. I also knew a more conventional cross section might be necessary to clarify the unusual view. ■ Underground information fell into three broad categories: foundations which support buildings, utility systems which feed them, and subways which help populate them. Each of these categories could have been a book in its own right. Taken all together and extended over an entire city, this information would have proved a daunting task for both writer and reader. To simplify the problem, and yet still cover the essentials, I created a fictitious urban intersection which I could then dissect and rebuild. ■ As usual, the project got into full swing with research. The initial obstacle was at the same time the book's ultimate justification, a notable

INVENTING POINT OF VIEW The most compelling aspects of Macaulay books are wit and the places he chooses to stand. When he looks up and draws from beneath a street or a wooden pile foundation (opposite and below), he quickly brings his readers into the information, and communicates the spirit of his own curiosity

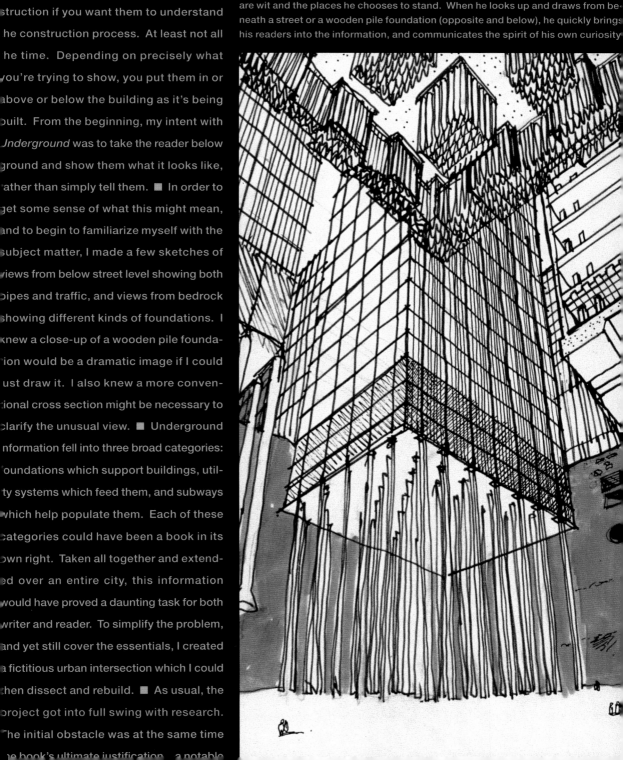

lack of accessible, up-to-date information on the subject. My three preceding books, *Cathedral, City* and *Pyramid,* had all begun in the library and were based entirely upon other people's conclusions. Almost all the information in *Underground* came directly from people responsible day in and day out for what goes on down there. I made phone calls and set up interviews. I asked hundreds of questions, most more than once, collected blue prints, filled sketchbooks and took hundreds of slides. In the end, as usual, I had far more material than I would eventually include. ■ First and foremost, like the earlier books, *Underground* had to entertain and to teach. This meant that it could not be written exclusively for the engineers and experts who had helped make it possible. On the other hand, I didn't want to offend them with inaccuracies or oversimplifications. While I was doing my research, I made endless drawings of the things I was learning, not only to see if I was actually learning them, but also to see what kind of visual imagery was developing. ■ As in all my books, when most of the research is done, the process of sorting, editing and assembling begins. Every effort is made to work with the words and the pictures at the same time. One usually helps me think about the other. It is the most efficient way of ensuring that they will support each other, and that redundancy will be minimized. Then, I pick a piece of information about which I feel fairly informed, and just go at it until I run out of steam. This results in a collection of solid, but completely disconnected chunks of written material and very crude pictures. I never try to work in a straight line from the beginning to the end of a book. I am usually not even sure what the beginning is until I've been at it for quite a while. As the book develops, many of the tiny images in the disconnected chunks serve as starting points for full-sized drawings. ■ As soon as enough chunks of material have been gathered, they are assembled into even

MAPPING SEQUENCE After lengthy interviews, research, site photography and sketches made from source material, the first topics of a subject were written and drawn in "chunks," or disconnected units (below). Then, the chunks were assembled in sequence and lengthened, shortened, or rearranged in overall book plans.

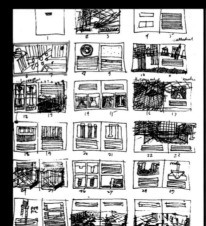

larger pieces. Then these pieces are assembled, and so on, and eventually I am able to produce the first overall plan of the book. The purpose of the plan is not just to see how long the book is going to be, but also to establish pacing. What is the distribution of information? What kinds of pictures are where? Too many cross sections in a row and, unless they are engineers, I've lost my audience. Too many dramatic images in a row and the information effect is lost. In *Underground*, one version of the book plan (opposite, bottom) shows red squares where my invented intersection reappears to serve as an opening drawing for each new subject. They still seem all over the place, too many of them, too arbitrarily spaced. In time, the content determined its own best size, the plan was revised accordingly, and its 128 pages became a book of 112 pages. ■ The single most time-consuming chunk of *Underground* involved the development of the hypothetical intersection (right). Putting the buildings in place was easy. It was the identifying, understanding, and locating each of the systems first that gave me nightmares. Without them I didn't know how wide the street would have to be, or where to place the buildings even though I knew what they were going to look like. First, I had to dissect the blueprints of various intersections and streets, isolate each system, and then locate them both horizontally and vertically in relation to each other. The sewer pipes always go below the water pipes to avoid contamination, and the electrical lines go near the top and away from the water lines as much as possible. Next, I invented the intersection in order to establish the perspective, and began the slow process of over-layering the various systems to make sure they would all fit in the space. ■ After fitting all the systems together, I realized we were too far away to see clearly what was going on. So, I moved us in a little closer. Unfortunately, the change in distance also necessitated a change in per-

INVENTING CONTEXT *Underground* required the compressing of much detail in a relatively short book. To simplify the compression without sacrificing essential detail, a hypothetical street intersection was invented (below). The city systems were individually researched, dissected, then carefully rebuilt to fit the space.

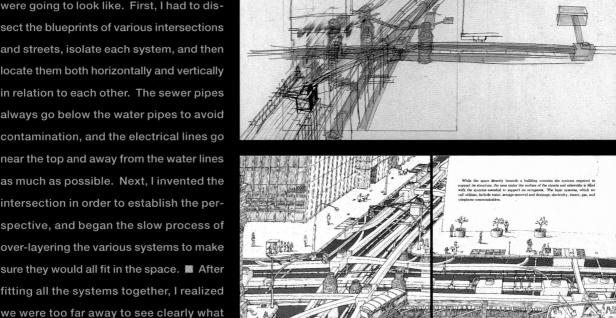

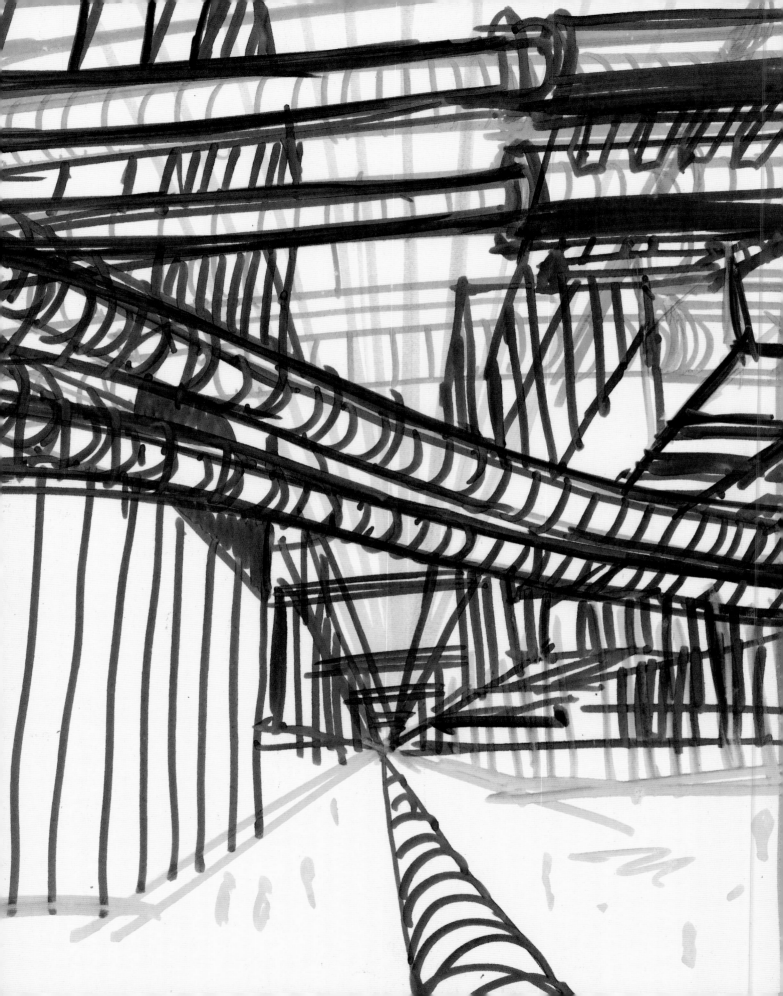

spective. That meant redrawing not only the road, but each of the systems and their manholes, catch basins, valve caps, and so on. The second color was introduced to help clarify this complicated image. The published drawing of the surface of the street had "clues" to systems, like manhole covers and leaking steam, which were circled, highlighted and numbered to serve as a kind of table of contents for the reader. If this was a computer program, you'd simply click on the circles. In the book, you turn to the

page indicated to learn more about that particular clue. ■ Technical information about this kind of subject almost always comes in the form of cross sections, elevations and plans—the visual language of the already-initiated. This language can be extremely dull, but it also can be very efficient. There are a number of ways in which cross sections can be effectively brought to life. The first is through page design. The second is dimensionality. The third is through whimsy. Yes, even cross sections can make you smile. I drew the water manhole as a sort of romantic ruin with a few scattered blocks (so you can appreciate its unique shaping), and, to show that it does not (cannot) fall in under great weight, an elephant strolls along the street. These little additions are informational, but primarily they are here to reward the reader who comes back and looks at these pictures again . ■ Perhaps the most important kinds of illustrations in the book are those that were derived from the very first sketches. The full-perspective and dramatic point-of-view drawings, like the marker sketch from below the intersection (opposite), not only interrupt the technical information, they catch the reader's imagination. The very last image in the book (following two pages) had to be memorable as well as encapsulate the preceding contents. By creating the appearance of a transparent street, the reader can clearly see the connections between the clues on the road and the systems buried below it.

EXTENDING POINT OF VIEW The unique viewpoints of the book continued, sometimes embellished with wit and surprising detail (like a frog in the electrical manhole, below). Sketches and final drawings show the invented intersection from below (opposite and bottom) and from above a transparent street (following pages).

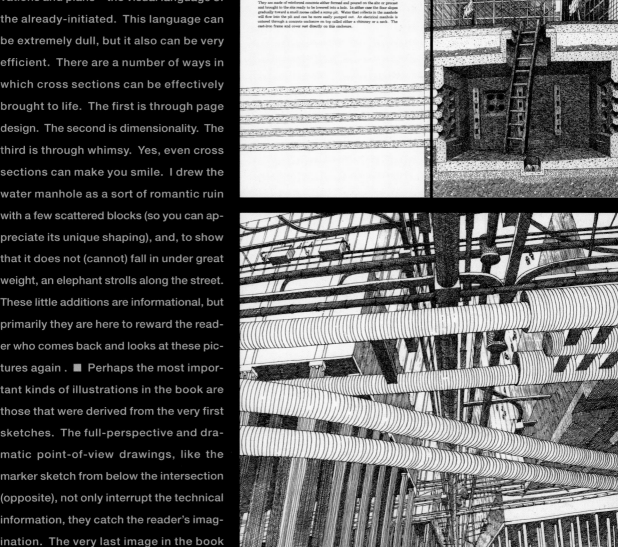

■ **THE AMAZING BRAIN** began as an article in a magazine called *Human Nature*. I made six illustrations to accompany a proposal by California Neurosurgeon Dr. Joseph Bogen to build a giant brain—a structure large enough to walk through so that visitors might become more familiar with what is supposed to be going on inside their skulls. A couple of years later, Robert Ornstein (Director of *Human Nature*) and Richard Thompson, both of Stanford University, produced a one hundred and fifty page text for an in-

troductory book on the workings of and the latest research into the human brain. I was asked to illustrate their work. ■ I began my research, as usual, with books. I soon realized, however, that in spite of the quality of much of the material, I was not getting a clear sense of the three-dimensional aspects of the brain. I bought a couple of brain models, one which could be taken apart and one of the ventricular system (basically a cast of the empty spaces inside the brain). They helped. After convincing a local doctor and teacher of my needs (and ignorance), I was given a human brain and permission to cut it up in the hospital's morgue. A sobering, but invaluable experience. The only problem was, the human brain isn't very well color-coded. In fact, it's all gray. Anyway, in my early attempts to understand its components, I made a series of pencil sketches in the morgue and back in the studio. ■ My last source of information was a computer-generated animation created from an enormous number of wafer-thin slices through a frozen brain, which were then traced and plotted and reassembled in color-coded lines. Putting all of the above together, I was finally able to form a still somewhat murky picture of the subject in my own brain. It was without a doubt the most difficult problem I have yet undertaken. ■ What to Illustrate? And, what kinds of pictures would most effectively support and amplify the text? Two kinds of images would be required. The first

INVENTING POINT OF VIEW *The Amazing Brain* was illustrated in three clusters. The first cluster shows the evolutionary growth of the brain in stages from its oldest part, the reptilian brain, placed in a kind of prehistoric dark swamp (below). Gradually, the brain "grows" in the drawing series and the sense of light increases.

were straightforward diagrams placed wherever they were needed. The second were more engaging images to excite the lay readers, or at least make them curious about what was in the text. I decided that these images should be concentrated in self-contained "clusters" rather than spread out. Not only was this a more normal way for me to think, it also seemed the best way of achieving some sort of visual and narrative impact. There would be three of these clusters and each would have its own primary func-

tion. The first would illustrate the anatomy of the brain and provide a reference to which the reader might return while reading the text. The second would show how the brain works by focussing on one fairly well understood process. The third would reinforce anatomical knowledge: where are things in relationship to each other, and what do they look like? ■ Since the three clusters were to be fairly short, I decided to create a full-size mock-up for each one. This forced me to really understand the subject matter, and also gave me a good idea of how many pictures would be necessary to do each job. ■ The first cluster (preceding two pages) was titled *The Amazing Garden*, or *A romantic view of the evolutionary growth of the brain with appropriate anatomical diagrams*. It was a "portfolio" of pseudo-classical drawings, accurately but romantically drawn in pen and ink to mimic (and pay tribute to) the engravings of illustrators such as Wandelaar. The drawings were explained with simple companion diagrams, and the brain's "growth" was echoed by the expanding size of the illustrations on each succeeding spread. The sense of light also increases from the darkened swamp, which is home to the brain stem or reptilian brain, to the final image where the completed brain is shown as the source of light. ■ The second cluster was titled *A Young Man Recognizes His Mother*, or *A simplified tour of the visual system for the busy reader*. It shows how the visual system

MAPPING SEQUENCE The second cluster in *The Amazing Brain* follows the steps in the brain's process of perceiving and recognizing an image. In another surprising twist, *David* (the sculpture) was chosen as the viewer. The first drawings were arresting (below), but more symbolic representations were finally used (opposite).

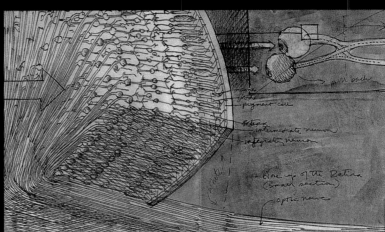

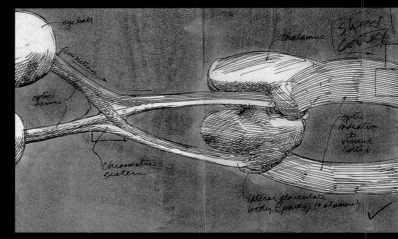

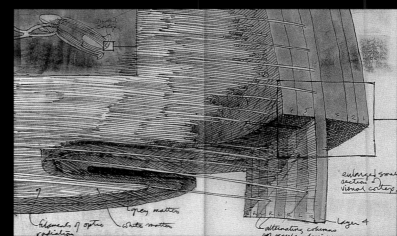

processes a perceived image step-by-step. But, first of all, why *David?* Because the subject matter relates to everyone who can see, I wanted a more or less universally recognized face. I went even further and chose a stone face to introduce a little humor. I hoped this would enliven, or at least lighten the somewhat complex explanation. ■ In my original mock-up, several steps in the process were over-explained. Obviously, I was still trying to understand the information while assembling the sketches. But, consistent in both mock-up and published versions of the cluster is a small close-up box, which indicates what is shown on the following page as we move through the eyes and into the cellular structure of the brain. The arrow extending from each box was intended to clarify this device. A major difference in the mock-up and the finished version is that, beginning on the second spread in the later book, the images suddenly "flip" over—the inversion reflecting how our brains process what we see. This had not occurred to me while doing the mock-up. But, I wanted to get the readers' attention by reminding them that the information they were reading was, at that moment, traveling from their eyes to their brains upside down. I realized the inversion could be confusing and a few folks might even return their books and complain about the "mistake". But it seemed worth the gamble. The arrows, which became much larger in the published version, serve the critical role of reminding readers that after inverting the book, they must read these pages in the right direction, which is right-to-left. ■ The earlier mock-up images are much more architectural and spatially arresting, and I still prefer them, but I felt the drama might be distracting. The movement of information from the visual cortex to other areas of the brain, for example, seemed overly complicated in the early version, and unnecessarily revisited the anatomical information of *The Amazing Garden*. I settled for a more sym-

MAPPING SEQUENCE (REVISED) In the final drawings, page-turning devices signal that the cluster has to be turned upside down at a specific point in order to reflect the brain's own inverting of images. A close-up box and an arrow isolate the section in each drawing that is enlarged and detailed on the following cluster page.

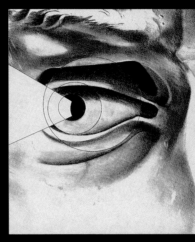
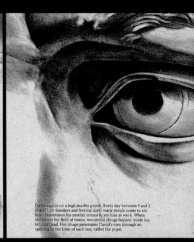

David stands on a high marble plinth. Every day between 9 and 2 IV and I on Sundays and festival days) many people come to see him. Sometimes his mother comes to see him at work. When she enters his field of vision, wonderful things happen inside his famous head. Her image penetrates David's eyes through an opening in the front of each one, called the pupil.

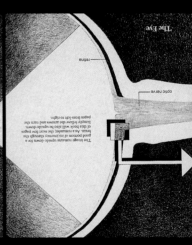

Immediately behind each pupil is a lens that focuses and projects the image on a light-sensitive layer of nerve cells called the retina, which lines the inside of the back of the eyeball. Since the image is inverted as it passes through the lens, you will have to turn the book upside-down to continue reading.

direction of light

The Eye

retina

optic nerve

pupil

cornea

The image remains upside-down for a good portion of its journey through the brain. As a reminder, the next few pages of this book will also be upside-down. Simply follow the arrows and turn the pages from left to right.

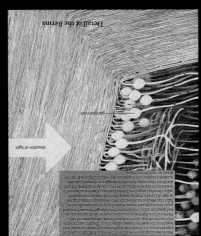
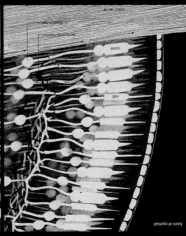

Detail of the Retina

direction of light

ganglion cells

optic nerve

bipolar cells

amacrine cells

cone

rod

back of eyeball

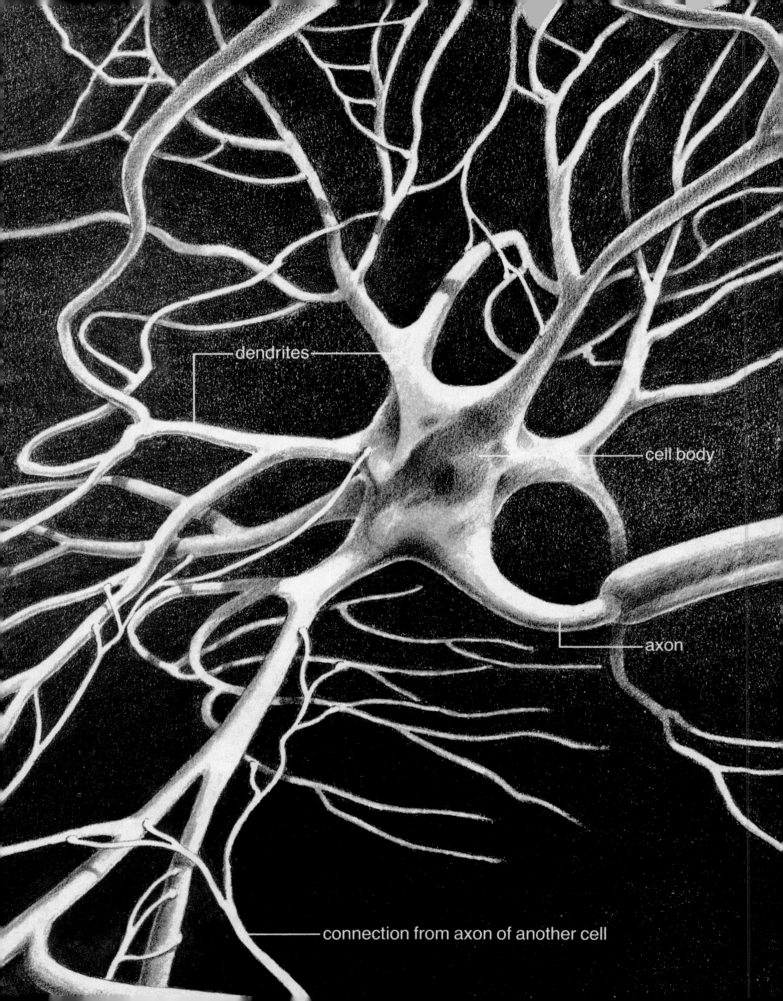

dendrites

cell body

axon

connection from axon of another cell

bolic representation. To tie together and punctuate the entire sequence I ended with *David* again, responding as he recognizes his mother. If the reader ends this section with a smile, I think they are more likely to go back and read it again. This is hardly rocket science, just common sense. ■ The third cluster was titled *A Modest Proposal*, or

The planning, construction and use of a giant brain for the edification and entertainment of us all. It was a considerably extended version of the original magazine article and, like the second cluster, it tells its story in both words and pictures. In cluster one we looked at a brain from the outside, in cluster two we saw the internal workings of the brain, but from a distance. Here at last, in cluster three, we are able to wander around inside the brain. We see first-hand what everything looks like, as if we were in a city museum. We go from exterior views of the construction of the brain museum, to a tour of some of the more impressive interior spaces. Preparing the sequence of images was very straightforward and changed very little from the original mock-up. The structure had to look solid and convincing in its urban setting, and I wanted to create some really dramatic images with strong lighting *à la* Hugh Ferris, so I worked entirely in pencil. As usual, I began with sketchbook doodles while still researching, which helped me get to drawing when the ideas were developed and supported by more knowledge. The goal was to place readers inside the architecture of the skull. In one drawing they stand behind the eyes with their backs against the pituitary stalk and look forward. In another they look back at the pituitary stalk (following two pages). Glass tubes, like those at Charles de Gaulle airport, connect the optic chiasm with the eyes (behind the skull bone on the right). In the distance, one sees different arteries wending their way to various parts of the brain museum.

EXTENDING SEQUENCE The brain's processing of an image continues with a drawing of one of the billions of cells and cell connections in the cortex (below and opposite). Because the cell has no definite top or bottom, the cluster pages are now turned right-side-up again. One of the billions of cell branch lines that carries nerve messages is shown stretching onto the right page. As before, the box slicing through it signals that a detail enlargement is coming next. Two versions of the cell line are shown here, the first mock-up drawing and the final drawing (bottom).

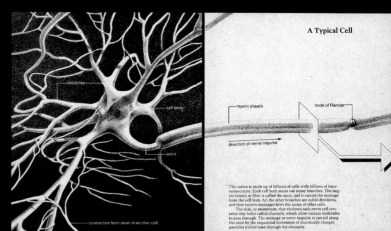

A Typical Cell

dendrites

cell body

axon

myelin sheath

node of Ranvier

direction of nerve impulse

connection from axon of another cell

The cortex is made up of billions of cells with billions of interconnections. Each cell body sends out many branches. The largest branch or fiber is called the axon, and it carries the message from the cell body. All the other branches are called dendrites, and they receive messages from the axons of other cells.

The skin, or membrane, that encloses each nerve cell contains tiny holes called channels, which allow certain molecules to pass through. The message or nerve impulse is carried along the axon by the sequential movement of electrically charged particles (called ions) through the channels.

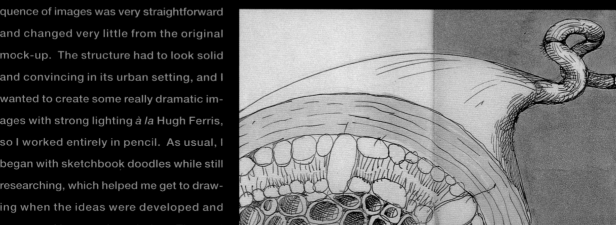

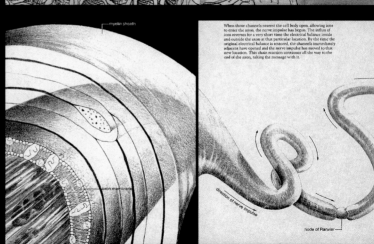

myelin sheath

axon membrane

When those channels nearest the cell body open, allowing ions to enter the axon, the nerve impulse has begun. The influx of ions reverses for a very short time the electrical balance inside and outside the axon at that particular location. By the time the original electrical balance is restored, the channels immediately adjacent have opened and the nerve impulse has moved to that new location. This chain reaction continues all the way to the end of the axon, taking the message with it.

direction of nerve impulse

node of Ranvier

INVENTING POINT OF VIEW The last cluster in *The Amazing Brain* places readers inside the skull, touring as if they were visitors in a city museum. Some of the
more impressive interior spaces are shown, with details like the pituitary stalk and
the tube-like optical connections. The exterior of the brain museum is on page 240.

Just below the aneurysm, the posterior communicating artery stretches toward the back of the brain. Above the aneurysm, the anterior choroidal artery ramp ascends into the left temporal lobe. At the rear of the cistern, dropping down from behind the optic chiasm, is the pituitary stalk, which connects the hypothalamus with the pituitary gland. Above the cistern are the two glass-enclosed optic nerves leading to the eyes.

CAMDEN Many years ago I decided Camden, New Jersey didn't *deserve* to be mapped. *Oh Peter, be serious.* But I was. At the time I was doing a book about the city's 67 well-known examples of really bad city planning. With lots of maps and lots of colors, the book was a typically cool *professional* product aimed at the few (140) city managers responsible for planning our largest cities. But—then I saw Camden. I saw that no book could possibly show how much chaos and misery the planning had added to the lives of thousands of people. A nice book might even *sanitize* it. So, I decided to build a giant blocky model of the city instead. A narrator would walk through it, lift buildings, shift highway ramps, point at flaws, and get *angry* about such insensitivity. Closed-circuit television would broadcast the message, a printed hand-out would clarify it. Effective solution? I don't know, the project never happened. All I do know is that Camden prompted my first urge to picture the bone plain truth in graphics, and erased my comfort with anything less.

■ **CALORIES** Even a *vital* science like nutrition has conventions that obscure its simplest principles. I ask you, exactly what is a "calorie" anyway? When I diagrammed nutrition for *American Health* magazine I got a chance to ask them. I heard that utterly useless definition, heat raising the temperature of a gram of water and all that. *Yes, yes,* I said. *But, can I hold a calorie? Is it a lump of energy like a lump of coal?* Signs of distress. Yes, the editor said. Food fuels your body with three groups of nutritional elements—carbohydrates, protein, and fat—which are measured in energy units called calories. *You mean, a calorie is a lump of fuel with three general ingredients?* Yes, he said. *Well. So. Draw one for me.* Sigh. He snatched up a pen, drew a pie shape with three parts, and labeled the parts *carbohydrate*, *protein,* and *fat.* Okay, he said, that's a calorie, all flattened out. It has three parts, always those three—nothing else, ever. The only thing is, *the parts vary in proportion according to the food*. Well, that was a Very Big Reveal to me. All calories are not the same. So counting *whole* calories means much less than counting calorie parts. And our pie symbols could clearly mark the parts.

MAPPING ELEMENTS The three groups of nutritional elements in calories vary greatly in different foods. So, counting *parts* of a calorie instead of the whole makes much more sense. Divided "pies" show calorie parts and signal a meal's hazards (opposite).

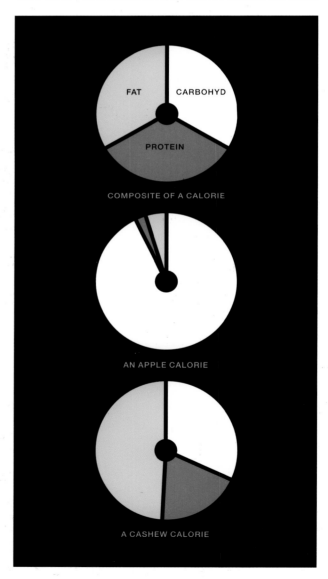

COMPOSITE OF A CALORIE

AN APPLE CALORIE

A CASHEW CALORIE

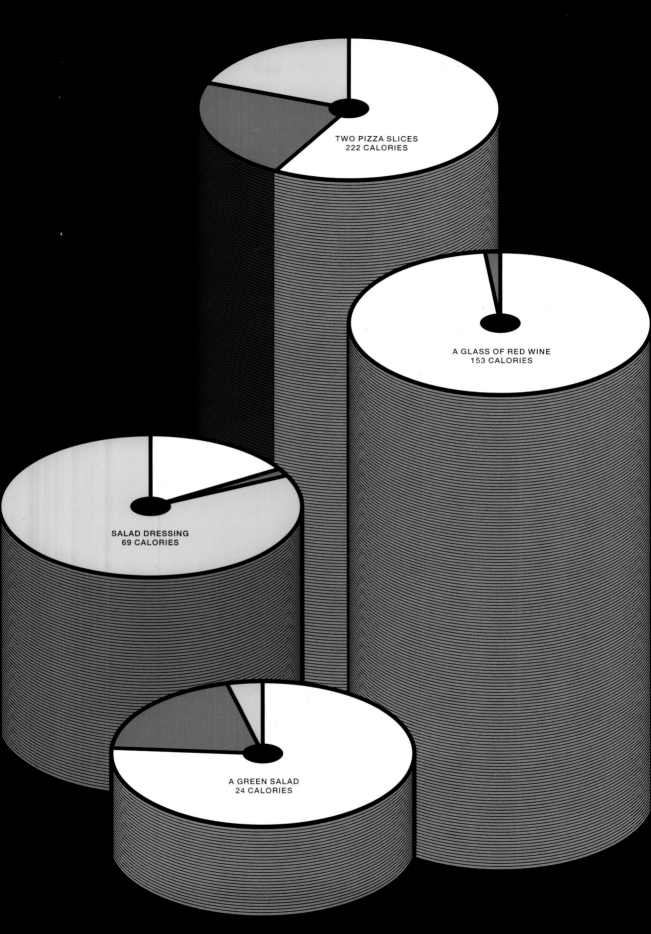

TWO PIZZA SLICES
222 CALORIES

A GLASS OF RED WINE
153 CALORIES

SALAD DRESSING
69 CALORIES

A GREEN SALAD
24 CALORIES

A CALORIE PORTRAIT OF A MEAL: PIZZA, RED WINE, GREEN SALAD, AND A (VERY HAZARDOUS) SALAD DRESSING

■ **PLATE TECTONICS** is a very young science. Constantly, with new insights and new discoveries, it seems to grow more complex every day. Far too often for me. But when I was asked to diagram a book about the subject, I suddenly had a need to know. With very long words, the author explained that the earth is covered with many thin irregular plates, which have carried the continents here and there for millions of years. Morocco was once connected to Nova Scotia, Antarctica was way over there, and so on. *Okay. But how can heavy things like continents float around like that?* He stopped. Starting again with stubborn grit, using short little words, he told me to picture the outer surface of the earth (continental crust) as a piece of paper wrapped around a basketball. He trotted off and found a world globe—this was not a basketball guy—and wrapped it with tracing paper. The paper slid easily around the globe. He described the warmth beneath the crust, and how the warm currents move like they do in a pot of boiling water, slowly circulating material under the crust to make the earth's plates separate and—

Eureka! Continents move! I said. He was very pleased. He pushed the sides of the paper together (two plates forced together), making it rise in the center in a raggedy line. *Mountains!* I screamed. He pulled at the paper until it split open. When plates are moved apart, new surface material pushes out, sometimes violently like the volcanic eruptions happening now on the bottom of the Atlantic Ocean. *Volcanoes under water? Right now?* Oh yes. Plates slide along each other too, moving vast land masses great distances. Mexico is moving along the San Andreas fault, headed for Alaska at the same rate your finger nails grow. All because of heat. ■ How simple. Rather, how simply can be expressed a basic principle that drives an inconceivably large and invisible science. Such clear models. With tracing paper on a small globe, plate tectonics was reduced to manageable scale in my mind and my diagrams were born. Later, of course, academic conventions of word and style were laid on top, but beneath them were solid understandings. And such an easy process: play dense, get a guy to explain the basics beneath his expertise (beneath *his* crust), and let *him* do the diagram designs.

MAPPING PROCESS The plates of the earth shift as the warm material beneath its crust circulates, not unlike boiling water in a pot (below). In the plumbing in our hearts, blocks are removed with drugs or catheter balloons, or they are by-passed (opposite).

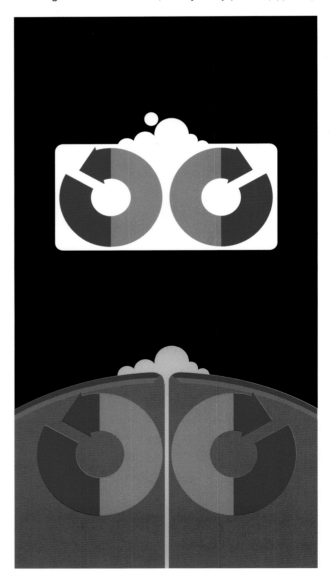

A BLOOD CLOT BLOCKS CIRCULATION TO PART OF THE HEART MUSCLE DURING A HEART ATTACK

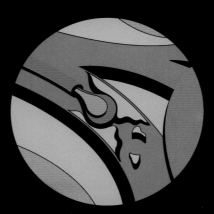

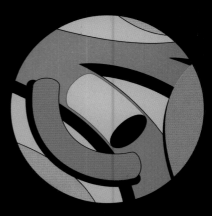

DRUGS CAN DISSOLVE THE CLOT

A CATHETER CAN BREAK UP THE CLOT

A BYPASS CAN DETOUR THE CLOT

■ **KEYNOTES** It seems that *Cliff Notes*, those beloved classics of literary avoidance, may be too dense for today's college students. So, Random House published *Keynotes*, a series of 100 skinny, six-page study guides of the world's great novels. I was asked to give the little things a gaudy cover and draw the tiny diagram that summed up the book's main characters and plot. These plot abbreviations had the gall to compress splendid literature into a few miniscule squares. But, while their simplifications were just stupendous, they were also very swift scans of their main ideas. ■ Content subtraction is a formidable skill; when sensibly compressed and reduced, content becomes a bare skeleton of essential ideas. Then, the essentials can be safely manipulated and enhanced—even animated. For example, I see plot diagrams *moving* as the action develops: *Bang!* One little character square shoots another little square. I see ingredients *joining* the process of cooking a recipe (bottom). I see surgical drawings moving too. How else could one bring the *thrust* of a catheter tube to life? (Just kidding.) But if the heart *pumps* and arterial blood *flows* as blocks are removed (preceding page), isn't the surgery made much more clear?

MAPPING ELEMENTS AND PROCESS The essential ideas of great novels were compressed into tiny interacting squares (below). The ingredients of a recipe were aligned with stages in the cooking process. In both, connecting the actors clarifies the action.

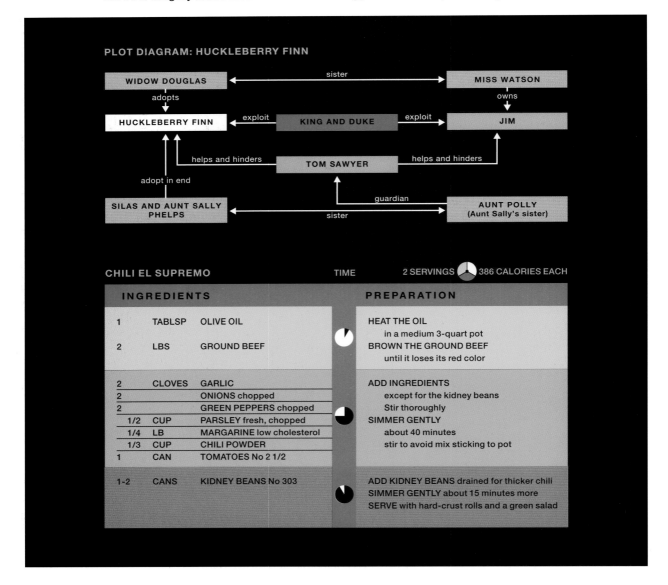

PLOT DIAGRAM: HUCKLEBERRY FINN

WIDOW DOUGLAS	←sister→	MISS WATSON
adopts↓		owns↑
HUCKLEBERRY FINN	←exploit— KING AND DUKE —exploit→	JIM
	helps and hinders — TOM SAWYER — helps and hinders	
adopt in end↑		
SILAS AND AUNT SALLY PHELPS	←sister→ guardian	AUNT POLLY (Aunt Sally's sister)

CHILI EL SUPREMO TIME 2 SERVINGS 386 CALORIES EACH

INGREDIENTS			PREPARATION
1	TABLSP	OLIVE OIL	**HEAT THE OIL** in a medium 3-quart pot
2	LBS	GROUND BEEF	**BROWN THE GROUND BEEF** until it loses its red color
2	CLOVES	GARLIC	**ADD INGREDIENTS** except for the kidney beans
2		ONIONS chopped	Stir thoroughly
2		GREEN PEPPERS chopped	**SIMMER GENTLY**
1/2	CUP	PARSLEY fresh, chopped	about 40 minutes
1/4	LB	MARGARINE low cholesterol	stir to avoid mix sticking to pot
1/3	CUP	CHILI POWDER	
1	CAN	TOMATOES No 2 1/2	
1-2	CANS	KIDNEY BEANS No 303	**ADD KIDNEY BEANS** drained for thicker chili **SIMMER GENTLY** about 15 minutes more **SERVE** with hard-crust rolls and a green salad

■ **CURRICULUM DICTIONARY** A very clever fellow once told me that one horse-power is equal to ten 75-watt light bulbs, 2637 pizza pies, or 3,122,756 calories. *What?* Yes. Because they share the same science definition of energy: doing *work* (how far you move an object) with *power* (how fast you move it). Those are measurements, he said, and all energy measurements can be compared. *So, how many pizzas will it take to heat my house?* How many rooms? he asked. Very interesting. ■ In time, the two of us travelled down a long and painful path on Dick and Pete's Excellent Adventure: the re-making of school dictionaries. He was Dr. Richard Venezky, an expert lexicographer. He felt conventional dictionaries were difficult, I felt they were armor-plated, bullet-proof monsters of opacity. We chose to attack school dictionaries because therein lies hope: the young learner finds pleasant reference a seductive friend. Random House was interested, committed money, and off we went. ■ At the same time, I got dunked in dictionary conventions when I re-designed the *American Heritage Dictionary* for Houghton-Mifflin. *Type styling only please, no rooting around in common sense. Reorganize definition entries? Are you crazy?*

MAPPING WORD RELATIONSHIPS In a school dictionary, complex definitions were divided into groups of similar senses, which were given labels. The labels created a vocabulary for electronic navigation, and gathered related words in topics (following pages).

CONVENTIONAL DEFINITION

watch (woch or wôch), 1 look attentively or carefully: *The medical student watched while the surgeon performed the operation.* 2 look at; observe; view: *Are you watching that show on television? We watched the kittens play.* 3 look or wait with care and attention; be very careful: *I watched for a chance to cross the street.* 4 a careful looking; attitude of attention: *Be on the watch for automobiles when you cross the street.* 5 keep guard: *The sentry watched throughout the night.* 6 keep guard over: *The police watched the prisoner.* 7 a protecting; guarding: *A man keeps watch over the bank at night.* 8 person or persons kept to guard and protect: *A call for help aroused the night watch.* 9 period of time for guarding: *a watch in the night.* 10 stay awake for some purpose: *The nurse watched with the sick.* 11 a staying awake for some purpose. 12 device for telling time, small enough to be carried in a pocket or worn on the wrist. 13 the time of duty of one part of a ship's crew. A watch usually lasts for four hours. 14 the part of a ship's crew on duty at the same time. 1-3,5,6,10 *v.,* 4,7-9,11-14 *n., pl.* **watch es.**

SENSE-LABEL DEFINITION (Phrases added)

watch (woch or wôch) pl **watches**
1. LOOK **a.** *verb:* look attentively or carefully: *The medical students watched while the surgeon performed the operation.* **b.** *noun:* a careful looking; attitude of attention: *Be on the watch for automobiles when you cross the street.* **c.** *verb:* look at; observe; view: *Are you watching that program on television? We watched the kittens play.* **d.** *verb:* look or wait with care and attention; be very careful: *I watched for a chance to cross the street.*
2. GUARD **a.** *verb:* keep guard: *The sentry watched throughout the night.* **b.** *verb:* keep guard over: *The police watched the prisoner.* **c.** *noun:* a protecting; guarding: *A man keeps watch over the bank at night.* **d.** *noun:* person or persons kept to guard and protect: *A call for help aroused the night watch.* **e.** *noun:* period of time for guarding: *a watch in the night.*
3. STAY AWAKE *verb:* stay awake for some purpose: *The nurse watches with the sick.*
4. DUTY **a.** *noun:* the time of duty of one part of a ship's crew: *A watch usually lasts four hours.* **b.** *noun:* the part of a ship's crew on duty at the same time.
5. INSTRUMENT *noun:* a device for telling time, small enough to be carried in a pocket or worn on the wrist.
PHRASES. **bird watcher:** someone who watches birds in their natural areas. **bear watching:** worth paying attention to. **clock watcher:** a worker anxious to stop working. **on the watch:** alert. **watch it:** be careful (usually a command). **watch one's smoke:** notice a quick action. **watch out:** be careful.

■ So naturally, the first thing we did in our school dictionary was re-organize the definition entries. Take the word *Watch.* It has 17 slightly or very different meanings, nouns and verbs, usually all mixed up in some order of common usage. *Look attentively* is mixed with *keep guard*, *device for telling time*, and *part of a ship's crew*. We felt that was confusing. So we separated the 17 meanings into five groups of similar-senses, giving each group a general sense label and a number to separate them (preceding page). ■ Group labels like *LOOK* and *GUARD* focussed the definition for faster searching. Even better, as more definitions were re-worked, the sense labels became a vocabulary which began to connect the entire data base upon which the dictionary was built. For example, the sense label *LOOK* connected *Watch* to other, slightly different definition entries like *Observe*, *Perceive,* and *Study*. When our printed dictionary turned electronic, this vocabulary could link definitions for travelling throughout the dictionary.

■ It worked in reverse too: word meanings that belonged together were gathered together. *Satire* gathered with *Parody* and *Irony*, *Typhoon* gathered with *Monsoon* and *Twister*. Isn't that nice? Each juxta-

UNIFYING WORD RELATIONSHIPS As related words were gathered by the similar-sense vocabulary, pictures were created to show their variances, like *Bodies of Water* (below). Or, if difficult to picture, word tables and diagrams were created (opposite).

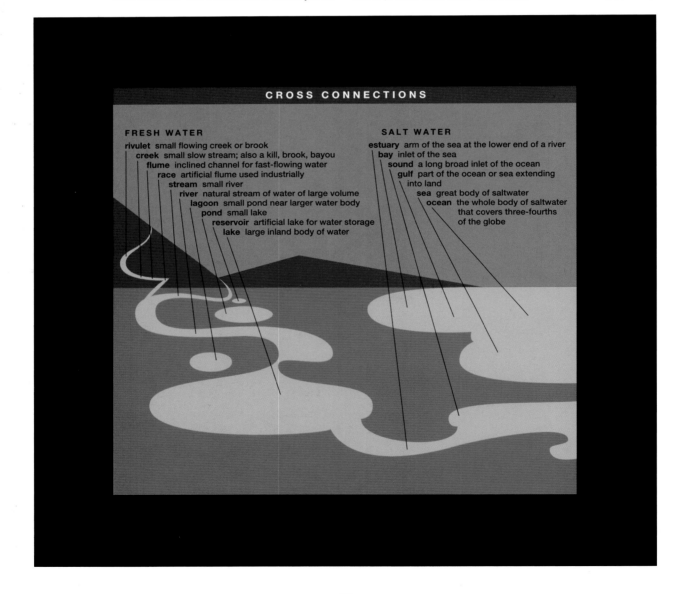

CROSS CONNECTIONS

FRESH WATER
rivulet small flowing creek or brook
  creek small slow stream; also a kill, brook, bayou
    flume inclined channel for fast-flowing water
      race artificial flume used industrially
        stream small river
          river natural stream of water of large volume
            lagoon small pond near larger water body
              pond small lake
                reservoir artificial lake for water storage
                lake large inland body of water

SALT WATER
estuary arm of the sea at the lower end of a river
  bay inlet of the sea
    sound a long broad inlet of the ocean
      gulf part of the ocean or sea extending
        into land
          sea great body of saltwater
            ocean the whole body of saltwater
              that covers three-fourths
              of the globe

PROSE

Prose literature has many forms. **Fiction** is writing produced by the imagination, unlike **non-fiction,** which is writing based on facts and real events. **Drama** is a form of prose designed to be performed on stage, by actors, in front of an audience, videotaped for broadcast on radio or television, or filmed for projection in movie theaters.

FICTION

tale
noun: a story or account of true or imagined events, passed down through generations by oral communication.
A **myth** is a tale originating in a preliterate society serving to explain the wonders of nature and man; a **legend** is a popular, modern myth believed to have historical basis. A **folk tale** is a story made up and handed down orally by the common people. A **fairy tale** is a folk tale about fairies and giants and a **tall tale** is a tale that exaggerates things.

moral
noun: a story with a conclusion meant to teach goodness or correctness of character and behavior.
A **parable** is a short, simple story, from which a moral lesson may be drawn; a **fable** is a fictitious parable and an **allegory** is a more complex parable in which people and things have a hidden meaning.

narrative
noun: a structured account of actual or imaginary events.
A **story** is a narrative intended to interest or amuse the hearer or reader; a **short story** usually describes a single event with few characters. A **novel** is a long story with a plot that unfolds through the actions, speech, and thoughts of the characters. A short or condensed novel with a moral or satirical ending is a **novella.**

fantasy
noun: fiction in which the characters are involved in imaginary or bizarre situations, unrelated to everyday life.
An **adventure** is a novel about a dangerous or risky undertaking. A **Gothic novel** is a medieval adventure emphasizing the supernatural and the grotesque. **Science fiction** is an adventure which takes place in the future, a **mystery** is about a puzzling crime and a **romance** is about idealized love.

irony
noun: a literary style in which words convey the opposite of their literal meaning for humorous effect.
A **parody** is a literary work that mimics and ridicules a serious author's writing, and a **satire** uses irony or wit to ridicule an idea or custom.

NON-FICTION

record
noun: events, ideas, and experiences put down in writing so as to create a permanent account.
History is a narrative record of important past events connected with a person, nation, or institution; a **chronicle** is more systematic than history in that it documents events in the order in which they took place. A **diary** is a personal chronicle, with entries written each day, of a person's experiences and observations. A **biography** is the life story of a person researched and written by another person; an **autobiography** is a biography written by and about the same person.

expression
noun: the act of conveying one's thoughts, feelings, or opinions through words, either written or spoken.
An **essay** is a short composition on a single subject, usually presenting the personal views of the author; a **review** is an essay in which the author expresses his or her opinions on a book, a play, a movie, etc. A **speech** is an essay presented verbally to an audience, or recorded in written form. A **letter** is a written communication addressed to another individual rather than the public, conveying personal or intimate information.

explanation
noun: a written or spoken account which serves to clarify, justify, or reason something.
An **exposition** is a speech or writing which explains a single process, thing, or idea; a **treatise** explains the relationship and connections between two or more ideas, and **discourse** is the verbal form of a treatise: a lengthy discussion of a subject or series of ideas.

DRAMA

entertainment
noun: a happening that is designed to interest, please, or amuse an audience: a **skit,** a short, comic sketch, is a form of light, often deliberately superficial diversion.
A show, performance, and spectacle are all terms for public entertainment. A **show** is the most general term in that it does not indicate content or place. A **spectacle** suggests that something unusual and sensational is presented. A **performance** implies that a dramatic or musical work is acted on a stage.

play
noun: a literary work that tells a story, usually of human conflict, by means of dialogue and action performed on stage. A **movie** is a filmed version of this kind of story projected on a screen in a movie theater.
A **comedy** is a play that is humorous in its treatment of theme and characters and has a happy ending; a **farce** is a comedy full of ridiculous happenings and absurd actions. A sentimental and romantic play is a **melodrama,** and a play leading to an unhappy, often disastrous ending is a **tragedy.** A **pageant** is an elaborate play often staged outdoors, celebrating a historical event. **Operas** and **musicals** are plays in which most of the text is set to music, characterized by elaborate costuming, scenery, and dance choreography. A musical features song and dance in a popular idiom. When a play is broadcast on the radio it is a **radio play** and when it is broadcast on television it is a **television play**.

TERMS USED IN PROSE

participant
noun: one who takes part or acts in a story, play, etc.
character is the term for a person portrayed in a story or drama. An **actor** is a participant in a play who takes on a dramatic role or character. The central or leading character is the **protagonist,** and a **hero** or **heroine** suggests a character in a play noted for exceptional physical or moral courage. The **antagonist** is a character who opposes and actively competes with the protagonist to create a **conflict** in the drama: a disagreement, struggle, or clash.

form
noun: style or manner of presenting ideas or concepts in a literary composition as distinguished from its content.
An **act** is one of the major divisions or sections of a play; a **scene** is a subdivision of an act in which the setting is fixed and the time continuous. An **episode** is a portion of a play which relates a number of scenes to form a coherent story in itself; a **flashback** interrupts the continuity of an episode to introduce earlier events. A **prologue** is a speech introducing the play, and an **epilogue** is a speech following the conclusion of a play. Both are addressed to the audience directly. A **climax** is the time of highest dramatic tension or a turning point in the action of a play. **Rising action** brings about the climax and **falling action** occurs after the play's climax and leads to the **resolution:** the part of the play in which the plot is explained. A **dialogue** is a conversational passage in a play or story, and a **monologue** is a speech or talk delivered by a single character.

content
noun: the meaning, significance, or substance of a literary composition as distinguished from its form.
A **plot** is the main story of a play, and the **subplot** is a secondary plot. A **theme** is the subject of the plot and a **setting** is the time, place, and environment in which the plot takes place. A **script** is a written text including the plot, dialogue, setting, and performance directions used by the director and actors of a play or film.

POETRY

Poetry can be defined by its **form** or by its **content.** The components of poetic form are explained below using some examples that show how a poem can be read to enhance its meaning. Opposite are content explanations and examples.

FORM

TERMS AND EXAMPLES

meter
The combination of **accented** and **unaccented syllables** that determine the rhythm in a poem. The **rhythm** of a poem is its flow of sounds having a regular measure or beat, which is heard most clearly when a poem is recited or read aloud. A foot is one line unit of the meter; or any combination of one accented and one or more unaccented syllables. An **iambic** foot is the combining of an unaccented syllable followed by an accented syllable. A line of verse with five iambic feet is described as iambic pentameter, and has a constant rhythm of five accents to a line. Blank verse (shown below in Shakespeare's *Hamlet*) is a poem consisting of unrhymed lines of iambic pentameter.

This above all: to thine own self be true,
And it must follow, as the night the day,
Thou canst not then be false to any man.
Farewell: my blessing season this in thee!

free verse
Poetry that does not follow a regular meter and has an irregular rhythm or no rhyme. **Haiku** and **Tanka** are forms of Japanese poetry, written in free verse, usually about nature. Haiku (shown in the example below) is composed of three or sometimes four lines that do not rhyme and contain seventeen syllables—five in the first and last lines and seven in the middle lines. Tanka has five lines—the first and third each have five syllables and the rest have seven syllables.

Does the sea have fun
Bobbing the swimmers around
Like so many corks?

rhyme
The correspondence of end sounds of two or more words, usually ending a verse line. In verse, the use of similar sounding words is used as a device of emphasis and as a means of defining a pattern of lines, or a **stanza.** A stanza is not only a fixed pattern of lines, but also a pattern of rhymes, or a **rhyme scheme.** The simplest stanza is that of **rhymed couplets** (shown below in Ted Hughes' poem *My Brother*) in which every two lines rhyme and form a verse paragraph. A **sonnet** is a poem written in fourteen lines of iambic pentameter with a prescribed rhyme scheme described as follows: **A-B-A-B-C-D-C-D-E-D-E-F-F;** the first line rhymes with the third, the second line with the fourth, etc. In its typical form a sonnet presents and develops its theme in the first twelve lines, and states the conclusion in the last couplet.

Pets are the hobby of my brother Bert.
He used to go to school with his mouse in his shirt.

His hobby it grew, as some hobbies will,
And grew and GREW and GREW until —

Oh don't breathe a word, pretend you haven't heard.
A simply appalling thing has occurred —

The very thought makes me iller and iller:
Bert's brought home a gigantic gorilla!

CONTENT

TERMS AND EXAMPLES

narrative verse
A poem that tells a detailed story in rhyme, following a rhyme scheme with lines arranged in verses or stanzas (see Sir Walter Scott's poem *Lochinvar* shown below). A descriptive poem is usually a short poem about a person, scene, situation, or occasion which reveals the author's feelings about what is being described.

Oh, young Lochinvar is come out of the west:
Through all the wide Border his steed was the best,
And save his good broadsword he weapons had none;
He rode all unarmed, and he rode all alone.

song
A short poem set to music. A **lullaby** is a poem set to soothing and lulling music, and a song belonging to the history and experiences of a certain culture is a **folk song.** A **lyric poem** (Robert Frost's *Stopping by Woods on a Snowy Evening* shown below) is characterized by its musical sound pattern, and its expression of personal emotion.

Whose woods these are I think I know
His house is in the village, though;
He will not see me stopping here
To watch his woods fill up with snow.

nonsense poem
A composition of words or syllables arranged primarily by meter and rhyme and not by sense, for humorous or whimsical effect (see below in *Jabberwocky*). A **tongue twister** in a poem is a series of words or syllables that are difficult to say quickly because of a succession of very similar sounds. A **limerick,** originating in Ireland, is a light, humorous, or nonsensical verse of five lines, usually with the rhyme scheme: **1-1-2-2-1** (see Edward Lear's limerick, bottom).

"Beware the Jabberwock, my son!
The jaws that bite, the claws that catch!
Beware the Jubjub bird, and shun
The frumious Bandersnatch!"

MIND'S EYE

Poetry can be identified by its rhythmic accents, or **meter scheme,** and by its similar line ending sounds, or **rhyme scheme.**

METER SCHEME	RHYME SCHEME	
There **was** an old **man** on whose **nose**	nose	1
Most **birds** of the **air** could re**pose;**	pose	1
But they **all** flew a**way,**	away	2
At the **close** of a **day,**	day	2
Which re**lieved** that old **man** and his **nose.**	nose	1

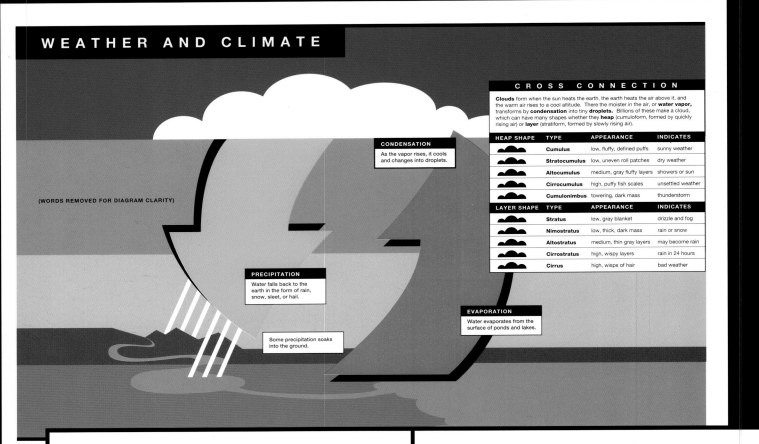

(WORDS REMOVED FOR DIAGRAM CLARITY)

CONDENSATION
As the vapor rises, it cools and changes into droplets.

PRECIPITATION
Water falls back to the earth in the form of rain, snow, sleet, or hail.

Some precipitation soaks into the ground.

EVAPORATION
Water evaporates from the surface of ponds and lakes.

CROSS CONNECTION

Clouds form when the sun heats the earth, the earth heats the air above it, and the warm air rises to a cool altitude. There the moister in the air, or **water vapor,** transforms by **condensation** into tiny **droplets.** Billions of these make a cloud, which can have many shapes whether they **heap** (cumuloform, formed by quickly rising air) or **layer** (stratiform, formed by slowly rising air).

HEAP SHAPE	TYPE	APPEARANCE	INDICATES
	Cumulus	low, fluffy, defined puffs	sunny weather
	Stratocumulus	low, uneven roll patches	dry weather
	Altocumulus	medium, gray fluffy layers	showers or sun
	Cirrocumulus	high, puffy fish scales	unsettled weather
	Cumulonimbus	towering, dark mass	thunderstorm

LAYER SHAPE	TYPE	APPEARANCE	INDICATES
	Stratus	low, gray blanket	drizzle and fog
	Nimostratus	low, thick, dark mass	rain or snow
	Altostratus	medium, thin gray layers	may become rain
	Cirrostratus	high, wispy layers	rain in 24 hours
	Cirrus	high, wisps of hair	bad weather

WEATHER COMPONENTS

Weather is the interaction of the **temperature, moisture, and winds** in the atmosphere. The activity occurs in the troposphere, the layer of the atmosphere closest to the earth. When the activity is noticeably swift, changeable, and violent, it is called one of the many forms of **storms.**

TEMPERATURE

Temperature is a measure by degree of the hotness or coldness in an object, body of water, or air. Air temperature, along with humidity and wind speed, effect our feeling of hotness or coldness in the surrounding air.

TERM	DEGREE	IDIOM
scorching	intensely hot, burning	a scorching attack
torrid	intensely hot, parched	with torrid passion
parched	intensely hot, dry	a parched thirst
boiling	intensely hot	with boiling anger
sweltering	oppressively hot	a nervous swelter
hot	heated, almost burning	hot under the collar
muggy	warm, damp, close	a muggy room
warm	moderately hot	a warm welcome
balmy	slightly warm	a balmy comfort
mild	gentle, not extreme	mild mannered
cool	moderately cold	a cool manner
nippy	chilling	a nippy response
chilly	noticeably cool	chilly suspicions
cold	very low temperature	passed out cold
frosty	briskly cold	a frosty reception
freezing	intensely cold	a freezing attitude
frigid	intensely cold, frozen	a frigid hello

MOISTURE

Moisture is the wetness in the air, caused by water vapor, and measured as humidity. **Water vapor** is evaporated water in gas-like state, and **humidity** is the amount of water vapor present at a given time, usually measured in relation to the maximum water vapor that the air can hold.

Warm air can hold more water vapor than cold air. As air cools, water vapor turns to water droplets or ice crystals, or **condenses** into clouds. When condensed water accumulates and becomes heavier than the air, it then falls as **precipitation** (rain or snow.)

TERM	EFFECT	IDIOM
raw	disagreeably damp	raw winter days
soggy	saturated with moisture	soggy prose
damp	high humidity	dampened enthusiasm
clammy	moist, cold, and sticky	clammy statistics
humid	oppressive moisture	a humid workout
moist	tolerable humidity	moist eyes
dry	a lack of humidity	a dry sense of humor
arid	excessively dry	arid miles of brushland

TERM	CONDENSATION	
cloud	masses of water or ice crystals in various forms	
fog	light cloud	
mist	fine water droplets suspended in fog	
smog	water vapor condensed with smoke or dust	
haze	particles of smoke or dust in the atmosphere	
steam	visible vapor, rising when air is cooler than ground	

TERM	PRECIPITATION	
dew	ground condensation when the earth is warm	
frost	ground condensation when the earth is cold	
hoar frost	furry looking frost	
rain	droplets collide to form drops and fall	
sprinkle	spatter of rain drops	
drizzle	light intensity rain, fine drops, almost mist	
dripping	average drops, coming down fast	
shower	short, light rainfall	
downpour	sudden, short, heavy rainfall	
deluge	heavy rainfall, almost torrential	
torrent	violent downpour	
sheet	heavy rainfall moving like a curtain	
pelting	large drops landing with force	
splashing	drops that split when they land	
pouring	large drops, coming down fast	
hail	clumps or small balls of frozen rain or snow	
hailstone	a single, large clump of hail	
snow	precipitation that falls as white ice crystals	
flurries	brief, light snowfall	
blizzard	sustained, heavy, very windy snowfall	

WIND

Wind is the natural, horizontal movement of the earth's air mass. Wind transports water vapor and spreads fog, clouds, and precipitation. Differences in temperature in the earth and atmosphere, which result in the changing high and low **air pressures**, create and drive the complex systems of wind.

Wind can be **laminar** (smooth and sheetlike) or it can be **turbulent** (erratic in direction or speed). An **eddy** is a whirling wind that flows against the main current, wind that shifts direction clockwise is a **veering wind** and wind shifting counter-clockwise is a **backing wind.**

An **air current** is an up and down, column-like movement of air within the wind. If this column descends rapidly, riders in an airplane will feel like their supporting air has disappeared; they are in an **air pocket.** Differences in a column's speed produces **bumpy air.**

If the wind or the air column has vastly different, adjacent speeds, it is called **windshear.** If the wind speed combines with the air temperature and cools the human body, the effect is called **windchill.**

FORMAL TERM AND EFFECT		*BSF	KPH
calm	smoke rises vertically	0	0-5
light air	smoke drifts slowly	1	1-5
light breeze	wind can be felt, leaves rustle	2	6-11
gentle breeze	twigs move, flag unfurls	3	12-9
moderate	dust blows, branches move	4	20-29
fresh breeze	wavelets form, trees move	5	30-39
strong breeze	large branches sway	6	40-50
near gale	trees sway, walking difficult	7	51-61
gale	twigs break, walking very hard	8	62-74
strong gale	shingles, branches blow down	9	75-87
storm	trees uprooted, severe damage	10	88-101

TERM AND EFFECT		IDIOM
breath	very slight wind	not a breath of scandal
puff	intermittent wind	puff up to full height
waft	slight, puffy wind	a waft of perfume
breeze	gentle, constant wind	breeze through it
gust	sudden, brief rush of air	a gust of emotion
swirl	forceful, circular	a swirl of events
eddy	circular, against current	eddies of people dancing
blow	strong, violent wind	blow hot and cold
blast	violent, constant gust	a blast of the siren
bluster	violent, sudden gusts	a bluster of protest

* BFS: Beaufort Scale Force (with kilometers per hour)

STORM

A **storm** is a disturbance of the atmosphere caused by a set of extreme weather conditions. It usually has high winds and precipitation. Storms can have a single extreme condition as in a snowstorm or windstorm, or multiple conditions as in a thunderstorm. The power of storms can be incredible. If all the energy from one hurricane in a single day could be converted into electricity, it would be enough to supply the whole of the United States for three years.

STORM	EFFECT	LOCATION
windstorm	high winds	any region
sandstorm	windstorm, clouds of sand	desert
whirlwind	rotating, spiral windstorm	over land
duststorm	dry, dust-laden whirlwind	arid regions
dust devil	tiny dust whirlwind	arid regions
twister	whirlwind, visible spiral air	over land
tornado	whirlwind, cone-shaped	over land
water spout	violent whirlwind	over water
squall	sudden, violent wind, rain	over land
tempest	extensive violent wind, rain	over ocean
cyclone	violent, rotating winds	tropics, ocean
hurricane	cyclonic, rotating winds	Atlantic Ocean
typhoon	cyclonic, rotating winds	Pacific Ocean
monsoon	periodic wind, torrential rain	Indian Ocean
blizzard	long, intense snowstorm	cold regions

MIND'S EYE

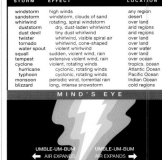

UMBLE-UM-BUM
AIR EXPANDS ←

UMBLE-UM-BUM
AIR EXPANDS →

Lightning is a giant spark of electricity that builds up in a thundercloud and zigzags to the ground and back as a *lightning bolt*. Lightning below the horizon illuminating the sky is *sheet lightning*, a glowing sphere is *ball lightning*, and a spray of lightning is *St. Elmo's fire*. **Thunder** is caused by superfast lightning that heats the air along its path to five times the heat of the sun, expanding the air at great speed and creating the familiar booming noises that Mark Twain described in the book *Huckleberry Finn* as ". . . rumbling, grumbling, tumbling . . . h–whack–bum! bum! bumble–umble–umbum–bum–bum–bum."

position clarifies the defining of each term. Gathering also helps locate a term when you don't know or can't spell it, instead of navigating back and forth in an alphabetic listing. Next, we designed ways to represent the gatherings. We made context pictures for easily pictured word groups like *Bodies of Water*, tables and typographic diagrams for less easily pictured groups like *Poetry*. Very quickly, our representations multiplied and grew to unwieldy size. They began to crowd the alphabetic section, making it jumpy and difficult to use. To accommodate them, we tacked on a group of pages after the alphabetic section and called it our topic section. ■ Well, not so easy, Sneezy. Topically arranged reference is neither familiar nor encouraged by American publishers. In fact, splitting the dictionary into two sections was to become our most provocative change. But how could we deny the logic? ■ Now we had word-group pictures and tables bunched together in topics, and a whole section to put them in. To organize it, we returned to our early rationale for deciding which major words should have major group

UNIFYING TOPIC RELATIONSHIPS Gradually, the pictures and tables of related word groups grew to become a whole topic section in the dictionary (opposite). To organize it, a grid of subject hierarchies and links was used, like the portion shown (below).

A DRAFTY MATRIX OF KNOWLEDGE (Partial)

	UNIVERSE	EARTH	LIFE
ORIGIN	Theories	Theories	Theories
	Big bang	Explosion	Simple life
	Expansion	Attraction	Evolutionary
	Accretion	Accretion	Spiritual life
	History	History	History
	Primitive	Primitive	Primitive
	Projected	Projected	Projected
STRUCTURE	Systems	Systems	Systems
	Galaxy	Mass/Core	Interaction
	Cluster	Physical	Regulation
	Solar	Convection	Anatomical
	Quasar	Cycle	Genetic
	Quark	Climate	Reproduction
	Hole	Weather	Eco-system
	Components	Components	Components
	Star	Atmosphere	Botanic
	Planet	Land mass	Biologic
	Asteroid	Mineral	Instinct
	Meteoroid	Element	Element
	Comet	Atom	Cell
ENERGY	Sustaining	Sustaining	Sustaining
	Interaction	Interaction	Interaction
	Gravity	Gravity	Gravity
	Light	Radiation	Radiation
	Expansion	Momentum	Synthesis
	Wave	Convection	Nutrition
		Magnetism	
	Decaying	Decaying	Decaying
	Thermal	Depletion	Degeneration
	Chemical	Pollution	Disease
BEHAVIOR	Innate	Innate	Innate
	Balance	Orbit	Survival
	Succession	Rotation	Selection
	Generation	Wobble	Branching
		Regeneration	
		Reaction	
	Learned	Learned	Learned
	Reactive	Reactive	Reactive
	Collective	Collective	Communing
	Tolerant	Tolerant	Resistant

pictures. For example, *Weather* had a picture because its terms are so numerous and so visual. As its basis, I chose to diagram the *Water Cycle* and its circling machinery of heat (opposite). Gradually, these intuitive choices evolved into an organizing mechanism: a hierarchical (top to bottom) and inter-linked (left to right) grid of topic pigeon holes for sticking every word in the dictionary—which covers, of course, everything we know. We called it Mother Matrix and a rickety thing it was, but it served our purpose. *Weather* fitted vertically as a topic group within *Earth Systems* beneath *Planet Earth* (diagram left). It linked horizontally to related subjects, like *Solar System* and *Eco-System*. (These hierarchies were not easily created, nor are they easily defended. But some kind of master scheme was needed to ensure free electronic travel throughout our data—just as it is in all such projects.) ■ Anyway, all to no avail. We presented our dictionary to loud frowns. It seemed to suit no reference category and had no generic name. The publisher said, if we can't name it, we can't sell it. *Well, how about Wooky?* I said. *That has a hairy flavor to it. How about calling it a Wooky?* They were not amused.

Earth

The earth is a great globe of rock surrounded by an envelope of air. It is one
of nine planets that travel through
space around the sun. The sun is a
star—one of billions in the Milky Way
galaxy. The Milky Way and billions of
other galaxies make up the universe.

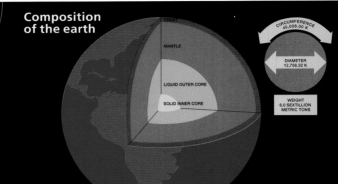

SOLAR SYSTEM: The
earth ranks fifth in
size among the sun's
nine planets, and, at
93 million miles, is
third in distance from
the sun. The sun is
third in distance from
the sun. The earth
travels 595 million
miles in just over 365
days and 6 hours.

PLANETARY SYSTEM:
The earth has one
orbiting moon which
is about a fourth the
size of the earth. Pluto
also has one moon,
Mercury and Venus
have no moons. All the
other planets have
two moons or more.

ATMOSPHERE: Air
surrounds the earth in
layers, and extends to
about 1600 kilometers
above it, where it
gradually fades into
space. All weather
takes place in the
troposphere, the layer
closest to the earth.

CRUST AND CORE: The
earth has a crust, or
topmost layer of solid
rock. The next mantle
layer is also solid rock,
but moves slowly under
heat and stress. The
outer core is molten rock
and the inner core is
believed to be solid iron.

SIZE AND SHAPE: The
earth is held nearly
round by gravity. But,
the earth also rotates,
creating an outward
push called centrifugal
force. The force is greatest at the equator Where
the earth bulges out as
it flattens at the poles.

Composition of the earth

CRUST

MANTLE

LIQUID OUTER CORE

SOLID INNER CORE

CIRCUMFERENCE
40,008.00 K

DIAMETER
12,756.32 K

WEIGHT
6.0 SEXTILLION
METRIC TONS

Terms

Earth science: the study of the earth
includes the sciences of:
  Geography: the study of the surface of the earth
  Geology: earth's history and composition
  Geochemistry: chemical properties of the earth
  Geophysics: the physical properties of the earth
  Meteorology: study of air and weather

Earth When and how did the earth begin?
This question has always fascinated people.
The earth is but one of nine planets that
make up our solar system, but to us it is by
far the most important planet. It is our
home. As far as we know, it is the only
planet that supports life.

The earth is constantly changing. It is
not the same as when it was first formed.
It does not look as it did several million years
ago or even 100 years ago. If you could re-

and how it is changing, scientists study the
land surface, the air, the oceans and the interior of our planet. The general term for
the study of earth is earth science. **Earth
science** is made up of several sciences that
are related to one another. Among them
are geography, geology, geochemistry, geophysics, meteorology, oceanography, and
paleontology.

The Ever-Changing Earth

world began. Most changes occur so slowly that the human eye does not notice
them. Over millions of years, mountains
are thrust up and worn down. The land is
steadily attacked by erosion—the slow
wearing away of the surface by water, air,
and ice. Rock is broken into tiny fragments,
which are carried away by rivers and
dumped into the oceans as sediment. Seas
creep in over the land, deposit sediment,
and draw back, making new land. Glaci-

ORBITS: As it rotates, the
earth travels around the
sun. The path that the
earth follows—called its
orbit—has the shape of
an ellipse, or slightly flattened circle. The earth
takes about 365 1/4 days
to complete its orbit.
This is the earth's year.

ROTATION: The earth
rotates, or spins, on its
axis from west to east.
The direction of the rotation makes the sun ap-
pear to rise in the east
and set in the west. A
complete rotation occurs
about every 24 hours,
which is the earth's day.

SEASONS: The earth's
axis is not at right
angles to the sun's
rays—it is tilted. In the
northern part of the
earth, summer arrives
when the North Pole is
tilted toward the sun,
and winter when tilted
away from the sun.

Motion of the earth

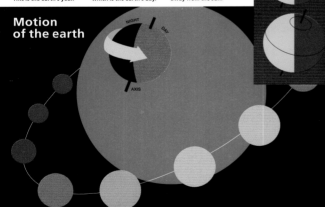

NIGHT

DAY

AXIS

LIGHT and HEAT: The sun
is a star and like every
star it is a very hot ball of
gas. As the gas burns,
energy is released in the
form of light, heat, and
other radiations. Because
the earth travels around
the sun in a stable orbit,
it receives a uniform

amount of energy from
the sun each year—just
the right amount for life
to develop. However, as
shown in the diagram
below, all parts of the
earth do not receive the
same amount of solar
heat because the earth
is round and not flat.

PROTECTIVE SHIELDS:
The earth's atmosphere
is essential to life. It
contains the oxygen we
breathe. It acts as a
shield that prevents too
many of the sun's rays
from reaching the earth's
surface and holds in the
solar heat that does.

RADIATION: Many of the
dangerous radiations
from the sun, such as
X-rays and cosmic rays,
are absorbed in the
ionosphere, an important
region of the earth's
atmosphere. Life would
not be possible if these
rays reached the earth.

Energy of the earth

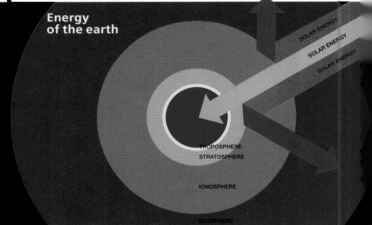

SOLAR ENERGY

SOLAR ENERGY

SOLAR ENERGY

TROPOSPHERE

STRATOSPHERE

IONOSPHERE

EXOSPHERE

earthquake. A volcano erupts, and hot,
molten (melted) rock pours out onto the surface. The lava hardens into new landforms.

Scientists study these changes and try to
understand the forces behind them. They
have taken giant strides forward in understanding the earth, but the answers to many
questions are still locked within our planet.

The Earth's Plates

Some of the changes on the earth's surface
are caused by movements of the crust. Ge-
ologists have determined that the crust is
made up of six large plates and a number

of smaller plates, each holding land masses, ocean regions, or both. This concept is
known as **plate tectonics**.

The plates move slowly with a sliding
motion. Two neighboring plates may move
apart. A rift (crack) opens between the
plates, and hot, molten rock from the
earth's interior wells up through it, forming a ridge. In another place two plates
may collide head on. One plate is forced
under the other, and a trench is formed.
Great mountains may be thrust up in such
a collision. It is believed that the Ap-
palachian Mountains were formed in this

way many millions of years ago, as were
the Alps, which are still rising slowly. Sometimes two plates slide slowly past each
other, their edges scraping. The edges may
catch and stick, pressing the plates together. A sudden release of the pressure
results in a jerking motion that causes an
earthquake.

Many details of plate movement are still
unexplained. But it is clear that these
movements do occur. And most scientists
agree that the forces of **convection** are
connected with the movement.

When you heat a pan of water, you set

up convection currents in the water. As
water at the bottom of the pan is heated,
it becomes lighter and rises. The cooler
water at the top is denser, and so it sinks.
The hotter water keeps rising, and the cooler water keeps sinking. This movement,
which goes round and round, produces a
convection current.

Many scientists think that something
similar takes place within the earth. The
lower part of the mantle is much hotter
than its top. As a result, convection currents are set up within the mantle. The hot
material, like the hot water, rises. The cool-

■ **THE NEW BOOK OF KNOWLEDGE** The job of an encyclopedia is to explain, isn't it? Well, how can that be done best? With vertically deep, exhaustively detailed explanations like the *Encyclopedia Brittanica*, or with horizontally broad, relational explanations like the *Curriculum Dictionary*? Maybe both? Yes, I think so, too. But, how does one build such a mass of linked knowledge? ■ The simplest mechanical linkage I have ever seen is in a toilet tank. I watch the water rush out, the stopper fall down, water rush back in, and the hollow ball float high to shut it off. I watch all the ways that machines use gravity for the good of me. But wait, why does the water rush in? I jump in the tank, swim down the pipe against the current to the main water tank, and find another cooperating force: tightly packed air is pushing hard to get more water back to the toilet. Oh, the clarity (and convenience) of clever links. ■ Grolier Publishers asked me to swim down the pipes of its encyclopedia. Clearly determined to look ahead, the editor Gerry Gabianelli asked if content could be arranged for both print and electron-

UNIFYING TOPIC ACCESS In a print version of a children's encyclopedia, subjects were displayed in three content layers for better access (opposite). Then, subjects were divided into topics that connected to related topics in the electronic version (bottom).

ic products. I said yes. (I *always* say yes.) We began with the subject *Earth*. For the printed pages, I placed content in three horizontal bands: detail on top, images in the middle, and text on the bottom. Then I separated *Earth* into a series of page-long topics to be read in order, first *Composition of the Earth*, then *Energy of the Earth*, then *Motion of the Earth*, and so on. I did this because: 1) I wanted more easily entered hierarchical pages in the print product, and 2) I wanted to lay foundations for a cross-navigational electronic product. ■ Topic separations created access routes *across* the subject. One can travel these routes or topic highways (or plumbing pipes) to various descriptions of the same topic. One can travel the *Motion* highway from *Motion of the Earth*, to *Motion of the Atom*, to *Motion of Heat* to better understand the realm of motion as a whole. ■ The topic highway system is a browser's delight; it links all subjects in a unified scheme of relationships. Imagine a topic like *centrifugal force* gaining clarity as you travel the *Motion* highway from *Earth* to *Orbiting Space Craft,* to *Hammerthrow.* Or, all the way to the Dictionary (*Yes!*) and the Latin root of centrifugal force: *center flee.*

■ **COSMIC COMICS** Driving as I was along my topic highways, a new thought struck. Why use words? Why not use other ways to link ideas, like pictures or symbols? Ways that represent ideas but liberate them from words, giving me visual tools to explore and compare any subjects I want? ■ In 1869, Dimitri Mendeleev drew a picture of kinships— the first accurate table of chemical elements. Each element was placed in a scheme according to properties it shared with other elements. Very logical, very elegant, and very bold. By plotting what was known, Mendeleev could predict and leave room for elements that wouldn't be found for years. ■ Then there was Richard Feynman, another bold relationist. When he found that current perceptions of physics could not accommodate new discoveries, he promptly redefined the perceptions. He too used diagrams to express his thoughts, strange and squiggly diagrams which became inseparable from the ideas themselves. Two bold guys seeking lasting relationships, both trying to draw the whole picture. ■ *Cosmic Comics* uses animated sequences to ex-

plore relationships between seemingly unrelated things. Not with words, not with special knowledge, but with analytic imagery. It applies a range of visual techniques, like cross-sections, comparative patterns, and unique points-of-view, to arbitrarily chosen subjects. The results are intriguing. When cross-sectioned, similar layers of concentric growth appear in eggs, pearls, raindrops, and even the earth itself. They have great differences, of course, but their growth *patterns* are so similar. Why is that? I don't know of any principles that explain the physics of growth—yet growth seems so basic to understanding everything. ■ Take a more dynamic natural event like lightning. A spark of lightning superheats its path to five times the heat of the sun, rudely spreading and colliding the air with great noise. Lightning is a giant heat machine making large masses move, just like the little heat machines moving pistons in a car engine (right). Sections through both also show concentric growth patterns—this time expanding energy instead of material. ■ Analytic techniques also explain the racing dominance of the hurdler Edwin Moses, or even the mystical zones of scoring in basketball. If you care.

EXTENDING TOPIC ACCESS The earth, an egg, and a pearl show similar concentric growth patterns when cross-sectioned (opposite). The expanding power of heat in lightning and a car engine is seen when the same analytic technique is applied. (below).

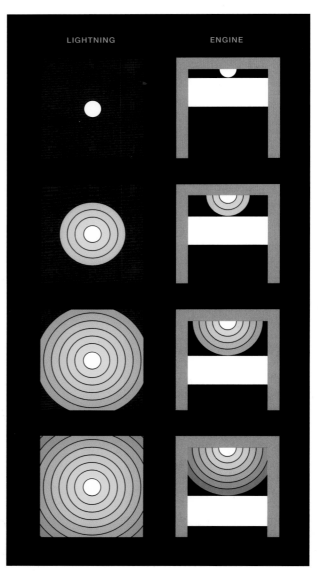

LIGHTNING ENGINE

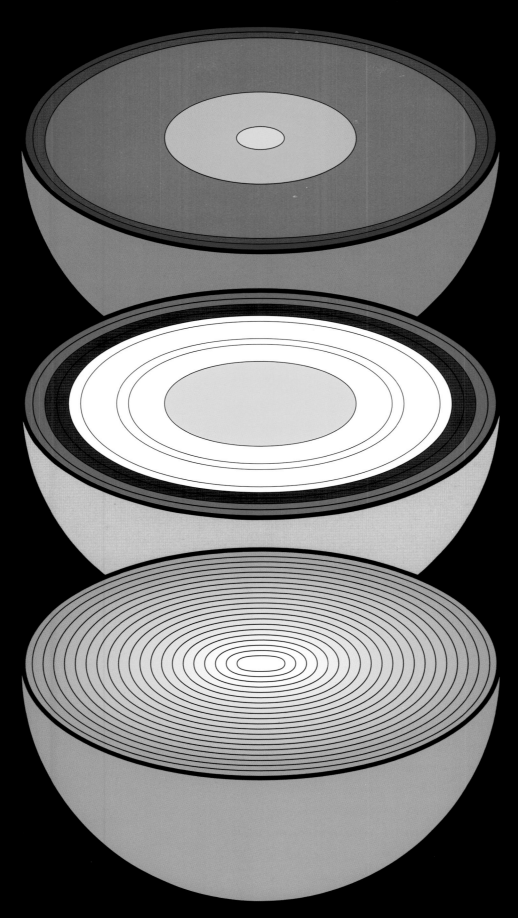

CROSS-SECTIONS SHOWING CONCENTRIC GROWTH PATTERNS IN THE EARTH, AN EGG, AND A PEARL

AS INFORMATION DESIGNERS, our first step always is to talk through the project with the entire project team: to decide what we're really trying to say with the piece we're working on. Out of those discussions comes a plan for how we can use text, illustration, and design as integrated parts to achieve those goals. In most cases, the graphic design itself is the last step in the process. The probing of the content is not only the primary step, but also the most interesting to us. In many of our projects, we work as project managers in addition to providing graphic design. Our role then, is to clarify purpose and create a piece that meets that purpose.

■ **THE AGFA'S DIGITAL COLOR PREPRESS** series started in 1990, when designers were just beginning to tackle the problems of color publishing with personal computers. Sanjay Sakhuja, proprietor of Digital Prepress International (DPI), a prepress shop in San Francisco, dealt with the resulting confusions every day. He found that he and his employees were spending more and more time teaching customers the basics of color publishing, and less and less on their prepress production work. ■ Sakhuja approached Agfa, a major vendor of digital prepress equipment, with an idea. He suggested that a short, easy-to-use visual guide to the processes might not only help him and other Agfa service bureau customers, but also enhance Agfa's market position and the whole digital prepress business. Agfa's Director of International Marketing saw his point and contracted Sakhuja to create the book. In turn, Sakhuja turned to us to manage the project, create an appropriate visual design, and produce it electronically. Arne Hurty, the infographic designer for *Macworld* magazine, would serve as the illustrator and technical advisor, and Steve Hannaford, editor of the fax newsletter *Prepress,* would write the copy. ■ In order to address illustrators and designers in a language they would find easy to understand, we all agreed that the book would rely heavily on visual explanations of concepts. This choice was reinforced by the topic itself; after all, the book was for designers who were trying to obtain certain visual results using the computer, and many of the illustrations would compare images created by using different processes. Given the book's expected role as a quick reference tool rather than a comprehensive, detailed text, we felt that well-executed infographics would be the most efficient way to explain the complex information. ■ We had 36 pages and five colors to work with,

CATEGORIZING REFERENCE A short, visual guide to electronic prepress work introduced color production issues and digital techniques to many designers who had little experience with either. Information was divided into discrete, spread-long topics and explained with words, diagrams, and samples of techniques.

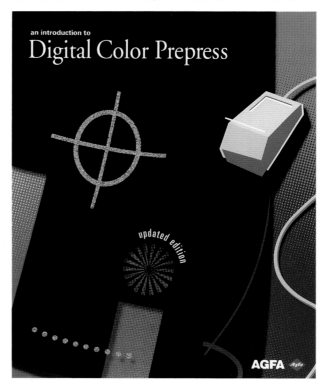

an introduction to
Digital Color Prepress

updated edition

AGFA

The colors we see in nature, on the computer screen, and on the printed page are as different as the sounds produced by the telephone, compact discs, and the human voice. Light comprises just a fraction of the electro-magnetic spectrum—most of which is detectable only by technological means, such as radio waves and infra-red light.

Sunlight produces color naturally when refracted and reflected, like the rainbow formed when a sunbeam passes through particles of water or glass. The human eye detects varying degrees of green, red and blue, the primary colors of which white light is composed—referred to in color science as the additive primaries.

Digital color is also a product of the additive primaries. Computer monitors project beams of red, green and blue light through a mesh or grid, forming tiny pixels (or picture elements) on a glass screen. The amount of data used to control the beams determines the complexity of each pixel, and consequently the total number of distinct tones that can be displayed. 24-bit color monitors produce over 16.7 million colors by employing 256 bits of color information to manipulate each beam. This range of colors is referred to as the RGB color space, or RGB model.

Printed color, or process color, is based on the reflective nature of pigments and paper. Process inks are made from cyan, yellow and magenta pigments that form black when combined at their strongest and purest, approaching white when their levels are reduced. Each pigment absorbs (or subtracts) some portion of the visible spectrum and reflects the rest. These subtractive primaries produce a range of color substantially different from the range created by combining beams of light onto a glass screen.

Source

Nature

Color Monitor

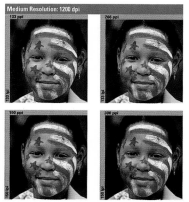

Printed Artwork

Range

The entire spectrum of light originates from the sun as pure white light, which is refract-ed and reflected by matter so that its compo-nent parts become visible.

A full color monitor can display over 16 million colors.

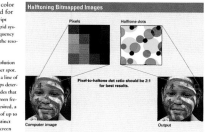

Many colors created by refracting light through a screen cannot be reproduced by combining inks on paper, nor can many CMYK or process colors be shown in RGB space.

Components

The visible spectrum is composed of many millions of colors, not all of which can be discerned by the naked eye.

Colors on computer terminals are made up of red, green and blue phosphors, which together create white light.

The components of process color are cyan, yellow, and magenta. Black is added to deepen shadows and to provide a true black for type and linework.

RGB colors and CMYK colors are created differently, and have their own peculiar characteristics that must be learned before they can be manipulated intelligently. To reproduce an RGB image in the CMYK environment, RGB colors have to be simulated on paper by special techniques. We speak of transforming color from one color space into another, but what we are actually manipulating is data, subjectively or mathematically, which indicates the CMYK elements that may be able to accomplish the job.

HLS and HSV are color models related to the RGB space. Colors are measured or defined by their hue and saturation, and their luminance or intensity value.

The discrepancies that arise as a result of color conversions have inspired the creation of complex color management systems, designed to minimize, if not overcome entirely, the inability of CMYK inks to reproduce the luminous colors of the RGB space. Now that desktop computers have grown powerful enough to manipulate the complex data these systems introduce, a number of software programs have recently been released that promise to make color specification between different color spaces very reliable.

An industry standard has emerged from work performed in 1931 by the CIE, or Commission Internationale de l'Éclairage. This group united the various color models into one three-dimensional space. Every visible color can be defined by a numerical value that measures hue, saturation and brightness, regardless of the space from which it originated. All of the new color management programs rely on the CIE standard.

Bitmapped grayscale and color images must be halftoned for printing purposes. PostScript screening algorithms employ a grid system based on the line screen frequency (lpi) that the user specifies, and the resolution of the output device.

Imagesetter and laser printer resolution is measured by the size of the laser spot. These are combined to produce a line of halftone dots, which in turn helps determine the number of distinct shades that can be created at specific line-screen frequencies. If a 60-line screen is desired, a 300-dpi laser printer uses a grid of up to 25 laser spots to represent 25 distinct gray levels. Increasing the line screen will sharpen the image, but reduces the size of the halftone dot and the number of distinct shades available.

The size of the halftone cell and the corresponding number of gray levels are determined by PostScript screening algorithms, which are designed to reproduce up to 256 gray levels, depending on the output device.

This arithmetic also applies to scanned images. Scanning devices use a pixel grid to reproduce an image, which will be used later to generate the halftone grid. The amount of information scanned is measured in pixels per inch (ppi), which is often incorrectly termed dots per inch. For a scanned image to print properly, especially a color scan, the number of pixels per inch should be twice the number of lines per inch. A 72-ppi scan will look fine on screen but does not contain enough information to produce a viable halftone. Image-editing programs can resample a scan—that is, add more data by intelligent guessing, also known as interpolation.

Halftoning Bitmapped Images

Pixels   Halftone dots

Pixel-to-halftone dot ratio should be 2:1 for best results.

Computer image   Output

Programs such as Photoshop use the computer's pixel information to transform the square pixels into a screen (or halftone) of much finer dots. The number of pixels per inch should be about twice the screen frequency used (lpi).

Medium Resolution: 1200 dpi

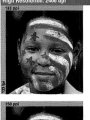

133 ppi   266 ppi

150 ppi   300 ppi

CMYK File Size Chart for Scanning (in Kilobytes)

inches	1	2	3	4	5	6	7	8	9	10
1	277	553	830	1080	1350	1620	1890	2160	2430	2700
	352	704	1030	1370	1720	2060	2400	2750	3090	3430
2	553	1080	1620	2160	2700	3240	3780	4320	4860	5400
	704	1370	2060	2750	3430	4120	4810	5490	6180	6870
3	830	1620	2430	3240	4080	4860	5670	6480	7290	8100
	1030	2060	3090	4120	5150	6180	7210	8240	9270	10300
4	1080	2160	3240	4320	5400	6480	7560	8640	9720	10800
	1370	2750	4120	5490	6870	8240	9610	11000	12400	13700
5	1350	2700	4050	5400	6750	8100	9450	10800	12200	13500
	1720	3430	5150	6870	8580	10300	12000	13700	15500	17200
6	1620	3240	4860	6480	8100	9720	11300	13000	14600	16200
	2060	4120	6180	8240	10300	12400	14400	16500	18500	20600
7	1890	3780	5670	7560	9450	11300	13200	15100	17000	18900
	2400	4810	7210	9610	12000	14400	16800	19200	21600	24000
8	2160	4320	6480	8640	10800	13000	15100	17300	19400	21600
	2750	5490	8240	11000	16500	16500	19200	22000	24700	27500

The diagram above shows the average size of CMYK scans (measured in kilobytes), based on the dimensions of the original document (measured in inches). Scanning resolution should be twice the intended line-screen frequency.

2770   Represents the digital file size in kilobytes of an image scanned at 266 ppi/133 lpi
3520   Represents the digital file size in kilobytes of an image scanned at 300 ppi/150 lpi

High Resolution: 2400 dpi

133 ppi   133 ppi

150 ppi   300 ppi

Color scans quickly use up large amounts of disk space. It is not unusual for scanning or image-manipulation programs to ask for more than 50 to 100 (or more) megabytes of free disk space in order to work with a color image—typically about three times as much space as the size of the image to be opened. These programs use virtual memory, creating temporary files (usually large, often invisible) on available (or specified) hard drives, to compensate for the limited amount of RAM normally available to the typical desktop computer system.

Transferring color scans to another location, or storing them for future use, requires large-capacity removable storage media. SyQuest drives offer removable cartridges that store 44 or 88 megabytes of data. "Floptical" technology is also catching on, with 20 megabyte disks for drives that also read and write to conventional floppies. Slow but relatively inexpensive digital tape systems also provide large-capacity storage.

Any process that uses up so much disk space so quickly will also benefit from large amounts of RAM. Eight megabytes is now the absolute minimum required for occasional scanning and retouching, but by next year even that may be too little to run an efficient workstation. Accelerator boards are also available now that specifically address the retouching techniques that go hand-in-hand with scanning. The amount of RAM needed depends on the model of computer and the kind of add-on boards being used.

See page 23 for a discussion of low-resolution scan placement as a way to speed up the production process.

For most scanners, resolution is measured in samples per inch (spi), though some scanners record only a certain number of pixels per image, no matter what size the image is. Generally, each sample in a scan is translated directly into a pixel (picture element) in the image file, so scanner resolution is sometimes referred to by pixels per inch (ppi). Some scanners, however, can create a much higher effective resolution than their actual sample rate by interpolation. This is done by adding extra pixels to the file, to which color values are assigned by calculating an average between the adjacent, sampled pixels. (This produces a lower-quality image than obtained with one-to-one sample-to-pixel scans.)

When a scanned image will be printed using conventional screening technologies, most experts recommend a sampling resolution at least 1.5 times the screen ruling of the printed image — for example, 225 samples per inch for an image to be printed at 150 lines per inch (lpi). For screen rulings below 133 lpi or for images with fine angles or curved lines, a scan resolution of two times the printed screen ruling is recommended. Lower scanning resolutions, generally equal to the effective resolution of the screen ruling, are possible with stochastic screening. Going beyond the recommended resolution creates bulkier files without any corresponding gain in image quality.

Reducing or enlarging an image file affects its resolution. To calculate the resolution required for a scan, one must multiply the resolution required for a given screen ruling by the image's printed scale. For example, an image to be printed with traditional screening using a value of 150 lpi, at 200% of its original size, would require a scan resolution of 450 spi (150 x 1.5 x 2).

Stochastic Screening — 150 ppi, file size: 1,776K

Conventional Screening 150 lpi — 150 ppi (1:1 ratio), file size: 1,776K

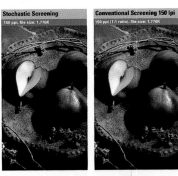

300 ppi, file size: 6,856K

300 ppi (2:1 ratio), file size: 6,856K

These images show the results of different screening methods using low-resolution (150 ppi, top) and high-resolution (300 ppi, bottom) scans. Stochastic screening generally requires a scan resolution equal to the screen ruling value that would be chosen if conventional screening were used instead. The recommended scan resolution for conventionally screened output is 1.5 to 2 times the desired screen ruling.

Up and Down Sampling

Most image processing programs provide ways to change the resolution of your file after you have scanned it: downsampling and resizing up will reduce the resolution, or upsampling and downsizing will increase it. This allows you to create greater image resolutions than your scanner is capable of producing. If the file has more resolution than you need for your printing method, it also allows you to discard extra pixels to reduce the image file size.

When you downsample, the software simply throws away the pixels it doesn't need. When you upsample, the software creates new pixels through interpolation: by averaging the values of the adjacent pixels. While maintaining the file's resolution, interpolation can tend to blur the image.

Resizing an image will also have an effect on the image file's resolution. Increasing an image's size generally decreases the image resolution: unless you upsample at the same time, the original pixels are simply packed more loosely. Conversely, downsizing an image will increase the image resolution: the original pixels are simply packed closer together. If you don't need the extra resolution, it's best to downsample the image as you reduce its size.

Original
File size: 1,960K
Image size: 2" x 2"
Resolution: 300 ppi

Downsampling
File size: 528K
Image size: 2" x 2"
Resolution: 150 ppi

Downsizing
File size: 1,960K
Image size: 1" x 1"
Resolution: 575 ppi

Downsizing and Downsampling
File size: 560K
Image size: 1" x 1"
Resolution: 300 ppi

Resized Up
File size: 2,000K
Image size: 3" x 3"
Resolution: 200 ppi

Resized Up and Upsampled
File size: 4,288K
Image size: 3" x 3"
Resolution: 300 ppi

Duotones, tritones, and quadtones are two-, three- and four-color halftone reproductions of black-and-white photos. Because a single color, such as black, can reproduce only a limited number of tones (usually about 50), adding extra ink colors can dramatically increase the subtlety and tonal range of a grayscale image. The extra ink colors can also be used to convey an artistic interpretation of a photographic subject, to make a photo look more dramatic, or simply to add color to a page.

Duotones are usually printed in black and a custom color. Traditionally, highlights, midtones and shadows were manipulated when halftone film was made for printing an image. Two negatives were produced, usually exposed differently. The artist had to visualize the results, because the final color effect couldn't be seen until it was printed. Now image-processing programs make it easy to see duotones on-screen before an image is finalized.

When a duotone is used to interpret a photo or add color to a page, the custom color may be either predominant or subtle. The black ink in printed halftones is "thinner" in appearance than the black generated with photographic emulsions. Printing a black-and-black or gray-and-black duotone extends the tonal range and allows deeper blacks for richer-looking reproductions.

With tritones and quadtones — three- or four-color black-and-gray reproduction, tonal range can be extended even further. A grayscale scan of a photo can also be converted to four-color mode, after which the individual process colors can be manipulated to create a colorful image that looks very different from the original photo.

Grayscale image

Pantone® 407 plate   Black plate

Duotone

Duotone: Magenta and Black

Tritone: Magenta, Yellow and Black

Quadtone: Cyan, Magenta, Yellow, Black

and a team whose members brought impressive knowledge and distinct skills to the project. To take advantage of the team's assets, we worked collaboratively throughout the process. As a first step, the team met to discuss the elements the book would contain and how they might be organized, focusing on methods of conveying the information graphically. The meeting resulted in a list of pre-press topics to be explained and concepts to be illustrated. Hurty took these back to his studio and emerged a few weeks later with a set of sketches for the illustrations. Using Hurty's illustrations as a starting point, Maria Giudice of the company *YO* created a design grid to hold the information. YO's plan for the book was distributed to Hurty for final illustrations and to Hannaford for the text. It included a developed table of contents and topic structure for the book, with Hurty's sketches in place and bullet points to guide the writer. It provided for a fair amount of content flexibility within a fairly rigid structure. Because Hurty's illustrations were mostly rectangular in shape, Giudice created a standard three-column page grid, with two columns set aside for graphics and one for text. Each topic could cover a page or a spread, but no more, allowing random access to subjects; readers can turn directly to the topic they want to know more about, with no need to read the information before or after it. Each topic is vertically labeled in a bleed tab on the side of the page for easy location by readers leafing through the short book. ■ The four process colors were used for illustrations and photography. The fifth color, a PMS gray, was used for page design elements such as topic title bars and the bleed tabs, differentiating page subjects from information elements. A process red color highlights new terms where

EXTENDING REFERENCE As the popularity of the original guide grew, a series of updates and new, more specific reference titles were produced. The format proved flexible and easy to apply. Topics like photograph resolution and color conversions were still confined to page or spread units to be read as separate references.

they are defined in the text. (All such terms are also defined in a glossary at the back of the book.) ■ The small text area forces a no-nonsense writing style. It also means that the type must be fairly small—and easy to read at small sizes. We specified 9.5/13 Garamond, with a larger, 12/13 size for the first sentence leading the reader into the text. ■ The heart of the book is the concise, visual portrayal of complex information. Taking such care with graphics is time-consuming and only possible in such short books, but it pays off by packing lots of information into very small spaces. Charts, photography, and infographics were mixed as each topic required. Captions were long if they had to be. They provided explanations for the illustrations and incorporated information not contained in the text, making the illustration columns completely self-contained.

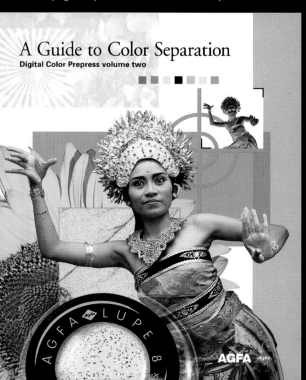

The "electronic darkroom" has brought dramatic changes to photography. Today, photographic businesses replace or supplement traditional darkroom equipment with computers, desktop scanners, image processing software, and output devices such as color film recorders. In addition, the latest filmless digital cameras have won acclaim for specialized uses.

With digital imaging becoming a mainstream technology, the question is not whether a photographer or lab should invest in some sort of digital system, but how extensive a first investment should be—and how quickly it will provide a return on the investment by generating new sources of revenue.

The first step in assembling a system is to examine reproduction requirements (output, resolution, color quality), and the costs of a computer, scanner, and camera system that will meet those needs. The cost of software, storage devices, a proofing system, modem, and related elements should be included. The value of existing systems (film, chemical processing, printmaking) and projections for savings in time, labor, and materials should be factored in.

The performance of different components in a computer system will likely be surpassed over time by newer products. But a well-planned system will enable improvements to be made incrementally over time, to keep pace with the industry and defer obsolescence. Combining the right electronic components with traditional photographic equipment can increase a photographer or lab's creative possibilities and broaden the range of services that they can offer.

At right are some typical components of a modern digital photo imaging system.

Cameras
Both film-based and filmless (digital or still video) cameras can be used in the electronic darkroom. Some digital camera backs attached to traditional cameras are tethered to and operated from the computer. Portable digital cameras in 35mm formats are also available.
Software
Color management software maintains color consistency between monitor, input and output devices. Image processing applications enable images to be modified. Page layout programs allow images to be integrated into publications. Compression software shrinks image files to more manageable sizes. Telecommunications programs send and receive files to and from other computers across phone lines. Databases can track images, customers and invoices.
Monitors and Video Cards
High-resolution monitors display from 256 to 16.7 million colors at one time. Basic models offer 8-bit color. Higher-quality units display 24-bit color, which usually requires either more video RAM, or a video card installed inside the computer. The largest screens usually require a video card, which may also accelerate the display.
Storage Devices
Electronic darkrooms can have enormous storage requirements. Magnetic hard disks provide fast access and a wide range of capacities. Removable disk cartridges (44 to 270 MB), magneto-optical cartridges (128, 650 MB, 1.3 GB), and CD-based systems in read-only and read-write configurations (650 MB) are alternatives. Digital audio tape (DAT) drives with multi-gigabyte capacity are generally used for archiving purposes.
Output Devices
PostScript laser printers render text, graphics and halftones in b&w, grayscale or color on plain paper. Dye sublimation printers, as shown, produce color output on special coated paper. Film recorders create continuous tone film "originals" of the highest quality. Imagesetters produce halftone color separations for offset printing.
Telecommunications
Modems enable digital files to be transferred over telephone lines.
Scanners
The wide range of scanners available today offer varying levels of performance and original image format handling. Most models connect directly to computers, and can be operated from within standard image editing programs.
Computers
Computers are usually distinguished by the speed of their microprocessor and the type of operating system. Processing speed is often affected by the actions of other system components, such as drives, modems, printers and scanners. When choosing a computer system, consider upgrade paths and expansion capabilities, such as RAM capacity and configuration options. Installing more RAM can increase productivity more effectively than a faster processor.

Conventional film cameras, long the mainstay of image capture, are being challenged by rapidly improving electronic cameras. In the past year, more than 20 new filmless camera models in all price ranges were introduced. Both types of devices share common components: lenses, aperture, shutter, and body, and many can be used for the same applications. But the similarities end there.

The advantages of film cameras are well known. The technology and process are mature, and operating expertise widespread. Modern film emulsions are sharper, more sensitive to light, have reduced grain, and capture vibrant color. But digital cameras produce images that can be transferred to computers for editing and output in a fraction of the time—sometimes in seconds. For many applications, where deadlines and convenience are important, electronic cameras are a viable alternative.

Decisions on what type of camera to choose depend on many criteria. As with any electronic component, you should consider a camera's performance, ergonomic design, cost effectiveness, method of image storage, and compatibility with existing systems. In particular, consider a device's dynamic range; some cameras have limited sensitivity, while others exceed the range of film. Most are classified according to film speed ISO ratings, between 50 and 800 ISO.

Because of rapid technological change, digital cameras have to pay for themselves relatively quickly. Sometimes, additional equipment is needed, such as special continuous frequency light sources for studio cameras. To protect investments in existing equipment, digital camera backs are available that fit onto certain traditional camera bodies.

Film Cameras

Studio Camera

Primary uses: Still life, portraiture, catalogs, brochures, advertising

Resolution: Most provide high resolutions
Input values: 50–100 ISO film speeds in grayscale or color
Cost: $$$ to $$$$
Advantages: View cameras provide built-in perspective controls; a bellows allows close focusing. Medium format roll film cameras are easier and faster to use.
Disadvantages: Large and bulky, awkward to use. Image is projected upside down and backwards on the viewfinder of some units. Requires a lot of light.

4 x 5 film transparency

35mm Single Lens Reflex Camera

Primary uses: Journalism, fashion, architecture, landscapes, catalogs, brochures, advertising

Resolution: Varies with film type and optics. Medium to high resolutions, sharp details.
Input values: 25–1,600 ISO film speeds in grayscale or color. Excellent tonal range capability with some emulsions.
Cost: $ to $$$
Advantages: Lightweight, versatile. WYSIWYG through-the-lens viewing and precise framing. Wide range of lenses and film types available.
Disadvantages: Noisy. SLRs have many moving parts, photographers cannot see the moment recorded.

35mm film slide

Electronic Analog Cameras

Still Video Camera

Primary uses: Still images for TV and multimedia

Resolution: 200,000–400,000 pixels
Typical file size: 900 K–1.2 MB
Input values: 8-bit grayscale, 24-bit color
Cost: $ to $$$
Advantages: Quick access to images, some allow interchangeable lenses.
Disadvantages: Some systems are bulky, awkward to use. Low resolutions, color quality acceptable, in some instances good for video applications.

2 x 3 inches at 300 DPI

Digital Cameras

Studio Digital Camera Back

Primary uses: Catalogs, advertising, studio still life, copying (30 x 40-inch prints, halftones)

Resolution: 4.2–40 million pixels
Typical file size: 12–90 MB
Input values: 8-bit grayscale, 30- to 42-bit color
Cost: $$$ to $$$$
Advantages: Largest, most light-sensitive CCDs. High resolutions and large reproductions possible. Good software-based camera controls and lenses.
Disadvantages: Expensive. Long exposures, limited subjects (still life) can be photographed. Large files require huge storage systems.

8 x 11.5 inches at 300 DPI

35mm Single Lens Reflex Digital Camera Back

Primary uses: Journalism, law enforcement, military, industrial

Resolution: 1.5 million pixels
Typical file size: 4.5 MB
Input values: 8-bit grayscale, 24-bit color
Cost: $$$
Advantages: Portable, easy to use, excellent ergonomics, reasonably priced. Produces smaller file sizes. New models use removable PCMCIA cards for storing up to 50 images.
Disadvantages: Difficult to use in low light. Limited dynamic range. Mid-range resolution limits enlargement sizes.

3 x 5 inches at 300 DPI

Point and Shoot Camera

Primary uses: Video presentations, small prints, electronic databases low resolution publishing

Resolution: 200,000–400,000 pixels.
Typical file size: 900 K–1.2 MB
Input values: 8-bit grayscale, 24-bit color
Cost: $
Advantages: Lightweight, easy and quiet to use. Affordable, quick access to images.
Disadvantages: Resolution is limited, but color quality can be acceptable. Imperfect optics, limited camera controls. Not a WYSIWYG viewing system.

1.5 x 2 inches at 300 DPI

Electronic cameras rely on two types of technology: analog-based still video, and digital. The still-video systems, which are based on camcorder technology, are best suited for low-resolution multimedia presentations. Digital cameras, however, have been built from the ground up to deliver higher quality.

A digital camera uses a CCD to capture color information. The size and number of elements in the CCD array determines resolution. Because of high cost, most CCD arrays are smaller than 35mm or 120mm film formats, which restricts the resolution of these devices. Some cameras are based on a static array CCD, which captures the image in a single, relatively fast exposure, and others use a linear or scanning array, which means they must be mounted on a tripod. Most studio cameras remain tethered to a host computer and rely on its hard disk to store downloaded images.

The resolution of digital cameras varies widely. Some point and shoot models capture only 307,200 pixels (640 x 480) of color data, while a few high-end models can record more than 40 million pixels. A fine-grain 35mm slide film has a resolution equivalent to 20 million pixels. But the most sensitive digital cameras are expensive, and their requirements for computing power and storage capacity are high.

Digital cameras improve with each generation, and can reduce long-term operating costs. They offer an attractive alternative for many business, industrial, and photojournalism applications. But the lower cost, versatility and ease of use of conventional cameras makes them the tool of choice for most assignments.

■ The treatment proved successful. For Agfa, the book not only increased the market's awareness of the company, it also created a new source of revenue. Demand for the book was so great that Agfa set up a separate 800 telephone number to manage the requests, and began charging $4, and then $10 each for copies. More than 300,000 have been printed so far for use in classrooms as well as design offices. The book's success also prompted Agfa to launch a series of updates based on the original design, and create a new division, Agfa Prepress Education Resources, to produce related materials. The Digital Color Prepress series now has five titles, with more planned. The design has proved extremely resilient; each new volume uses the basic grid in various ways, as works best for the volume's information. The consistency of the design has given the series a signature look, and also makes the development of later titles relatively easy. The second volume, for example, was planned in a day and a half. ■ **CREDITS:** Creative direction and design: *YO*, San Francisco; Technical direction and concept: Sanjay Sakhuja, *Digital Prepress International*, Eugene Hunt, *Agfa*; Writing: Linnea Dayton, Darcy DiNucci, Steve Hannaford; Illustration: Arne Hurty, Steve McGuire; Photographers: Various. ■ **THE PEACHPIT PRESS WEB SITE** design was our first project for the world-wide Web. Peachpit, a publisher of computer books in Berkeley, California, wanted to use the Web not only to support on-line book sales, but also to serve a public relations purpose: conveying Peachpit's role as a friendly source of information of all types about computers and desktop publishing. ■ Graphic design for the Web, at least for the time being, has severe limitations. Though most of the "browser"

MAPPING CONTENT A 1:2 ratio of text area to graphics in the original guide format supplied room for many visual techniques. It also encouraged the team of writers, illustrators, and designers to invent compact visual methods of conveying information. The short booklets are packed with an amazing amount of information.

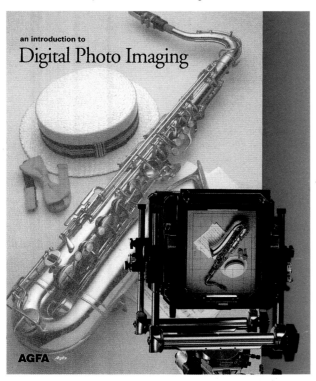

software that readers use to view published texts uses standard defaults for text elements (such as 12-point Times), the reader can change the default font at any time, and the designer has no control over it at all. The line width of the text the reader sees is determined by how wide the reader opens the browser window. And of course, not all browsers support graphics or every text style. For the most part then, the browser text is 12-point Times, flush left, with various-sized, Times Bold headings. Graphics must be used sparingly, since many readers access the Web through relatively slow modem connections. ■ Designing for the Web, at least in these early days, means shrugging off attempts to control the "graphic design" and focus on the interface: how the reader understands and accesses the contents of the publisher's site and its network of pages. The most important aspects of a successful web site are organization and navigation—the design must support both. ■ Peachpit's staff came to us with a description of the kinds of information they felt the site should contain. A Features section would offer chapters or tutorials from Peachpit's books and other information of general interest. A Titles section would present Peachpit's current catalog, giving the reader detailed information about the books and offering them a chance to order. A section about the company itself would introduce Peachpit, its personnel and its authors. The site would also provide readers a chance to contact the company and participate in forums. ■ Discussions with the project group developed a consensus of activities the readers want at the site, resulting in six main sections rather than the original four. We also determined that our solution must help readers anchor themselves in the amorphous world of cyberspace: they should at all times know that they were on a Peachpit

TRANSLATING IMAGE AND IDENTITY Designing a site for the world-wide Internet means preparing an electronic doorway for potential customers to enter a company. Peachpit Press needed to convey its friendly image and information about itself, as well as to sell books. Because the defaults of browser software force a standard text approach and limit graphics, the success of the site depends on how quickly and easily users can interact with it.

page, know what else Peachpit had to offer, understand where they were in the overall page structure, and how to navigate to other destinations. ■ The design result was a three-tiered navigation structure on each Web page. Each level is identified by icons, text, or color-coded buttons. The top screen bar identifies the company and displays a "home" icon that, when clicked, takes the reader to Peachpit's home page. The second tier presents six icon buttons that represent each of the site's six sections; clicking on any one of them takes you to that section's "lobby," or introductory page. A third tier names the section the reader is currently visiting and offers color-coded buttons for moving into that section. The illustrations are by John Grimes, who has become identified with Peachpit through his work on several of its books and releases. His drawings, the publisher felt, conveyed the friendly, informal imagery with which the company identifies. The web site URL code is http://www.peachpit.com ■ **CREDITS:** Project Director: Nolan Hester, *Peachpit Press*; Editorial Consultant: Darcy DiNucci; Technical Consultant: Glenn Fleishmann, *POPCO;* Designers: *YO*, San Francisco; Illustrations: John Grimes and Robin Chin

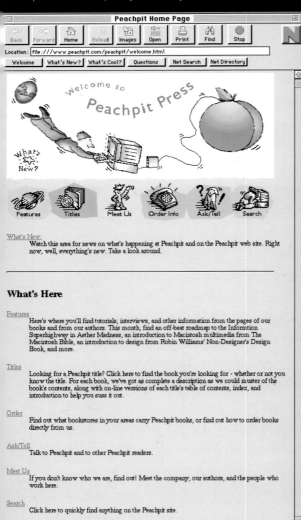

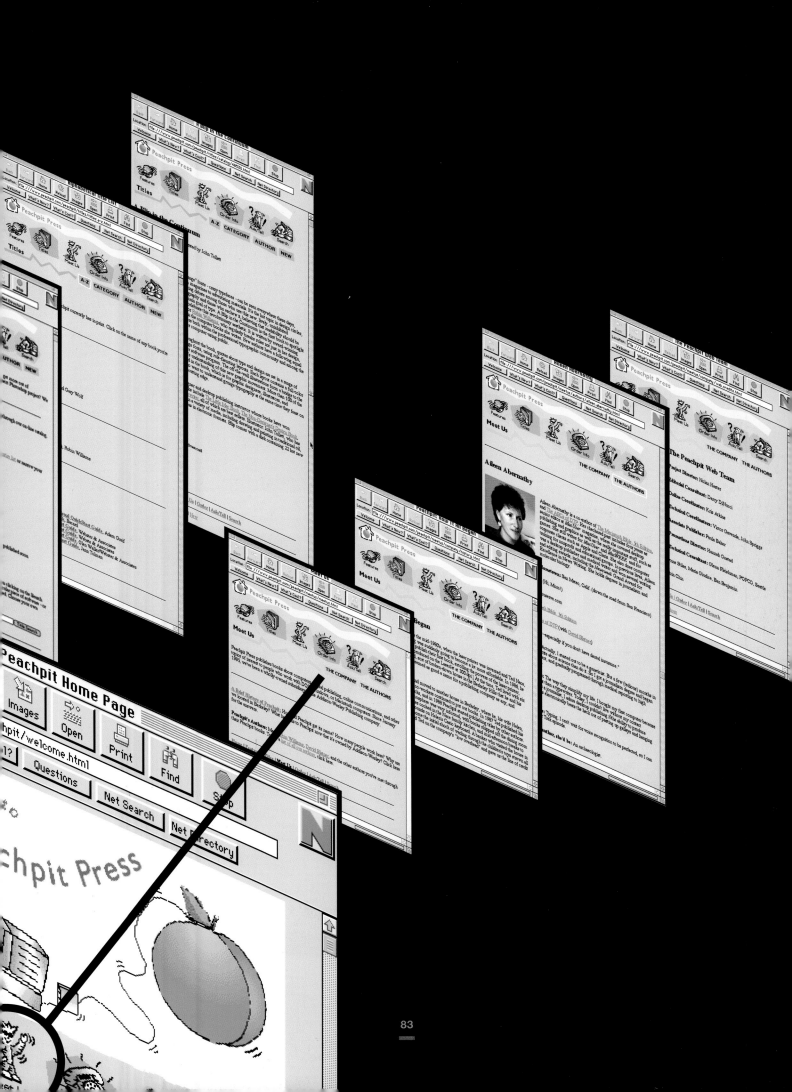

THE INFORMATION FACTORY Since 1967, The Diagram Group in London has produced 251 books with over 32,000 pages of integrated text and illustrations, published in 34 countries and 40 languages. ■ Diagram's work has focussed on resolving, reorganizing and representing facts in a diagrammatic and captioned form. "Information you can trust in a visual form you can understand," says Bruce Robertson, manager of the firm's writers, researchers, designers and illustrators. Once described as a salty sea dog designer with principles and a wish to do something useful, Robertson, his partners and Diagram moved from single illustrations to entire reference books, to packaging their own book ideas. ■ Along the way, they evolved a distinctly simple (and widely copied) style "by setting out to have no style at all," Robertson says. "Low budgets forced us to devel-

REFINING REFERENCE The word for the Collins Gem reference series is *brief*. The encyclopedia (below), described by Robertson as "an OXO (meat extract cube) digest, a boiled down information tool kit from which readers pick the bits they want," is a two-color, one volume, 660-page response to the demand for low-cost popular reference. "The size of a pack of fags, but twice as thick, with every key fact you'll ever want. And 1500 diagrams."

op a line style that would *last*. We also felt that first impressions of information were vital, so we wanted a form that was *clear*— single ideas in short sentences with diagrams that expressed them immediately."

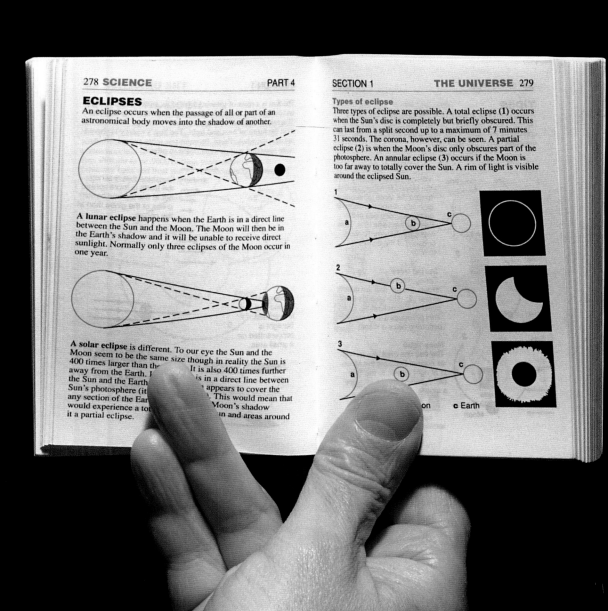

infatuated with the ideas contained in their subjects," Robertson
says. "As I was with *Handtools of Arts and Crafts*. But sadly it was
published at the end of 3000 years of man's use of hand tools. It
never sold well, except to people who gain pleasure (and little reward) from working with their hands." The tools are categorized
by the crafts they serve, then sub-categorized by the separate operations within each craft. Step-by-step diagrams show the use
of over 2000 tools. In effect, the book uses tools to sum up the incredible range of crafts that we have evolved throughout history.

8 Car

Virtually the [...]
to all sculptu [...]
dimensional, [...]
relief. With ca [...]
with a solid b [...]
carves away [...]
to leave a ple [...]
carved sculpt [...]
and their uses [...]
strong, large [...]
portions of ur [...]
progressively [...]
is refined. Al [...]
selves, such [...]
the knives use [...]
in some way, [...]
the abrasive-[...]
Until the 20th [...]
in the Wester [...]
representatio [...]
in sculpture have taken the art form to previously
inconceivable limits. Sculpture can now be
vigorously stylized, totally abstract, or even
kinetic. The sculptor Henry Moore has described
the feeling of freedom that came over him when
he first made a hole entirely through one of his
sculptures, and this new sense of freedom of
expression in sculpture is one of this century's
most significant contributions to the arts.

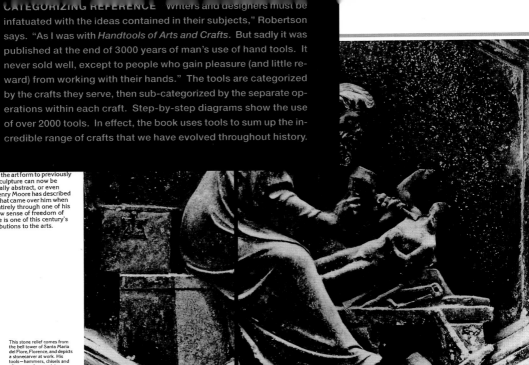

This stone relief comes from
the bell tower of Santa Maria
del Fiore, Florence, and depicts
a stonecarver at work. His
tools—hammers, chisels and
pliers—can be seen lying
beside his work.

Wood sculpture 2

Tools for carved sculpture

Mallets are wooden hammers
used for driving **chisels**
through the wood when
carving. As they are made of
wood, mallets are unlikely to
splinter or split the chisel
handles as a metal hammer
might do. Mallet weights vary
from very light (such as those
of beechwood) to very heavy
(such as lignum vitae). As the
work progresses, and more
delicate chisels are chosen for
the carving, a lighter mallet is
used for striking the chisels so
that they will not cut into the
wood too deeply.

The **mallet** is held in the
carver's stronger hand so that
he controls the blow accurately;
the **chisel** is held in the other
hand and is struck with the
mallet (above). Both hands
should be behind the point of
the chisel at all times.

Woodcarving tools must be
kept extremely sharp at all
stages of the work. A properly
sharpened blade is more
efficient and also safer,
since its path through the wood
is more predictable and it is
less likely to slip and damage
the carver or the carving.

1 Rectangular **washita stone**
for sharpening chisels and any
other tools with straight blades.
2 Gouge slip, a curved stone
used for sharpening both
gouges with the bevel on the
inside (in-cannel) and those
with the bevel on the outside
(out-cannel).
**3,4 Sharpening point and
triangle;** these shaped and
tapered stones are useful for
sharpening tools with complex
cutting surfaces.
5 Tool honer used to sharpen
a variety of carving tools.
6 Strop, a wooden block
covered in leather, for
producing a really sharp finish
on blades.

The surface of the slip stone is
oiled, and then the tool to be
sharpened is moved over its
surface, held at the exact angle
of the desired bevel. A curved
gouge (above) is moved in a
figure of eight, to ensure that
all parts of the bevel are
sharpened equally.

Files, rasps and **scrapers**
are all used to abrade and
refine the surface of the wood
once it has been carved or
sculpted to the required shape.
All the tools come in grades
varying from coarse to fine; the
coarse grades are used on the
surface first, and then the finer
grades produce an even
smoother finish.
1 Coarse flat file; the
blade is made of steel and
shaped into many small gouge-
like cutters that pare off the
unwanted material as the file
moves over the surface.
2 Coarse round file.
3 Cabinet rasp.
4 Round rasp.
5,6,7,8 Riffler rasps in a
variety of shapes. These slim
rifflers are useful for reaching
into awkward corners and
curves.
9,10,11,12 Riffler files.
13 Rasp brush for cleaning
the teeth of rasps and files
when they become clogged
with sawdust.
14 Curved rasp; this can be
fitted round the hand and used
for smoothing curves that are
difficult to reach with a straight
rasp.
15 Cabinet scraper for
paring down large flat surfaces.

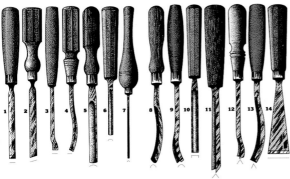

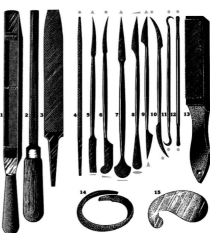

Chisels and **gouges** are used
for the majority of the carving
work in wood sculpture; they
can be guided by hand, or
struck with a **hammer** or a
mallet. The shape and size of
the blade determine the
character of the mark made on
the wood.

1 Straight chisel.
2 Skew chisel or **corner
chisel;** the end of the blade is
cut across at an angle.
3 Short bent chisel.
4 Spade.
5 Gouge, a chisel with a blade
that is curved in section.

6 Fluter, a gouge with a
deep channel.
7 Veiner, a very narrow
gouge.
8,9 Long bent gouges.
10 Macaroni tool, a chisel
with three straight edges.
11 Parting tool, a chisel
with a V-shaped section.

**12 Short bent parting
tool.**
13 Long bent parting tool.
14 Fishtail tool; the large
blade spreads from the neck
into a flat triangular shape.

©DIAGRAM

Leather decoration 1

Leathercarving is a craft that has become very popular in recent years. The leather for carving needs to be fairly thick, so that the knives will not cut right through it and so that there is some scope for modeling. All the tools used must be kept very sharp, otherwise they will not leave a clean impression on the surface.

The shield shown (right) is of cut and embossed leather, and was made in Italy in the 16th century. The technique used is that known as "cuir-bouilli," in which the leather is first boiled to soften it before being shaped.

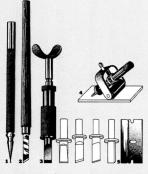

1 Tracer, a metal point used for transferring patterns or shapes onto the leather.
2 Incising knife with beveled blade.
3 Swivel knife with interchangeable blades; this is a very versatile leathercarving tool.

4 Swivel knife sharpener; the knife is screwed into the holder, which keeps it at the correct angle while it is run across the sharpening stone.
5 Razor blade for delicate cutting work.

6 Leathercarving knife with interchangeable blades. The different blades are used for cutting a variety of different strokes into the leather.

7,8,9,10,11,12 Modeling tools forged from stainless steel. These tools are used for pressing down and shaping outlines when carving patterns into leather; each head produces a particular mark on the leather surface.

300

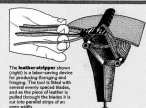

The **leather-stripper** shown (right) is a labor-saving device for producing thonging and fringing. The tool is fitted with several evenly spaced blades, and as the piece of leather is pulled through the blades it is cut into parallel strips of an even width.

A **turntable,** such as the one above, is a valuable accessory when leathercarving. The leather piece is placed on the top, and the turntable can be spun to present a new part of the work to the carving tool, so that the leather need not be picked up.

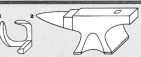

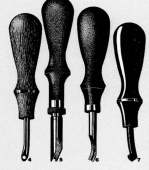

Racers or **races** are cutting tools with horseshoe-shaped cross-sections; the outside of the curve is sharpened so that it cuts a groove in the leather as the tool moves across the surface.
1 Double-ended racer.
2 Screw or **adjustable racer;** the straight edge can be used as a guide at the side of the leather piece so that the line cut by the racer head will be parallel to the edge of the leather.
3 Compass racer, used for cutting grooves in the shape of a circle.

4 Gouge used for cutting channels in leather, either for decoration or as an aid to folding.
5 Adjustable gouge; this tool is capable of gouging grooves of various depths. The groove depth is altered by turning the guide ring on the handle.

6 Edge beveler or **edge shave** for rounding off and smoothing cut edges of leather.
7 Edge cutter, used to ensure that borders are cut accurately.

©DIAGRAM

301

Shaping, sewing, finishing

Leather can be shaped, stitched, glued, colored and dressed in an almost infinite variety of ways. Shaping can be achieved by folding, by hammering over a former, or by stitching several pieces of leather together. Dye can be applied to an entire article, or may be painted on in patterns, and smooth leather can be polished or waxed.

The print on the right illustrates some leather gloves that were made and sold at the turn of the century. Gloves are articles that are often made in fine leatherwork, and they present many challenges to the leatherworker because they require small, strong seams and very accurate shaping.

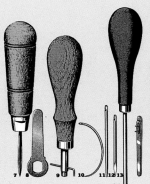

1 Bone folder used for making folds in leather.
2 Creaser for producing firm, neat creases.
3 Double creaser with adjusting screw so that the width between the creases can be altered.
4 Horseshoe-shaped former for making jewel-cases etc.

5 Bracelet bender used in shaping bracelets; the leather is hammered over the curved shape.
6 Curved sewing awl.
7 Harness awl, an awl with a chuck and wrench for fitting alternative heads.
8 Awl wrench.

9 Stitching awl used for placing stitch holes.
10 Curved leather needle.
11 Harness needle with blunt end.
12 Glover's needle.
13 Collar awl.
14 Lacing needle.

304

1 Last has multiple heads and is particularly useful for clinching nails in leather footwear.
2 Anvil is used as a base for hammering and shaping, and as a hard surface for eyelet and grommet setting.

Leather articles can be easily colored and dyed.
3 Wool dauber, a piece of sheepskin used for applying dye.
4 Hole dauber with pointed end for coloring the insides of punched holes.
5,6 Dye brushes.
7 Glue brush.

8 Lacing pliers, used to grip lacing so that it can be pulled tight.
9 Open-ended thimble with large indentations to take the thick needle heads.
10 Lacing pony; this tool holds pieces of leather while they are being stitched together.

11 Thimble palm used for pushing needles through the leather.
12 Wool for applying dyes, waxes and other dressings.
13 Shine brush for polishing up glossy finishes.

14 Edge slicker, used to smooth leather edges; the slicker is run down the cut surface.
15 Sole scraper, a tool for roughening leather surfaces (such as the soles of shoes) before they are cemented.

©DIAGRAM

305

TRANSFORMING REFERENCE "For all of us to communicate ideas and understand them, we use a method of mental pictures. Diagrams are just thoughts with a line around them." Thoughts were communicated without visible lines when the simple line drawings from the Group's book *Woman's Body* were transformed into embossed, braille diagrams by a charity for blind Japanese women. Robertson discovered it accidentally in Tokyo and he was thrilled. "It doesn't come any higher than that for me. Thousands of women in Japan who had never *seen* shapes, forms, or colors, were given 'images' of the things happening inside their bodies."

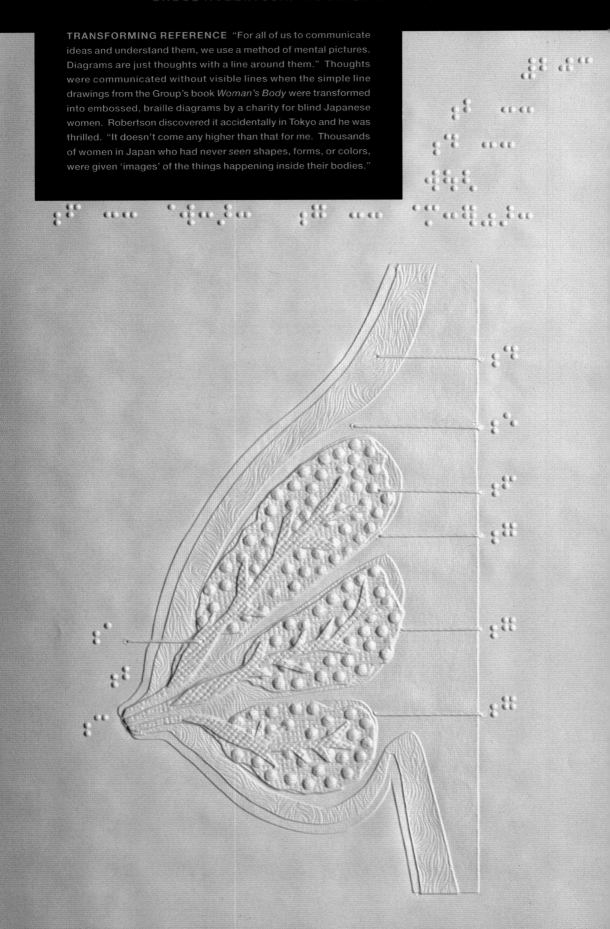

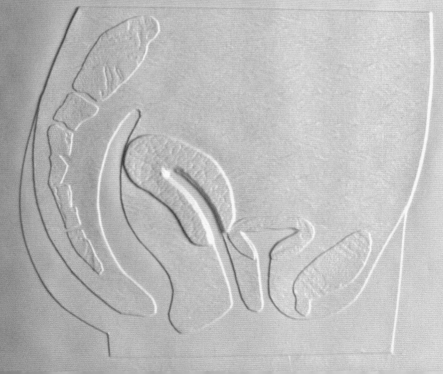

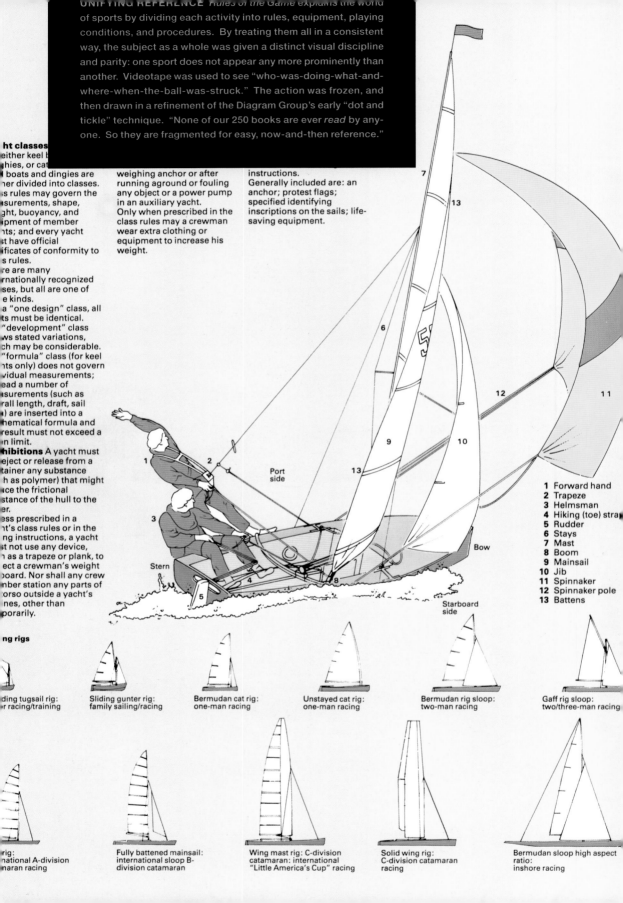

ht classes either keel b
hies, or cat
boats and dingies are
her divided into classes.
s rules may govern the
asurements, shape,
ght, buoyancy, and
ipment of member
nts; and every yacht
st have official
ificates of conformity to
s rules.
re are many
rnationally recognized
ses, but all are one of
e kinds.
a "one design" class, all
ts must be identical.
"development" class
ws stated variations,
ch may be considerable.
"formula" class (for keel
nts only) does not govern
vidual measurements;
ead a number of
asurements (such as
rall length, draft, sail
) are inserted into a
hematical formula and
result must not exceed a
n limit.

hibitions A yacht must
eject or release from a
tainer any substance
h as polymer) that might
ce the frictional
stance of the hull to the
er.
ess prescribed in a
t's class rules or in the
ng instructions, a yacht
st not use any device,
h as a trapeze or plank, to
ect a crewman's weight
board. Nor shall any crew
mber station any parts of
orso outside a yacht's
nes, other than
porarily.

weighing anchor or after
running aground or fouling
any object or a power pump
in an auxiliary yacht.
Only when prescribed in the
class rules may a crewman
wear extra clothing or
equipment to increase his
weight.

instructions.
Generally included are: an
anchor; protest flags;
specified identifying
inscriptions on the sails; life-
saving equipment.

Port
side

Stern

Bow

Starboard
side

1 Forward hand
2 Trapeze
3 Helmsman
4 Hiking (toe) stra
5 Rudder
6 Stays
7 Mast
8 Boom
9 Mainsail
10 Jib
11 Spinnaker
12 Spinnaker pole
13 Battens

ng rigs

ding tugsail rig:
r racing/training

Sliding gunter rig:
family sailing/racing

Bermudan cat rig:
one-man racing

Unstayed cat rig:
one-man racing

Bermudan rig sloop:
two-man racing

Gaff rig sloop:
two/three-man racing

rig:
national A-division
maran racing

Fully battened mainsail:
international sloop B-
division catamaran

Wing mast rig: C-division
catamaran: international
"Little America's Cup" racing

Solid wing rig:
C-division catamaran
racing

Bermudan sloop high aspect
ratio:
inshore racing

9

Offshore yacht racing

Competitors race sea-going keel yachts over offshore courses. Yachts are divided into classes, and races range from short afternoon events to great round-the-world races lasting seven or eight months.

Class IV

Class V

Class III

Class I

Class II

Basic standards The hulls and equipment of offshore racing yachts must meet certain basic standards.
Hulls must be self-righting, strongly built, and fully watertight. They must be properly rigged and ballasted, and completely seaworthy.
Equipment must function properly and be readily accessible. Specifications vary according to the type of yacht and the category of course. They cover:
a) structural features such as hatches, cockpits, and lifelines;
b) accommodation, such as bunks, galley, and the provision of drinking water;
c) navigation equipment, such as compass and spare compass, charts, piloting equipment, radio direction finder, lead line or sonar, log, and navigation lights;
d) general equipment, such as fire extinguishers, bilge pumps, anchors, first aid kits, foghorns, radar reflectors, and fuel shutoff valves;
e) safety equipment, such as life jackets, whistles, safety harnesses, life rafts, life buoys, distress signals, heaving lines, ship's dinghy, and white flares;
f) emergency equipment, such as spare navigation lights and power source, storm sails, emergency steering equipment, tools and spare parts, portable sail numbers, and radio receiver.

Average crew of 6/8 aboard 37ft yacht

1 Navigation lights
2 Stern lights
3 Lifelines
4 Bow rail (pulpit)
5 Stern rail (pushpit)
6 Life buoy
7 Lift raft pack
8 Cockpit
9 Compass
10 Hatches
11 Winches
12 Rudder
13 Ballasted keel
14 Propeller (auxiliary engine)
15 Storm sails
16 Back stay radio aerial

Electronic aids Permitted electronic aids are: speedometer and log; sonar; wind speed and direction indicator; radio receiver; radio direction finder (but not automatic or self-seeking); radio transmitter (for private business, emergencies, or for race reporting when included in the sailing instructions); repeating compass. The only permitted links are between radio receiver and direction finder, and between compass and compass repeaters.

Yacht classes Yachts are divided according to their ratings into offshore classes. The five largest ones are:
I (33–70ft)
II (29–32.9ft)
III (25.5–28.9ft)
IV (23–25.4ft)
V (21–22.9ft)
Organization The international body for the sport is the Offshore Racing Council, and most offshore races are run under its International Offshore Rule and special safety regulations.

Race categories There are four categories, according to the course's distance from the shore.
Category 1 races are of long distance and are well offshore. Yachts must be completely self-sufficient for extended periods, capable of withstanding heavy storms, and prepared to meet serious emergencies without outside assistance.
Category 2 races are of extended duration, along or not far from the shoreline or in large unprotected bays or lakes. A high degree of self-sufficiency is required, but with the reasonable probability of outside aid in a serious emergency.
Category 3 races are across open water, most of it relatively protected or close to the shoreline. This category includes races for small yachts.
Category 4 races are short, close to the shore in relatively warm or protected waters.
Race awards Prizes are generally awarded:
a) to a winner in each class (based on corrected times – calculated from the yachts' ratings and race times);
b) to the first boat to finish the course.

Yacht ratings Each yacht has a rating, obtained by inserting its measurements (length, beam, depth, girth, sail area, and many others) into a complex formula (the International Offshore Rule). Measurement is in two stages: hull measurements when the yacht is ashore during building or in winter; freeboard and some other measurements when afloat in full commission. Ratings are expressed in feet or meters and are used to divide yachts into offshore racing classes. Rating certificates are compulsory and must be renewed after alterations or a change of ownership.

Owner's responsibility The safety of a yacht and her crew is the sole responsibility of the owner. He must do his best to ensure that the yacht is thoroughly seaworthy, properly equipped, and manned by an experienced crew who are physically fit to face bad weather.
It is the sole responsibility of each yacht to decide whether or not to start or continue in a race.
Inspection A yacht may be inspected at any time. If she does not comply with official specifications her entry may be rejected, or she may be disqualified or subjected to some other penalty prescribed by the national authority or sponsoring organization.

Prohibitions (in Europe) are:
a) automatic, mechanical, or wind vane devices for steering;
b) engine or power pump, except for charging batteries, pumping bilges, or supplying power for weighing anchor or heaving off (full details must be reported if the engine is used in a grave emergency);
c) electronic aids other than those permitted in the regulations.
(If a yacht has any prohibited devices, these must be sealed inoperable before a race.)

222

223

9

Surfing

A surfer's basic equipment is a board, normally made to his individual specifications, with which he attempts to ride waves as they approach the shoreline. In competitions surfers may be required to ride a number of waves. Each performance is scored separately, and the points from the best waves are totaled to give a final score.

Officials The number of officials depends on the size of the competition and may include judges, a referee, a starter, and an official supervising the event.
Starting On the starter's signal the competitors enter the water and paddle out to their appropriate positions.
Duration Heats will be of 15–25 minutes duration, whilst finals will be of 30–45 minutes. Heat times depend upon surf conditions. Surfers may catch as many waves as they wish in the allocated heat time. Depending on number of competitors in the heat the final total of waves counted for determining heat position will be 3 or 4, with 5 waves counted in the final.

Scoring Competitors are awarded points for each wave they ride. They score between 0.1–10 (with 0.1 increments) on the following criteria.
Riders will be given maximum points for performing in the most difficult part of the wave, selected for quality and size, for the longest time at the fastest speed using the widest range of functional maneuvers involving the highest degree of difficulty:
1 making the wave
2 beating sections
3 tube rides
4 turns, cut backs and reentries
5 nose walking (longboard – over 9ft – category only).
Points may be lost for interference or other offenses.

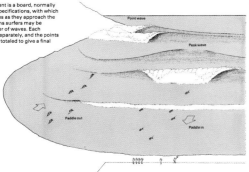

Point wave

Peak wave

Paddle out

Paddle in

Interference A competitor must not:
interfere with a rider who has wave possession (left);
interfere with the previous heat when paddling out;
surf in the contest area unless actually competing.
After a heat competitors must return at once, either kneeling or prone.

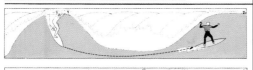

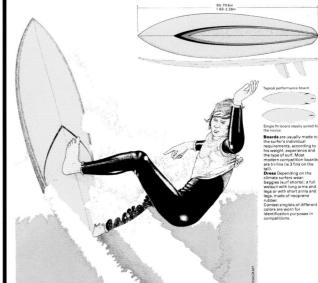

5ft–7ft 6in
1.63–2.28m

Typical performance board

Single fin board ideally suited for the novice

Boards are usually made to the surfer's individual requirements, according to his weight, experience and the type of surf. Most modern competition boards are tri-fins (ie 3 fins in the tail).
Dress Depending on the climate surfers wear: baggies (surf shorts); a full wetsuit with long arms and legs or with short arms and legs, made of neoprene rubber. Contest singlets of different colors are worn for identification purposes in competitions.

Wave possession Whenever possible, a wave should only be ridden by one competitor.
A competitor is entitled to priority on a wave if he:
is closest to the curl (6);
stands up before any other competitor paddles towards that wave;
is nearest the peak on a peak wave.
Should there be a contestant on either side of a peak wave (7) then each surfer has possession of his own side.

Penalties Offenses are penalized by loss of points or disqualification from the competition.

207

203

THE WEATHER PAGE began in 1981. It was an idea generated by the original team of planning editors gathered in Washington, D.C., to produce prototypes of what would become *USA TODAY*. The charge was simple: What would it take to distinguish a new, nationally distributed newspaper from a host of competitors, both local and other would-be national newspapers? One idea, which remains to this day, was to do a much more comprehensive job of reporting weather, an area often overlooked by local newspapers. The team produced prototypes of a weather page in both color and black and white, and tested them. Predictably, the color version won. ■ By contrast to what newspapers do with weather, what local TV news broadcast *doesn't* devote a major portion of on-air time to reporting weather? What makes it so interesting? After all, can't we look out the window and see the same thing the TV guy is reporting? But, people watch this stuff all the time. Let a major snowstorm be forecast for the Washington, D.C. area, and everyone—and I mean everyone—is glued to the TV, getting the latest update. Newspapers ignored this interest in 1982, and today, 13 years later, most still do. This has caused a sizeable portion of their potential audience to look elsewhere for the information. ■ Weather news sells. And, it is one of the country's great unifiers. If it's snowing in the Northeast, the Northeast is interested, but so are the many residents of Miami who moved there to escape the ravages of northern winters. When I worked for *The Miami News* in the late 1970s, one of the biggest-selling stories we could print was a winter storm in New York. "New York Hit By Major Snowstorm" would read the Page 1 headline. Single copy sales went up. Happened every time. The only bigger story would be "Snow In Miami" (which actually happened, although barely enough to coat a windshield.) ■ The needs of today's newspaper readers are many and complex. Commodity traders in Chicago are interested in the winter storm approaching Chicago, but also in drought conditions in the corn belt and unseasonal freezes affecting coffee plantations in South America. South Carolina trucking companies are concerned about weather in the Rockies. School bus drivers, suntan lotion manufacturers, state highway departments, and electric utility companies all want to know about forecasts. ■ We live in an extremely mobile society, and we need information about other places. Weather is just one of those needs, but an important one. For example, we have a special group of readers called Road Warriors. They travel a great deal, often over 100,000 miles a year. They are heavy users of *USA TODAY*, and they rank The Weather Page as one of the pages they look at most often. If they are any indication, more and more people are willing to use visuals to obtain information. ■ Now, how to do a comprehensive job of reporting weather? And how to show it visually in a manner that would be attractive, entertaining and educational to all gender, age, geographical and other groups? And how could we design such a page that would be relatively easy to produce? ■ One big problem we faced was finding a source for good weather data, forecasts, and explanations. Most newspapers get their information from the National Weather Service, which issues generalized, computer forecasts every 12 hours. On the other hand, private weather services can update forecasts as wanted by their clients. To give us what we hoped would be a competitive edge, we went with a private service and its slightly more personalized forecasts. Also, the private service could provide better material for the graphic feature in the center of The Weather Page that explains some aspect of that day's weather. ■ Another daunting task was finding the manpower needed to create this page daily. In 1982, we spent an average of 23 person-hours to produce each weather page. In those days, we had to cut amberlith overlays for each color, and each of the city names was positioned and pasted down by hand. How could we produce this thing every day? ■ It would be easy to say that we just drew a U.S. map and threw some color on it. From a 13-year perspective, that's what it looks like we did. Actually, the original Weather Page was ugly. It didn't contain a lot of information, the colors were too harsh, the page didn't look like the rest of the paper, and there was no sense of visual urgency. But the readers loved it, which is probably more an indictment of poor weather reporting in other newspapers, rather than tribute for the job we did. Surveys showed that readers found it easy to read, entertaining, informative, and "fun," a word often used by

PLANNING THE WEATHER PAGE To produce a much more comprehensive and visually understandable daily weather report, USA TODAY organized a full page of graphics, topical features and forecast text. Pages from 1981 and 1990 (below) show both consistencies and multiple adjustments. A color-banded temperature map of the U.S. has always been the lead and "anchor" for the page, and information is displayed in layers of prominence.

them to describe reading USA TODAY. ■ By 1990 we had redrawn the large map more accurately (without that huge eastern bias), making it cleaner and using the available space more wisely. More cities

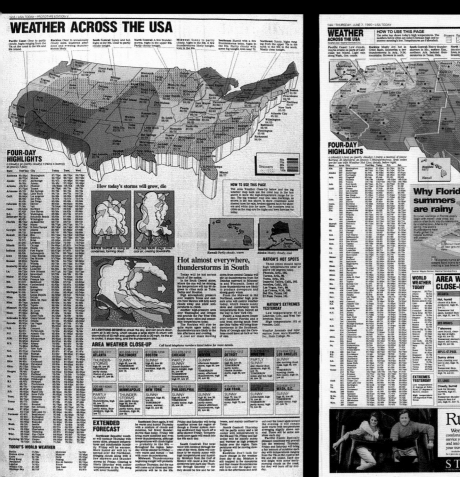

were located on the map due to the huge (and still continuing) demand from many readers, chambers of commerce, governors, tourism bureaus, my neighbor, and so on. In 1982, we had a little over 100 cities, by 1990, we had about 130, in 1994 over 190. We had increased the Area Weather Closeups from eight in 1982, to 28 in 1990, to 52 in 1994. By 1990, the page contained an advertisement to help pay the freight and provide more visual interest. ■ We redesigned The Weather Page again in 1993 with several goals in mind: 1) to show a more global view of the U.S., one that did not isolate it from the rest of the continent (unlike the early years, we now circulate the U.S. domestic edition in Canada and parts of Mexico, plus there are foreign editions for Asia and Europe); 2) redraw the map to make it more contemporary; 3) add more information, and cities to the map; 4) isolate the precipitation outlooks (precipitation patterns on the map made city information difficult to read); 5) add more Weather Area Closeups, now called Top Travel Destinations; 6) add another day's forecasts to the foreign cities; 7) make the page more consistent visually; 8) add more color; 9) maintain the graphic feature ex-

plaining the weather; and 10) utilize technology to make the page easier to produce.

■ But from the very beginning, our primary goal was to make the weather understandable. To do that, we utilized a famil-

UNIFYING PAGE AND STYLE A recent Weather Page and its diagram (below) show continuing revisions within a fixed page architecture. The weather feature beneath the map, and the Snapshot features used elsewhere in the newspaper (all opposite), have grown in sophistication. The comprehensive nature of The Weather Page was extended to special subject pages, like those which detail the America's Cup and an aircraft carrier (following pages).

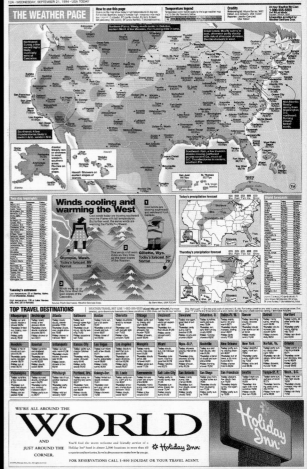

lar, iconic point of reference: the U.S. map. It's simple, straightforward and quickly understandable to most readers. The map also anchors the page visually, it is the introduction to the page, or the "lead" of the story. The colors used to identify temperature bands are also quickly understandable. The colors go from white (below 10 degrees) to deep red (over 100 degrees.) Aren't those the colors we would associate with those temperatures? The temperature legend removes any doubt. ■ The map gives readers information on different levels. At first glance, you can tell easily if the nation is enjoying reasonable or unreasonable weather. If the map shows a lot of dark red, perspiration pops out on your brow. If the map has very pale colors—a lot of white, cerise and blue—you start reaching for a sweater and coat. The map also can be fairly specific. For example, if you're headed to North Carolina's Outer Banks for the weekend, a look tells you it's going to be in the 70s. Coupled with your general knowledge of seasons, you understand that the nights are going to be relatively cool. You won't plan to do a lot of swimming and will pack a sweater for the trip to dinner. ■ The temperature color bands also tell you which end of the temperature range you're on. If you look at Richmond, Virginia, and it lies in the midst of the yellow-orange color band (temperature in the 70s), you know that Richmond is likely to be near 75. The message is reinforced by text reporting that Richmond's forecast high will be 75. If you see that Dallas-Fort Worth lies on the southern edge of the yellow-orange band, very close to the orange-red band

A storm that won't let go

Remnants of Tropical Storm Allison, which hit Texas last Monday, will continue drenching parts of the East through at least Wednesday.

1 Counterclockwise winds around low-pressure center are dying . . .

3 Another high pressure area helps block rain from moving east

4 Third high pressure area helps block rain from moving west

2 . . . but winds around high pressure continue pumping humid air in to feed rain

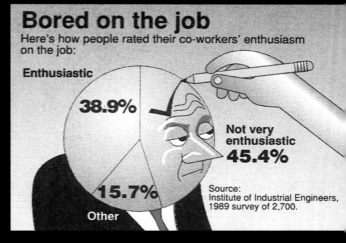

Bored on the job

Here's how people rated their co-workers' enthusiasm on the job:

Enthusiastic
38.9%

Not very enthusiastic
45.4%

15.7%
Other

Source:
Institute of Industrial Engineers, 1989 survey of 2,700.

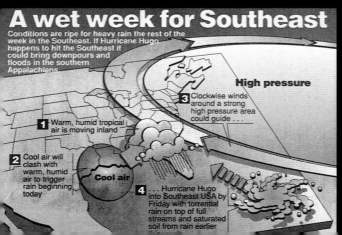

A wet week for Southeast

Conditions are ripe for heavy rain the rest of the week in the Southeast. If Hurricane Hugo happens to hit the Southeast it could bring downpours and floods in the southern Appalachians.

High pressure

3 Clockwise winds around a strong high pressure area could guide . . .

1 Warm, humid tropical air is moving inland

2 Cool air will clash with warm, humid air to trigger rain beginning today

Cool air

4 . . . Hurricane Hugo into Southeast USA by Friday with torrential rain on top of full streams and saturated soil from rain earlier

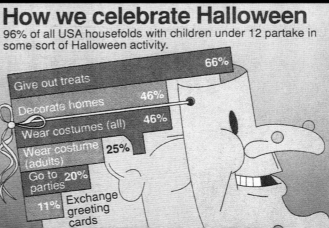

How we celebrate Halloween

96% of all USA housefolds with children under 12 partake in some sort of Halloween activity.

Give out treats — 66%
Decorate homes — 46%
Wear costumes (all) — 46%
Wear costume (adults) — 25%
Go to parties — 20%
Exchange greeting cards — 11%

America's Cup 1987

Here's USA TODAY's guide to watching the America's Cup matches, to the course off Fremantle, Australia, and to the sailing terms, tactics and equipment involved in racing 12-meter yachts.

The USA's mega-million dollar hopes of winning back the America's Cup are down to one 12-meter yacht and a best-of-seven race off Fremantle, Australia, that began Tuesday.

Skipper Dennis Conner, in *Stars and Stripes*, is sailing against *New Zealand*. The winner will challenge the Royal Perth Yacht Club for the 27-inch Cup, nicknamed *The Auld Mug* and forged of 8.4 pounds of silver.

The Australians also are in their final races to select a boat to defend the Cup.

A final best-of-seven race, to decide the next holder of the Cup, begins Jan. 31.

Competing to be in the America's Cup final races is a new experience for the USA sailing teams.

The New York Yacht Club won the first race in 1851, in the waters off Great Britain with Queen Victoria in attendance, and held the trophy for 132 years. It was guaranteed the defender's place in the finals, and held the competition in East Coast waters.

That all ended when the Australians won it — from Conner — in 1983.

The United States' effort to win back the Cup began almost immediately after the '83 loss. Eventually, six USA syndicates — from New York to Chicago to San Diego — prepared boats and raised about $50 million.

Four Australian syndicates, spending $50 million in all — have competed to be the defender.

The process of picking a challenger began in September, with six USA yachts expected to dominate a field of 13 boats. They had tradition, the most experience, the best backing and enjoyed design help from experts at NASA, McDonnell Douglas and Boeing.

But the New Zealand entry — manned by a young crew with just 10 months experience together and a 25-year-old skipper, and utilizing a revolutionary fiberglass hull — has rolled over the opposition. Going into the defender finals, it had won a record 37 races and lost only one, to Conner.

Hulls weren't supposed to be the story at Fremantle. The winged keels introduced by the winning Australians in '83 were the high-tech element for most of this year's Cup field, along with computers — which assisted with everything from sail and boat design to weather forecasts to on-board information.

Where the money comes from

- National campaign 10%
- Regional companies' goods and services 8%
- National companies' goods and services 5%
- Regional companies' cash 20%
- Individuals 57%

Where the money goes

- Boat-building 20%
- Sailing program 25%
- Logistics 8%
- Design 23%
- Contingency 9%
- Miscellaneous 9%

Computer-cut sails

Sail design has been a matter of trial-and-error. But with computers, a sailmaker can get an advance look at the stress that will be put on a sail. Left, stress lines lead to the sail's bottom corner. By cutting the sail into pieces (right), stress is spread out.

- Stress pattern
- Clew
- Clew

How a sail works

A mainsail operates most of the time like an airplane wing — its curve speeds the air moving across one side of it, creating suction on the back of the sail and pulling the boat along. Using another sail in front creates a 'slot' that boosts the speed of the air across the mainsail — moving the boat faster.

- Thrust
- Thrust
- Thrust
- Genoa sail
- Wind direction
- Main sail
- Yacht

Source: USA TODAY research

By Bob Laird, USA TODAY

Anatomy of a 12-meter

One of the top designers of turn-of-the-century America's Cup winners used to carve soft wood into the shape of a possible boat, and then run his hands over it get the proper 'feel' of the hull design. But computers do the work now. A "12-meter yacht" actually is about 65 feet long — the name comes from a complex equation used to measure the boat. Each designer tinkers — a bigger sail or a smaller hull or a taller mast — in hopes of gaining speed and manuverability.

- Mast
- Mainsail — The largest sail behind the mast.
- Boom
- Jib, genoa — Smaller sails, set forward of the mast.
- Transom (stern)
- Rudder
- Waterline
- Keel
- Deck
- Profile plan
- LWL
- Body plan
- Half-breadth plan

What's a 12-meter yacht? Here's the math:

Formula:

$$\frac{L + (2 \times D) + \sqrt{s} - F}{2.37} = 12 \text{ Meters}$$

- Add the length of the hull along the waterline (LWL), twice difference between the skin and overall 'girth' at the middle (d), and the square root of sail area (S);
- Subtract from that the height of the deck above the water (F);
- Divide that answer by 2.37.

As long as the answer comes out to 12 meters, the boat could race for the America's Cup.

Tacking duel in 1983

Here's the final race downwind in the 1983 America's Cup duel. *Australia II* trailed the USA entry *Liberty* when they rounded a buoy and turned to have the wind coming from behind them. At the end of the duel, *Australia II* had caught up with and passed *Liberty* — and never again trailed.

- Windward marker
- Australia II jibes (turns)
- Wind
- Wind
- Liberty jibes
- Australia II bears off and pulls ahead

Tacking

Tacking is when a sailboat zigzags to change direction, to best use the wind and to change direction.

- Bowman
- Spinnaker pole
- Forward hatches — Access to hull sail storage area
- Sewerman
- Deck beam
- Hullskin
- Ribs

Construction of the hull

Twelve-meter yachts had hulls of wood until the mid-1970s, when aluminum came into use. This year, the yacht *New Zealand* is built of fiberglass — lighter and stiffer than a metal hull. A hull is designed much like that of an airplane — streamlined, with a thin skin supported by a stiff framework of 'ribs' inside.

- Pits — Where a crewman stands to control the jib or genoa sail
- Gooseneck — The fitting that secures the boom to the mast
- Mastman
- Boom — Holds the bottom edge of the mainsail
- Tailer
- Grinders
- Tactician
- Navigator
- Mainsail trimmer
- Tailer
- Coffee-grinders — Winches that raise, lower sails
- Helmsman
- Ballast keel — Made of lead, its weight allows the boat to keep upright when the wind is blowing from the side
- Steering wheels — Twin wheels, so the skipper can steer from either side
- Antenna — For navigational or radio equipment
- Mainsheet traveller — A track for a line that helps control the boom and mainsail
- Racing compass — Often recessed into the deck, it enables the on-board tactician to know the boat's critical angles during the race
- Rudder — A moveable plate attached to the wheels, it steers the boat
- Keel wings — Enable more ballast to be carried lower on the keel and allow a boat to use less ballast overall, improving the boat's stability and speed

The course

The America's Cup course off Fremantle, in the Indian Ocean, has eight legs, curving around buoys where most of the tactical battles take place — with the first leg always heading into the wind. (The courses off Newport, R.I, had only six legs.) The course is up to the Royal Perth Yacht Club, holders of the Cup.

- Start
- Leeward mark
- 3.5 nautical miles
- Wing mark
- Windward mark
- Finish
- Perth
- Course
- Australia
- Fremantle
- Marina
- Wind
- Australia
- Perth

HOW AN AIRCRAFT CARRIER WORKS

Where the carriers are

Red Sea
1 Saratoga, 2 John F. Kennedy,
3 America

Persian Gulf
4 Midway
5 Ranger
6 Theodore Roosevelt

0 300
miles

Ship personnel

About 5,250 men (women are not assigned to carriers) run *America* and its airplanes. Exact numbers change daily.

250	Pilots and flight officers
2,200	Squadron support, from maintenance to administration
460	Hangar and flight deck crews
240	Major aircraft maintenance
520	Engineering
125	Combat information center
150	Deck department, from steering ship to lookouts and maintenance
30	Navigation department
35	Air traffic controllers
250	Food service
65	Medical and dental
190	Supply
140	Electronic technicians
210	Weapons handlers
85	Marines, who handle security
300	Miscellaneous

Flight and hangar deck crew

Men working on the flight and hangar decks wear colored shirts and helmets indicating their jobs:

Yellow shirts direct movement of aircraft.

White shirts handle safety-related jobs, including final inspections of airplanes.

Green shirts hook planes to catapults and handle arresting wires

Purple shirts fuel planes

Brown shirts are plane captains who watch over individual planes.

Blue shirts chock and chain planes into position, drive tractors that pull airplanes.

Red shirts handle all weapons and ammunition

Silver suits handle aircraft crashes and fires.

How to take off

Launching (and landing) only takes place after the ship is turned into the wind. Each of the four catapults can launch an F-14 every 1 minute and 45 seconds — for a total rate of about one plane every 30 seconds off the ship.

1 Missiles and bombs are armed

2 Plane taxis into position

3 Planes are hooked to catapults. A fully powered aircraft is held on the deck by a hold-back bar, which releases when the catapult launches the plane

4 **Pilot** salutes when he's ready to go.

5 **Catapult officer** touches hand to deck and points forward.

6 A button is pressed that releases steam at about 500 pounds per square inch into catapult.

Size

The length is about 3 football fields placed end to end.

Football field

1,048 ft.

252 ft.

The catapult

A fully loaded F-14 weighs about 67,000 pounds. It can be launched from a dead stop to 165 mph in space of 250 feet and just over 2 seconds

Shuttle
A wheeled car rolling on a track underneath a slot in the deck. The launch bar on the nose gear of plane is connected to it.

Pistons
Attached to the shuttle, they are forced forward when steam from the ship's boilers is forced into the tubes holding them.

Shuttle track

Water brakes
Stop pistons within five feet.

How a catapult works

Shuttle track

Piston Shuttle Mechanical grab wire brings shuttle back into position for next launch. Water brake

What's inside

Supply
Flight deck
Hangar deck
Combat information center
Ready rooms
Eating areas
Aircraft maintenance
Sleeping areas
Engineering
Auxiliary machinery room
Diesel generator
Fuel
Sleeping areas
Magazine (munitions storage)

17 stories

How to land

1 Pilot lines up with flight deck centerline.

2 Pilot knows he is on correct glide path if an amber light on the deck, known as the ball, is lined up with a horizontal row of green lights. If the ball is too high, so is the plane.

3 Plane hits deck at approximately 160 mph.

4 Pilot immediately pushes engines to full power in case he misses the four arresting wires and needs to take off and try again — known as the bolter.

5 When the plane's tail hook catches one of the arresting wires, plane is brought to an abrupt stop within 350 ft.

6 A man signals the pilot to cut power and raise hook, then directs jet clear to be refueled, re-armed, and remanned.

Six aircraft carriers are among the approximately 100 U.S. Navy ships involved in Desert Storm. These super ships — floating cities with more than 5,000 people each — are key players in the air attack on Iraq. Here's a look at the USS America:

The island

Air Boss controls planes taking off, landing and within five nautical miles of ship.

Captain located on bridge

Landing signal officer guides planes

Arresting wires

Flight deck officer in charge of people on deck.

Aircraft handler controls movements of planes on flight and hangar decks.

2 planes at a time can be raised to flight deck level.

Elevator No. 2
Elevator No. 3
Elevator No. 4
Elevator No. 1

Bomb elevators
Bridge
Ready rooms
Hangar deck

Jet blast deflectors

Jet blast deflectors protect crew and other planes from jet exhaust.

Bomb elevators

No. 1 catapult
No. 2 catapult
No. 3 catapult
No. 4 catapult

Safety net

Life rafts surround ship

Aircraft refueling stations
Many are scattered around the ship. Aircraft taxi up to pumps and their tanks are filled using long hoses.

Safety net

99

A carrier battle group

Carriers travel in a group of ships commanded by a rear admiral on board the carrier. Battle groups include:

Cruiser
Supply ship
Fuel ship
Frigate
Ammunition ship
Destroyer
Frigate
Cruiser
E-2C Hawkeye
Cruiser
Helicopter
Destroyer
Frigate

Jets are often airborne during high-threat times.

During flight operations, a helicopter is constantly alert to retrieve any "men overboard" or downed aircrew

The ball
Yellow light appears to move up and down to alert incoming pilots whether they are too high or too low. This shows pilot to be too low.

Close-in protection

The Phalanx close-in weapon system

Computer guided high-speed Gatling guns can destroy an incoming missile before it hits the carrier. They are located several places on the ship.

Aircraft on board

The USS America has an airwing of nine squadrons, totaling 75 to 85 aircraft.

SH-3H Sea King
Helicopter locates and attacks submarines, also provides search and rescue. (6 on board)

F/A-18 Hornet
The single-seat jet fights enemy planes in the air and bombs targets on the ground. (20-24 on board)

A-6E Intruder
Low-level attack bomber flies in all weather and carries a crew of 2. (10 on board)

S-3A Viking

F-14 Tomcat
The two-seat, twin-engine fighter flies offensive missions and also defends the battle group. It carries Sparrow and Sidewinder missiles, and long-range Phoenix missiles. (20-24 on board)

E-2C Hawkeye
Subsonic jet seeks out and attacks submarines with torpedoes and depth charges. (10 on board)

EA-6B Prowler
Four-seat jet jams enemy radar. (4 on board)

Rotating radar dome provides airborne early warning of enemy aircraft, and airborne traffic control. (4 on board)

Graphic by Sam Ward, research by Lori Sharn, USA TODAY

Source: U.S. Navy, National Air & Space Museum, Boeing Co.

ous), you know quickly that the area is going to be closer to the 80s than the 70s. ■ We try to make every story in the newspaper exist for a reason. That reason is usually news driven: If it happened in the past 24 hours, or will happen within the present 24 hours or might happen in the next 24 hours, you should read about it in *USA TODAY*. We apply the same reasoning to everything on The Weather Page. We aim to make all the information current, "hot" and interesting. It is this sense of story urgency throughout the newspaper that drives sales and reader satisfaction. ■ **THE WEATHER FEATURE** is an informational graphic in the middle of The Weather Page. It changes every day, and has become a fixture for both casual and dedicated readers. It begins with a question What's happening in the weather today or tomorrow that we can explain to readers? I might be an approaching hurricane, or why it's raining today on the western slope of the Rockies and not the eastern slope. The weather feature graphic is almost always produced live and published the next day. It is the only part of the page done by an artist, the rest is completely generated by computer. The "decorating" of these graphics in a light-hearted manner captures the readers' eye and entertains them a bit, making the information appear less academic, less scientific, and hopefully more attractive to casual readers as they graze through the paper. ■ **SNAPSHOTS** After The Weather Page and the weather feature graphic, Snapshots get more attention than any other feature in *USA TODAY*. Like every other feature in the newspaper, we try to peg them to something current. A small staff is dedicated to originating, researching and editing them. The ideas come from everywhere: "over the transom," from public relations firms research companies, polling companies, even my brother-in-law. ■ Each of the 13 *USA TODAY* staff artists spends a fair amount of time each week conceptualizing and illustrating Snapshots. We allow about three hours to complete each one. While a majority of Snapshots are done at least 24 hours in advance, some are done on deadline. We publish four Snapshots each day, in one year we will produce about 1100, and over the 2-year history of the paper we've produced over 13,000. ■ Each Snapshot fits within a rigidly fixed rectangle that speeds production, anchors each section front, and is visually consistent. They follow the same Helvetica typography schedule as the rest of the newspaper's graphics, and we use a fairly limited palette of colors but still, each artist's individuality shines through and gives the Snapshots distinct, separate personalities. ■ Snapshots are part of our strategy to establish a consistent identity for the paper, one that sets *USA TODAY* apart from other newspapers. They are a clea some would say persistent) signal that *USA TODAY* is a visual newspaper. Readers obviously want more news in a visual way, it is more entertaining and it does a better job of communicating. While imparting valuable information (U.S. postage costs relative to those of other nations, how medical costs will increase by the year 2000), readers think of these nuggets as fun to read and understand. Regardless of some opinions, there is just no comparison between the come-hitherness of a properly illustrated informational graphic and that of a flat, dimensionless bar chart. The information might be the same, but the illustrated one is seen and remembered by more readers. ■ **SPECIAL PAGES** Full-page graphics are done to show subjects in great detail. They are often bird's-eye views to help orient people to the context of the subject. The *America's Cup 1987* page illustrated a typical boat during the Cup competition in Perth, Australia. It explains many things, like how a sailboat can sail against the wind, what it looks like inside, how the competition is run, and how computers are used to design and cut sails. ■ The aircraft carrier special page has a remarkable history. Just prior to the Gulf War, we knew that the U.S. would soon deploy aircraft carriers in combat areas near Iraq. The editors wanted to show an aircraft carrier, and explain their workings. How large are they? How many people work on one? What about armaments? Food? To help us, we had a model of the *USS America*, a nuclear-powered carrier, along with reference materials and advice from the military. We chose a view that would have impact and still allow the inclusion of other visual aspects. As luck would have it, the day before the page was published the U.S. announced that the *USS America* and five other carriers would be committed to the war. This gave us an unexpected but important news peg. As always in our graphics, we maintained an order to the page: headline, "lead,"

EXTENDING PAGE AND STYLE Weather has been an extremely productive field for *USA TODAY*, and its style of visualizing the subject has achieved near-iconic status. In 1992, *The Weather Book* was published (below and following two pages), with hundreds of illustrations drawn directly from The Weather Page itself. The qualities of book printing relaxed the limitations of newspaper reproduction, and a softer range of colors and contrasts was introduced, sometimes with full-page drop-out graphics. The book is now in its tenth printing.

a body of information—in this case lots of facts and visual details—and a closing (the plane flying off the deck). We are told that a framed copy of this page now hangs on the boardroom wall of the *USS America*.

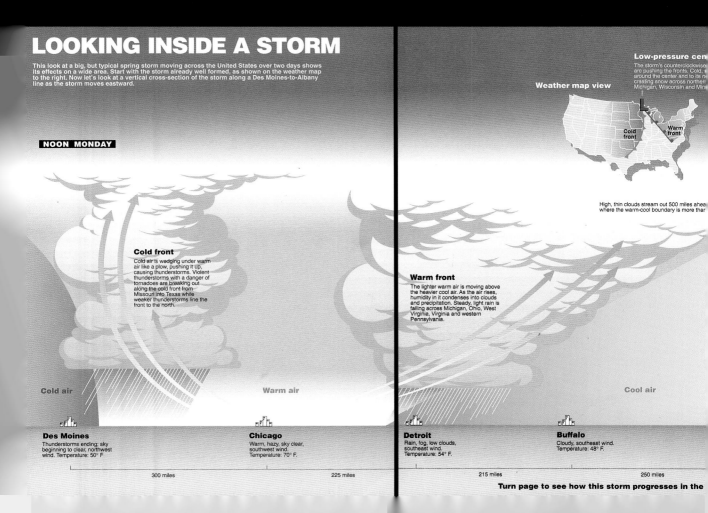

LOOKING INSIDE A STORM

This look at a big, but typical spring storm moving across the United States over two days shows its effects on a wide area. Start with the storm already well formed, as shown on the weather map to the right. Now let's look at a vertical cross-section of the storm along a Des Moines-to-Albany line as the storm moves eastward.

NOON MONDAY

Low-pressure cen
The storm's counterclockwise
are pushing the fronts. Cold,
around the center and to its n
creating snow across northern
Michigan, Wisconsin and Min

Weather map view

Cold
front

Warm
front

High, thin clouds stream out 500 miles ahea
where the warm-cool boundary is more than

Cold front
Cold air is wedging under warm air like a plow, pushing it up, causing thunderstorms. Violent thunderstorms with a danger of tornadoes are breaking out along the cold front from Missouri into Texas while weaker thunderstorms line the front to the north.

Warm front
The lighter warm air is moving above the heavier cool air. As the air rises, humidity in it condenses into clouds and precipitation. Steady, light rain is falling across Michigan, Ohio, West Virginia, Virginia and western Pennsylvania.

Cold air   Warm air   Cool air

Des Moines
Thunderstorms ending; sky beginning to clear, northwest wind. Temperature: 50° F

Chicago
Warm, hazy, sky clear, southwest wind. Temperature: 70° F.

Detroit
Rain, fog, low clouds, southeast wind. Temperature: 54° F.

Buffalo
Cloudy, southeast wind. Temperature: 48° F.

300 miles   225 miles   215 miles   250 miles

Turn page to see how this storm progresses in the

TRACKING A STORM

Here's what happens to the storm from the previous page during the next 24 hours.

Warm front

Cold front

MIDNIGHT TUESDAY

The cold front is moving through Chicago. The warm front passed Detroit in the last two hours. Steady rain is moving eastward into New England. Thunderstorms along the cold front have weakened, but lightning is still flashing in the sky southward into Louisiana.

Des Moines

Clear, chilly night, northwest wind. Temperature: 25° F

Chicago

Thunderstorm, wind changing from southwest to northwest. Temperature: 30° F.

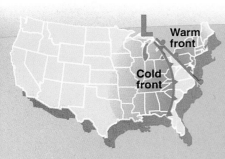

Warm front

Cold front

NOON TUESDAY

An occluded front has formed near the storm's center. Heavy snow is falling across northern Michigan into Canada. Lighter snow is falling west of the Great Lakes. Steady rain has spread eastward across the Northeast and New England. Thunderstorms are dumping heavy rain on the mountains of western Virginia and North Carolina. A severe thunderstorm watch is posted for South Carolina, Georgia and northern Florida.

Des Moines

Clear, chilly, west wind. Temperature: 40° F.

Occluded front

MIDNIGHT W

The occluded front n
south as the New Je
intense with thunders
downpours mixed in
steady rain. Snow is
northern New Englan
its thunderstorms ha
Coast over the Atlan
about 600 miles ahe
the west are moving

Des Moines

High thin clouds, halo around the moon. Calm wind. Temperature: 33° F.

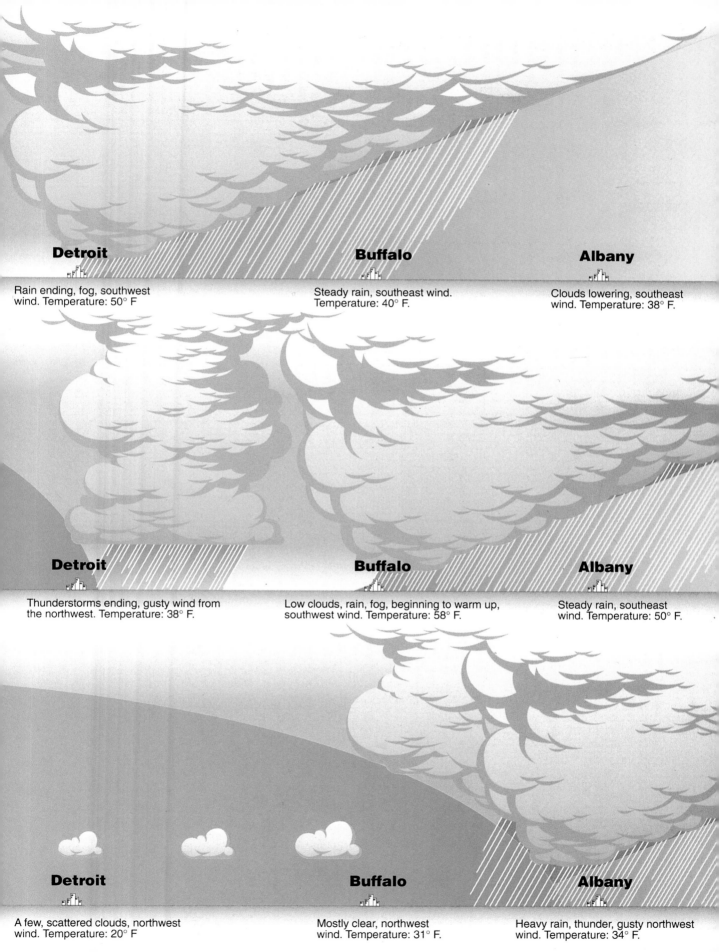

Detroit

Rain ending, fog, southwest wind. Temperature: 50° F

Buffalo

Steady rain, southeast wind. Temperature: 40° F.

Albany

Clouds lowering, southeast wind. Temperature: 38° F.

Detroit

Thunderstorms ending, gusty wind from the northwest. Temperature: 38° F.

Buffalo

Low clouds, rain, fog, beginning to warm up, southwest wind. Temperature: 58° F.

Albany

Steady rain, southeast wind. Temperature: 50° F.

Detroit

A few, scattered clouds, northwest wind. Temperature: 20° F

Buffalo

Mostly clear, northwest wind. Temperature: 31° F.

Albany

Heavy rain, thunder, gusty northwest wind. Temperature: 34° F.

JOHN GRIMWADE

THE TOPKAPI PALACE Lefts and rights. The shortest route past the things that shouldn't be missed. Key landmarks shown along the route, sometimes as much for their orientation value as for their noteworthiness. Topkapi is a dimensional map, not an architectural drawing, its whole purpose is to support a text with numbered references. It is very selective, but that reflects its relevance to a story in *Condé Nast Traveler*. Graphics in a travel magazine are tightly edited, and have quite different functions than graphics in a guide book. Everything here is secondary to the red "walk" line. I added icons to give a hint

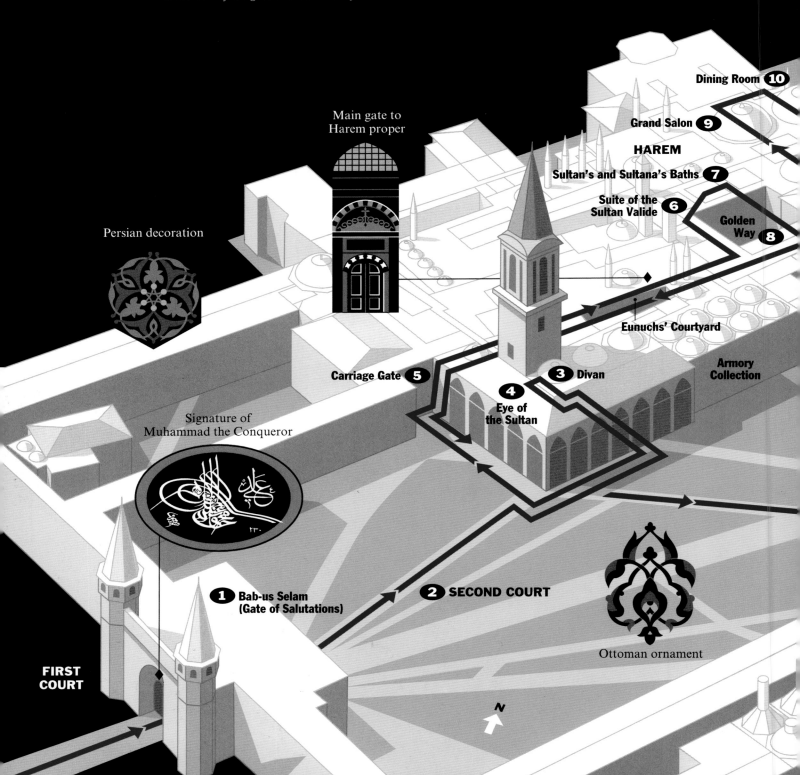

Dining Room ❿

Grand Salon ❾

HAREM

Sultan's and Sultana's Baths ❼

Suite of the Sultan Valide ❻

Golden Way ❽

Main gate to Harem proper

Persian decoration

Eunuchs' Courtyard

Armory Collection

Carriage Gate ❺

❸ Divan

Signature of Muhammad the Conqueror

❹ Eye of the Sultan

❶ Bab-us Selam (Gate of Salutations)

❷ **SECOND COURT**

Ottoman ornament

FIRST COURT

N

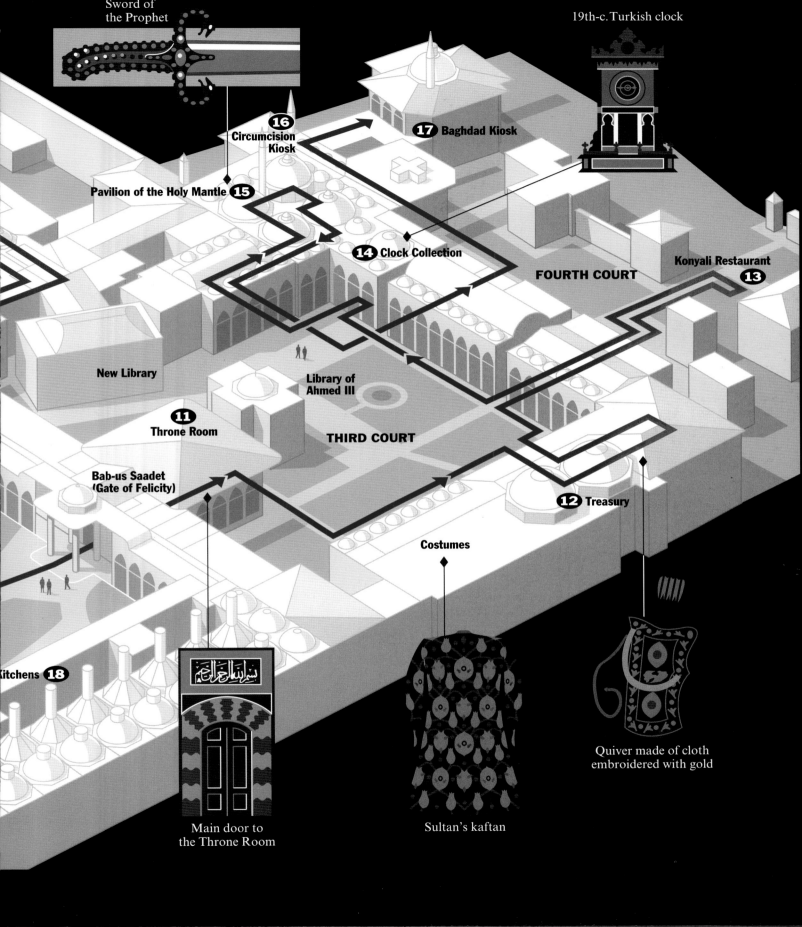

Sword of
the Prophet

19th-c. Turkish clock

16 Circumcision
Kiosk

17 Baghdad Kiosk

15 Pavilion of the Holy Mantle

14 Clock Collection

Konyali Restaurant

13

FOURTH COURT

New Library

Library of
Ahmed III

11 Throne Room

THIRD COURT

Bab-us Saadet
(Gate of Felicity)

12 Treasury

Costumes

Kitchens **18**

Main door to
the Throne Room

Sultan's kaftan

Quiver made of cloth
embroidered with gold

the way. Original reference for these was mixed, like color and monochrome photog... shot from different angles, but I drew them in a rigid two-dimensional style to be... sistent graphically, and to place them on a different visual layer. Often graphics... run as planned; the route line became more complicated as the project progresse... cause of a problem with doorways that were not in use, thus the later stages of the... became rather convoluted. ■ **CREDITS:** Design Director: Diana LaGuardia. ■

MAPPING SEQUENCE Tour walking lines are dimensionally diagrammed for magazine stories about the Ottoman Empire's *Topkapi Palace* (preceding pages), and in pocket-sized, "sixty minute" museum guides. With coordinated text and graphics, the guides show the route of a tour, and the art and architecture along it. The Vatican Museum tour is shown in overview (below middle and opposite), and in segments with numbered text references (bottom).

VATICAN MUSEUM GUIDE The ... view (opposite) is a map that sets up ... ries of detailed diagrams in a *Condé ...Traveler* sixty-minute museum guide ... walk line is complex, but is shown to ... the tour in the context of the Vatican ... ings and the bus route that brings vi ... from St. Peter's. The features of a re ... map have been pulled up and to the ... to create the buildings, with detail a ... from photographs. The execution i ... liberately simple to show only what's ... ed to support the guide's opening ... This doesn't mean I don't need a sta ... reference, I like to see everything I ca ... fore deciding what to leave out. ■ M ... proach to information graphics is tha ... is often much more. From the ma ... background material available, I try ... tract the lines and shapes necessary ... across an editorial point. To do that ... tempt to split information visually int ... ers of importance. If the diagram is ... cessful, the reader will know where t ... first, and can easily take in the rest ... message. Sometimes, when absorb ... a project, I start to cloud the inform ... with needless detail, but, the obje ... comments of colleagues soon leads ... visions. It's our responsibility to re ... ber that there are readers who are n ... miliar with the material on the receivin ... of every graphic we do. ■ **CREDITS** ... sign Director: Diana LaGuardia; Bo ... design by Christin Gangi, Michael Po ...

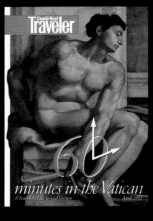

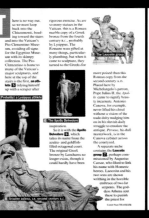

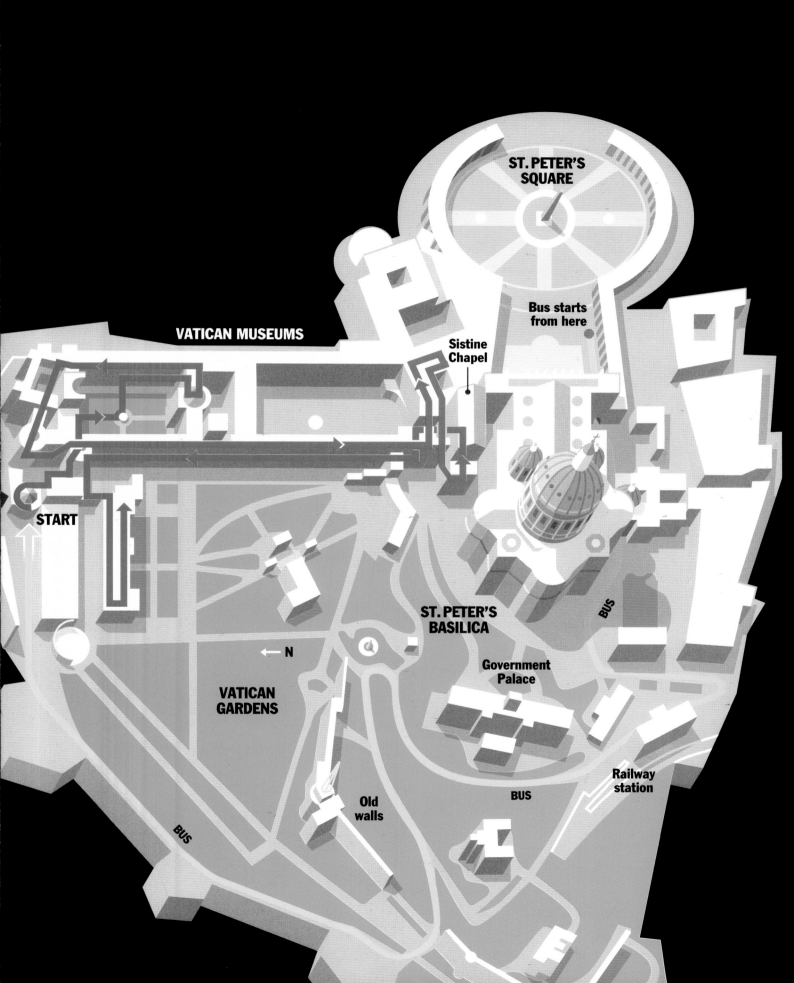

THE LARGER LESSERS

GRANDE-TERRE

GUADELOUPE

Grande-Anse

St-François

BASSE-TERRE

Pointe-à-Pitre

LA DÉSIRADE

Trois Rivières

MARIE-GALANTE

Basse-Terre

Grand-Bourg

Terre-de-Haut

Terre-de-Bas

ILES DES SAINTES

GUADELOUPE–LES SAINTES
● Ferries (590-91-13-43): 2 crossings daily; $12–$15; 30 min. to 1 hr.

GUADELOUPE–LA DÉSIRADE
● Ferries (590-83-32-67 or 20-02-30): 2 crossings daily; $8.75; 45 min.
● Air Guadeloupe: 2 flights daily; 20 min.

GUADELOUPE–MARIE-GALANTE
● Emeraude Express: 4 crossings daily; $15; 45 min.
● Air Guadeloupe (590-82-28-35): at least 3 flights daily; 20 min.

MARIE-GALANTE–LES SAINTES
● Emeraude Express: Tues. or Thurs., times vary; $12; 40 min., then on to St-François

■ **MAPS FOR ISLAND HOPPING** A lighter approach. This is part of an 11-page section in *Condé Nast Traveler* on boat and plane connections in the Caribbean. First comes an opening locator page, then each spread with a different island group. During an editorial meeting, I sketched the rough outline of this very literal solution, with boats and planes hopping between islands. Later, after more resolved roughs and discussions with designers, that plan was carried out. Over five spreads, the projections in the graphics rotated to occupy different areas of the page layouts, and the colors of the skies changed to show travel from dawn through the day to dusk. This created variations in presentation, but stylistically everything remained constant. ■ These are not island maps, but graphics of island links. (In the past, we have covered the Caribbean in considerable detail using more conventional maps). A lengthy text was a necessary part of the equation when dividing up the space because each island group had to be contained in one spread. A team effort by editor, designer and graphic artist was needed to make the whole package work. For everybody's sake, I roughed out the whole sequence at full size, like a storyboard, so we could get a good idea of the overall flow of the section and see it in the context of the whole magazine. ■ **CREDITS:** Design Director: Diana LaGuardia; Art Director: Christin Gangi; Designer: Michael Powers.

MAPPING CONTEXT AND SEQUENCE In *Condé Nast Traveler*, an article described boat and plane connections between five island groups in the Caribbean. Shown are graphics for the Lesser Antilles group (opposite) and another spread (below). A locator page begins the article, globe projections rotate to relieve repetition, and sky colors change to suggest travelling all day long.

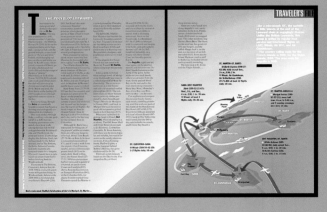

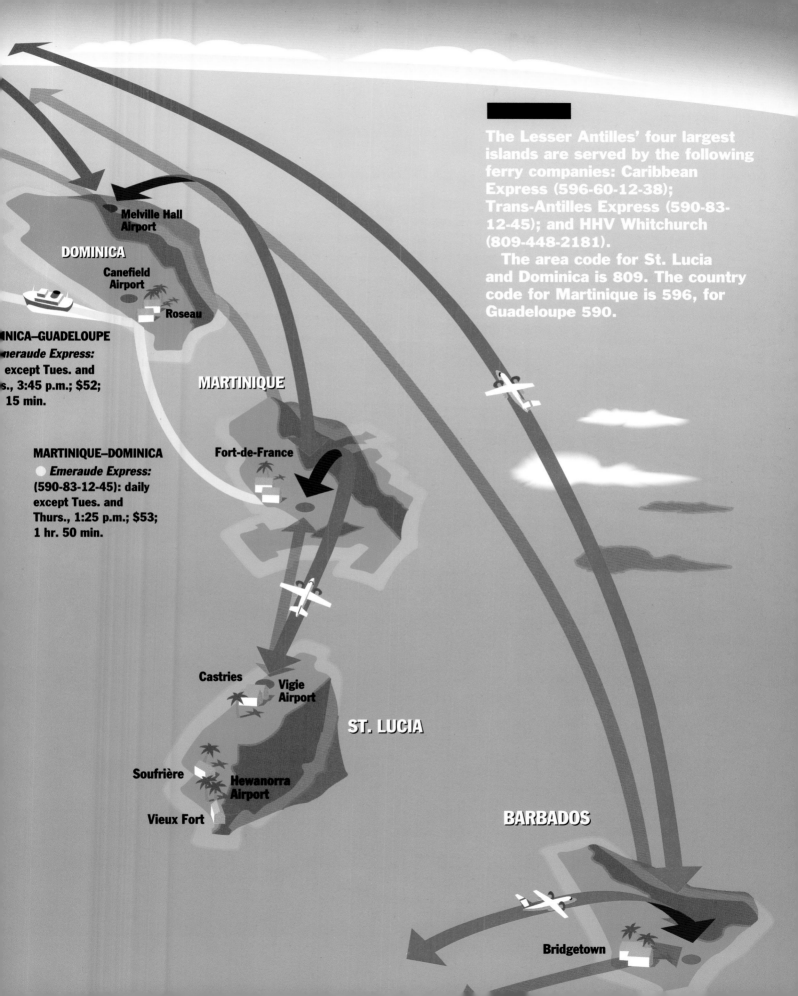

The Lesser Antilles' four largest
islands are served by the following
ferry companies: Caribbean
Express (596-60-12-38);
Trans-Antilles Express (590-83-
12-45); and HHV Whitchurch
(809-448-2181).

The area code for St. Lucia
and Dominica is 809. The country
code for Martinique is 596, for
Guadeloupe 590.

**Melville Hall
Airport**

DOMINICA

**Canefield
Airport**

Roseau

NICA–GUADELOUPE
neraude Express:
except Tues. and
s., 3:45 p.m.; $52;
15 min.

MARTINIQUE–DOMINICA
● *Emeraude Express:*
(590-83-12-45): daily
except Tues. and
Thurs., 1:25 p.m.; $53;
1 hr. 50 min.

MARTINIQUE

Fort-de-France

Castries

**Vigie
Airport**

ST. LUCIA

Soufrière

**Hewanorra
Airport**

Vieux Fort

BARBADOS

Bridgetown

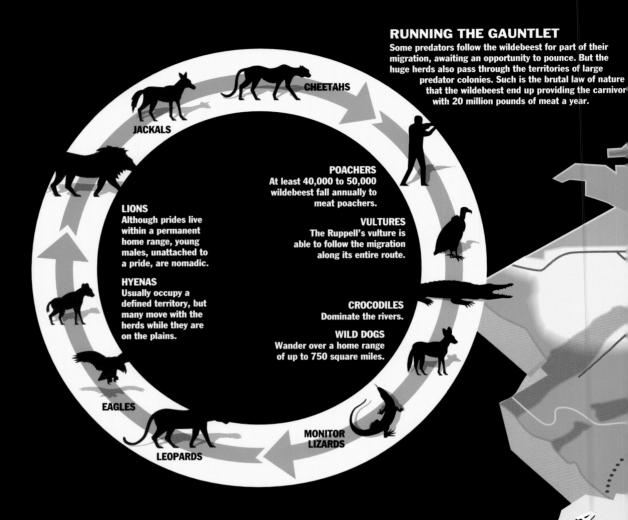

RUNNING THE GAUNTLET

Some predators follow the wildebeest for part of their migration, awaiting an opportunity to pounce. But the huge herds also pass through the territories of large predator colonies. Such is the brutal law of nature that the wildebeest end up providing the carnivores with 20 million pounds of meat a year.

CHEETAHS

JACKALS

LIONS
Although prides live within a permanent home range, young males, unattached to a pride, are nomadic.

HYENAS
Usually occupy a defined territory, but many move with the herds while they are on the plains.

POACHERS
At least 40,000 to 50,000 wildebeest fall annually to meat poachers.

VULTURES
The Ruppell's vulture is able to follow the migration along its entire route.

CROCODILES
Dominate the rivers.

WILD DOGS
Wander over a home range of up to 750 square miles.

EAGLES

LEOPARDS

MONITOR LIZARDS

AFRI

TANZANIA

MAPPING CONTEXT AND SEQUENCE A magazine feature about Wildebeest migration in Kenya and Tanzania uses a diagram to represent the migration's year-long, circular, 500-mile route. A small schematic locates the area on the African continent, and text on the diagram supports the regularity of the round-trip. The ecosystem's grazing order of heavy to lightweight animals is shown, and the long gauntlet of predators the Wildebeest herd must face.

■ **WILDEBEEST MIGRATION** A Gatefold. This graphic is but one part of a large magazine feature on Wildebeest migration. I was involved in the earliest editorial discussions of the various components of the story, so I could participate in decisions about the use of graphics. Clearly we needed a fairly detailed map, with elements that showed the various animals that prey on the wildebeest herd as it moves in its annual circle through Tanzania and Kenya. These predators had no specific positions on the map, so I made a rigid circle and placed them around it. This mirrors the wildebeest route, yet reinforces the idea that this part of the graphic is schematic. The other side of the gatefold was filled by a striking photograph of a wildebeest in motion. ■ I'm always trying to integrate my graphics into the larger editorial plan so they don't look like they have been derived from another source. Good communications between writer and artist is one positive factor. Another is the *Condé*

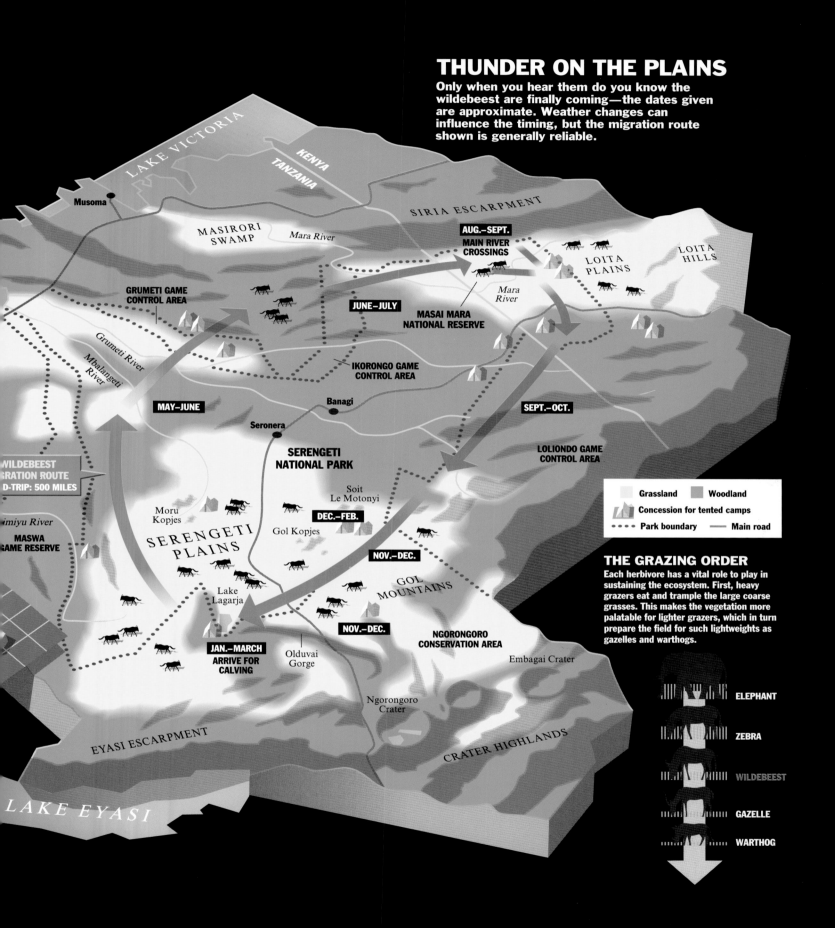

THUNDER ON THE PLAINS

Only when you hear them do you know the wildebeest are finally coming—the dates given are approximate. Weather changes can influence the timing, but the migration route shown is generally reliable.

LAKE VICTORIA

KENYA

TANZANIA

Musoma

MASIRORI SWAMP

Mara River

SIRIA ESCARPMENT

AUG.–SEPT. MAIN RIVER CROSSINGS

LOITA PLAINS

LOITA HILLS

GRUMETI GAME CONTROL AREA

Mara River

JUNE–JULY

MASAI MARA NATIONAL RESERVE

Grumeti River

Mbalangeti River

IKORONGO GAME CONTROL AREA

MAY–JUNE

Banagi

SEPT.–OCT.

Seronera

SERENGETI NATIONAL PARK

LOLIONDO GAME CONTROL AREA

WILDEBEEST MIGRATION ROUTE
ROUND-TRIP: 500 MILES

imiyu River

MASWA GAME RESERVE

Moru Kopjes

Soit Le Motonyi

DEC.–FEB.

Gol Kopjes

SERENGETI PLAINS

Lake Lagarja

NOV.–DEC.

GOL MOUNTAINS

NOV.–DEC.

NGORONGORO CONSERVATION AREA

Embagai Crater

JAN.–MARCH ARRIVE FOR CALVING

Olduvai Gorge

Ngorongoro Crater

EYASI ESCARPMENT

CRATER HIGHLANDS

LAKE EYASI

Legend:
- Grassland
- Woodland
- Concession for tented camps
- ···· Park boundary
- — Main road

THE GRAZING ORDER

Each herbivore has a vital role to play in sustaining the ecosystem. First, heavy grazers eat and trample the large coarse grasses. This makes the vegetation more palatable for lighter grazers, which in turn prepare the field for such lightweights as gazelles and warthogs.

ELEPHANT

ZEBRA

WILDEBEEST

GAZELLE

WARTHOG

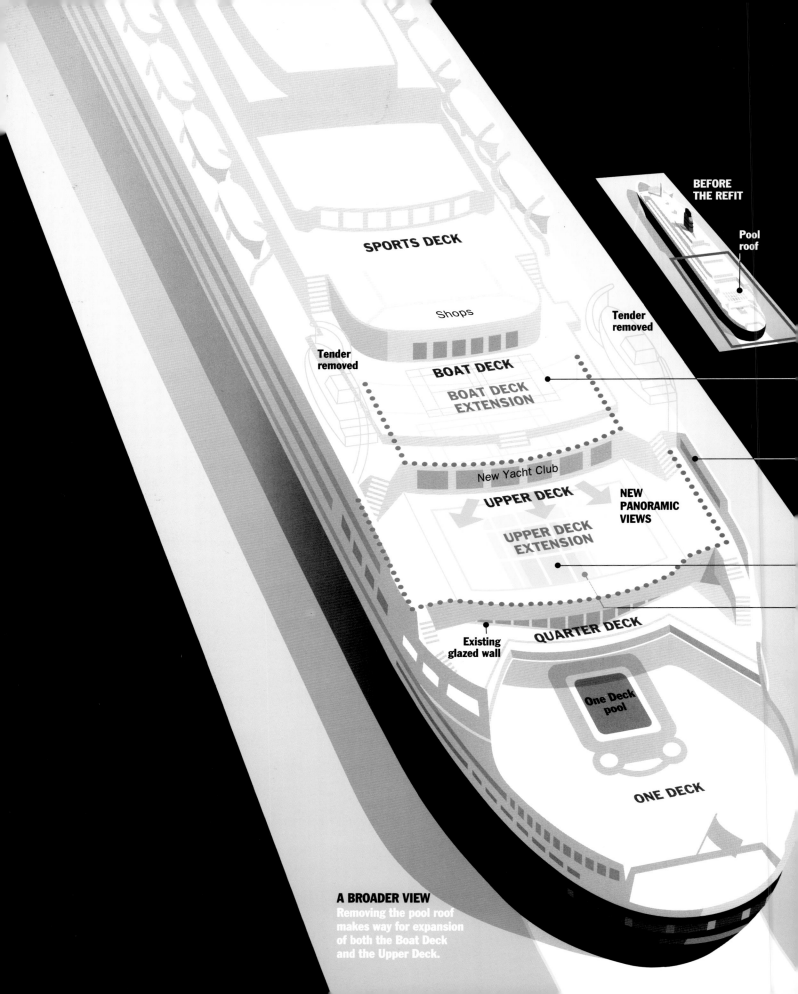

SPORTS DECK

Shops

BEFORE THE REFIT

Pool roof

Tender removed

Tender removed

Tender removed

BOAT DECK

BOAT DECK EXTENSION

New Yacht Club

UPPER DECK

NEW PANORAMIC VIEWS

UPPER DECK EXTENSION

Existing glazed wall

QUARTER DECK

One Deck pool

ONE DECK

A BROADER VIEW
Removing the pool roof makes way for expansion of both the Boat Deck and the Upper Deck.

Nast Traveler approach of involving editor, writer, designer and graphic artist in the planning of graphic projects. Also, there are frequent dialogues between the designer and the artist during development of artwork and final layouts. This two-way process is invaluable—many times it has led me to question a particular graphic approach and then switch to a better solution. ■ **CREDITS:** Design Director: Diana LaGuardia; Art direction by Christin Gangi.
■ **REFITTING THE QE2** Getting technical. This kind of graphic presents unique problems, particularly in a travel magazine. It shows alterations to a very important cruise liner about which many of our readers might well be interested. But I didn't want the diagram to be to technically intimidating. I also wanted to make something appear real when it only existed in plans. Also, because all the detail is at the stern of the ship, I included a small locator—as I would use for a map—which serves to show the ship prior to the refit. ■ Features like these are news stories, but our long lead time for printing and distribution means that they must be prepared well in advance. Some time before beginning the artwork, I had been on board the QE2 while it was docked in New York, and the alterations were described by a Cunard representative. Later, large plans were sent to us from a studio in London which was designing the alterations. Our researcher also found a very large model of the ship in the Cunard offices, plus cruise brochures, which gave me many details for the drawing. Then, very near our deadline, the designers in London drew the correct positions of various elements on top of a fax of my virtually finished drawing, and I modified the artwork to match. The limited colors used here reflect the approach we take for graphics in the front of the magazine, where they often run opposite full-page, very busy advertisements. ■ **CREDITS:** Design Director: Diana LaGuardia; Designer: Flavia Schepmans.

— **Sports Center moved up from Upper Deck to Boat Deck extension**

— **Glazed sidescreens added on sides of Upper Deck**

— **Roof over pool removed and replaced with decking**

— **Quarter Deck pool removed**

Plastic surgery for the *QE2*
A face-lift as cruise-ship rivalry heats up
By Wendy Perrin

A BOOMING CRUISE industry expects 5.2 million North Americans to take cruises in 1995—that's a 152 percent increase over ten years ago. To accommodate them all, at least 7 new luxury ships are expected to be launched this year, and another 20 by the end of 1998.

But while other cruise lines scramble to build new vessels, Cunard Line is revamping its older ones. The *Queen Elizabeth 2*, its flagship, just got a twenty-fifth birthday present: a $45 million makeover that includes a restructured stern allowing for uninterrupted ocean vistas. "New face, old soul," say the company's ads, because the revamp also emphasizes Cunard's and the *QE2*'s history.

The *QE2* is one of only three classic vessels still sailing (the others are the *Rotterdam* and the *Norway*, formerly the *France*) and the only cruise ship that still routinely crosses the Atlantic. She is also the only one with a class structure: First-class passengers drink and dine apart from those in "transatlantic class."

The redesign includes a new observation lounge, a pub à la Knightsbridge, a bar for first-class passengers, two informal cafés, a library that has doubled in size, and modernized cabins.

The *QE2*, which had taken on a well-worn air, was a hodgepodge of styles and colors. The new decor has a formal, traditional feel and highlights the ship's British heritage. Some public areas are furnished in dark woods and rich Victorian reds and greens. *(Continued on page 34)*

32

SPORTS DECK

Shops

Tender removed

BOAT DECK

BOAT DECK EXTENSION

New Yacht Club

UPPER DECK

UPPER DECK EXTENSION

Existing glazed wall

QUARTER DECK

One Deck pool

ONE DECK

A BROADER VIEW
Removing the pool roof makes way for expansion of both the Boat Deck and the Upper Deck.

BEFORE THE REFIT

Pool roof

Tender removed

Sports Center moved up from Upper Deck to Boat Deck extension

Glazed sidescreens added on sides of Upper Deck

NEW PANORAMIC VIEWS

Roof over pool removed and replaced with decking

Quarter Deck pool removed

GRAPHICS by JOHN GRIMWADE

MAPPING CONTEXT A graphic had to represent significant changes in the refitting of the QE2 cruise ship when the changes existed only in plans. A visit to the ship, various cruise brochures, verbal descriptions by the refit designer, and a large model of the ship were needed to create the simple schematic and its locator.

e manufacturing revolution

ny U.S. companies have
rhauled their factories in recent
rs and are now producing goods
ramatically different ways.

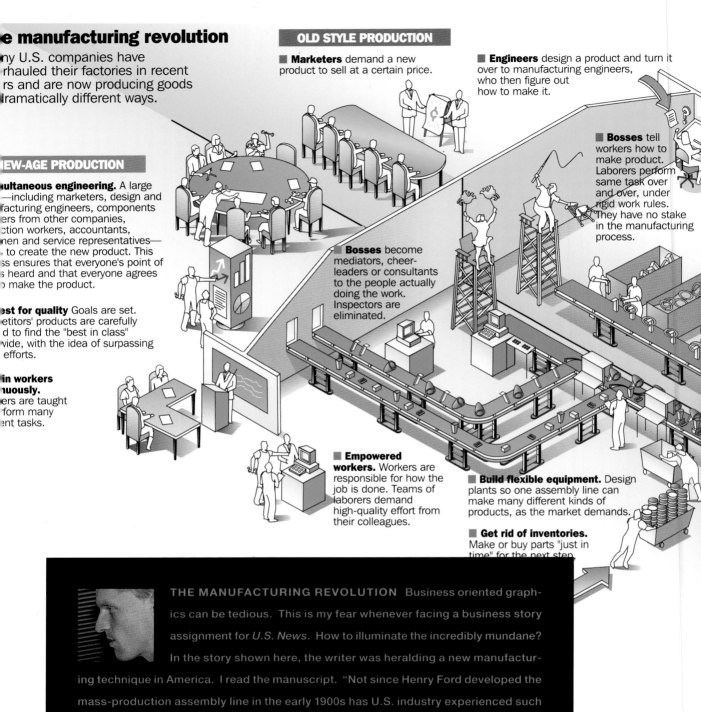

NEW-AGE PRODUCTION

ultaneous engineering. A large
—including marketers, design and
facturing engineers, components
ers from other companies,
ction workers, accountants,
nen and service representatives—
. to create the new product. This
ss ensures that everyone's point of
s heard and that everyone agrees
o make the product.

est for quality Goals are set.
etitors' products are carefully
d to find the "best in class"
wide, with the idea of surpassing
efforts.

**in workers
nuously.**
ers are taught
form many
ent tasks.

Marketers demand a new
product to sell at a certain price.

Engineers design a product and turn it
over to manufacturing engineers,
who then figure out
how to make it.

Bosses tell
workers how to
make product.
Laborers perform
same task over
and over, under
rigid work rules.
They have no stake
in the manufacturing
process.

Bosses become
mediators, cheer-
leaders or consultants
to the people actually
doing the work.
Inspectors are
eliminated.

**Empowered
workers.** Workers are
responsible for how the
job is done. Teams of
laborers demand
high-quality effort from
their colleagues.

Build flexible equipment. Design
plants so one assembly line can
make many different kinds of
products, as the market demands.

Get rid of inventories.
Make or buy parts "just in
time" for the next step.

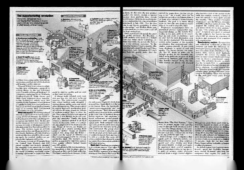

THE MANUFACTURING REVOLUTION Business oriented graphics can be tedious. This is my fear whenever facing a business story
assignment for *U.S. News*. How to illuminate the incredibly mundane?
In the story shown here, the writer was heralding a new manufacturing technique in America. I read the manuscript. "Not since Henry Ford developed the
mass-production assembly line in the early 1900s has U.S. industry experienced such
a change in production techniques." Well,
I didn't care whether he was right or not,
the guy was really enthusiastic and the
story sounded like it might be fun. A large
graphic illustration was needed to explain
this new process. The story cited some of
the companies which were using the new
techniques, like Xerox, GM, and Motorola

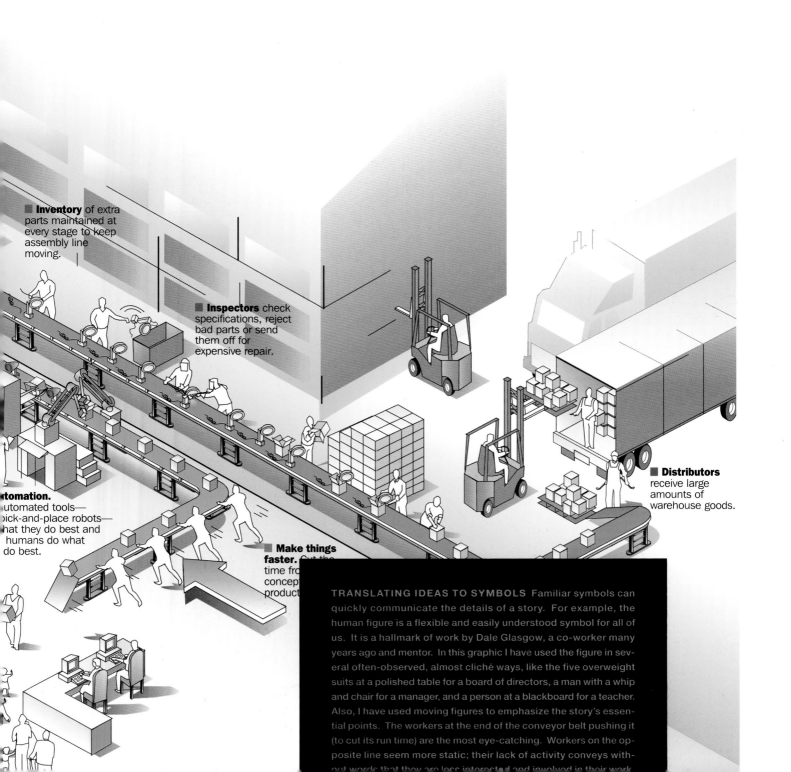

■ **Inventory** of extra parts maintained at every stage to keep assembly line moving.

■ **Inspectors** check specifications, reject bad parts or send them off for expensive repair.

■ **Distributors** receive large amounts of warehouse goods.

tomation.
utomated tools—
ick-and-place robots—
hat they do best and
humans do what
do best.

■ **Make things faster.** Cut the
time fro
concept
product

TRANSLATING IDEAS TO SYMBOLS Familiar symbols can quickly communicate the details of a story. For example, the human figure is a flexible and easily understood symbol for all of us. It is a hallmark of work by Dale Glasgow, a co-worker many years ago and mentor. In this graphic I have used the figure in several often-observed, almost cliché ways, like the five overweight suits at a polished table for a board of directors, a man with a whip and chair for a manager, and a person at a blackboard for a teacher. Also, I have used moving figures to emphasize the story's essential points. The workers at the end of the conveyor belt pushing it (to cut its run time) are the most eye-catching. Workers on the opposite line seem more static; their lack of activity conveys with-

Some of their factories had automated robots, and we had photographs, but I decided not to use them. Instead, the diagram was designed to be comprehensive and schematic enough to work for all the companies. ■ The manuscript kept mentioning the word "change." I thought that a sense of change might best be suggested by a side-by-side comparison. Most readers of *U.S. News* know what a typical assembly line looks like, so it would seem that comparing an assembly line of the future beside one of the past would clearly and understandably highlight the changes that have evolved since the early 1900s. With the main points of the story fresh in my mind, I sketched up a few ideas and asked the writer to develop a dozen or so factoids to accompany the parallel comparison. ■ I sketched with pencil and paper in the old fashioned way—this was way back in 1990. Today I would use a three-dimensional computer modeler and be able to develop many different perspectives for a factory floor in half the time. The diagonal shape of the final graphic allowed for the inclusion of more text than a horizontal one, and it held the page together without the need for additional art or photographs.

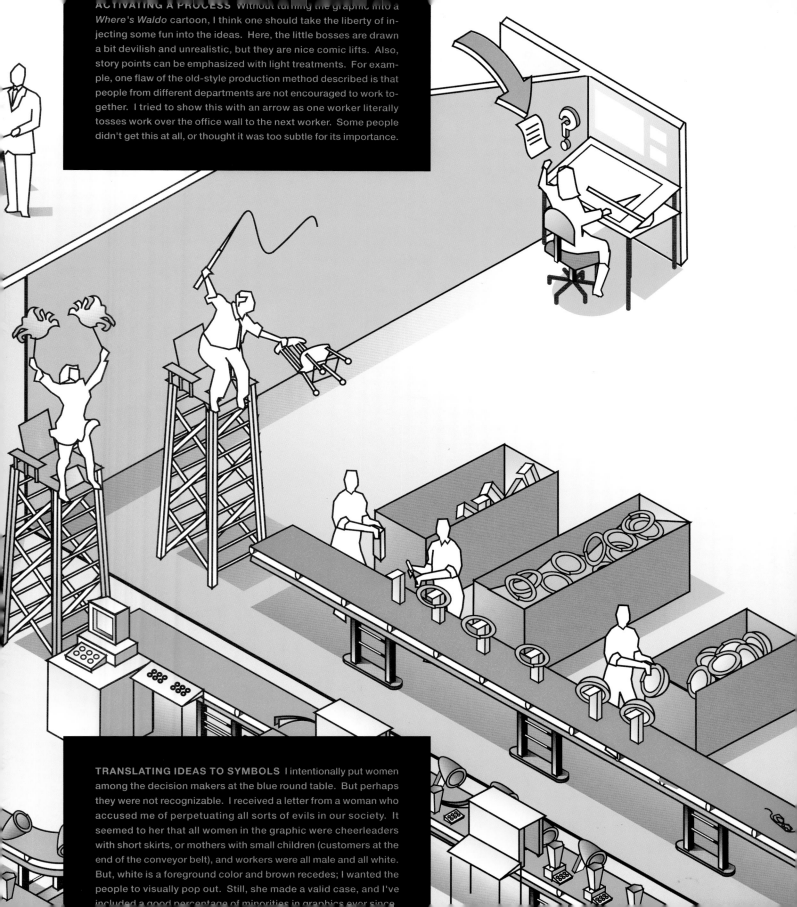

ACTIVATING A PROCESS Without turning the graphic into a *Where's Waldo* cartoon, I think one should take the liberty of injecting some fun into the ideas. Here, the little bosses are drawn a bit devilish and unrealistic, but they are nice comic lifts. Also, story points can be emphasized with light treatments. For example, one flaw of the old-style production method described is that people from different departments are not encouraged to work together. I tried to show this with an arrow as one worker literally tosses work over the office wall to the next worker. Some people didn't get this at all, or thought it was too subtle for its importance.

TRANSLATING IDEAS TO SYMBOLS I intentionally put women among the decision makers at the blue round table. But perhaps they were not recognizable. I received a letter from a woman who accused me of perpetuating all sorts of evils in our society. It seemed to her that all women in the graphic were cheerleaders with short skirts, or mothers with small children (customers at the end of the conveyor belt), and workers were all male and all white. But, white is a foreground color and brown recedes; I wanted the people to visually pop out. Still, she made a valid case, and I've included a good percentage of minorities in graphics ever since

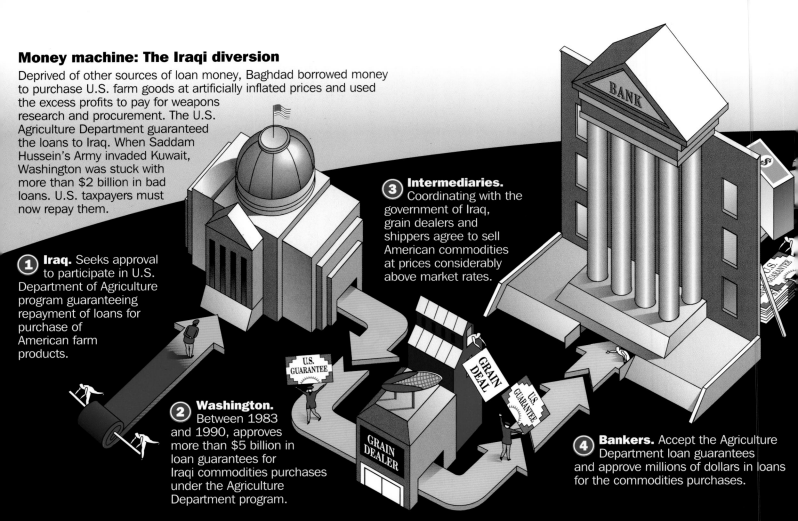

Money machine: The Iraqi diversion

Deprived of other sources of loan money, Baghdad borrowed money to purchase U.S. farm goods at artificially inflated prices and used the excess profits to pay for weapons research and procurement. The U.S. Agriculture Department guaranteed the loans to Iraq. When Saddam Hussein's Army invaded Kuwait, Washington was stuck with more than $2 billion in bad loans. U.S. taxpayers must now repay them.

1 Iraq. Seeks approval to participate in U.S. Department of Agriculture program guaranteeing repayment of loans for purchase of American farm products.

2 Washington. Between 1983 and 1990, approves more than $5 billion in loan guarantees for Iraqi commodities purchases under the Agriculture Department program.

3 Intermediaries. Coordinating with the government of Iraq, grain dealers and shippers agree to sell American commodities at prices considerably above market rates.

4 Bankers. Accept the Agriculture Department loan guarantees and approve millions of dollars in loans for the commodities purchases.

■ **GRAPHICS AT THE PENTAGON** If you don't think information graphics are important, you are probably not reading this book. But even colleagues of mine were shocked by what this story says about the importance of visual communication. ■ Not long ago, I received a call from the Joint Chiefs of Staff office at the Pentagon. The main duty of the joint Chiefs is to advise and brief the President on military matters. A week or two before this conversation, the JCS had briefed the President on how they planned to rescue pilot Scott O'Grady, whose plane had been shot down while flying reconnaissance over Bosnia. According to the story, JCS Chairman General John Shalikashvili felt they had almost failed in their attempt to sell the President on the rescue mission. The reason—the graphics they used in the briefing were inadequate. At a subsequent meeting, the General held up copies of *Time* and *US News* and asked his staff why Pentagon graphics fell short of the newsweekly standard. ■ So, deep inside the Pentagon, I sat and mulled over their questions. (I could tell you a lot more, but according to their

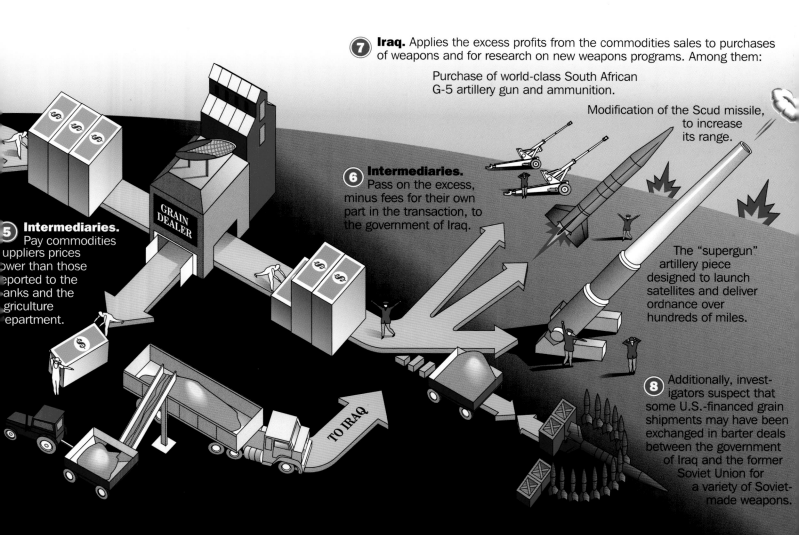

7 Iraq. Applies the excess profits from the commodities sales to purchases of weapons and for research on new weapons programs. Among them:

Purchase of world-class South African G-5 artillery gun and ammunition.

Modification of the Scud missile, to increase its range.

6 Intermediaries. Pass on the excess, minus fees for their own part in the transaction, to the government of Iraq.

5 Intermediaries. Pay commodities suppliers prices lower than those reported to the banks and the agriculture department.

GRAIN DEALER

TO IRAQ

The "supergun" artillery piece designed to launch satellites and deliver ordnance over hundreds of miles.

8 Additionally, investigators suspect that some U.S.-financed grain shipments may have been exchanged in barter deals between the government of Iraq and the former Soviet Union for a variety of Soviet-made weapons.

instructions, I'd probably have to kill you). The reasons their graphics suffered when compared to news magazines were readily apparent even to Admirals and Generals. First, almost all their graphs were flat and two-dimensional. Any kind of perspective was rarely explored. Second, there were considerable time constraints. When lives are on the line, you can't unseal a new, three-dimensional software package and start to experiment. And third, artistic license is rarely issued in the military. ■ Anyway, I agreed to help and instruct the graphics people at the Pentagon however I could, for the good of my country and a small fee. But, my superior officers at *US News* had a problem with the appearance of a journalist (yes, artists are journalists too) taking money from an organization about which they report. So in the end, I took the job without the small fee.

■ To think that a rescue mission was nearly postponed because the graphics couldn't deliver the message is quite amazing. Communicating ideas is what journalism is all about. In many cases, the quality of the graphics can either make or break that mission.

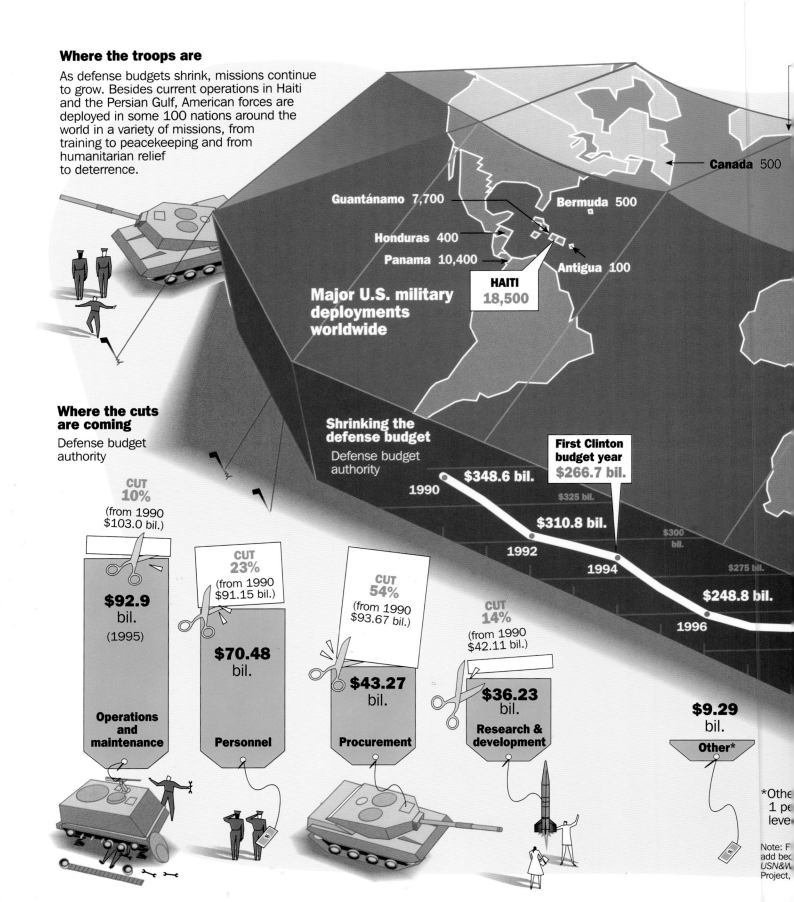

Where the troops are

As defense budgets shrink, missions continue to grow. Besides current operations in Haiti and the Persian Gulf, American forces are deployed in some 100 nations around the world in a variety of missions, from training to peacekeeping and from humanitarian relief to deterrence.

Major U.S. military deployments worldwide

Guantánamo 7,700
Honduras 400
Panama 10,400
Bermuda 500
Antigua 100
Canada 500
HAITI 18,500

Where the cuts are coming

Defense budget authority

Shrinking the defense budget
Defense budget authority

First Clinton budget year $266.7 bil.

1990 $348.6 bil.
$325 bil.
1992 $310.8 bil.
$300 bil.
1994
$275 bil.
$248.8 bil.
1996

CUT 10%
(from 1990 $103.0 bil.)
$92.9 bil. (1995)
Operations and maintenance

CUT 23%
(from 1990 $91.15 bil.)
$70.48 bil.
Personnel

CUT 54%
(from 1990 $93.67 bil.)
$43.27 bil.
Procurement

CUT 14%
(from 1990 $42.11 bil.)
$36.23 bil.
Research & development

$9.29 bil.
Other*

*Othe
1 pe
leve

Note: F
add bed
USN&W
Project,

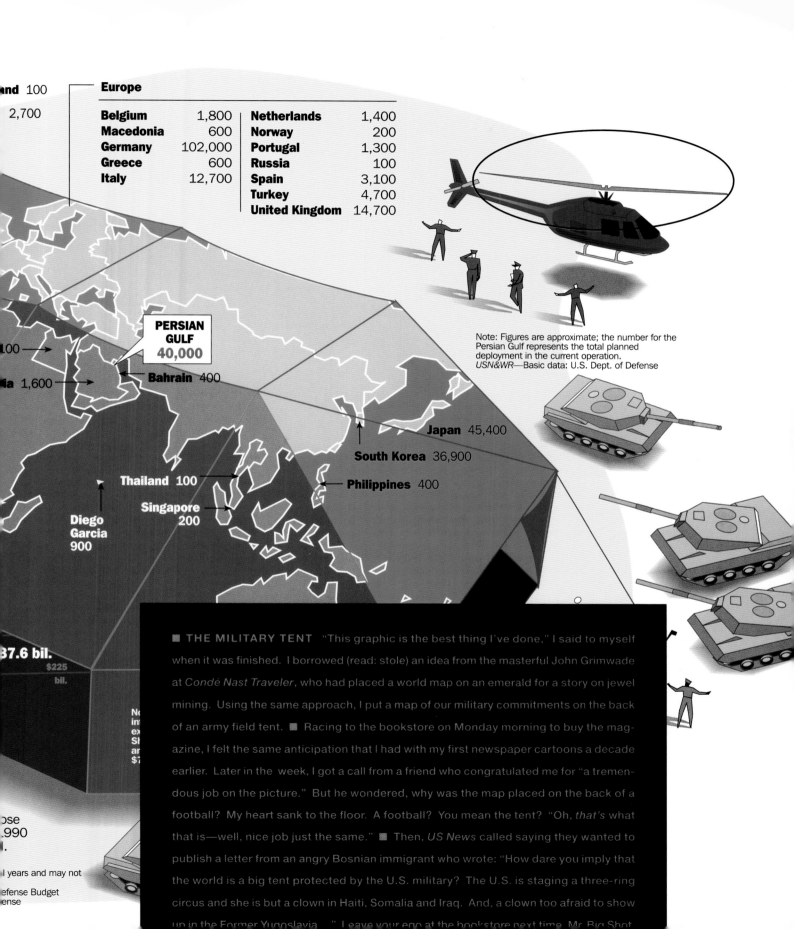

Europe

...and	100		
	2,700		
Belgium	1,800	Netherlands	1,400
Macedonia	600	Norway	200
Germany	102,000	Portugal	1,300
Greece	600	Russia	100
Italy	12,700	Spain	3,100
		Turkey	4,700
		United Kingdom	14,700

PERSIAN GULF **40,000**

...100 →

...ia **1,600** →

Bahrain 400

Note: Figures are approximate; the number for the Persian Gulf represents the total planned deployment in the current operation.
USN&WR—Basic data: U.S. Dept. of Defense

Japan 45,400

South Korea 36,900

Thailand 100

Philippines 400

Singapore 200

Diego Garcia 900

37.6 bil.
$225 bil.

...ose
.990

l years and may not

efense Budget
ense

■ **THE MILITARY TENT** "This graphic is the best thing I've done," I said to myself when it was finished. I borrowed (read: stole) an idea from the masterful John Grimwade at *Condé Nast Traveler*, who had placed a world map on an emerald for a story on jewel mining. Using the same approach, I put a map of our military commitments on the back of an army field tent. ■ Racing to the bookstore on Monday morning to buy the magazine, I felt the same anticipation that I had with my first newspaper cartoons a decade earlier. Later in the week, I got a call from a friend who congratulated me for "a tremendous job on the picture." But he wondered, why was the map placed on the back of a football? My heart sank to the floor. A football? You mean the tent? "Oh, *that's* what that is—well, nice job just the same." ■ Then, *US News* called saying they wanted to publish a letter from an angry Bosnian immigrant who wrote: "How dare you imply that the world is a big tent protected by the U.S. military? The U.S. is staging a three-ring circus and she is but a clown in Haiti, Somalia and Iraq. And, a clown too afraid to show up in the Former Yugoslavia..." I leave your ego at the bookstore next time, Mr. Big Shot

THE FRAUDS OF BCCI The investigation by *Time* magazine into the fraudulent dealings of the Bank of Credit and Commerce (BCCI) was published in 1991. The diagram for the story pictures the strands of the bank's global web. It also fairly represents the process of evolving graphics at the magazine. ■ Although the story had been developing for some months, our weekly production schedule all but prohibits work on a particular subject until the week of publication. Stephen Koepp, the editor in charge of this story, described to me a version of the connections between BCCI and its clients as he understood it. This is the sketch he drew while we talked (right top). It grew during our discussion, with parts added as he thought of them. There were still gaps in the information, even though we were discussing the diagram on the Wednesday before Friday's midnight deadline. ■ I transferred Steve's sketch to a full-size magazine spread (right middle). The organizing principle imposed on the information was a flow from left to right, starting with the bank's headquarters at the left, and then fanning out to the right as the BCCI connections became more complex. I made room for photographs of the main players (boxes with an x), even though I had no idea if they could be obtained. Also, I played with the form of lines connecting the boxes. Should they be stair-stepped from one to another, conforming to the arrangement of boxes, or should they be sweeping diagonally and dynamically across the space? ■ Almost immediately, I translated this hand-drawn version into computer terms (right, bottom). Now I could see everything more clearly, and could make easy distinctions between types of connections. For instance, overt transactions were solid lines, undercover ones were dotted lines. The flow of the information was still the most obvious one, left to right. Had I not made the first quick

TRANSLATING IDEAS The process of diagram-making for *Time* magazine is seen in a story about bank fraud with (from top) the editor's original sketch, its hand-drawn translation in the magazine's format, and its first computer rendition—all done in one day.

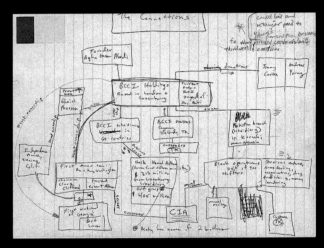

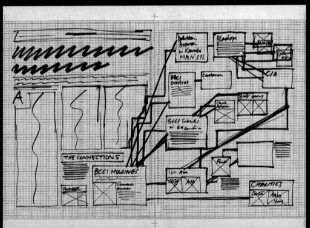

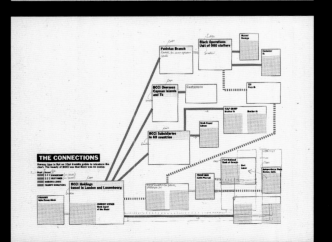

sketch by hand, enabling me to grasp the scope of the project and see its place on the printed page, this computer version would not have been achieved so easily. I went home for the night. ■ Next morning, on the train ride back to Manhattan (hence the wiggly lines), I doodled a different way of organizing the elements (below top). While a left-to-right arrangement had been a good first choice to help make the information easier to grasp, it precluded one level of the complexity of the BCCI connections—the

geographic locations of people and properties. The train doodle showed me that it was possible to arrange the boxes around a globe, and still keep their relationship to one another. Just visible in the sketch is a second new idea: that this was all the brainchild of one man. (I mistakenly drew a head with an Arab headdress; the founder of BCCI was a Pakistani.) ■ The commuter doodle was then drawn on the computer, placing the elements in their real geographic locations. It was now lunchtime on Thursday. Debby Wells, the diagram's researcher, needed a number of hours to check the facts against the written story, which itself was being edited to fit the space in the magazine. Meanwhile, I found a photograph of the bank's founder to use as reference for the background head. ■ On Friday night, with all research completed, legal questions answered and the drawing done, the final file was placed in the layout with Agha Abedi's profile jutting into the text. The layers of information in the diagram were carefully given graduated tones and colors according to their importance. The tones grew in strength starting from the base page (headlines and text), up through the profile, the map, to the top layer—the connections. ■ The story's diagram was not intended to simplify the contents of this complex web of connections by, for instance, leaving some of them out. It was intended to simplify the *understanding* of such complexity within the context of a general interest magazine.

TRANSFORMING IDEAS The process continued the next two days with new thoughts. A world globe introduced geography as a new organizing principle (doodle and computer drawing below), and a man's profile was added—the source of all the shenanigans.

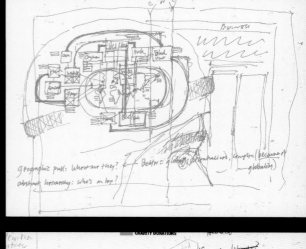

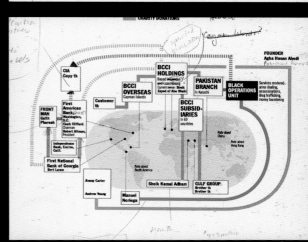

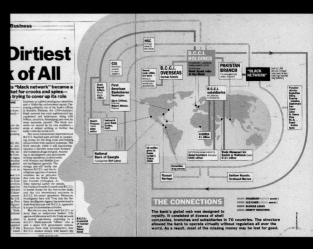

■ **TOOTHPASTE** During lectures I gave in the mid 1980s, I tried to explain graphically how much toothpaste is used every day in the United States. If you could squeeze
this amount out of tubes, you would create a white line 3000 miles long. After a few lectures, when I actually squeezed a whole tube of toothpaste onto a long roll of black
paper, I realized there was a better way. Audiences could understand the 3000 mile-
long quantity if I asked them to *imagine* a map of the country, and "draw" a white line
across it from coast to coast. Everyone has the shape of the U.S. in their minds already,
and they know it's about 3000 miles wide. The key to understanding the information
was to get people to picture the graphic for themselves: they *see* the amount in relation
to something they already know. So, I stopped the theatrical antics and got people to
conjure up their own images. Sometimes the best infographic can be just the idea of it.

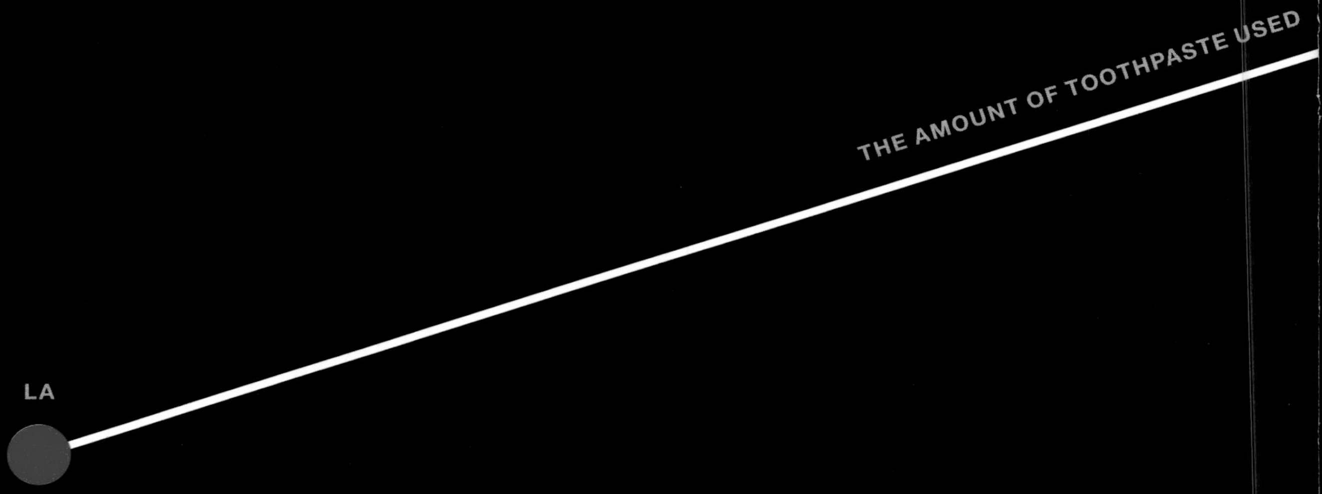

THE AMOUNT OF TOOTHPASTE USED

LA

EVERY DAY IN THE UNITED STATES

NY

There are 5,000 indigenous cultures in the world. Th[e]
facing possible extinction. The causes range from
In addition, most indigenous groups

NORTH
AMERICA

SOUTH
AMERICA

Innu
Canada
(1,200 left)
Military exercises
are forcing them
to leave their
homes

Hawaiians
Hawaii
(200,000–220,000 left)
Their land has been
lost to tourism and
energy projects

Lacandon
Maya
Mexico
(500 left)
Displaced by timber
industry and
cattle ranching

Kuna
Panama
(45,000–50,000 left)
Threatened
by logging

Guaja
Brazil
(400 left)
Threatened by
deforestation

Wau-Wau
Brazil
(1,000 left)
Devastated by
logging, mining
and settlers

Kogi
Colombia
(3,000–5,000 left)
Displaced by drug
trafficking

Waorani
Ecuador
(1,000 left)
Forced to abandon
their traditions

Juruna
Brazil
(150 left)
Relocated
by the
government

Nambiquara
Brazil
(600 left)
Displaced
by settlers

[...T]URES A series of posters intended for sec-[ondary]
[cla]ssrooms was produced for the *Time Education*
[po]ster *Endangered Cultures* estimates a total of
[...c]ultures in the world, then places and counts the
[peopl]e remaining in cultures now facing extinction. It
[...s] many threats the groups are facing, and the dif-
[...]e in maintaining rights to their own lands. Icon-[ic]
[d]escriptive marginalia represent the rich variety
[...]tures, and the traditions and survival tools (the
[...]es, the Aborigine boomerang) that may be lost.

Inuit
Alaska
Canada
Denmark
Greenland
(92,000 left)
Fighting over
their land
rights

Inuit hunters
wear goggles
with tiny slits to
protect the eyes
from the glare of
the snow. The
spear and rope
are used to
catch seals.

Iroquois
Canada
U.S.
(1,200 left)
Devastated by
pollution

The Iroquois
were originally
a league of
six Indian tribes—
Mohawk, Oneida,
Ondonaga, Cajuga,
Seneca and
Tuscarora. This
is a traditional
costume made
from European
cloth.

Hopi
Arizona
(7,000–9,000 left)
Devastated by
uranium mining
and nuclear testing

This Hopi girl
wears her hair
in traditional
butterfly style.

Yanomami
Brazil
Venezuela
(20,000 left)
Threatened by
illegal miners

A Yanomami
boy holds the
long bow and
arrows that
are still used
for hunting.

Tuareg
Sahara
(3,000,000 left)
Affected by
nuclear testing

Tuareg means
'people of the
veil'. They
wear long
black veils
around their
heads to shade
them from
the desert sun.

Expert
desert
Bushm[en]
live by
wild an[imals]
and ga[thering]
plants.

ows some of these groups of people——ones that are
tion and illegal mining to environmental pollution.
g for the rights to their homelands.

Saami
Scandinavia
(51,000 left)
Devastated by the effects of
the Chernobyl nuclear disaster

ASIA

Akha
China
Myanmar
Thailand
(360,000 left)
Have lost their
territorial rights

MIDDLE
EAST

Bhil
India
(120,000 left)
Displaced
by land
development

Tadvi
India
(10,000 left)
Displaced
by dam
projects

Jumma
Bangladesh
(600,000 left)
Victims of
massacres

Lumad
Philippines
(2,100,000 left)
Threatened by
logging, mining
and energy
projects

Onge
India
(100 left)
Relocated
by the
government

Dayak
Malaysia
(520,000 left)
Displaced
by logging

Yali
Indonesia
(40,000 left)
The government
is taking their
homelands

Hupla
Indonesia
(3,500 left)
Displaced
by mining

Vedda
Sri Lanka
(800 left)
Displaced by
a national park

Mentawa
Indonesia
(50,000 left)
Displaced
by logging

OCEANIA

Maoori
New Zealand
(400,000 left)
Disputes over
ownership of
their land

Nuba
Sudan
(44,000 left)
Caught in the
civil war

Gondi
India
(2,000,000 left)
Displaced by
deforestation

Aborigines
Australia
(170,000 left)
Disputes over ownership
of their land

Ainu
Japan
Russia
(16,500 left)
Fighting for
the right to
their own land

Pygmies
Central Africa
(150,000 left)
Displaced by
settlers and
industry

*This Nuba girl
carries water
back to her
family's
home every
day in the dry
season in
order to
survive.*

*Aborigines, the first Australians,
are expert hunters and fishers.
This Aborigine man uses a
boomerang to steady and aim
his spear. He can also use the
boomerang as a weapon for
hunting. The curve of the wood
enables the boomerang to make
a circular flight in the air, and
return to the thrower.*

*Older Ainu
people color
around their
mouths with a
dark stain. Here
ceremonial
beads are
worn with a
patterned coat
that resembles
a Japanese
kimono.*

*Pygmy is a term
used to describe
groups of people
whose average
height is less
than 4' 11".
African Pygmies
live in forests.*

*Gondi women wear a
variation of the
traditional Indian sari.*

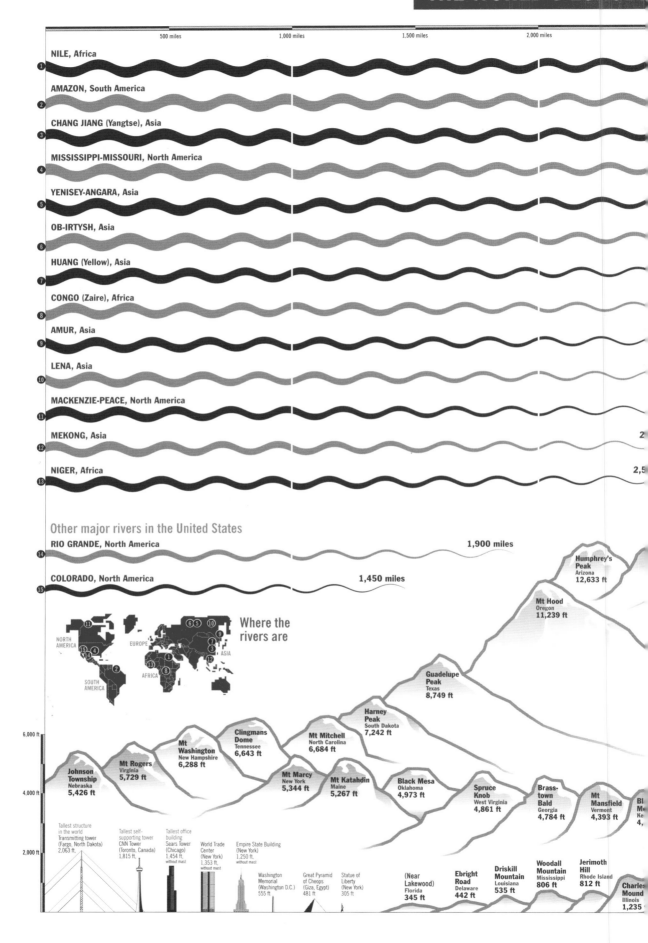

	500 miles	1,000 miles	1,500 miles	2,000 miles

1 NILE, Africa

2 AMAZON, South America

3 CHANG JIANG (Yangtse), Asia

4 MISSISSIPPI-MISSOURI, North America

5 YENISEY-ANGARA, Asia

6 OB-IRTYSH, Asia

7 HUANG (Yellow), Asia

8 CONGO (Zaire), Africa

9 AMUR, Asia

10 LENA, Asia

11 MACKENZIE-PEACE, North America

12 MEKONG, Asia 2

13 NIGER, Africa 2,5

Other major rivers in the United States

14 RIO GRANDE, North America 1,900 miles

15 COLORADO, North America 1,450 miles

Where the rivers are

NORTH AMERICA

EUROPE

ASIA

AFRICA

SOUTH AMERICA

Humphrey's Peak Arizona 12,633 ft

Mt Hood Oregon 11,239 ft

Guadelupe Peak Texas 8,749 ft

Harney Peak South Dakota 7,242 ft

Clingmans Dome Tennessee 6,643 ft

Mt Mitchell North Carolina 6,684 ft

Mt Washington New Hampshire 6,288 ft

Mt Rogers Virginia 5,729 ft

Mt Marcy New York 5,344 ft

Mt Katahdin Maine 5,267 ft

Black Mesa Oklahoma 4,973 ft

Spruce Knob West Virginia 4,861 ft

Brass-town Bald Georgia 4,784 ft

Mt Mansfield Vermont 4,393 ft

Johnson Township Nebraska 5,426 ft

Bl Me Ke 4,

6,000 ft

4,000 ft

2,000 ft

Tallest structure in the world Transmitting tower (Fargo, North Dakota) 2,063 ft,

Tallest self-supporting tower CNN Tower (Toronto, Canada) 1,815 ft,

Tallest office building Sears Tower (Chicago) 1,454 ft, without mast

World Trade Center (New York) 1,353 ft, without mast

Empire State Building (New York) 1,250 ft, without mast

Washington Memorial (Washington D.C.) 555 ft

Great Pyramid of Cheops (Giza, Egypt) 481 ft

Statue of Liberty (New York) 305 ft

(Near Lakewood) Florida 345 ft

Ebright Road Delaware 442 ft

Driskill Mountain Louisiana 535 ft

Woodall Mountain Mississippi 806 ft

Jerimoth Hill Rhode Island 812 ft

Charles Mound Illinois 1,235

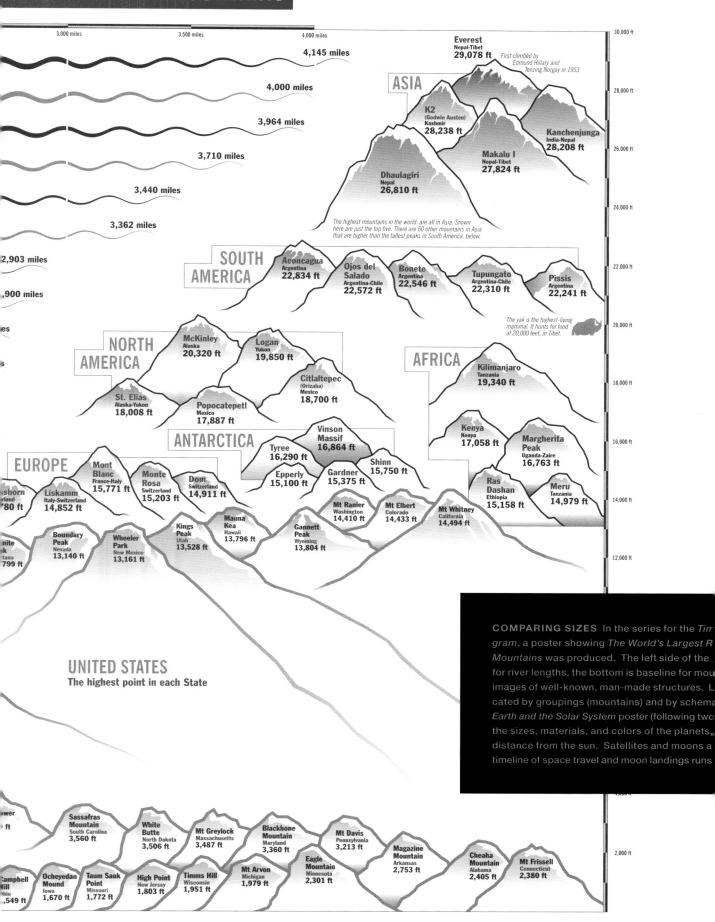

3,000 miles

3,500 miles

4,000 miles

4,145 miles

4,000 miles

3,964 miles

3,710 miles

3,440 miles

3,362 miles

2,903 miles

,900 miles

ASIA

Everest
Nepal-Tibet
29,078 ft

*First climbed by
Edmund Hillary and
Tenzing Norgay in 1953*

K2
(Godwin Austen)
Kashmir
28,238 ft

Kanchenjunga
India-Nepal
28,208 ft

Makalu I
Nepal-Tibet
27,824 ft

Dhaulagiri
Nepal
26,810 ft

*The highest mountains in the world. are all in Asia. Shown
here are just the top five. There are 60 other mountains in Asia
that are higher than the tallest peaks in South America, below.*

**SOUTH
AMERICA**

Aconcagua
Argentina
22,834 ft

**Ojos del
Salado**
Argentina-Chile
22,572 ft

Bonete
Argentina
22,546 ft

Tupungato
Argentina-Chile
22,310 ft

Pissis
Argentina
22,241 ft

*The yak is the highest-living
mammal. It hunts for food
at 20,000 feet, in Tibet.*

**NORTH
AMERICA**

McKinley
Alaska
20,320 ft

Logan
Yukon
19,850 ft

AFRICA

Kilimanjaro
Tanzania
19,340 ft

Citlaltepec
(Orizaba)
Mexico
18,700 ft

St. Elias
Alaska-Yukon
18,008 ft

Popocatepetl
Mexico
17,887 ft

ANTARCTICA

**Vinson
Massif**
16,864 ft

Kenya
Kenya
17,058 ft

**Margherita
Peak**
Uganda-Zaire
16,763 ft

Tyree
16,290 ft

Shinn
15,750 ft

EUROPE

**Mont
Blanc**
France-Italy
15,771 ft

**Monte
Rosa**
Switzerland
15,203 ft

Dom
Switzerland
14,911 ft

Epperly
15,100 ft

Gardner
15,375 ft

**Ras
Dashan**
Ethiopia
15,158 ft

Meru
Tanzania
14,979 ft

shorn
land
'80 ft

Liskamm
Italy-Switzerland
14,852 ft

Mt Ranier
Washington
14,410 ft

Mt Elbert
Colorado
14,433 ft

Mt Whitney
California
14,494 ft

nite
k
799 ft

**Boundary
Peak**
Nevada
13,140 ft

**Wheeler
Park**
New Mexico
13,161 ft

**Kings
Peak**
Utah
13,528 ft

**Mauna
Kea**
Hawaii
13,796 ft

**Gannett
Peak**
Wyoming
13,804 ft

UNITED STATES
The highest point in each State

COMPARING SIZES In the series for the *Tim*
gram, a poster showing *The World's Largest R*
Mountains was produced. The left side of the
for river lengths, the bottom is baseline for mou
images of well-known, man-made structures. L
cated by groupings (mountains) and by schema
Earth and the Solar System poster (following two
the sizes, materials, and colors of the planets
distance from the sun. Satellites and moons a
timeline of space travel and moon landings runs

wer
ft

**Sassafras
Mountain**
South Carolina
3,560 ft

**White
Butte**
North Dakota
3,506 ft

Mt Greylock
Massachusetts
3,487 ft

**Blackbone
Mountain**
Maryland
3,360 ft

Mt Davis
Pennsylvania
3,213 ft

**Magazine
Mountain**
Arkansas
2,753 ft

**Cheaha
Mountain**
Alabama
2,405 ft

Mt Frissell
Connecticut
2,380 ft

**Eagle
Mountain**
Minnesota
2,301 ft

Campbell
Hill
hio
,549 ft

**Ocheyedan
Mound**
Iowa
1,670 ft

**Taum Sauk
Point**
Missouri
1,772 ft

High Point
New Jersey
1,803 ft

Timms Hill
Wisconsin
1,951 ft

Mt Arvon
Michigan
1,979 ft

30,000 ft

28,000 ft

26,000 ft

24,000 ft

22,000 ft

20,000 ft

18,000 ft

16,000 ft

14,000 ft

12,000 ft

2,000 ft

Our Solar System has a central star (the Sun)
of 61 moons, or satellites. Most of th
earthlike—small and rocky. The next four are
outermost planet, Pluto, is different from th
than a planet. The Solar System also

SUN

Our sun is
a medium-
size star.
At its core,
where the
temperature
is 27 million
degrees
fahrenheit,
hydrogen is
converted
into helium
by nuclear
fusion.
The energy
produced is
heat and light.
The sun is five
billion years
old, and will
probably shine
for another five
billion years.
DIAMETER:
870,000 miles

The Sun and
the nine planets,
with their
satellites, are
all drawn to
the same scale.

At the far right,
the Earth is
enlarged for
a closer view.

MERCURY

Small and
heavily cratered
by meteorites,
this planet is
almost airless.
It rotates very
slowly, so that
one day on
Mercury is as
long as 176
days on Earth.
The surface is
very hot (800˚F)
on the sunny side,
and very cold
(−270˚F) on the
side facing away
from the Sun.
DIAMETER:
3,100 miles
DISTANCE
FROM THE SUN:
36 million miles

VENUS

This planet's
dense
atmosphere
makes it the
hottest in our
system, and
also the
brightest in the
sky (after the
Sun and Moon).
There are many
large volcanoes
on Venus; some
may be active.
DIAMETER:
7,700 miles
DISTANCE
FROM THE SUN:
67 million miles

EARTH

The only planet
known to
support life. The
atmosphere
protects us from
most of the
Sun's damaging
radiation, but
keeps in enough
heat to stop the
surface
temperature
from falling too
low. 70% of the
Earth's surface
is covered by
water.
DIAMETER:
7,913 miles
DISTANCE
FROM THE SUN:
93 million miles

1 moon

MARS

Iron-rich dust on
Mars gives it a red
appearance. There
are canyons 3,000
miles long which
were made by
water, but the only
water now is in the
polar icecaps.
DIAMETER:
4,216 miles
DISTANCE
FROM THE SUN:
142 million miles

7 moons

ASTEROID BELT
Between Mars and
Jupiter is a belt of
asteroids - rock and
iron fragments - which
are between one to
a thousand miles across.
When asteroids collide
parts may chip off
(meteoroids) and enter
the Earth's atmosphere
where they can be viewed
as shooting stars. On
rare occasions, they
crash into Earth as
meteorites.

JUPITER

The largest planet, it was first observed 300 years ago. Jupiter is a ball of
gas eleven times the size of Earth, and it has a faint ring of gas encircling
it. The Red Spot is a spiral of clouds three times wider than Earth.
DIAMETER
86,700 miles
DISTANCE
FROM THE SUN:
484 million miles

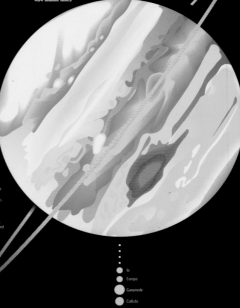

Io
Europa
Ganymede
Callisto

16 satellites

SATURN

This planet has an atmosphere of hydrog
comprise many tiny ringlets of icy lumps,
small particles to chunks many feet wide
seen from Earth with binoculars.
DIAMETER
71,500 miles
DISTANCE
FROM THE SUN:
887 million miles

18 satellites

THE MARCH INTO SPACE

1957	1958	1959	1960	1961	1962	1963	1964	1965	1966	1967	1968	1969	1970	1971	1972	19
Soviets launch *Sputnik 1* ("Fellow Traveler"), the first human-made satellite to orbit Earth; the space race begins.	First U.S. space vehicle (*Pioneer 4*) reaches the moon. Soviet *Luna 2* impacts the moon.			Soviets send the first human, cosmonaut Yuri Gagarin, into space. Alan Shepard is the first U.S. astronaut in space.	U.S. astronaut John Glen orbits Earth.					Three U.S. astronauts die in explosion on launch pad.		U.S. astronauts reach the Moon.				

that orbit it. They are accompanied by a total
wo kinds: the four nearest the Sun are
are composed of gas with a metallic core. The
onsists of ice, and may be more like a comet
ls, comets, meteoroids, gas and dust.

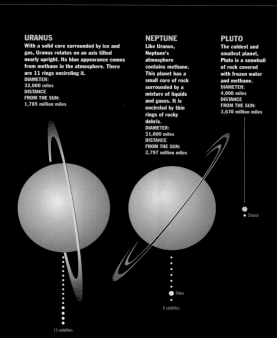

URANUS
With a solid core surrounded by ice and
gas, Uranus rotates on an axis tilted
nearly upright. Its blue appearance comes
from methane in the atmosphere. There
are 11 rings encircling it.
DIAMETER:
32,000 miles
DISTANCE
FROM THE SUN:
1,785 million miles

NEPTUNE
Like Uranus,
Neptune's
atmosphere
contains methane.
This planet has a
small core of rock
surrounded by a
mixture of liquids
and gases. It is
encircled by thin
rings of rocky
debris.
DIAMETER:
31,000 miles
DISTANCE
FROM THE SUN:
2,797 million miles

PLUTO
The coldest and
smallest planet,
Pluto is a snowball
of rock covered
with frozen water
and methane.
DIAMETER:
4,000 miles
DISTANCE
FROM THE SUN:
3,670 million miles

• Charon

• Triton

8 satellites

15 satellites

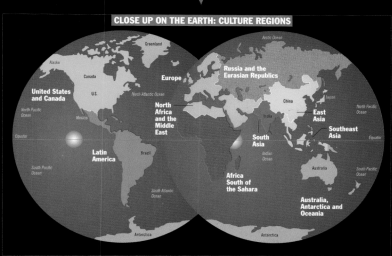

CLOSE UP ON THE EARTH: CULTURE REGIONS

Arctic Ocean

Greenland

Alaska

Canada

Europe

Russia and the
Eurasian Republics

United States
and Canada

U.S.

North Atlantic Ocean

China

Japan

North Pacific
Ocean

North
Africa
and the
Middle
East

India

East
Asia

North Pacific
Ocean

North Pacific
Ocean

Mexico

Southeast
Asia

Equator

South
Asia

Equator

Latin
America

Brazil

Indian
Ocean

Africa
South of
the Sahara

Australia

South Pacific
Ocean

South Pacific
Ocean

South Atlantic
Ocean

Australia,
Antarctica and
Oceania

Antarctica

Antarctica

A total of 12 men have walked on the Moon

Neil Armstrong, Edwin Aldrin	Apollo 11	July 1969
Charles Conrad, Alan Bean	Apollo 12	November 1969
Alan Shepard, Edgar Mitchell	Apollo 14	February 1971
David Scott, James Irwin	Apollo 15	July 1971
John Young, Charles Duke	Apollo 16	April 1972
Eugene Cernan, Harrison Schmitt	Apollo 17	December 1972

The **MOON**
has a diameter
of 2,155 miles,
which is just over
a quarter of
the size of
the Earth's

| 1976 | 1977 | 1978 | 1979 | 1980 | 1981 | 1982 | 1983 | 1984 | 1985 | 1986 | 1987 | 1988 | 1989 | 1990 | 1991 | 1992 | 1993 | 1994 |

1977
U.S. *Voyager
2* begins its
12-year
journey to
the edge of
the solar
system.

1979
Sunspot
activity
burns up
Skylab;
debris
crashes to
Earth (no
injuries).

1981
U.S. launches
first space
shuttle.

1983
Sally Ride
becomes the
first U.S.
woman to
head into
space.

Guion Bluford, Jr.,
is the first
African
American
into space.

1986
Space shuttle
Challenger
explodes,
killing seven
astronauts.

Soviets launch
their first space
station, *Mir*.

Costa Rican-
born Franklin
Chang-Diaz is
the first Latino
into space.

1988
U.S. resumes
the space
shuttle
program.

1990
U.S. launches
the Hubble
space
telescope.

1993
U.S. sends
Endeavour
to repair the
Hubble
telescope.

1994
U.S. and Russia
plan joint
space venture,
including
docking of U.S.
shuttle with
Mir space
station.

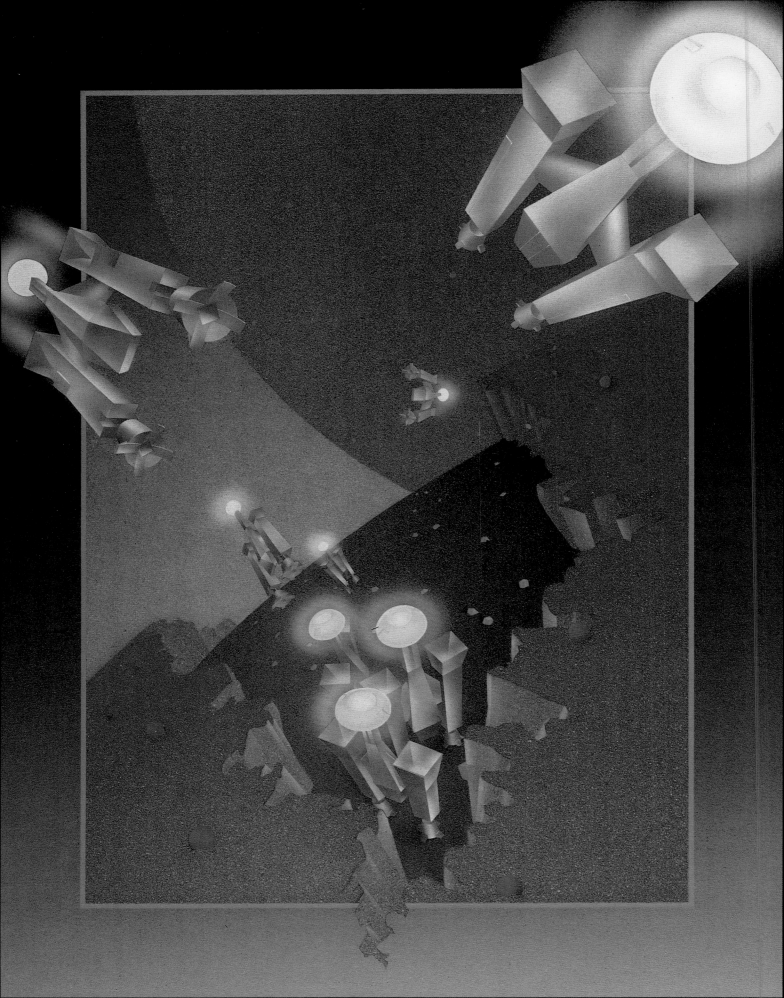

CENTOCOR ANNUAL REPORT One of the first of many maxims I learned from Richard Wurman (almost literally at his knee; it was 22 years ago) was, "People only understand something relative to something they already understand." To which I added my own modest corollary: "The best way to show how something works is not necessarily to show what it looks like." From the combination of these two statements can be derived, I think, a rationale and a checklist for all functional diagrams and non-geographic cartography: how does it work; how can you use it; what does it feel like; how can you relate to it? ■ Centocor is a monoclonal antibody-based biotechnology company for whom my firm produced annual reports. First, a little science to explain the metaphors used in the illustrations shown. *Antibodies* are the response by the body's immune system to the presence of *antigens,* which are features on the surface of cells that reveal that they are diseased or controlled by a hostile bacterium. Antibodies have a lock-to-key relation-

TRANSLATING BIOTECHNOLOGY A Star Wars metaphor was created to visually dramatize the cultivating of antibodies to combat hostile antigens on the surface of cells in the body. Good is arrayed against evil as a flight of antibodies locates and locks on the antigens in a fissure of a recently dead heart cell (opposite). Antibodies intercept a fusillade of lethal endotoxin missiles from dying bacteria before they can unleash their deadly effect (below).

ship to the specific antigens that stimulate them. *Monoclonal* refers to the exact duplicative process by which clones of a desired antibody are sowed and harvested. In this report, the objective was to create

a dramatic vision of the future possibilities of monoclonal antibody-based biotechnology and pharmaceuticals. ■ Having avoided high school biology and physics, done poorly at chemistry, and almost failed college geology and astronomy, I have long felt that metaphor was the key to understanding science. And, interior pictures of the body don't offer many clues to how it works—the processes are invisible. So, after having the principles and functions of Centocor's products of the future explained by a number of gracious, patient scientists, the metaphor that came to me was *Star Wars* (Lucas, not Reagan). The antibody became the colonizing spaceship discovering new planets, the warrior for good arrayed against evil, the scout leading armored divisions into battle, the protector of space stations about to be boarded by a fleet of enemy fighters. The captions, which the client and I wrote jointly, reinforce the metaphor through the use of an active, Star Wars vocabulary. ■ The results altered my point of view. My confidence in geometric, abstract, symbolic vocabularies changed to my later and current belief in the effectiveness of metaphor.

■ **CREDITS:** Concept and design direction: Joel Katz; Design: Joel Katz and Daniel Picard; Artwork: Daniel Picard and Stacey Lewis; Firm: Katz Wheeler Design.

EXTENDING THE METAPHOR The Star Wars continue as antibodies inside a blood vessel scramble to occupy sites on a group of activated platelets, blocking the formation of a potentially lethal blood clot (below). Immuno-combination molecules, armed with macrophages and killer T-cells, close in to attack a cancer cell (opposite). With these Centocor report images, captions described the body processes in both Star Wars and biotechnological terms.

dees at the Fifth International Pediatric Nephrology Symposium held in Philadelphia in 1980, was used as the basis for discussion in many of the symposium's breakout sessions. The importance of its data, which was new at the time, was of less interest to me than the application of a familiar graphic notation vocabulary to a kind of process data to which it was not customarily applied. ■ Visualizing process data—arranging the components of time—is a crucial and difficult aspect of graphing. I was told the usual way of dealing with the poster's kind of information—the ability of a newborn infant's kidneys to deal with insufficiencies and oversufficiencies of salt, water and acid—is to use leveled or angled lines across a graph to indicate a continuing and indefinite process. For example, kidneys maintaining the balance of inflow and outflow would all be represented by a horizontal line. Whether the inflow was theoretically insufficient (normal),

or oversufficient would be indicated by the horizontal line's position on the y-axis. ■ We decided that the information would be more clearly understandable, and the variations between infant kidneys of different "ages" more easily compared, if we graphed the data as if the kidneys' objective was to reduce the quantity of salt, water, or acid to baseline over the 24-hour period required to maintain health. Thus, the slope of the graph clearly indicates that functional kidneys slow down to conserve insufficiencies, and speed up to get rid of oversufficiencies. Any graph that does not end at baseline indicates a serious health problem. When a sense of graphic volume is added to the graph, the kidney's objective is much more clear: get rid of everything that came in, no more and no less. So, the new method of notation was able to reveal the processing of volumes, both in and out, in a direct and visual way, reducing the need for mentally gymnastic, numerically-driven conclusions. ■ For this work, the International Paediatric Nephrology Association (IPNA) made me an honorary life member, one of the awards of which I am most proud. ■ CREDITS: Design: Joel Katz; Airbrush artwork: James Manos; Design firm: Katz Wheeler Design.

TRANSLATING NEPHROLOGY Traditionally, a simple straight or angled line graph showed the balance or imbalance (outflow versus inflow) of volumes processed by the kidneys of a newborn infant (below, left column). The line represented a continuous, ongoing process—the essential message was the position of the line, high or low, on the y-axis. But, knowing that the basic objective of the kidneys is to reduce the processing of volumes to baseline over a 24-hour period, led to a better, more informative picture of the kidneys' process (right column). The new graphs appeared on a poster (opposite) and became the basis for seminar discussion.

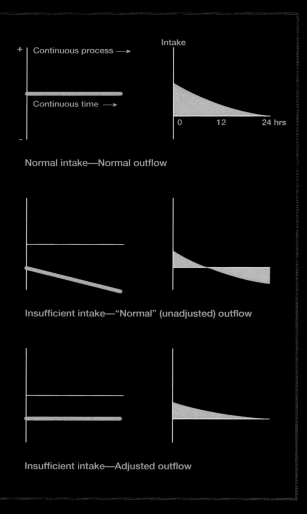

Normal intake—Normal outflow

Insufficient intake—"Normal" (unadjusted) outflow

Insufficient intake—Adjusted outflow

This poster presents a developmental concept of three critical renal tubular functions; sodium balance, water balance, and acid excretion. Preservation of balance (homeostasis) is depicted as a function of developmental age, under conditions of normal, increased, and decreased intake of sodium, water, and acid. Failure to restore homeostasis after an increased or decreased intake is shown as a net positive or negative balance between 24 and 48 hours after challenge, and is depicted in red as a state of disease. The degree of imbalance is indicated by the height of the bars above or below the plane of balance.

Ce placard présente une idée développementale de trois fonctions importantes des tubules rénaux: la balance de sodium, la balance d'eau et l'excretion d'acide. L'homéostase est présenté en fonction de l'âge développementale, sous conditions de l'apport normal, augmenté ou diminué de sodium, de l'eau et de l'acide. L'incapacité de restorer l'homéostase après l'apport augmenté ou diminué est présenté comme une balance (nette) positive ou négative entre 24 et 48 heures après la provocation; ceci est décrit en rouge comme état malade. Le degré de déséquilibre est indiqué par l'hauteur des barres au-dessus ou au-dessous du plan de balance.

Dieses Plakat illustriert das Entwicklungsprinzip der drei wichtigsten tubulären Funktionen der Niere: Natrium-Haushalt, Wasser-Regulation und Säure-Ausscheidung. Erhaltung dieser Regulationen(Homöostase) ist als Funktion des somatischen Alters dargestellt unter Bedingungen von normaler, erhöhter und erniedrigter Zufuhr von Natrium, Wasser und Säure. Krankheitszustände sind rot gekennzeichnet und bedeuten Unfähigkeit die normale Homöostase zu bewahren unter erhöhter oder erniedrigter Zufuhr von Natrium, Wasser und Säure und sind dargestellt als positive oder negative Bilanz gemessen 24 bis 48 Stunden nach entsprechener Belastung.

Su questo affisso si vuole rappresentare, lo sviluppo delle tre funzioni tubulari renali, cioe, l'equilibrio del sodio, l'equilibrio dell'acqua, e l'escrezione d'acidi. La preservazione dell'equilibrio (omeostasi) viene rappresentata come funzione dell'età, questo in condizioni normali oppure in casi dove l'ingestione di sodio, acqua ed acidi sia aumentato oppure diminuito. Il mancato restauro delloomeostasi entre il 24 e 48 ore sequenti alla provoca viene considerato come stato di malattia e viene mostrato qui in rosso. Il grado di equilibrio viene indicato qui, dall'altezza delle sbarre al di sopra e al di sotto della linea d'equilibrio.

このポスターにはナトリウム バランス、水バランス、酸の損消という三つの大切な腎尿細管の機能が発育成長時にいかにして行きかという概念が示してあります。つまりナトリウム、水、及び酸の摂取が正常である時、増加又は減少した時にこのバランスがいかに保たれるかということ(ホメオスターシス)を発育令に応じて図示されています。これらの物質の摂取が多すぎたり、少なすぎたためにホメオスターシスを回復できなくなった状態は24時間後、48時間以内に正味の正又は負のバランスとして網的状態を赤で示しています。バランスのズレの度合は棒グラフの高さとして上(正)又は下(負)に示してあります。

Este cartel presenta un concepto del desarrollo de tres funciones criticas en el sistema tubular del riñón: equilibrio del sodio, del agua, y de la excreción de acidos. La conservación de estos equilibrios (homeostasis) se representa como una función de la edad del desarrollo, bajo condiciones de consumo de agua, sodio y acido, normales, aumentadas y disminuidas. El fracaso de restaurar la homeostasis despues de consumir estas substancias en cantidades abnormales, altas y bajas, esta representado como un equilibrio neto positivo o negativo entre 24 y 48 horas siguiendo al reto, y esta pintado en rojo como un estado de enfermedad. El grado de desequilibrio esta indicado por la altura de las barras arriba y debajo del nivel de equilibrio.

Developmental
Nephrology

Fifth
International
Pediatric
Nephrology
Symposium

6-10 October 1980

Philadelphia
Pennsylvania

Design: Katz Wheeler

© October 1980

■ **DEVELOPMENT MARKETING MAPS FOR PENN'S LANDING** These two map spreads are from a brochure aimed at marketing waterfront sites for development. The map series starts with a satellite photograph of the region, and ends with the map shown of the eastern half of Center City in Philadelphia, indicating the development site and its road connections. ■ It is the five-county map that is of most interest to me. For many years I have revered the work of Harry Beck for the London Underground, in which natural as well as man-made resources conformed to 45°/90° diagrammatic notation. It suddenly struck me that geographic and diagrammatic vocabularies were not necessarily incompatible. When appropriately assigned, the payoff is significant: a geographic, virtually geographic, or faux geographic base has credibility and the comfort of familiarity, and it can be related to normal and strictly geographic "gas station" maps. The combination responds effectively to showing the congestion of central cities, true time and distance realities, and it is easily followed and understood. ■ Convincing in its geographic verisimilitude, this map actually uses a sliding scale: Philadelphia city is about twice the scale of the surrounding counties, and the scale of the counties diminishes very slightly at their extremities.

MAPPING SITE DEVELOPMENT A brochure was produced to market waterfront building sites in Center City, Philadelphia. The five-county map (below) uses a combination of geographic and diagrammatic vocabularies. While convincing in geographic appearance, it actually uses sliding scales to enlarge areas with more congested detail. Other maps focus on the site area (opposite); historical and contemporary images leaven the pages throughout.

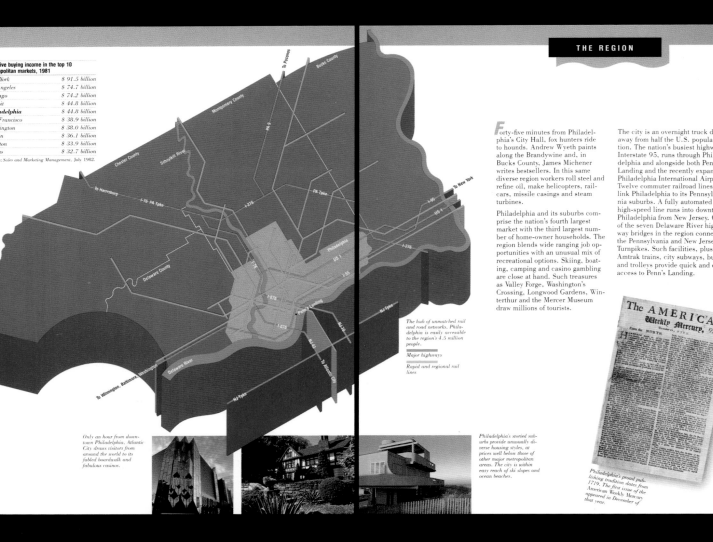

THE REGION

five buying income in the top 10 politan markets, 1981	
York	$ 91.5 billion
ngeles	$ 74.7 billion
go	$ 74.2 billion
t	$ 44.8 billion
delphia	$ 44.8 billion
Francisco	$ 38.9 billion
ington	$ 38.0 billion
n	$ 36.1 billion
ton	$ 33.9 billion
s	$ 32.7 billion

: Sales and Marketing Management, July 1982.

Forty-five minutes from Philadelphia's City Hall, fox hunters ride to hounds. Andrew Wyeth paints along the Brandywine and, in Bucks County, James Michener writes bestsellers. In this same diverse region workers roll steel and refine oil, make helicopters, railcars, missile casings and steam turbines.

Philadelphia and its suburbs comprise the nation's fourth largest market with the third largest number of home-owner households. The region blends wide ranging job opportunities with an unusual mix of recreational options. Skiing, boating, camping and casino gambling are close at hand. Such treasures as Valley Forge, Washington's Crossing, Longwood Gardens, Winterthur and the Mercer Museum draw millions of tourists.

The city is an overnight truck d away from half the U.S. popula tion. The nation's busiest highw Interstate 95, runs through Phi delphia and alongside both Pen Landing and the recently expan Philadelphia International Airp Twelve commuter railroad lines link Philadelphia to its Pennsyl nia suburbs. A fully automated high-speed line runs into downt Philadelphia from New Jersey. (of the seven Delaware River hig way bridges in the region conne the Pennsylvania and New Jerse Turnpikes. Such facilities, plus Amtrak trains, city subways, bu and trolleys provide quick and a access to Penn's Landing.

The hub of unmatched rail and road networks. Philadelphia is easily accessible to the region's 4.5 million people.

Major highways

Rapid and regional rail lines

Only an hour from downtown Philadelphia, Atlantic City draws visitors from around the world to its fabled boardwalk and fabulous casinos.

Philadelphia's storied suburbs provide unusually diverse housing styles, at prices well below those of other major metropolitan areas. The city is within easy reach of ski slopes and ocean beaches.

The AMERICA
Weekly Mercury,

Philadelphia's proud publishing tradition dates from 1719. The first issue of the American Weekly Mercury appeared in December of that year.

But, the relationship of the diagram to the geography, and the relationship of each aspect in the diagram to every other, are true. ■ The dimensionality of these maps is entirely decorative, fitting nicely with what I call the Caesar Condition. Like Gaul, all information is divided into three parts: information, which must be communicated; misinformation, which must not be communicated; and uninformation, where one can play.

■ **CREDITS:** Design: Joel Katz; Artwork: Stacey Lewis; Firm: Katz Wheeler Design.

■ **HEADS-UP MAPS / PENNSYLVANIA DEPARTMENT OF TRANSPORTATION**

I first became interested in maps when I had to design a book of them for Geneva, Switzerland. In them I had color coding, but otherwise only cosmetic control; as the noncartographer-designer, I remained a prisoner of geography, even for issues like circulation and movement which are experiential and time-distance based rather than geographic. We have been doing maps for the Pennsylvania Department of Transportation for 10 years. They fall pretty much into three categories: static maps, which show an area in which certain things are happening (construction, closures and the like); detour maps, which are movement-driven and show how one gets from point A to point B when the usual route is closed), and road-resource diagrams, which show a length of road with all its exits, connections and signing. Because each of these map types has unique information and functions, each occupies a different position in the spectrum

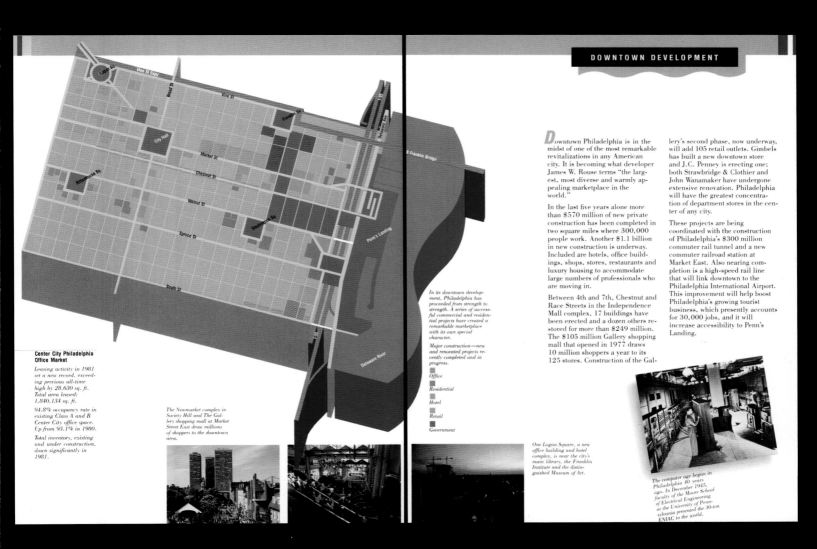

DOWNTOWN DEVELOPMENT

Center City Philadelphia Office Market

Leasing activity in 1981 set a new record, exceeding previous all-time high by 28,630 sq. ft. Total area leased: 1,840,134 sq. ft.

94.8% occupancy rate in existing Class A and B Center City office space. Up from 93.1% in 1980.

Total inventory, existing and under construction, down significantly in 1981.

In its downtown development, Philadelphia has proceeded from strength to strength. A series of successful commercial and residential projects have created a remarkable marketplace with its own special character.

Major construction—new and renovated projects recently completed and in progress.

■ Office
■ Residential
■ Hotel
■ Retail
■ Government

The Newmarket complex in Society Hill and The Gallery shopping mall at Market Street East draw millions of shoppers to the downtown area.

One Logan Square, a new office building and hotel complex, is near the city's main library, the Franklin Institute and the distinguished Museum of Art.

Downtown Philadelphia is in the midst of one of the most remarkable revitalizations in any American city. It is becoming what developer James W. Rouse terms "the largest, most diverse and warmly appealing marketplace in the world."

In the last five years alone more than $570 million of new private construction has been completed in two square miles where 300,000 people work. Another $1.1 billion in new construction is underway. Included are hotels, office buildings, shops, stores, restaurants and luxury housing to accommodate large numbers of professionals who are moving in.

Between 4th and 7th, Chestnut and Race Streets in the Independence Mall complex, 17 buildings have been erected and a dozen others restored for more than $249 million. The $105 million Gallery shopping mall that opened in 1977 draws 10 million shoppers a year to its 125 stores. Construction of the Gal-

lery's second phase, now underway, will add 105 retail outlets. Gimbels has built a new downtown store and J.C. Penney is erecting one; both Strawbridge & Clothier and John Wanamaker have undergone extensive renovation. Philadelphia will have the greatest concentration of department stores in the center of any city.

These projects are being coordinated with the construction of Philadelphia's $300 million commuter rail tunnel and a new commuter railroad station at Market East. Also nearing completion is a high-speed rail line that will link downtown to the Philadelphia International Airport. This improvement will help boost Philadelphia's growing tourist business, which presently accounts for 30,000 jobs, and it will increase accessibility to Penn's Landing.

The computer age began in Philadelphia 40 years ago. In December 1945, faculty of the Moore School of Electrical Engineering at the University of Pennsylvania presented the 30-ton ENIAC to the world.

from the geographic to the diagrammatic. ■ We did our first heads-up map for Penn-DOT about five years ago. In these maps, the direction of travel is always towards the top of the map. In this way, a right turn on the map represents a right turn in reality. The sight of exasperated drivers and their loyal navigators turning their maps around in frustration in order to orient themselves (and then, of course, not being able to read any type on the map), is eloquent testimony to the need. John Ogilby tried to address the perceptual reality that your travelling direction is always ahead of you in his *Britannia,* an atlas of scroll maps of English roads, in 1675. Ahead of you was always up, the north arrow serves to tell you what compass direction you were taking. His maps were terrific if you were going, say, from London to Liverpool, (the type was right side up), but less so if you were going from Liverpool to London. ■ The map shown below was our third heads-up. When held vertically, it avoids what I call the Ogilby Syndrome (the concept is brilliant, but the execution works only half the time) by printing the type both

right side up and upside down. Type running the long dimension doesn't really need to be repeated, as we have all learned to read either up or down, personal preference notwithstanding. ■ Virtually all of

MAPPING DIRECTION In "heads-up" maps for the Pennsylvania Department of of Transportation, the direction of travel is always towards the top of the map. A right turn on the map will be a right in your car. These maps are bi-directional; if you want to go in the opposite direction, you simply turn the map around. Text is repeated for reading easily no matter how the map is held. The map shown extends onto the following page: it is 35.5 inches long.

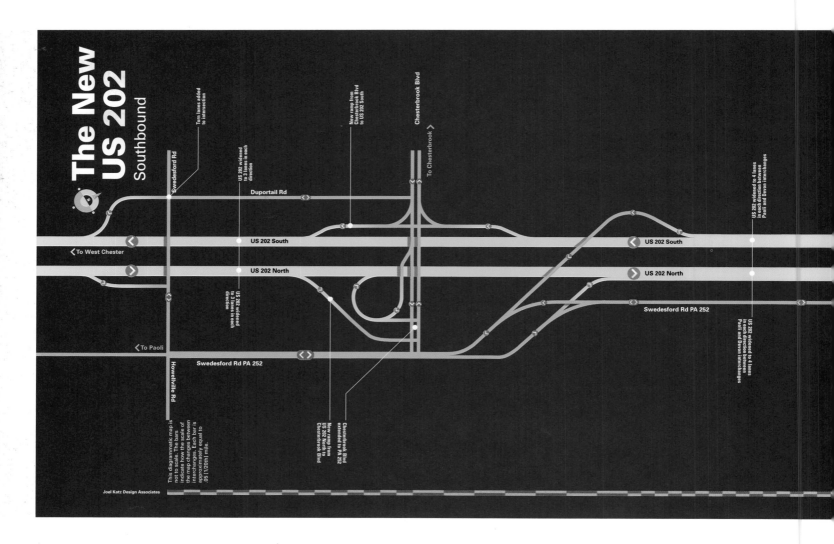

The New US 202
Southbound

Joel Katz Design Associates

This diagrammatic map is not to scale. The bars indicate how the scale of the map changes between interchanges. Each bar is approximately equal to .05 (1/20th) mile.

To West Chester

To Paoli

Swedesford Rd

Howellville Rd

Duportail Rd

Turn lanes added to intersection

US 202 widened to 3 lanes in each direction

US 202 widened to 3 lanes in each direction

New ramp from Chesterbrook Blvd to US 202 South

New ramp from US 202 North to Chesterbrook Blvd

Chesterbrook Blvd extended to PA 252

Chesterbrook Blvd

To Chesterbrook

Swedesford Rd PA 252

US 202 South

US 202 North

US 202 South

US 202 North

Swedesford Rd PA 252

US 202 widened to 4 lanes in each direction between Paoli and Devon interchanges

US 202 widened to 4 lanes in each direction between Paoli and Devon interchanges

our work for PennDOT folds down to roughly 4"x 9". This map unfolds to 35.5" high. It reveals the changes that are going to be made to a 4.25-mile stretch of a very busy suburban route with an extremely congested expressway interchange. In addition to being bi-directional, it incorporates other features I have evolved as a cartographer. It has a changing scale between interchanges to permit the small but very complex lengths of road to be enlarged, and long featureless lengths of road to be reduced. The difference in scales is quite dramatic. Color bands are used to code road types and route names. Color blending signals the transitions between one route or type of road and another.

■ **CREDITS:** Design and electronic artwork: Joel Katz; Design firm: Joel Katz Design Associates. ■ **URBAN ICONS** My urban icons project is more about process than product, the process of exploring functional and geometric, rather than geographic, relationships of city sites. It indulges and reinforces my anti-geographic bias (that the world is flat, that the sun moves around the earth, that trains travel in a straight line), and gives me the opportunity to create icons for cities rather than deities. My impetus was the serendipitous combination of two experiences. One was the design of dinnerware for The Rittenhouse Hotel in Philadelphia, based on the city's 1682 plan by William Penn and Thomas Holme; the other was a visit to the archeological crypt under the *parvis* of Notre Dame in Paris. I was struck in both cases by the geometries conceived—some

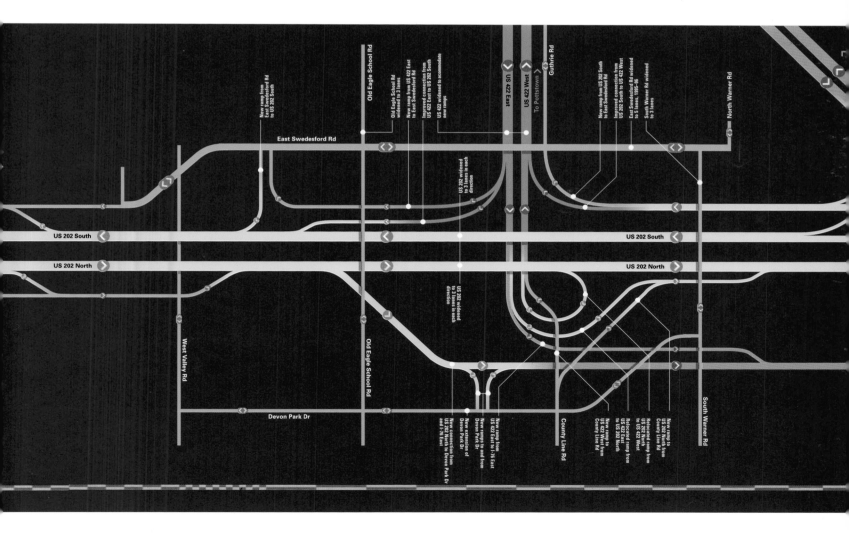

intentionally, most "accidentally"—by the original settlers/ builders/planners, which were added to, reinforced, obscured, or redefined by centuries of development. Like Philadelphia, present-day Paris may be perceived as maintaining its original organizational "intention," while Rome and London may not. ■ I develop an urban icon with a process I call fictional archaeology. I begin with a circular outline of a city (homage to the earliest walled Paris), then I explore the relationships among its geographic features, open space, movement axes and important structures. I do this with a reflective study of maps and views from historical sources, and personal perceptions. Begun in 1988, the icons have begun to share certain symbolic elements, as well as literary and historical allusions: Venice is split into a yin-yang by the Grand Canal, Rome's Aurelian wall is reconstructed as a cross. Although scale is fluid, the relationship of elements remains true, not unlike successful diagrammatic movement maps. ■ **CREDITS:** Concept and design: Joel Katz. ■ Final note: Every individual in a design office, I believe, participates in a shared enterprise of values simply by virtue of his or her presence. To anyone who worked on these projects whose name I have inadvertently omitted, and to all those with whom I have worked over the years—colleagues, clients, and printers—my deepest thanks and appreciation.

MAPPING RELATIONSHIPS Icons of historic cities were created to show functional and geometric relationships. Organized symbols for natural features, spaces, movement axes, and prominent structures represent cities like Rome and London (opposite).

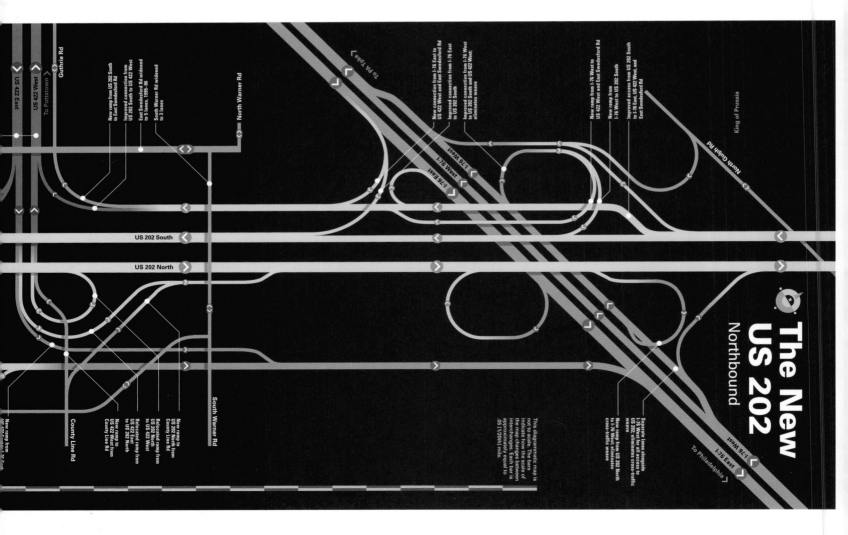

The New US 202
Northbound

ROMA

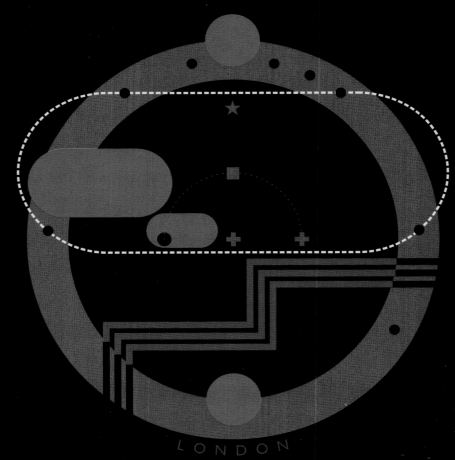

LONDON

LOUVRE

PROJECTS THAT INVOLVE making complex information understandable come to us in all shapes and sizes. Sometimes the project is a massive publication system or a series of textbooks. It can be a complicated retail branding or identity program. Often it is a wayfinding and signage system for a complex building. However, some basic design principles apply across all categories, and generally, the more complicated the problem, the simpler the solution must be. ■ These projects take years to complete. They are a true test of communication design, patience and tenacity, and leave little room for creative self-indulgence. ■ Our experience shows that there are two steps to solving these problems successfully. First is to "engineer" the solution correctly, focusing on the invisible infrastructure until the raw concept emerges. Second is to provide a visible "architecture" which communicates how the system works and engages people to try it, trust it and ultimately rely on it. ■ Understanding the users and appreciating their lack of sophistication by employing the obvious are often key to finding the right solution. Designers sometimes have a fear of being "too obvious." But, when solving complex problems, the obvious may be just what the end user needs. ■ **SIGNAGE AT THE LOUVRE** After winning an international competition to design a signage system for the Louvre, we faced the daunting task of moving eight million visitors annually through one of the world's most complicated museums. ■ To make things worse, we had to consider its multi-lingual audience, the contrasting architectural styles of I.M. Pei's "pyramid" and the old palace, and the constant relocation of the museum's collections. After considering many ap-

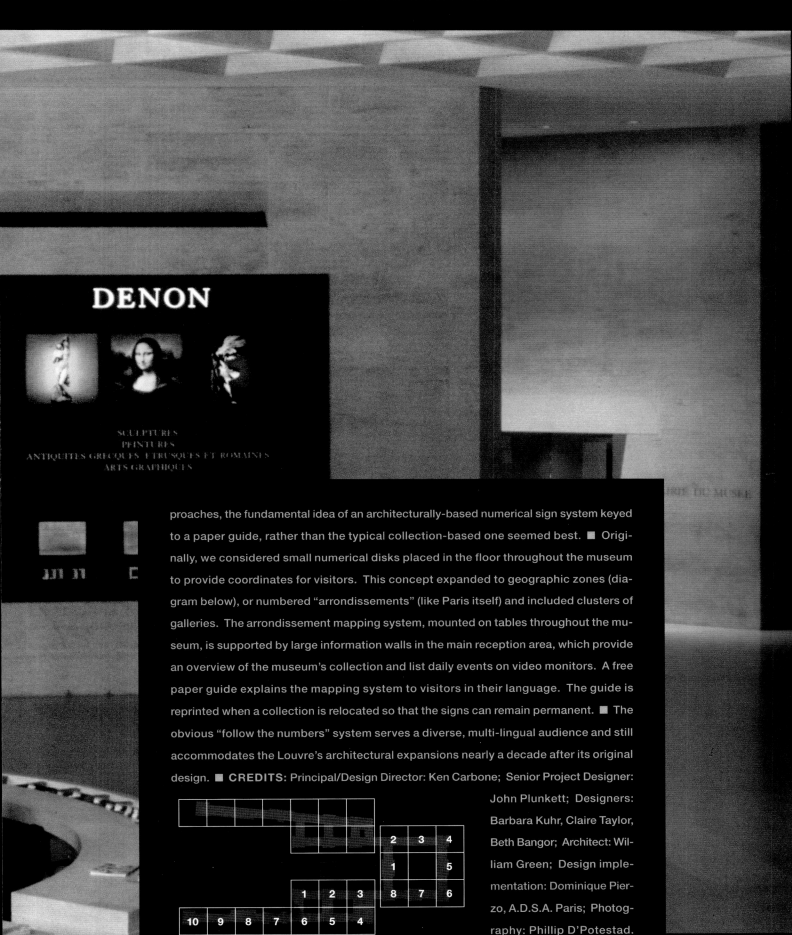

DENON

SCULPTURES
PEINTURES
ANTIQUITES GRECQUES, ETRUSQUES ET ROMAINES
ARTS GRAPHIQUES

proaches, the fundamental idea of an architecturally-based numerical sign system keyed to a paper guide, rather than the typical collection-based one seemed best. ■ Originally, we considered small numerical disks placed in the floor throughout the museum to provide coordinates for visitors. This concept expanded to geographic zones (diagram below), or numbered "arrondissements" (like Paris itself) and included clusters of galleries. The arrondissement mapping system, mounted on tables throughout the museum, is supported by large information walls in the main reception area, which provide an overview of the museum's collection and list daily events on video monitors. A free paper guide explains the mapping system to visitors in their language. The guide is reprinted when a collection is relocated so that the signs can remain permanent. ■ The obvious "follow the numbers" system serves a diverse, multi-lingual audience and still accommodates the Louvre's architectural expansions nearly a decade after its original design. ■ **CREDITS:** Principal/Design Director: Ken Carbone; Senior Project Designer: John Plunkett; Designers: Barbara Kuhr, Claire Taylor, Beth Bangor; Architect: William Green; Design implementation: Dominique Pierzo, A.D.S.A. Paris; Photography: Phillip D'Potestad.

■ SIGNAGE FOR WORLD BANK Designing a signage program for the new World Bank headquarters in Washington D.C. provided similar challenges to those at the Louvre. ■ This building, designed by Kohn Pedersen Fox, takes up a full city block, accommodates 5000 people in multi-national offices, and has thirteen floors above grade and five below. ■ Our "zone" plan for wayfinding, located at primary orientation points throughout the building, is designed to present the complex structure in a simple and understandable way. It gives an overview of the building, divides the building into eight parts and reinforces the pinwheel circulation path developed by KPF. Each of the eight zone parts represents a "block" of one hundred numbers or office "addresses." ■ Stylistically, the signs reflect KPF aesthetic in form, materials and finishes, yet provide enough contrast to the building's environment to serve their purpose as clear guideposts. ■ **CREDITS:** Principal/Design Director: Ken Carbone; Associate/Design Director: Claire Taylor; Designer: Kamol Prateepmanowong; Photography: Jeff Goldberg.

13

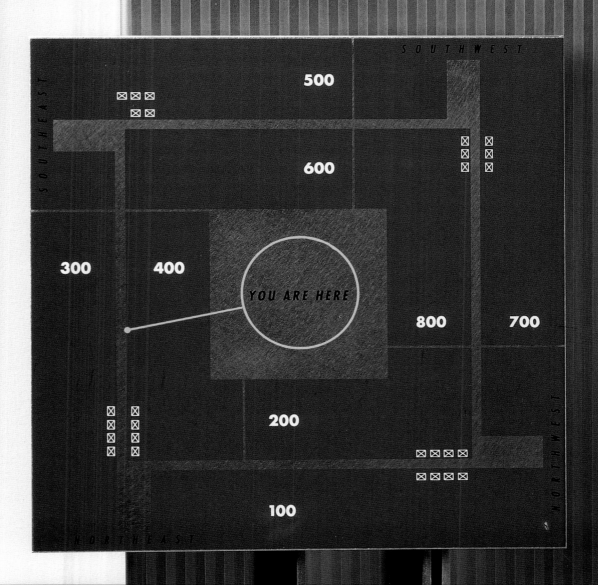

Putnam
Investors
Fund

Putnam
Global
Growth
Fund

Putnam
Voyager
Fund

A strategy that lets you chart
a course for growth

100% increase in just 10 years

Putnam Voyager invests in smaller compan...
grow over time and in larger, more establish...
This combination has proven an effective w...

ABOVE-AVERAGE GROWTH. Th...

well-suited for aggressive-growth investo...

accept som...

GROWTH OF A $10,000 INVESTMENT $45,047
Class A share performance
▨ Account value if you had let
   income and capital gains grow
▨ Account value if you took
   income in cash $42,341

■ **PUTNAM INVESTMENTS** Putnam Investments is a Boston-based, mutual fund
company which manages over $109 billion in investments for nearly 4.5 million individ-
ual and 304 institutional investors. ■ Our look at the company's communications program revealed the need for fundamental changes in how they sold their products and
services. These included changing the company name from The Putnam Companies
to Putnam Investments to better reflect their business. Additionally, we consolidated
the company's five satellite divisions into four coherent parts. Most importantly, we
identified a significant opportunity in re-defining how they sold over 80 of their investment products. ■ Our research showed that the language of investing is intimidating
to most customers. We suggested that Putnam simplify their rates literature, and develop four investment strategies based on how people actually invest. These became
the cornerstone of Putnam's marketing efforts. Color-coded brochures with simple
photographic icons distinguished the strategies, succinct and understandable language
was established as editorial policy. Our program created a new standard in the fund industry, and proved that good design can make a significant contribution to a company's success. ■ **CREDITS:** Principal/Design Director: Leslie Smolan; Designers: Alyssa
Adams, Hannah Smotrich, Justin Peters, Allison Muench; Photography: Peter Medilek

RALPH APPELBAUM

ACTIVATING PUBLIC SPACE *to echo a museum's message and provoke multiple levels of response.* ■ In our recent work for the American Museum of Natural History and the United States Holocaust Memorial Museum, we have experimented with ways to activate the total environment, including pathways and transitional spaces, in service of the interpretive experience and communications goals. We look for architectural and environmental metaphors for the key pedagogical concepts behind an exhibition, so that space traditionally left neutral is given voice. This approach casts a broader informational net to engage the receptivities of different visitors. We feel the results are seen in people's sense of immersion, attention span, and enhanced memory of their experience, provoking them to discuss the exhibit with others and engage in activities such as reading more on the subject, visiting related sites, or becoming more involved with the museum. ■ **AMERICAN MUSEUM OF NATURAL HISTORY—THE MAMMAL HALLS** The Lila Acheson Wallace Wing of Mammals and Their Extinct Relatives opened in May 1994, and comprises the first third of our renovation of the Museum's renowned fossil collections. The renovation, to be completed in 1996, will unite the Museum's mammal and primitive-vertebrate holdings with its world-famous dinosaur collection in a sequence of six light-filled halls on the building's entire top floor. ■ The process of planning, designing, and constructing the halls entailed the rearrangement and reinterpretation of the collection to reflect a current approach to understanding vertebrate evolution—which differs greatly from the views held when the collection was last organized. It also aims to involve the visitor by emphasizing that scientific knowledge is not a fixed plateau from which to view prehistory—but a great detective game. ■ The Museum expressed several essential goals that called for broad, strategic design responses. These became governing principles of our design work — and they are among the first qualities of the exhibition that visitors notice. ■ *Creating a Spatial Metaphor.* As Dr. Lowell Dingus, Project Director, AMNH, describes the process, "The breakthrough in our thinking about these halls occurred early in the development of our plans. We were wrestling with how to make these halls different from all the others. Both of us had been around to visit many contemporary exhibits about evolutionary history, and although each had its distinctive and creative elements, they basically revolved around the same organizing principle—a walk through time. In order to break out of this mold and provide our exhibition with a distinctive signature, we'd have to come up with a different way of presenting the information. But how? We hit upon the idea that people are naturally interested in their family history, especially in a country of immigrants like the United States. In a very real sense, evolutionary history simply represents an extrapolation of one's family history, no matter what kind of organism you are. So, we decided to see if we could take the basic concept of a family tree and spatially expand it . . ."

■ This family tree, or cladogram, thus became the main circulation path and alcoves, so that visitors actually walk and

ACTIVATING SPACE Visitors to the new mammal halls may walk the black terrazzo path in the exhibit halls for a highlighted tour of evolution—activating the circulation space itself, space that has traditionally been left neutral. Scientist Stephen Jay Gould wrote: ". . . They have created this new icon at gigantic scale, so that we can perambulate along the tree of life and absorb the new scheme viscerally by walking, rather than only conceptually by reading."

Mammals whose foot has a

HOOF

belong to a group called ungulates.

The hoof evolved when the bone at the end of one or more toes broadened and became overlaid with a thick

horny covering made of material like your nails.

Ungulates include pigs, camels, deer, horses, rhinos, whales, elephants, sea cows, and their relatives. Clearly, some of these animals, such as whales, no longer have hooves, but evidence shows that the mammals from which they evolved did. Consequently, they belong to the ungulate family.

What is the hoof for?

Located at the end of the foot, they obviously play a role in locomotion.

In many ungulates, such as horses and deer, the number of toes on the foot has been reduced to only one or 2. These toes must provide traction and a stable foundation for the animal when it walks or runs.

pigs, deer, cattle, and their relatives

ARTIODACTYLS

TRICONODONTS,
MULTITUBERCULATES,
MONOTREMES,
AND MARSUPIALS

The extent of the Museum's renowned fossil collection permits a comprehensive story of evolution on earth to be told, using lively mounts and a minimum of barriers. Wire frames are used to fill in the bodies of animals where the complete fossil record is lacking.

PLACENTA

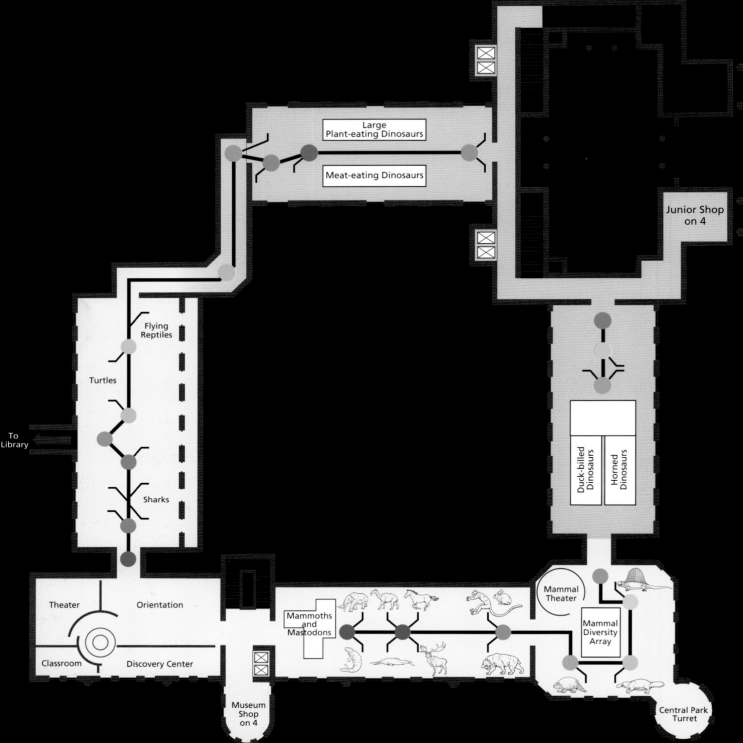

Large
Plant-eating Dinosaurs

Meat-eating Dinosaurs

Junior Shop
on 4

Flying
Reptiles

Turtles

To
Library

Sharks

Duck-billed Dinosaurs

Horned Dinosaurs

Mammal
Theater

Theater

Orientation

Mammoths
and
Mastodons

Mammal
Diversity
Array

Classroom

Discovery Center

Museum
Shop
on 4

Central Park
Turret

experience a branching system as they learn about one. This was one way of activating public space (circulation space) that would otherwise be neutral, harnessing it in support of the exhibition's message. ■ *Linking Great Collections in an Interpretive Loop.* The Museum was planning to redo its fourth-floor mammal halls, but it was clear that the nearby dinosaur halls needed updating as well; and primitive vertebrates were consigned to an alcove where only a fraction of the collection could be displayed. Because of the longtime presence of a library on the fourth floor, there had been no thought that these great evolutionary stories could come into a more dynamic relationship, spatially and interpretively. ■ During masterplanning, we realized that the library, which needed renovation anyway, could be moved to expanded space in a new building—freeing the top floor for a truly big story of vertebrate evolution. As the Museum was already committed to some renovation, we proposed adding primitive vertebrates to the program and uniting them with the dinosaurs and mammals by means of a circulation loop through the whole fourth floor. Next year visitors will be able to tour the world of vertebrate paleontology, from early fish to much closer ancestors, and perceive relationships with greater immediacy and clarity. ■ *The Architecture as a Hidden Asset.* The Muse-

ACTIVATING A DIAGRAM The scientific diagram depicts the nodes and branching pattern of evolutionary characteristics (below). It was transformed into the actual layout of the exhibit hall, with the nodes as stations on the main path and animal fossils as illustrative exhibits along the sides (opposite, lower right). A walking loop through the entire fourth floor was created for visitors to experience the full story of evolution from fish to mammals.

um was aware of the dim and fusty ambiance of its former fossil halls, which tended to make visitors feel like fossils, too. To match the new interpretation, the institution wanted a new look. ■ As we began to

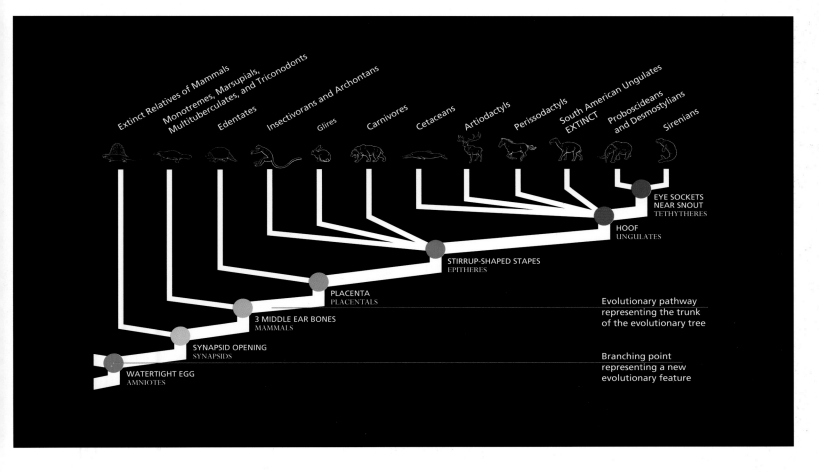

analyze the architecture underlying the old exhibits, it was a bit like finding happiness in one's own backyard. We realized that the original 19th-century grandeur of the halls—buried beneath a century's build-up of confining, light-blocking renovations—would be a beautiful metaphor for the grand adventure of evolutionary science. The restored Victorian volumes and details aptly refer to the time when museums were getting started—when scientists and patrons sought to impart the spirit of a great quest to the public and to students. At the same time, by keeping these soaring spaces airy, light-filled, and free of casework, we make reference to the new scientific approach. ■ *The Specimen as the Star.* The curators were concerned that the installation techniques never upstage the specimens, which should be observed as freely as possible. This concern about visual access to the fossil skeletons is one we more than took to heart. We sought a physical design that would be transparent, so that one's first impression on entering could be the beauty of the fossil skeletons and the perception that the circulation path forms a diagram. Buried structure in the floor supports the minimal glass barriers, and groups of specimens on open platforms were installed where possible. The colors and materials—stone, steel and glass—are quiet and harmonious. There is actually a wealth of graphics and text, but they are compressed into small packages and discreet places, so that one can soak up information without interrupting a primary visual dialogue with the collection. ■ **CREDITS:** Photographs: © Scott Frances/Esto; Editorial assistance: Peter Morais and Cheryl Filsinger.

UNIFYING SPACE AND SCIENCE The 19th-century architectural grandeur of the renovated halls became "a metaphor for the grand adventure of evolutionary science." Minimal casework allows maximum access to the skeletons—the stars of the exhibit.

Glyptotherium

an armored mammal

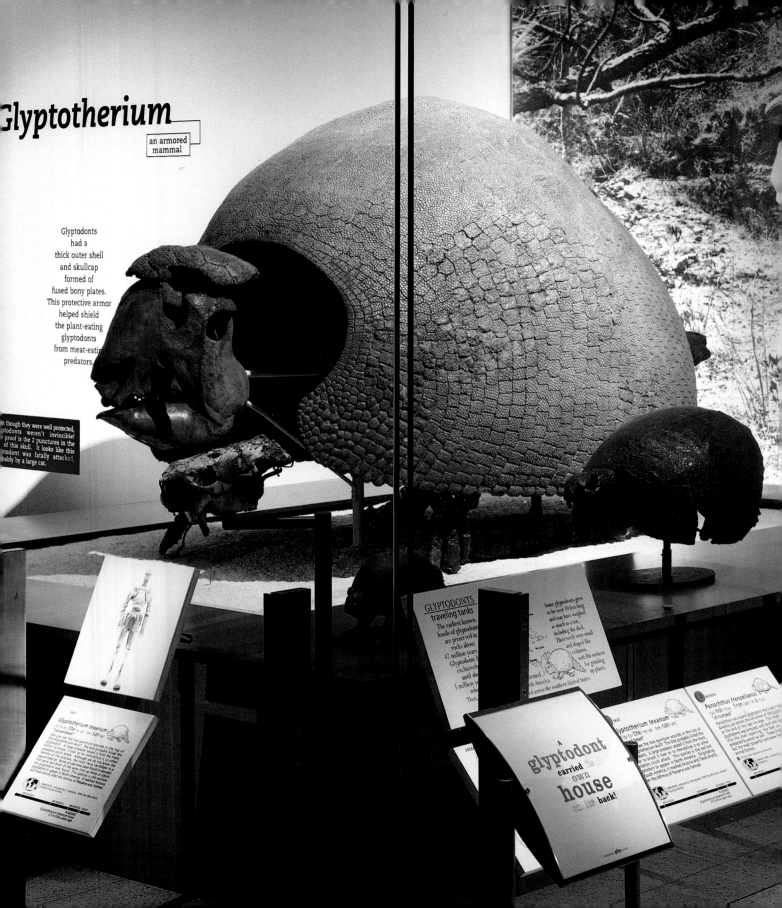

Glyptodonts
had a
thick outer shell
and skullcap
formed of
fused bony plates.
This protective armor
helped shield
the plant-eating
glyptodonts
from meat-eating
predators.

Even though they were well protected,
glyptodonts weren't invincible!
The proof is the 2 punctures in the
top of this skull. It looks like this
glyptodont was fatally attacked,
probably by a large cat.

GLYPTODONTS
traveling tanks

The earliest known
fossils of glyptodonts
are preserved in
rocks about
47 million years

Glyptodonts
exclusively
until abo
3 million y
whe

Then

Some glyptodonts grew
to be over 10 feet long
and may have weighed
as much as a ton,
including the shell.
Their teeth were small
and shaped like
columns,
with flat surfaces
for grinding
up plants.

A
glyptodont
carried its
own
house
on its **back!**

Glyptotherium texanum

Panochthus frenzelianus

ods and sauropods

ODOMORPHS

FINGERED
HAND

The Museum's well-known, beloved dinosaurs are presented in
relation to their evolutionary nodes in the second phase of the renovation. These nodes encourage awareness that evolution is not
a strict timeline, but more like a puzzle of shared characteristics

Theropod dinosaurs include all saurischians
except sauropods and their early relatives.
The advanced feature of theropods is the

3-TOED
hind
FOOT

The central 3 toes are large,

while the first
and fifth toes
are small
or absent.

This foot was probably an adaptation for pursuing
prey. The 3-toed foot of many theropods
survived as the 3-toed foot of birds.

The Museum's grand, historic architecture, "buried beneath a century's build-up of confining, light-blocking renovations," enhances
the hall's progressive methods of evolution interpretation in airy,
light-filled spaces atop the American Museum of Natural History.

allosaurs and tyrannosaurs

CARNOSAURS

The 3-fingered hand
is the common ancestor of

TANURANS

■ **RONALD REAGAN PRESIDENTIAL LIBRARY** Some would say that a presidential library is the ultimate exercise in Making the Complex Clear; others would say it's simply impossible. In fact, it's a little of both. Documenting any presidency isn't solely about official papers: it's about capturing the essence of a man and his beliefs—or at least as much as possible. Clearly, that was our challenge in designing the 22,000 square feet of public exhibition space for the Ronald Reagan Presidential Library in Simi Valley, California. ■ The museum exhibition traces his life from boyhood through the presidency. But the "story" is more than where he came from and what he did; it's about what he became over the years, and why, and how that affected his political party, his fellow countrymen and the world. ■ Every president ultimately addresses a di-

verse audience, and our task was to make certain that we told a consistently clear story. Information was layered to bring the messages of The Great Communicator to the many different kinds of people that might visit the library on a given day—professors and school children, senior citizens and international tourists, Americans and immigrants, dignitaries and dissidents, men and women from all walks of life. Each person sees in Ronald Reagan something different: leadership, compassion, humor, strength, bravado. ■ We wanted visitors to leave with more than a set of disconnected, albeit inter-

DOCUMENTING A PRESIDENTIAL LIFE In the Ronald Reagan Presidential Library, a sequence of galleries represents the man's diverse character, values, ideas, and achievements. Visitors enter through the Hall of Presidents (lower left, opposite page). Shown clockwise are the Prosperity Gallery, the timeline in the Peace and Freedom Gallery, memorabilia in the Voices of Freedom Gallery, and the interactive video theater: *Meet the President.*

esting experiences. We wanted to give them access to larger ideas, using and interrelating interactive and dynamic material with static materials. Our goal was to entertain so that we could inform. ■ To that end, the museum was divided into a series of galleries, each to show part of the Reagan story: the Early Years Gallery combines memorabilia and photographs of his

life through the Hollywood days. The Prosperity Gallery uses photographs, quotes and charts to show how Reagan's policies affected inflation, taxes, and jobs. In the Peace and Freedom Gallery, a timeline displays material from his eight-year presidency. ■ This museum had to have the man himself in it. An interactive video theater allows visitors to Meet the President, using touch-sensitive monitors to choose questions for him to answer. Not every question deals with the serious business of leading the Western World: There's a humor category, so that his famous jokes—and his inimitable delivery—are not lost. ■ An exhibit like this must be many things—bold and intelligent, tasteful and dignified, and of extremely good quality. However, Ronald Reagan also enjoyed widespread personal appeal. Therefore the environment, while technologically sophisticated, was designed to be warm, comfortable and very "human." The road from

Dixon, Illinois to the Oval Office—and beyond—is long and complex. But clearly, it's a great story. ■ CREDITS: Project principals: Michael Donovan, Nancye Green, Susan Berman, Stuart Silver, Susan Myers.

DOCUMENTING COMPASSION Ronald Reagan's efforts to respond to issues of human rights are shown in the Voices of Freedom Gallery. Free-standing vitrines contain personal memorabilia and biographies of 13 dissidents who fought for their political and religious beliefs. One displays a Russian priest's photograph and the miniature bible he used in prison (below). A steel wall is etched with the names of victims of persecution around the world.

VIDEO

1900

1930

Touch the arrows to move the timeline.
To see a story about 3M's history,
touch a picture.

Return to
Main Menu

Forward

More about 3M
1902 - 1919

William L. McKnight

In 1906, William L. McKnight
tried to get work at 3M as a
laborer. A year later, the
persistant youth was hired as a

M Scrapbook

Done

1900

MCo

1930

Where we came from ...

Touch here to explore 3M's
history from 1902 to
the present.

Where you'll find
us ...

Touch here t...

■ **THE 3M COMPANY** How do you create a comprehensible, engaging overview of a transnational company that makes over 60,000 products—from sandpaper to fiber optic connectors? 3M asked us to help them accomplish this in an exhibit at its head-quarters in St. Paul, Minnesota. The goal was to give visitors a broad understanding of the company, encouraging them to say, "I never knew that about 3M," or "I never thought about things in quite that way before." ■ As a way of achieving that response, we created stories about 3M's markets, products and core competencies using a variety of media to communicate broad themes. Key exhibit components are two interactive programs. *3M's World* allows navigation through stories and information that describe and interrelate 3M's markets and products, and convey 3M's history, culture, and values. *3M Innovation* illustrates how 3M products have evolved over time as new markets,

DOCUMENTING A COMPANY The architecture of the interactive programs offers both entertaining and information-intensive options. *3M's World* (architecture below) is a comprehensive overview in two parts: "Where we came from" (history, culture and values), and "Where you'll find us" (markets and products). Short videos are installed along each story path. *3M Innovation* also explores the company's inventive nature in two paths (following two pages), with a quiz called "The Innovation Challenge" and "One Idea Leads to Another" (leading to a multilayered information chart.)

product ideas, and technical capabilities have created opportunities and 3M's culture has actively promoted innovation. ■

CREDITS: Project Principals: Michael Donovan, Susan Berman, Madeleine Butler.

VIDEO

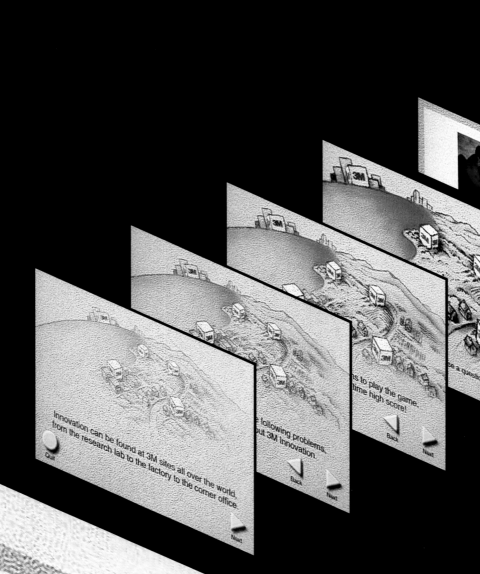

■ **THE ROCHE EXPERT SYSTEM** Industries that are highly regulated need to warehouse vast amounts of data to accommodate changing regulatory requirements. In the case of the pharmaceutical industry, there is also the need to understand the performance of a drug throughout its life cycle. Our client F. Hoffmann-LaRoche, in collaboration with Donovan and Green and Richard Saul Wurman, has found a means of utilizing stored data to create a vehicle that disseminates the company's drug development knowledge. ■ The Roche Expert System provides a means of sharing knowledge across all scientific functions at Roche. Its core structure is a six-volume document that serves as a repository for synthesized worldwide regulatory requirements from the agencies that must approve new drug applications and continuously monitor a drug's use. The Expert System pairs this regulatory information with the contributed experiences and knowledge of Roche's drug development experts. ■ There are six Expert System sections. Each section represents a scientific area: Drug Discovery; Toxicology; Pharmacoeconomics; Pharmacodynamics and Drug Metabolism; Clinical Development; and Chemistry, Manufacturing, and Controls. The six sections are interconnected by three constants in drug development: 1) the six key questions that are asked throughout the process, 2) the time-course and milestones of development (from identification of a new compound to approval of the final drug form), and 3) the studies and research results contributed by each scientific area to the ongoing development process. ■ The best way to understand the Expert System is to imagine using it. Imagine for a moment that you are an expert in reproductive toxicology at Roche, working as part of a team to develop a new drug. Before you begin, you need specific regulatory information to ensure the validity of your preclinical studies. Your first step is to refer to the Toxicology Section of the Expert System. The System's Index is designed

DOCUMENTING PROCESS The Roche Expert System is a six-volume document designed to disseminate the company's drug development knowledge. Access to data is various, including the key questions that are asked throughout the development process.

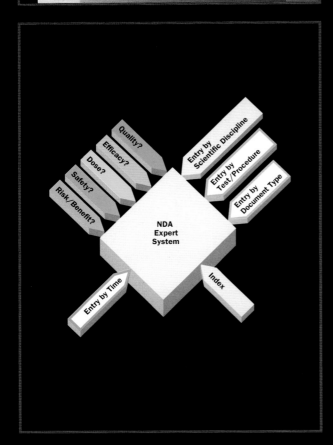

to let you choose from several routes to access the information you want (diagram opposite). You can enter by your area of study, track the development timeline, or (following this example) ask a key question about the safety of the drug. You will find that the Index lists safety-related issues by color-coding them purple. You scan the Table of Contents, and locate the entry for reproductive studies, and find the purple page numbers. Turning to the appropriate page (below), you find a small insert on the left that maps the questions that must be asked about the risk of a drug to humans. One

highlighted question pertains to a drug's effect on reproduction; it indicates that you're in the right place. Now, what does the Expert System provide? ■ The column on the right half of the page contains the regulatory guidelines for the studies you'll have to undertake to determine any adverse effects your drug may have on reproduction. These guidelines are anno-

TRANSLATING PROCESS Six key questions are used to navigate the System as a whole (diagram below). A page from the Toxicology volume shows regulatory guidelines, with links to source references and information available from the Roche community.

Drug Discovery	Toxicology	Preclinical Pharmacokinetics and Pharmacodynamics	Chemistry Manufacturing and Controls	Clinical Research
E? What is efficacy and why?				
S? What is safety and why?				
R|B? What is the risk/benefit ratio?				
D? What is dosing and why?				
Q? What is the quality and why?				
C|P? What is the cost/performance ratio?				

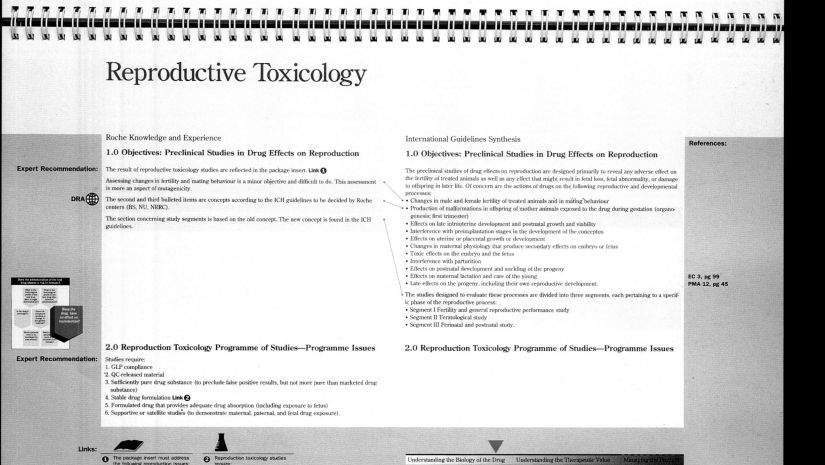

Reproductive Toxicology

Roche Knowledge and Experience

1.0 Objectives: Preclinical Studies in Drug Effects on Reproduction

Expert Recommendation: The result of reproductive toxicology studies are reflected in the package insert. **Link ❶**

Assessing changes in fertility and mating behaviour is a minor objective and difficult to do. This assessment is more an aspect of mutagenicity.

DRA 🌐 The second and third bulleted items are concepts according to the ICH guidelines to be decided by Roche centers (BS, NU, NRRC).

The section concerning study segments is based on the old concept. The new concept is found in the ICH guidelines.

2.0 Reproduction Toxicology Programme of Studies—Programme Issues

Expert Recommendation: Studies require:
1. GLP compliance
2. QC-released material
3. Sufficiently pure drug substance (to preclude false positive results, but not more pure than marketed drug substance)
4. Stable drug formulation **Link ❷**
5. Formulated drug that provides adequate drug absorption (including exposure to fetus)
6. Supportive or satellite studies (to demonstrate maternal, paternal, and fetal drug exposure).

International Guidelines Synthesis

1.0 Objectives: Preclinical Studies in Drug Effects on Reproduction

The preclinical studies of drug effects on reproduction are designed primarily to reveal any adverse effect on the fertility of treated animals as well as any effect that might result in fetal loss, fetal abnormality, or damage to offspring in later life. Of concern are the actions of drugs on the following reproductive and developmental processes:
- Changes in male and female fertility of treated animals and in mating behaviour
- Production of malformations in offspring of mother animals exposed to the drug during gestation (organogenesis; first trimester)
- Effects on late intrauterine development and postnatal growth and viability
- Interference with preimplantation stages in the development of the conceptus
- Effects on uterine or placental growth or development
- Changes in maternal physiology that produce secondary effects on embryo or fetus
- Toxic effects on the embryo and the fetus
- Interference with parturition
- Effects on postnatal development and suckling of the progeny
- Effects on maternal lactation and care of the young
- Late effects on the progeny, including their own reproductive development.

The studies designed to evaluate these processes are divided into three segments, each pertaining to a specific phase of the reproductive process:
- Segment I Fertility and general reproductive performance study
- Segment II Teratological study
- Segment III Perinatal and postnatal study.

2.0 Reproduction Toxicology Programme of Studies—Programme Issues

References:

EC 3, pg 99
PMA 12, pg 45

Links:

❶ The package insert must address the following reproduction issues:
- Teratogenicity
- Effect on fertility
- Effect on late-fetal and postnatal development.

❷ Reproduction toxicology studies require:
- QC-released material
- Sufficiently pure drug substance
- Stable drug formulation.

	Understanding the Biology of the Drug		Understanding the Therapeutic Value		Managing the Profile		
Drug Discovery	**Phase 0**	**Phase I**	**Phase II**	**Phase III**	**Phase IV**		
	NPRP	EIM		FDDP	Pre-NDA	NDA	Post-NDA

contributes answers to the key questions during a drug's development process. Over time, the answers become study reports and documents that help support a drug's approval. An overview tracks the interdependent process, and marks it with documenting "events." Procedural phases and products are shown in the separate section volumes with a sliding timeline (diagram below).

may want to know an expert in pre-clinical pharmacokinetics who can help you with a study protocol. You consult the Expert System Team Directory. It lists everyone who has contributed to the Expert System, how and where to reach the contributors, and it provides detailed descriptions of their expertise—with photographs so you

Understanding the Biology of the Drug	Understanding the Therapeutic Value	Managing the Product
Drug Discovery **Phase 0** **Phase I**	**Phase II** **Phase III**	**Phase IV**
NPRP EIM	FDDP	Pre-NDA NDA Post-NDA

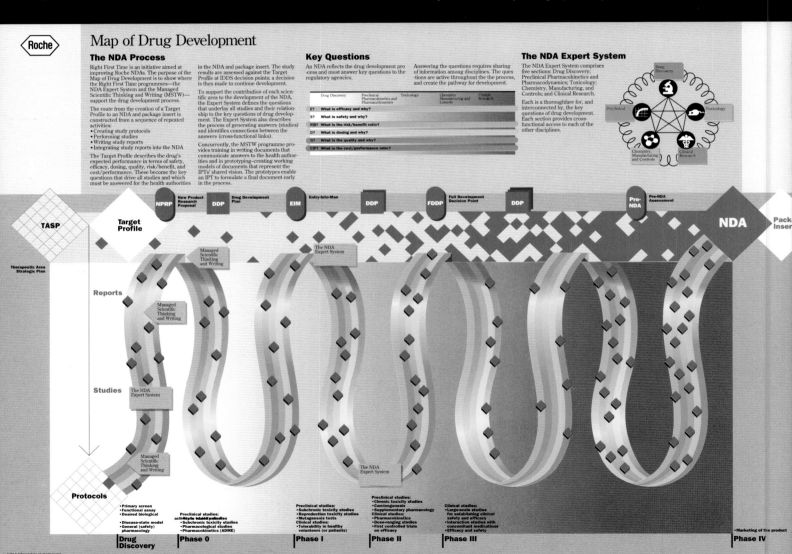

Roche

Map of Drug Development

The NDA Process

Right First Time is an initiative aimed at improving Roche NDAs. The purpose of the Map of Drug Development is to show where the Right First Time programmes—the NDA Expert System and the Managed Scientific Thinking and Writing (MSTW)—support the drug development process.

The route from the creation of a Target Profile to an NDA and package insert is constructed from a sequence of repeated activities:
- Creating study protocols
- Performing studies
- Writing study reports
- Integrating study reports into the NDA

The Target Profile describes the drug's expected performance in terms of safety, efficacy, dosing, quality, risk/benefit, and cost/performance. These become the key questions that drive all studies and which must be answered for the health authorities

in the NDA and package insert. The study results are assessed against the Target Profile at IDDS decision points; a decision is then made to continue development.

To support the contribution of each scientific area to the development of the NDA, the Expert System defines the questions that underlay all studies and their relationship to the key questions of drug development. The Expert System also describes the process of generating answers (studies) and identifies connections between the answers (cross-functional links).

Concurrently, the MSTW programme provides training in writing documents that communicate answers to the health authorities and in prototyping—creating working models of documents that represent the IPTs' shared vision. The prototypes enable an IPT to formulate a final document early in the process.

Key Questions

An NDA reflects the drug development process and must answer key questions to the regulatory agencies.

Answering the questions requires sharing of information among disciplines. The questions are active throughout the the process, and create the pathway for development.

	Drug Discovery	Preclinical Pharmacokinetics and Pharmacodynamics	Toxicology	Chemistry Manufacturing and Controls	Clinical Research
E?	What is efficacy and why?				
S?	What is safety and why?				
R/B?	What is the risk/benefit ratio?				
D?	What is dosing and why?				
Q?	What is the quality and why?				
C/P?	What is the cost/performance ratio?				

The NDA Expert System

The NDA Expert System comprises five sections: Drug Discovery; Preclinical Pharmacokinetics and Pharmacodynamics; Toxicology; Chemistry, Manufacturing, and Controls; and Clinical Research.

Each is a thoroughfare for, and interconnected by, the key questions of drug development. Each section provides cross-functional access to each of the other disciplines.

Drug Discovery — Preclinical — Toxicology — Chemistry, Manufacturing and Controls — Clinical Research

TASP | Target Profile | NPRP — New Product Research Proposal | DDP — Drug Development Plan | EIM — Entry-Into-Man | DDP | FDDP — Full Development Decision Point | DDP | Pre-NDA — Pre-NDA Assessment | NDA | Package Insert

Therapeutic Area Strategic Plan

Reports — **Studies** — **Protocols**

Managed Scientific Thinking and Writing

The NDA Expert System

Drug Discovery
- Primary screen
- Functional assay
- Desired biological
- Disease-state model
- General (safety) pharmacology

Phase 0
Preclinical studies:
activity in related models
- Subchronic toxicity studies
- Pharmacological studies
- Pharmacokinetics (ADME)

Phase I
Preclinical studies:
- Subchronic toxicity studies
- Reproduction toxicity studies
- Mutagenesis tests
Clinical studies:
- Tolerability in healthy volunteers (or patients)

Phase II
Preclinical studies:
- Chronic toxicity studies
- Carcinogenesis
- Supplementary pharmacology
Clinical studies:
- Pharmacokinetics
- Dose-ranging studies
- First controlled trials on efficacy

Phase III
Clinical studies:
- Large-scale studies for establishing clinical safety and efficacy
- Interaction studies with concomitant medications
- Efficacy and safety

Phase IV
- Marketing of the product

| **Drug Discovery** | **Phase 0** | **Phase I** | **Phase II** | **Phase III** | **Phase IV** |

know who will be receiving your call. In the Roche Expert System, the validity of the core documents are dependent on the constant flow of information and recommendations contributed by users from each of the scientific functions. All users are provided with response forms to make their contributions easy. They receive Expert System updates in team newsletters, and they can also communicate by e-mail. The next step for the Expert System is to provide the Roche drug development community with an on-line system for faster delivery, richer content, and direct interaction. ■ CREDITS: The

ACTIVATING PARTICIPATION The value of the system depends on the constant flow of contributed information. To increase participation, teams receive directories, response forms, and newsletters reporting results of collaborations in the Roche community.

team that created, developed, implemented, and supported the Roche Expert System from F. Hoffmann-LaRoche included Dr. Clive Meanwell, Dr. Helmut Giersiefen, Steve Roper and Dr. Lutz Wevelsiep. Donovan and Green Principals: Nancye Green and Marge Levin. Project team: Thom Kam, Ray Sysko, Larry Wolfson, Lisa Yee, Lisa Mullineaux, and Marjorie Nelson.

UNDERSTANDING FURNITURE SYSTEMS Office furniture systems present a basic dilemma: simple systems offering few choices are easy to order, complex systems that solve lots of space problems are hard to order. When you account for all the different components, materials, and size variations, it's not unusual to find a furniture system that offers 20,000 choices. For a really robust system, that number can climb to 100,000. ■ This complexity means that specifiers—interior designers, architects and facility managers—must understand the ins and outs of various systems and keep track of the available choices, or they risk costly and schedule-breaking errors with every order. Traditionally, a price list helps them contend with these challenges and prepare orders. But, to provide a higher level of product understanding, my team at Agnew Moyer Smith has helped the Steelcase company replace price lists with a new format—specification guides. ■ The project began in 1989 with research by Elizabeth Keyes (Watzman & Keyes), a consultant to Steelcase. Elizabeth and her team interviewed furniture specifiers, talked about existing specifying tools, and asked them what worked and what didn't work. The answers were clear and consistent. They wanted: a single source ("Tell me everything I need to know in one place"), visual information ("Give me pictures, diagrams and graphics without long explanations in text"), a safety net ("Make it hard to make mistakes, and easy to do it right"), clear landmarks and paths to follow ("Make it clear where I am and how I get to related topics"), different paths for novices and experts ("Give me a streamlined path once I become an expert"), consistency ("Keep the same information structure so new product lines aren't a mystery"), and bad news up front ("Tell me if there's something the product can't do.") In response to the specifiers' wish list, we developed our first format for specification guides in 1990. Since then, we've produced dozens of additions to this library and refined our original design. ■ Two basic sections make up every specification guide. The Understanding section is a textbook of product features and functions. The Specifying section is a reference for product variations, prices and style numbers that enables the specifier to create a "shopping list." Each chapter in the Understanding section begins with an illustrated overview of

CATEGORIZING PRODUCT REFERENCE Steelcase product guides are divided into two sections: Understanding and Specifying (above). An annotated product drawing is the lead element on every Understanding page (opposite bottom), with recurring topics, like details, connections, and wiring, always appearing in the same order. Color-coded bands on the Specifying pages separate standard product features from the options (opposite top).

Non-Tackable Panels

Tip: To price a panel with two surface materials in different price groups, add the two panel surface prices together and divide by two.

Tip: Traces pattern is available on the top cap, end trim, and/or base covers. A single additional charge is applied regardless of where the Traces pattern is located.

Tip: If you want the panel fabric to match the fabric on change-of-height panel connectors, power poles, cable poles, or fillers, check to see that the fabric you want is available on that product before you specify the panel fabric. Some fabrics are not available because they are not suitable for wrapping thin pieces.

	Standard Includes	Required to Specify
▶Need help? Product details, page 16	• Panel with two surfaces: textured paint or vertical surface fabric • Top cap, end trim, and plain base covers: paint • Top cap height: medium • Universal connector package	1 Style number 2 Color number for surface 1 3 Color number for surface 2 4 Paint color number for top cap, end trim, and base covers 5 Options, if selected below ▶See *Surface Materials Foldouts.*

	Options	Price	Required to Specify
Surface Materials ▶*Surface Materials Foldouts*	**Top cap, end trim, and base covers** • Wood on low or medium top cap only • Customīz stain on wood top cap • Traces pattern on paint	 Prices at right Prices at right Prices at right	 *with wood top cap* and select wood color number See *Surface Materials Reference* price list. Select paint color number and Traces pattern number for top cap, end trim, and/or base covers.
Top Cap ▶Page 30	**Height** • Low (reduces panel height by 3/4") • High (increases panel height by 1")	 No cost +$ 11	 Replace second *"M"* in style number with *"L"*. Replace second *"M"* in style number with *"H"*.
	Knockouts • Cable knockout on medium top cap	 +$ 12	 ▶Add top cap style number to panel specifications, page 203.
Electrical ▶Pages 44–48	**Factory-installed powerway** • 3-circuit powerway with power base covers • 4-circuit (3+D) powerway with power base covers	 +$112 +$124	 Add suffix *"P3"* to panel style number. Add suffix *"P4"* to panel style number.
	Field-installed powerway • For use in New York City	 +$ 12	 ▶Must specify powerway for field installation only, page 198, and add power base cover style number to panel specifications, page 199.
	Factory-installed power base covers • Substituted on non-powered panels 24 5/16"W – 60 5/8"W only • For use in Chicago	 No cost	 ▶Add power base cover style number to panel specification, page 199. ▶Add power base cover style number to non-powered panel specification, page 199.
Related Products	• Panel connectors and brackets • Panel accessories • Panel wiring and cabling		▶Pages 184–186 ▶Pages 190–192 ▶Pages 193–209

Specification Information

• Width	• Style Number	• Base Prices: Textured Paint	Fabric Price Group 1	Fabric Price Group 2	Fabric Price Group 3	Fabric Price Group 4	• Options (Add $ to Base Price): Wood Top Cap	Customīz Stain on Wood Top Cap	Traces Pattern on Top Cap, End Trim, and/or Base Cover	• Shipping Weight
41 1/4"H Panels										
18 5/16"W	**MPNTM-4118**	$246	$292	$300	$352	$378	+$ 50	+$ 10	+$111	33 lbs
24 5/16"W	**MPNTM-4124**	$252	$304	$314	$376	$404	+$ 55	+$ 10	+$118	39 lbs
30 5/16"W	**MPNTM-4130**	$256	$320	$330	$400	$426	+$ 62	+$ 11	+$124	44 lbs
36 5/16"W	**MPNTM-4136**	$271	$339	$351	$421	$449	+$ 67	+$ 11	+$131	51 lbs
42 5/16"W	**MPNTM-4142**	$288	$360	$372	$456	$488	+$ 75	+$ 12	+$133	57 lbs
48 5/16"W	**MPNTM-4148**	$313	$417	$429	$515	$551	+$ 86	+$ 12	+$138	64 lbs
60 5/8"W	**MPNTM-4160**	$353	$477	$493	$599	$641	+$109	+$ 13	+$162	75 lbs
52 3/8"H Panels										
18 5/16"W	**MPNTM-5318**	$210	$264	$272	$328	$352	+$ 50	+$ 10	+$113	39 lbs
24 5/16"W	**MPNTM-5324**	$250	$298	$306	$368	$394	+$ 55	+$ 10	+$123	45 lbs
30 5/16"W	**MPNTM-5330**	$263	$331	$343	$411	$439	+$ 62	+$ 11	+$131	53 lbs
36 5/16"W	**MPNTM-5336**	$279	$351	$363	$435	$467	+$ 67	+$ 11	+$133	61 lbs
42 5/16"W	**MPNTM-5342**	$305	$391	$403	$483	$517	+$ 75	+$ 12	+$138	67 lbs
48 5/16"W	**MPNTM-5348**	$322	$414	$426	$512	$546	+$ 86	+$ 12	+$142	75 lbs
60 5/8"W	**MPNTM-5360**	$372	$506	$522	$634	$678	+$109	+$ 13	+$162	93 lbs
64 11/16"H Panels										
18 5/16"W	**MPNTM-6518**	$227	$287	$295	$353	$379	+$ 50	+$ 10	+$133	46 lbs
24 5/16"W	**MPNTM-6524**	$266	$336	$348	$416	$444	+$ 55	+$ 10	+$142	55 lbs
30 5/16"W	**MPNTM-6530**	$289	$381	$393	$473	$505	+$ 62	+$ 11	+$149	66 lbs
36 5/16"W	**MPNTM-6536**	$322	$414	$426	$512	$546	+$ 67	+$ 11	+$155	71 lbs
42 5/16"W	**MPNTM-6542**	$347	$437	$451	$539	$575	+$ 75	+$ 12	+$158	83 lbs
48 5/16"W	**MPNTM-6548**	$370	$480	$494	$594	$636	+$ 86	+$ 12	+$162	91 lbs
60 5/8"W	**MPNTM-6560**	$433	$573	$591	$711	$761	+$109	+$ 13	+$182	110 lbs
80 1/2"H Panels										
18 5/16"W	**MPNTM-8018**	$312	$434	$448	$536	$574	+$ 50	+$ 10	+$138	58 lbs
24 5/16"W	**MPNTM-8024**	$334	$440	$454	$562	$602	+$ 55	+$ 10	+$144	66 lbs
30 5/16"W	**MPNTM-8030**	$354	$446	$460	$586	$628	+$ 62	+$ 11	+$155	75 lbs
36 5/16"W	**MPNTM-8036**	$401	$541	$557	$665	$711	+$ 67	+$ 11	+$158	85 lbs
42 5/16"W	**MPNTM-8042**	$421	$559	$575	$691	$739	+$ 75	+$ 12	+$162	92 lbs
48 5/16"W	**MPNTM-8048**	$450	$616	$636	$764	$818	+$ 86	+$ 12	+$166	102 lbs

Non-Tackable Panels

Non-tackable panels are constructed with two steel pans that are joined together.

Panels surface is covered with textured paint or vertical surface fabric.

Stress skin construction encloses a layer of corrugated honeycomb between two steel pans.

End trim finishes the vertical edge of the panel.

Base-end door slides up to provide access to base cavity and has a knockout for routing cables through a panel run.

Leveling glides adjust to install panels on uneven floors.

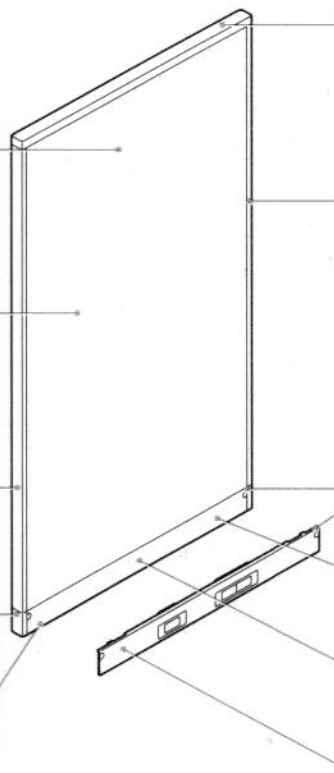

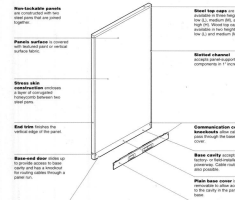

Steel top caps are available in three heights–low (L), medium (M), and high (H). Wood top caps are available in two heights–low (L) and medium (M).

Slotted channel accepts panel-supported components in 1" increments.

Communication cord knockouts allow cables to pass through the base cover.

Base cavity accepts a factory- or field-installed powerway. Cable routing is also possible.

Plain base cover is removable to allow access to the cavity in the panel base.

Power base cover, with knockouts for receptacles, is provided when you specify powered panels. You can also have the factory substitute power base covers on non-powered panels if you plan to add powerways in the field. Power base covers are removable to allow access to the base cavity.
▶Page 46

Product Details

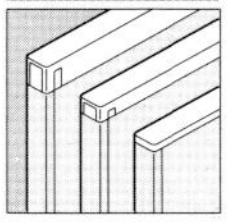

Top caps come in three height options that will alter the panel height according to the top cap selected. See dimensions table below.
▶Page 30

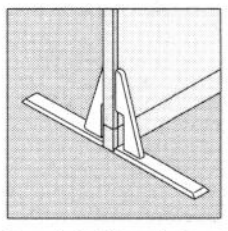

Panel stabilizer feet are designed to provide additional support for panels when they aren't stabilized by components. Each foot extends 16" from the side of the panel.
▶Page 40

Actual Dimensions

Depth (thickness)	2"		
Width	18 5/16", 24 5/16", 30 5/16", 36 5/16", 42 5/16", 48 5/16", or 60 5/8"		
Low top cap height	5/8"		
Medium top cap height	1 3/8"		
High top cap height	2 3/8"		
Leveling glide range	1 11/16"		
Height	with low top cap	with medium top cap	with high top cap
41"H panel	40 1/2"	41 1/2"	42 1/4"
53"H panel	51 5/8"	52 3/8"	53 3/8"
65"H panel	63 15/16"	64 11/16"	65 11/16"
80"H panel	79 3/4"	80 1/2"	81 1/2"

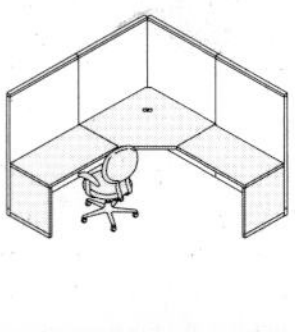

Connections

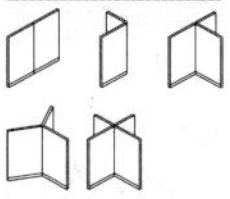

Universal connector package, shipped with every panel, joins panels of the same height in a straight line or in L-, T-, Y-, or X- configurations.
▶Page 31

Connectors are available to attach panels to adjacent panels, walls, and freestanding furniture.
▶Page 32–36

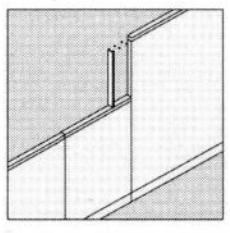

Change-of-height panel connector provides a finished edge when panels of varying heights are joined in a straight line, L-, T-, or X-configuration. It will not work with fillers, power poles, or cable poles that are in a T-configuration.
▶Page 38

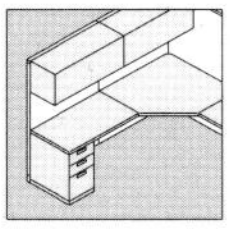

Panels can support components, including worksurfaces, shelves, and overhead storage bins.

Panel-run stability recommendations vary depending on the width of the panel run and use of panel-supported components or freestanding furniture.
▶Page 53–55

Wiring & Cabling

Base or end power-ins bring power to the panel run by connecting at a designated receptacle location or at the end of a run.
▶Page 42

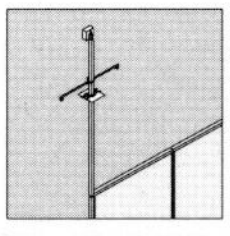

Power poles and cable poles attach to the panel end or at L- and T-connections. They bring power or communication cables from the ceiling.
▶Page 43

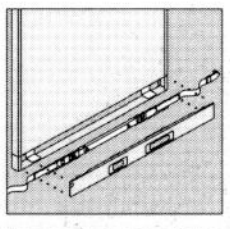

Powerways can be factory or field installed in the base cavity. Three-circuit or four-circuit (3+D) powerways are available. Power base covers with receptacle openings are standard on powered panels. *Exception: 18"W panels accommodate pass-through powerways. These panels are shipped with two plain base covers. Pass-through powerways are shipped in a separate carton for field installation.*
▶Page 44

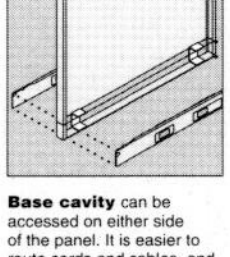

Base cavity can be accessed on either side of the panel. It is easier to route cords and cables, and to field install powerways, on the surface-one side because the C-shape foot opens to that side.

Panel-base end grommet is available to fit in the base-end door knockout to protect cords and cables.

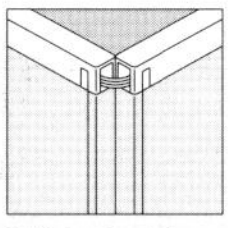

Cable knockout allows for cable routing through steel medium or high top caps. *Exception: Wood top caps and steel low top caps do not allow cable routing.*
▶Page 30

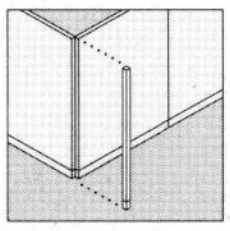

Fillers conceal cables running vertically and aesthetically fill in the space at L- and T-connections. Fillers should be used on panels that are the same height.
▶Page 39

Wire separator is available, field installed, to separate telecommunication cables from the powerway.

All panels are UL listed.

Surface Materials

Top cap
• Paint (standard)
• Traces pattern (option on paint)
• Wood (option on low and medium top caps)
• Customīz stain (option on wood)

End trim
• Paint (standard)
• Traces pattern (option on paint)

Base cover
• Paint (standard)
• Traces pattern (option on paint)

Panel surface
• Textured paint
• Vertical surface fabric
Tip: If a panel has different surfaces, use these guidelines:
The first surface you specify is considered to be surface one.
The second surface you specify is surface two.
End trims, left, right, or both, are specified while you're facing surface one.
Factory-installed powerways are always installed with the green end of the powerway on the left-hand side as you face surface one.
▶Page 44

Slotted channel
• Black paint only

Leveling glides
• Black only

Panel-base end grommet
• 6000 Black vinyl only

Pricing

To price a panel with surface materials ot different prices, add the two prices together and divide by two.

Appliation Topics

Base Covers and Receptacles
▶Page 46

Panel Creep
▶Page 49

How Connectors Affect Panel-Supported Components
▶Page 51

How Connectors Affect Power Flow
▶Page 52

Wiring and Cabling
▶Page 145–165

Cable Capacities
▶Page 164

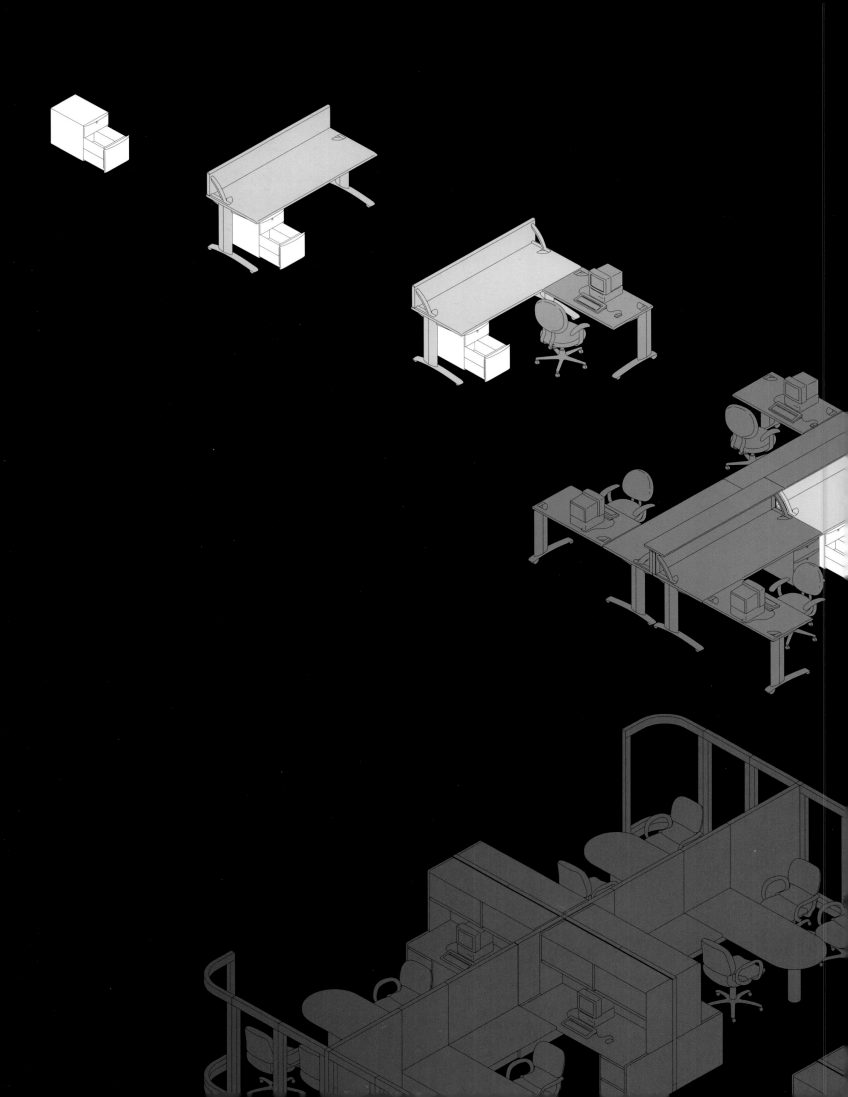

a specific product line, showing all the choices available within that product category. These matrices give specifiers quick reference to product dimensions—the key information they need to start developing a space plan. The matrix pages also function as an illustrated table of contents. ■ A product drawing festooned with call-outs is the

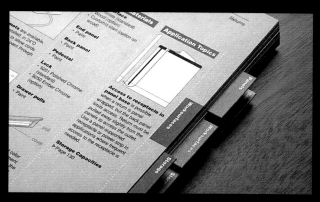

lead element on every Understanding page (preceding page, bottom). The call-outs express what an expert would tell you if showing the product for the first time. They also provide a vocabulary guide by starting with the name of the item being described. (If I could start over, I would push harder to improve the clarity of some of the component names.) ■ Each paragraph of Understanding text starts with a bold lead-in phrase to indicate what subject will be addressed. This tends to put sentences in the active, instead of the passive voice, and helps eliminate arbitrary differences in the writing style. Best of all, the phrases tell readers what the text is about without forcing them to read the entire paragraph. ■ Specifiers are highly visual people who find drawings a very comfortable way to receive information. Thus, hundreds of drawings in each guide show how product parts look, function, and connect. We evaluated perspective, oblique, and

MAPPING CONTENT RELATIONSHIPS For browsing and quick navigation to related topics, highlighted page references, and bold lead-in phrases are used. Extended tabs locate the beginnings of chapters (above top), and the covers of the biggest guides fold out flat to continually display lists of surface materials. The guides have a consistent 30° isometric drawing standard to allow related product drawings to "fit" together like the furniture does (below).

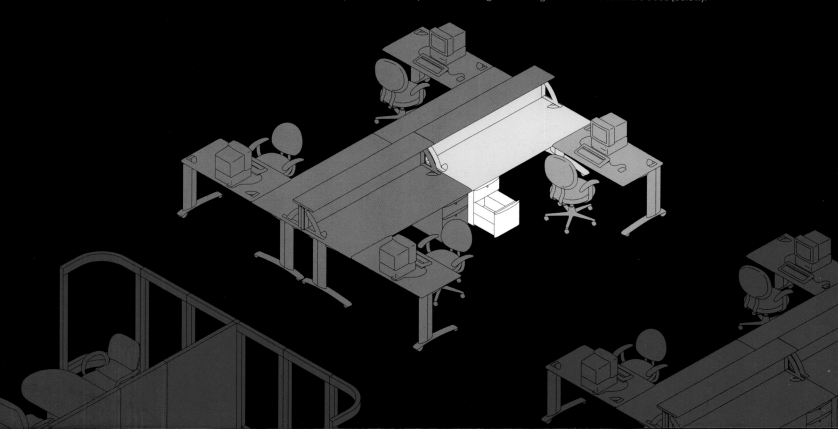

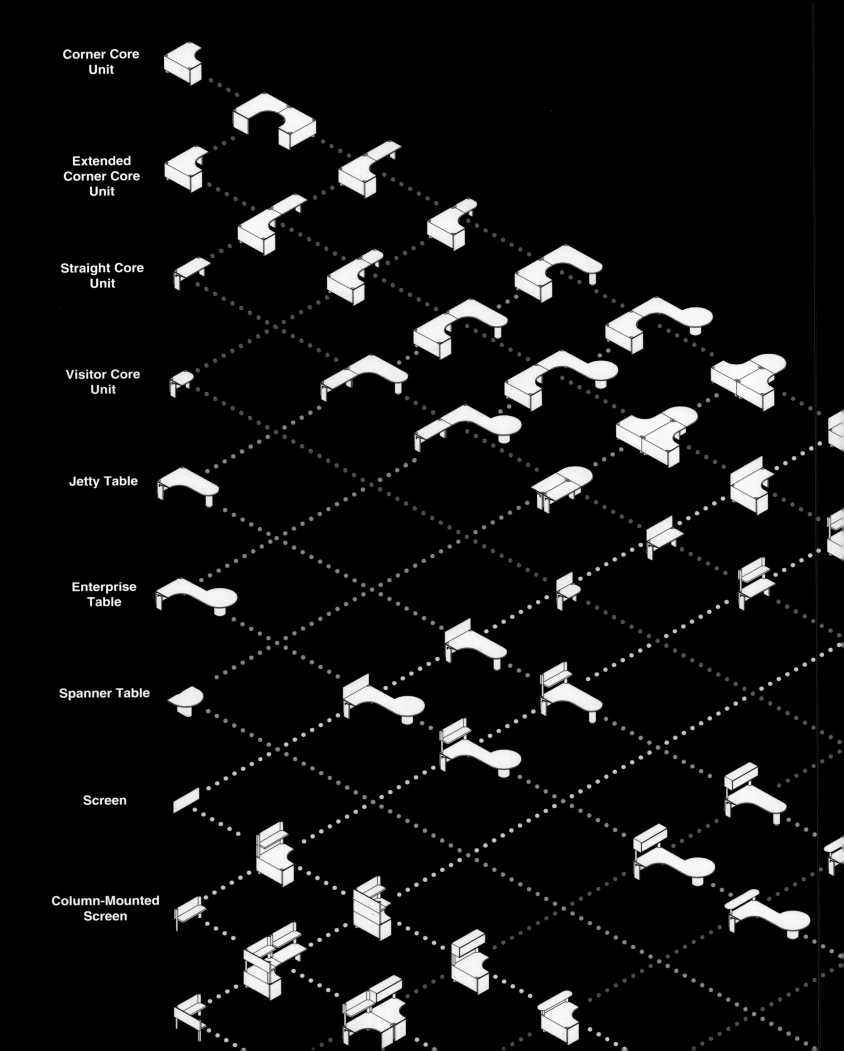

Corner Core Unit

Extended Corner Core Unit

Straight Core Unit

Visitor Core Unit

Jetty Table

Enterprise Table

Spanner Table

Screen

Column-Mounted Screen

onfigurations in the new Context product line, a map was creat- ed (opposite). Lines extend from the product's basic components (n the left column) to intersections where they are joined. A blank intersection means that the components cannot be connected. Again, the consistent isometric drawing standard in the guides al- lows the "fitting" of products and emphasizes interchangeability.

other drawing systems before finally choosing 30° isometric. It retains a true, measurable scale along all three axes, and most clearly depicts things made up of 90° angles—like furniture. Then, because our drawings fit together the same way the furniture does, we could draw the components of the system separately at the same scale, and combine them later to create worksta- tions and clusters—even an entire floor's furniture layout (see preceding page). To help the reader grasp the size of unfamiliar components, we limited the number of drawing scales used; the products similar in size appear at the same scale. ■ Special diagrams are frequently needed to explain special products. One diagram (below) was developed for a radically new furniture product called Context. It reveals all of the system's com- ponents at a glance, and how they relate. ■ Every Specifying page (page 175) contains a detailed list of features in a basic product, along with the exact steps that are required to create an accurate specification of them. Color-coded bands—black for the basic product and red for options—separate product features. Often, more than a dozen op- tions can be specified, but not all of them apply to every product. To make sure the reader understands this, we list all the available options on the same specifying page as the basic product—a simple but significant improvement over earlier price lists which scattered the options. ■ **ELECTRONIC FURNITURE GUIDES** Based on what we learned about structuring information in the printed specification guides, we designed an electronic version of them. It has an interface that gives users an immediate visual

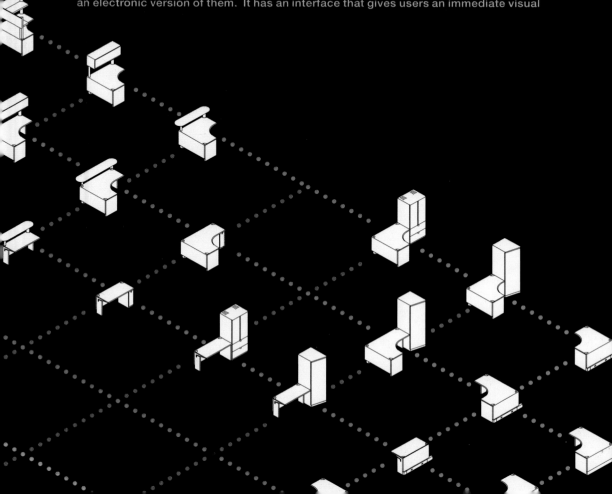

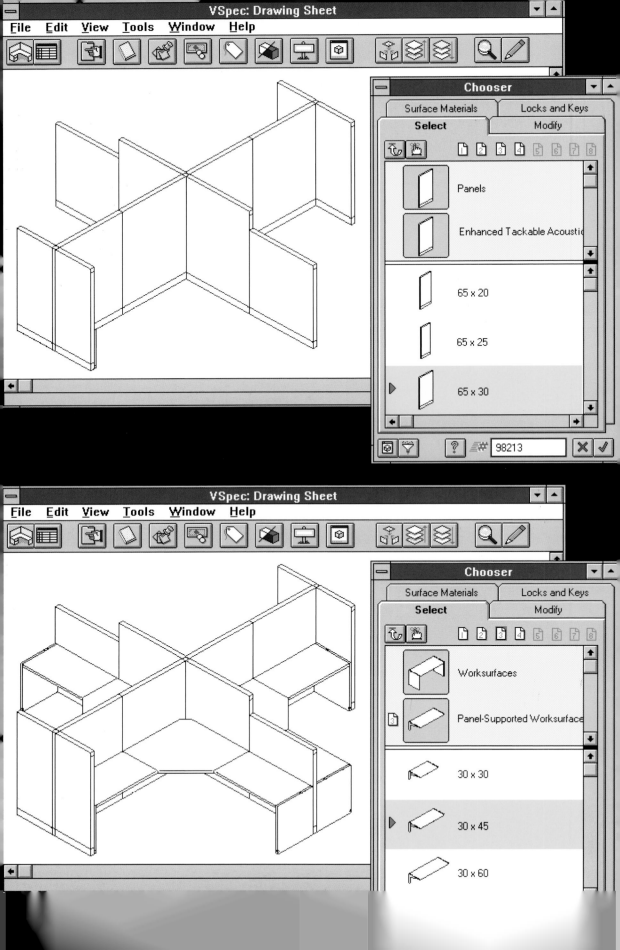

response; as they select furniture, they instantly see pictures of their choices, the configurations they are building, and the surface materials they choose—all in the context of an office layout drawing. At the same time, the computer builds a text-based shopping list of what the user has selected. ■ The interface is comprised of two primary screens: a drawing sheet for selecting and configuring components visually, and a work sheet that displays in text every item on the drawing sheet. This is useful for analyzing

TRANSFORMING PRODUCT REFERENCE The guides were translated to CD-ROM with an interface for selecting and building clusters of furniture. During that process, the program builds a shopping list of the selections made (below). On the drawing sheet, or "home base," selections are made from the "chooser" catalog, and then dragged into place to create units or entire space plans.

master orders, exploring pricing alternatives, tracking orders and so forth. ■ On the drawing sheet, tools can be opened from the toolbar and appear at the top of the screen in much the same way that designers place triangles, swatch books, or calculators on traditional drawing sheets. The Understanding Module can be opened and also appears at the top. Its information comes directly from the files we first created for the printed guides. Navigating the system is dramatically simplified by the fact that all the printed guides have parallel hierarchies, uniform drawing scales, and consistent text organizations and syntax.

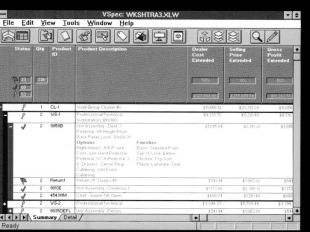

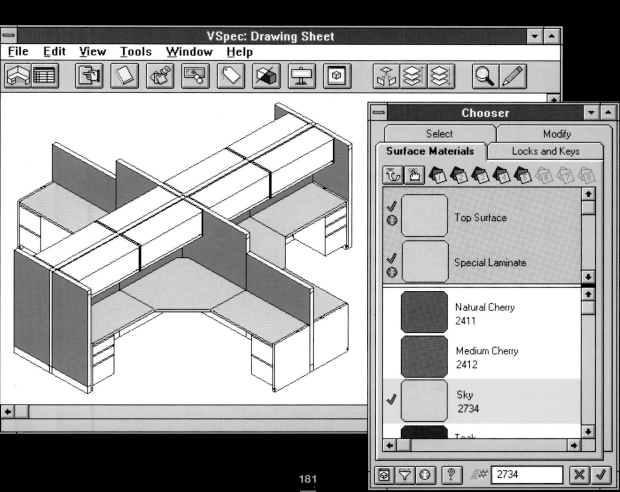

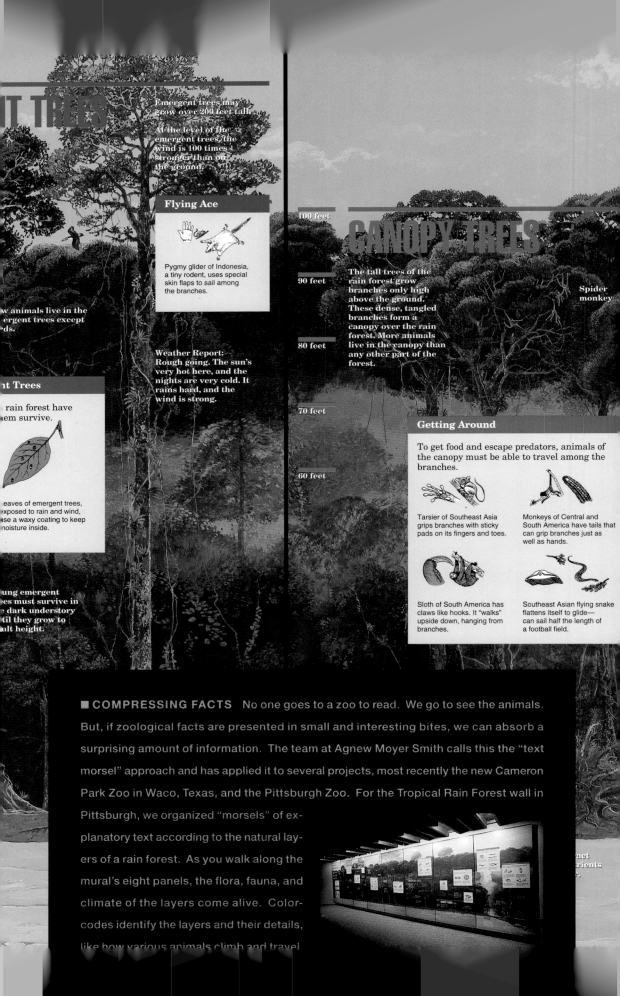

Emergent trees may grow over 200 feet tall.

At the level of the emergent trees, the wind is 100 times stronger than on the ground.

Flying Ace

Pygmy glider of Indonesia, a tiny rodent, uses special skin flaps to sail among the branches.

…w animals live in the …ergent trees except …ds.

Weather Report: Rough going. The sun's very hot here, and the nights are very cold. It rains hard, and the wind is strong.

…nt Trees

… rain forest have …em survive.

…eaves of emergent trees, …xposed to rain and wind, …se a waxy coating to keep …moisture inside.

…ung emergent …es must survive in … dark understory …til they grow to …lt height.

100 feet

CANOPY TREES

90 feet

The tall trees of the rain forest grow branches only high above the ground. These dense, tangled branches form a canopy over the rain forest. More animals live in the canopy than any other part of the forest.

Spider monkey

80 feet

70 feet

Getting Around

To get food and escape predators, animals of the canopy must be able to travel among the branches.

60 feet

Tarsier of Southeast Asia grips branches with sticky pads on its fingers and toes.

Monkeys of Central and South America have tails that can grip branches just as well as hands.

Sloth of South America has claws like hooks. It "walks" upside down, hanging from branches.

Southeast Asian flying snake flattens itself to glide— can sail half the length of a football field.

■ **COMPRESSING FACTS** No one goes to a zoo to read. We go to see the animals. But, if zoological facts are presented in small and interesting bites, we can absorb a surprising amount of information. The team at Agnew Moyer Smith calls this the "text morsel" approach and has applied it to several projects, most recently the new Cameron Park Zoo in Waco, Texas, and the Pittsburgh Zoo. For the Tropical Rain Forest wall in Pittsburgh, we organized "morsels" of explanatory text according to the natural layers of a rain forest. As you walk along the mural's eight panels, the flora, fauna, and climate of the layers come alive. Color-codes identify the layers and their details, like how various animals climb and travel

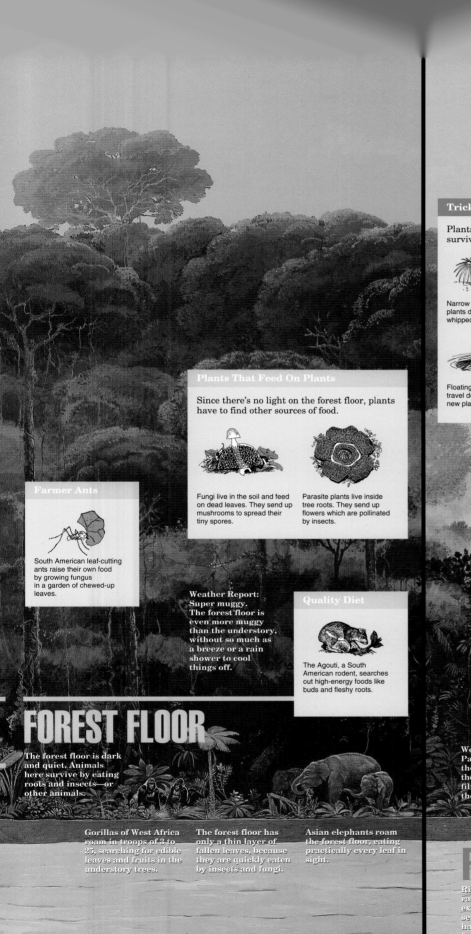

Plants That Feed On Plants

Since there's no light on the forest floor, plants have to find other sources of food.

Fungi live in the soil and feed on dead leaves. They send up mushrooms to spread their tiny spores.

Parasite plants live inside tree roots. They send up flowers which are pollinated by insects.

Farmer Ants

South American leaf-cutting ants raise their own food by growing fungus in a garden of chewed-up leaves.

Weather Report: Super muggy. The forest floor is even more muggy than the understory, without so much as a breeze or a rain shower to cool things off.

Quality Diet

The Agouti, a South American rodent, searches out high-energy foods like buds and fleshy roots.

FOREST FLOOR

The forest floor is dark and quiet. Animals here survive by eating roots and insects—or other animals.

Gorillas of West Africa roam in troops of 3 to 25, searching for edible leaves and fruits in the understory trees.

The forest floor has only a thin layer of fallen leaves, because they are quickly eaten by insects and fungi.

Asian elephants roam the forest floor, eating practically every leaf in sight.

Tricks of the River Plants

Plants of the rain forest have special ways to survive in or near rivers.

Narrow leaves of riverbank plants don't tear easily when whipped by rushing water.

Many plants send roots upward for the oxygen they can't get from watery soil.

Floating seeds of some plants travel downstream to start new plants.

Giant water lily heats up its flowers at night, attracting beetles that pollinate it.

Tricks of the River Creatures

River creatures of the rain forest have ways to survive in a watery home.

Long-toed jacana bird, found on all continents, can travel on river's surface by walking across plants.

Lungfish of Africa Amazon can wait dry spells by hiber in the mud.

South American water opossum keeps its young in a waterproof pouch.

African electric ca sends a powerful through the water stun prey.

In many areas, r overflow each ye and flood the lar

Sunlight breaks through at the river, and plants form a solid wall of greenery along the banks.

Weather Report: Partly sunny. Since the river cuts through the rain forest, sunlight filters down to reach the water.

The capybara, a of the Amazon, l in family groups has webbed feet swimming.

RIVER

Rivers cut through the rain forest, carrying excess water to the sea. They create a habitat very different from the rest of the rain forest.

Manatee of Africa and South America is the size of a small car but eats only plants.

VOICES OF THE 30s *Voices* is a unique CD-ROM. It is an educational database and curriculum for high school English and History classes about Western expansion, the Depression, and the Dust Bowl in the United States in the 1930s. It is also a set of activities, a living database, and a "library in a box." *Voices* was originally designed by two high-school teachers and used in their classrooms for almost five years before becoming a commercial product. Our goals were to maintain the rich content and activities, reshape the product so that others could understand how to use it, and exceed the quality of other interactive multimedia products. ■ *Voices* has many special features for classrooms. Teachers and students are encouraged to add new materials and commentary, allowing the database to "grow" better and more valuable over time. Plus, students can use the materials in the database to create custom "multimedia book reports" and present them to their classes. ■ *Voices* was reorganized to group similar kinds of content together. We flattened the hierarchy as much as we could by categorizing everything as either a Resource or an activity (called Themes.) These categories also signalled the two main uses of the product: research and critical thinking. The separation of Resources and Themes is introduced by a road with two groups of billboards (below), reinforcing the idea of taking a journey into the 30s. The division is also natural; the Resources are content, shipped to the buyer as a vast database, while the Themes are activities in the form of questions for students to respond to and think about. Very few interactive products challenge students to think, contribute, and create. In the classroom, this is almost all they should be doing. ■ All text in the interface is active, with built-in searching capabilities. To support browsing, users can click on a word and move to another occurrence of the same word, or pursue more sophisticated searches. *Voices* was designed to be used in the classroom, but not as the center of the learning experience. Related books, movies, and other materials not found in the program are referenced. The Themes are mostly things to do away from the computer. For example, activities in the section about the Okies ask students to remember their own experiences of moving, or encountering prejudice. ■ When students add their own materials to the program, they are automatically indexed and linked to the existing Resources. There are few precedents for integrating new material in interactive media, especially on CD-ROM. ■ Students can use the RouteMaker tool to create a sequence of screens of their own to show and share with others. All the rich media in *Voices* can be assembled and rearranged in custom multimedia products. This creative component is also rare in interactive media. ■ Finally, a six-minute movie was

SEPARATING FUNCTION AND CONTENT is critical in interactive media. In *Voices of the 30s*, bottom screen bars clearly remove access tools from screen content. Tools also appear in floating windows for quick moving to other sections without going through the program's hierarchy. Backgrounds use images drawn from the contents (below), and provide subtle clues to navigation.

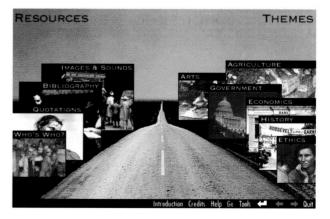

IMAGES & SOUNDS
Five Waifs

Five waifs — four young children caring for infant — sitting in doorway of cabin. Considered stereotype of "Okies." Ozark County Mountains, Missouri, 1940.

John Vachon, photographer

Source
In this Proud Land, plate 75, p. 84

LC-USF 34-61043

Related Topics
Family, Social History, Photos, Depression, Okies

Images   Sounds   Video   Zoom In   Index   Comments   Help   Go   Tools   Quit

Images   Sounds   Video   Zoom Out   Index   Comments   Help   Go   Tools   Quit

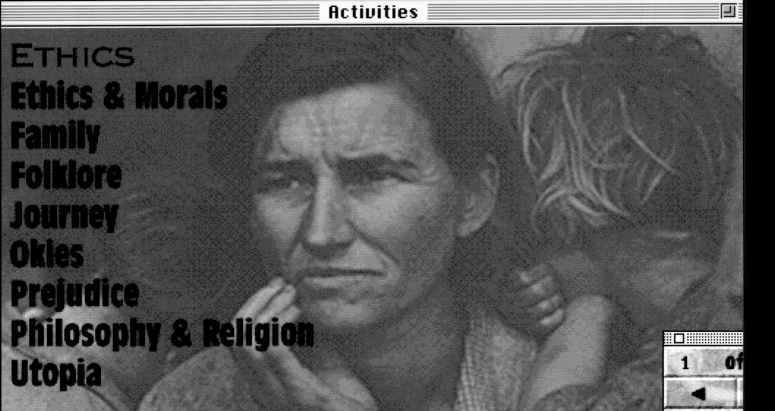

ETHICS
Ethics & Morals
Family
Folklore
Journey
Okies
Prejudice
Philosophy & Religion
Utopia

1   of

FAMILY

voice of: **Florence Thompson**

Florence Thompson & Daughters 1936

created to introduce *Voices*, using imagery from the program and interviews from people who lived through the 30s. It captures the attention and emotions of the students while introducing the program's key concepts. ■ **CREDITS:** Executive Producer: Kristina Hooper-Woolsey; Writing, research, content expertise: Pat Hanlon, Bob Campbell; Instructional design: Pat Hanlon; Producer, interaction design, programming, project management: Abbe Don; Information, interaction, visual design: Nathan Shedroff; Photography, production: James Cottle. ■ **DEMYSTIFYING MULTIMEDIA** is a book and CD-ROM commissioned by Apple Computer to explain the process of creating multimedia products. We concentrated on describing the development *process*, leaving tools and software explanations to other books. We wanted a timeless reference resource to help users in a rapidly changing industry. It has now become a standard for developers and students. ■ After considering different book organizations, we settled on arranging the content by *Process*, or the series of steps needed to create a successful product. But, for better access, we also indexed it by *Roles* (the responsibilities and skills needed), and by *Projects* (the prototypical categories of products.) ■ We deliberately tried to describe a successful development process and coax it into the reader's mind, replacing any competing process. The process is compelling because it is both described and infused into the structure of the book. ■ The book's secondary organizations are represented by categorized indices. The *Role index* describes different process roles, each having a description, highlighted responsibilities, case studies and interviews, an icon, and employment information. The icons work as data filters throughout the book, making it easy to browse and find related material. Similarly, the *Project index* categorizes descriptions of various projects and establishes its own family of icons. ■ The book pages were designed with color-coded chapters, illustrations, and jump words, and used the icons to layer the role and project information on relevant pages. Open space, marginalia, and non-grid visuals give the book an airy, free-form look. ■ **CREDITS:** Text, information and visual design, illustration: Nathan Shedroff; Text: Ken From; Text, project management: J. Sterling Hutto; Content: Henri Poole; Writing, research: Mark Beaulieu, Chris Okon; Photography: James Cottle; Illustration: Kathleen Egge; Production by Drue Miller.

SEPARATING KINDS OF CONTENT is also critical to clarify complex information. In *Voices*, screen content is divided by purpose: text, video, and images on the right, titles, authors, sources, and topic links on the left. *Demystifying Multimedia* (below, following pages) separates content by the process steps of creating multimedia, and also by references to roles and kinds of projects.

How to Use This Book

Icons at the top of left-hand pages indicate the different roles associated with the information on these pages.

This book is process oriented, taking you from the beginning, organizing steps of a project through prototyping, production, testing, and distribution. The navigation bars at the top of each page tell you the page number and project phase.

The text has been written to clearly explain the often complex terms and processes in the multimedia industry. Industry "buzz words" are explained both when used and in the combined Glossary/Index at the end of the book.

Twelve basic project types are described in 12 special two-page spreads following the roles indexes. Use these spreads as summaries of some of the key differences between different kinds of projects and as guides to the rest of the book from the perspective of these projects.

The book has been color coded to help visually identify each section.

Margin notes, box stories, and quotes from industry professionals provide related and expanded information from different points of view.

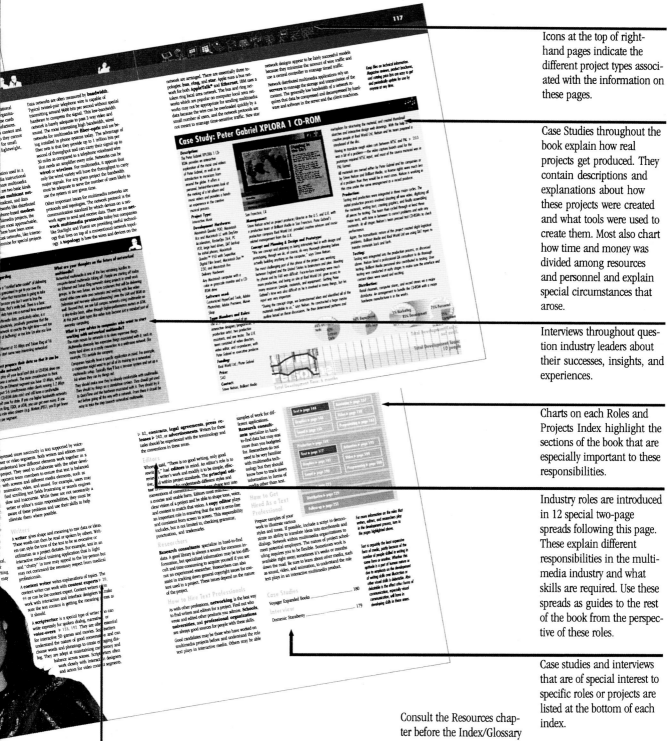

Icons at the top of right-hand pages indicate the different project types associated with the information on these pages.

Case Studies throughout the book explain how real projects get produced. They contain descriptions and explanations about how these projects were created and what tools were used to create them. Most also chart how time and money was divided among resources and personnel and explain special circumstances that arose.

Interviews throughout question industry leaders about their successes, insights, and experiences.

Charts on each Roles and Projects Index highlight the sections of the book that are especially important to these responsibilities.

Industry roles are introduced in 12 special two-page spreads following this page. These explain different responsibilities in the multimedia industry and what skills are required. Use these spreads as guides to the rest of the book from the perspective of these roles.

Case studies and interviews that are of special interest to specific roles or projects are listed at the bottom of each index.

Consult the Resources chapter before the Index/Glossary for lists of books, magazines, tools, conferences, and organizations that cover the multimedia industry.

"Jump" words in the text point to other pages where related topics are explained.

ENCYCLOPÆDIA AFRICANA, the prototype for an interactive database of linked text, images, sounds, and video, was designed and produced by Dynamic Diagrams over a five month period. The final encyclopedia is planned to be a very large electronic database covering all aspects of African culture dispersed around the world. Its development is expected to take several years. This prototype was designed to illustrate how existing multimedia technology could be used to present such material in ways that are both visually exciting and easy to access. ■ We worked with an editorial team led by professors K. Anthony Appiah and Henry Louis Gates, Jr. and their colleagues at Harvard University's W.E.B. Du Bois Institute for Afro-American Research. As designers, we found ourselves acting as catalysts in the editorial process. Every sketch and visualization we presented led to further discussions and new specifications for the prototype. ■ Our basic method was to design by addition. We began by defining the requirements of the different languages for the kinds of material to be included: written stories, timelines, and maps. Each of these could be illustrated by still images, videos and audio. We then created basic layouts for the written stories that would make up the majority of the encyclopedia. The layouts helped define the optimal legibility of text on the screen in terms of font, size, line spacing, and column width. The final screen layout was created by the size and placement of the resulting text block, its relation to illustrations, and the instruments needed for interactive access and control. ■ A basic color scheme was developed in parallel with the

screen layout. Key colors were selected from the brown/red/beige range to express the warm ambiance of the material we were using. Contrasting yellow and green colors were selected for highlighting the text and icons of linked information. ■ In general, the icons and border treatment for the instruments of control were made as delicate and non-aggressive as possible. The designer must clearly distinguish the interactive from the non-interactive areas on the screen. We always seek to efficiently present the content of the program, not the buttons to be clicked. ■ Controls were grouped in the screen borders around the content areas. Global controls such as lists of content, searching, and help links to general information found throughout the encyclopedia were placed on the left margin. Specific information about each article as it appeared, and links to paths related to that article, were placed on the top of the screen. In articles and maps, the right margin was reserved for local icons linking to the specific information being presented on the screen. In timelines these links were distributed across horizontal colored bands. ■ Creating the *Encyclopædia Africana* prototype afforded

PLANNING STORY PATHS The *Encyclopædia Africana* is planned to be a linked, interactive database of images, video, sound, and text representing all aspects of African culture throughout the world. The database is divided into eight chapters. The screens (below) show a path looping through linked stories found in different chapters. From the title and contents (opposite left), the user selects the *Warfare* chapter, then a topic within it, then follows the story and its link to a related story in *Philosophy and Religion*. Further links lead to interactive maps that relate the migration of religious ideas to music, which lead to multimedia timelines in the *Art* chapter. This path appears in the program's architecture (following pages) with a blue line linking detailed screens.

us the opportunity to exercise design control over a complex project, while at the same time call on the enormous talents of the editorial team. Each stage of the design was accomplished through team effort. In the case of the jazz timeline, for example, the editorial staff provided us with

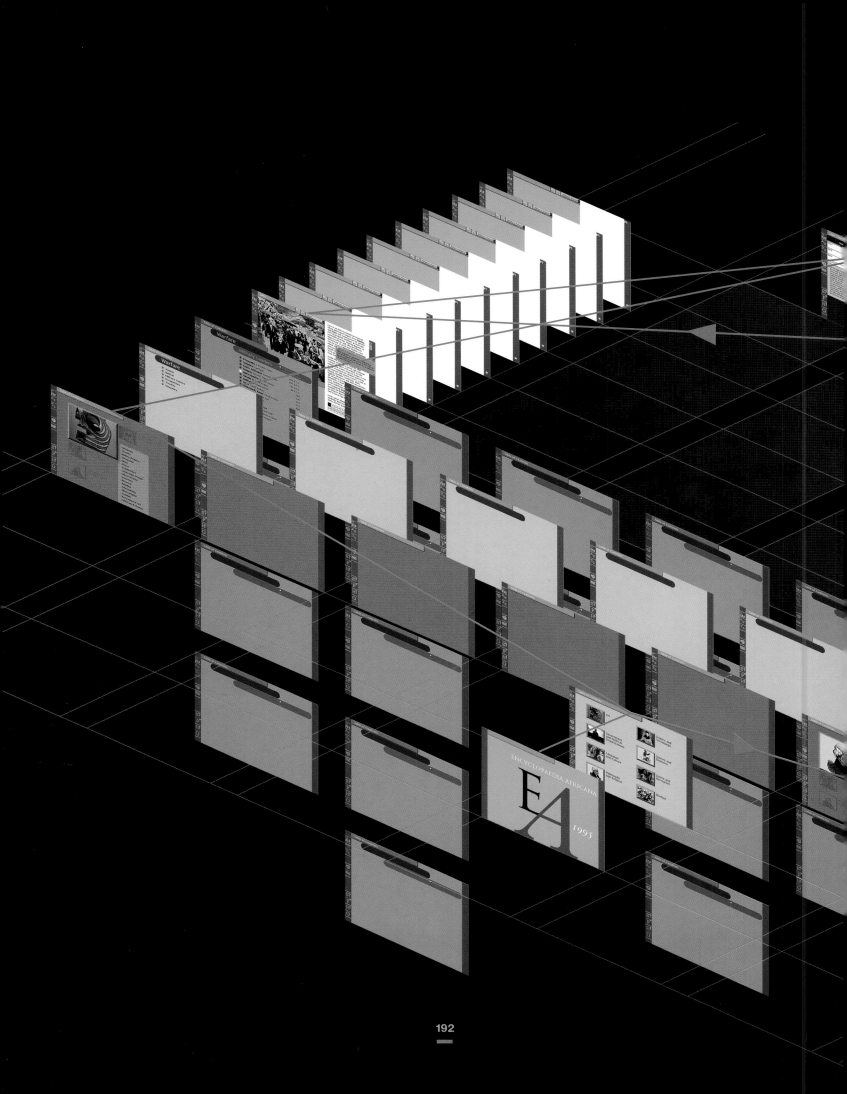

a summary article, and a broad selection of both photographic and video material defining the scope of the segment. We proceeded to visualize this content in a timeline format, grouping important cities, musical styles, and musicians in their appropriate periods. This led to further refinements in the content of the story, and searches for additional photographs, videos, and studio
recordings. The result was a timeline divided into three chronological time periods, each period having two musical styles
fully populated with multimedia examples.

PLANNING A GLOBAL DATABASE A plan of the
chitecture illustrates circulation through it (below).
contents screens are shown (opposite lower left), wh
branch to one of eight chapters. The highlighted scr
line show a path through related stories found in sev
(preceding two pages). Closeups of one of the inte
and the multimedia timeline screens (following two
the placement of navigation controls on the screen
al controls are constant on the left side, information
story, its relations, and local information are on the

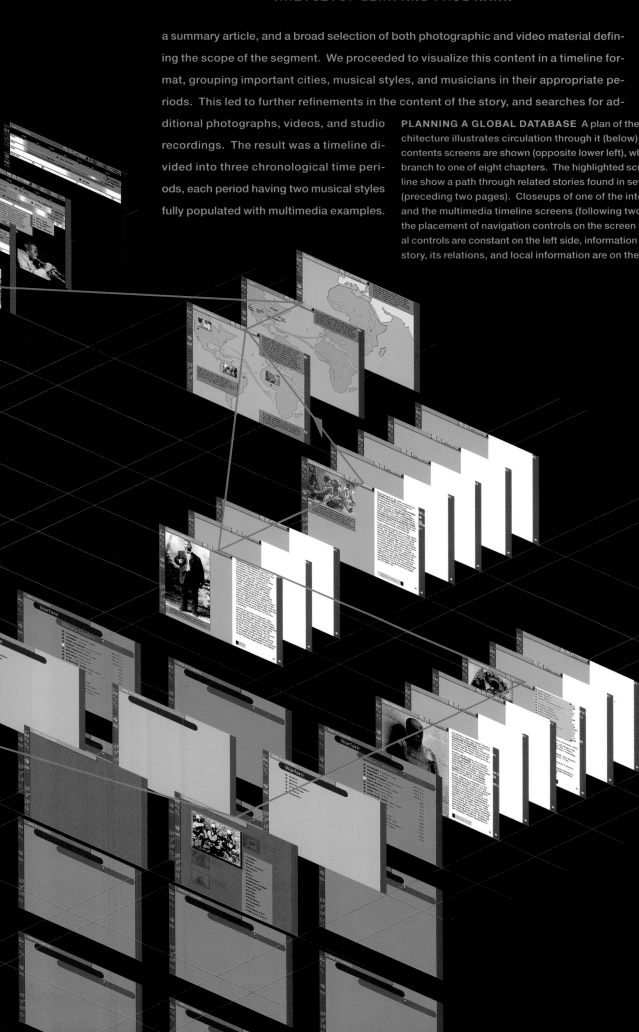

Diffusion

Chicago

New York

New Orleans

Jazz Timeline

	1890		95		1900

Place

Style

Style

Musicians

Ragtime

Jazz, a complex marriage of African rhythmic conceptions and European instrumentation and musical forms, was created by black musicians in New Orleans in the early 1900s and spread north to Chicago, New York and the rest of the United States in the 1920s.

ew Orleans
ntext
rgence of
of numerous
d active
, Caribbean,
an cultures,
the hybridity
s, traditions,
ns such as
narches that
re peculiar
nt roles in the

Jazz Timeline

Place

Style

Style

Musicians

1890

95

1900

05

1910

Ragtime

New Orleans

Early Jazz

1910

15

1920

Stride

Chicago

New York

Dixieland

1890
1920
1920
1960
1960
Present

Music

Stride

Chicago

New York

Dixieland

1890
1920
1920
1960
1960
Present

Music

Born into poverty in New Orleans and first taught cornet at a local reform school, Louis Armstrong became one of the most celebrated musicians in jazz history, bringing a new level of creativity and energy to solo improvisation in the early 1920s and going on to lead some of the most important pioneering ensembles of all time, the Hot Fives and Hot Sevens; an international jazz celebrity by the 1930s, Armstrong remained at the forefront of jazz music until his death in 1971.

rmstrong sings, scats
ys trumpet in a
n of "Dinah," at a
ance in Copenhagen,
k on October 21, 1933
rst European tour.
no: Louis Armstrong,"
sic, Video Enterprises,
ords Inc., 1989.)

KRZYSZTOF LENK AND PAUL KAHN

■ **THE MONGOLIAN FELT TENT** (as described by Paul Kahn) In the spring of 1994, I was attending a symposium on Central Asia at the University of Toronto. I heard from my friend James Bosson that the first show of Mongolian art to come to North America was being mounted by the Asian Art Museum of San Francisco for exhibit the following year. I had been interested in Mongolian history, literature and culture for several decades. I saw the opportunity to contribute the design skills of Dynamic Diagrams to the show as one that would not happen twice in my lifetime. With the support of the Asian Art Museum, we began to identify what could be done on a computer that could add to the show *Mongolia: The Legacy of Chinggis Khan.* ■ We decided that we did not want to duplicate a printed catalog or digitize the artwork on display. The printed page is a far better medium for an art catalog, and the artwork itself would be available to the museum visitor in the galleries. But there was much more about Mongolia that would not fit on gallery labels and wall graphics. We wanted to give the museum visitor access to some additional dimensions of Mongolian culture. ■ We found the answer in the most contemporary object in the show, a Mongolian *ger*. The show would feature the circular felt tent, known in America as a yurt, which was set up in the museum's interior courtyard. What was this thing? What was it made of? How was it built? We imagined these questions in the mind of the museum visitor. I knew of the extraordinary photographs and video taken by ethnographer Carole Pegg during her many field sessions in Mongolia, which included footage of the felt-making process and the stages in putting up a new tent. We built our computer application, *The Mongolian Felt Tent*,

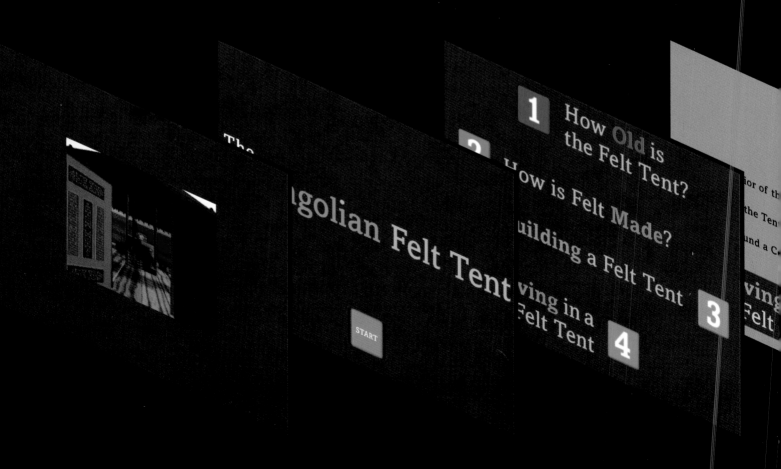

around Carole's photographic material. We created a three-dimensional model of the tent on the computer from book illustrations and photographs, populated it with furniture, musical instruments, and everyday household and religious objects, and then rendered it from different points of view. We collected historical paintings, etchings and photographs, designed interface controls, and selected and cropped photographs. We developed an animated game which simulated the steps of building the *ger*. We photographed the interior of a tent belonging to a Mongolian-American and stitched the pictures together into a Virtual Reality movie. One former Peace Corps volunteer loaned us her horsehead fiddle, and another made sure all the Mongolian words were pronounced correctly. It was a labor of love. ■ Having artistic control over such a project gave us the opportunity to demonstrate our theory of multimedia: use computer technology to create synergy by combining several forms of information signal. Most museum visitors have no idea how felt is made on the steppe. The process was shown in seven stages. The still pictures represent a process which is described in an audio nar-

PLANNING A LINEAR DATABASE A multimedia, interactive program was produced to add a cultural dimension to an exhibit of Mongolian art. *The Mongolian Felt Tent* is a story divided into four chapters: the tent's history, material, construction, and its use. The chapters are arranged sequentially, with each having easily accessible supplementary material. The close-ups below show entry through the program's title and content screens (opposite). Then, four screens are shown from the chapter *Living in a Felt Tent*: its own contents screen and then three sub-chapters. As seen in the program's architecture (following pages), the chapters are planned in line, but users can view them any way they wish. Video, audio, 3D animation, and games are sprinkled throughout.

ration. The same verbal material can be absorbed more slowly by reading the text of a caption on the screen. The sound and motion of the process itself are captured in a video clip. Giving the user control to manipulate and combine these four signals is the goal of interactive multimedia.

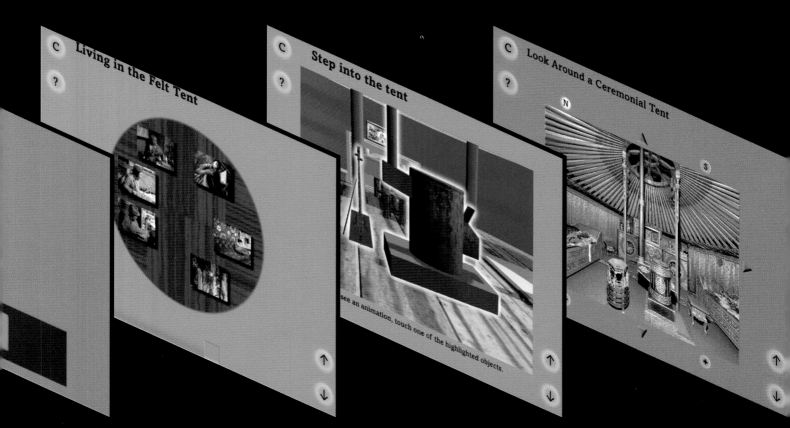

KRZYSZTOF LENK AND PAUL KAHN

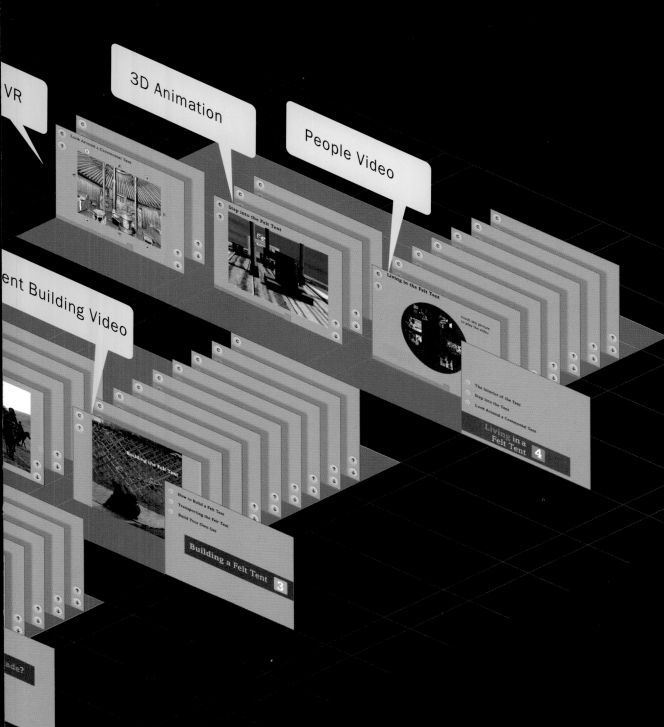

■ **INSO CORPORATION** For many years the electronic spelling-checkers, grammar-checkers, dictionaries, and thesauri developed by Houghton Mifflin's Software Division have been smoothly incorporated in many word processors and desktop publishing systems. In 1994, the independent company of InfoSoft International (later renamed Inso Corporation) was created from the former software division to specialize in electronic linguistic tools. Their first new product was IntelliScope, a software tool for analyzing, parsing, and tagging text in many languages. ■ Because of its linguistic sophistication, the program is difficult to explain to non-professionals. We were asked to design a poster to show its mechanisms. We asked them to provide samples of IntelliScope at work which could be used as poster components. As usual, the job became more complicated than expected; we also produced a twenty-page brochure to show the software's many features. In both poster and brochure, we used typographic structures to clearly distinguish two levels of text, and a second color to highlight the details.

The text samples display the software's major features, promoting the concept of text as an image in the most literal sense.

MAPPING A LANGUAGE Inso Corporation produces IntelliScope, a software tool for analyzing, parsing, and storing text in many languages. To promote its many sophisticated analytic mechanisms, text examples were used on a poster and brochure.

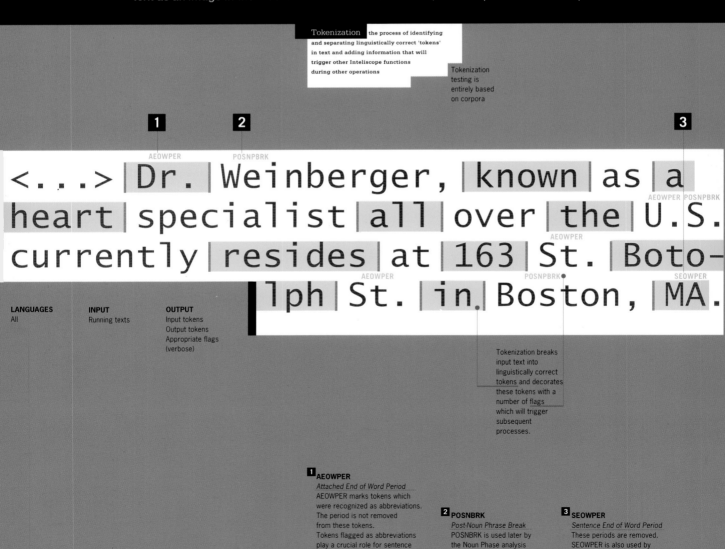

Tokenization the process of identifying and separating linguistically correct 'tokens' in text and adding information that will trigger other Inteliscope functions during other operations

Tokenization testing is entirely based on corpora

1 AEOWPER **2** POSNPBRK **3**

<...> |Dr. |Weinberger, |known |as |a heart |specialist |all |over |the |U.S. currently |resides |at |163 |St. |Botolph |St. |in |Boston, |MA.

AEOWPER POSNPBRK
AEOWPER
AEOWPER POSNPBRK
SEOWPER

LANGUAGES
All

INPUT
Running texts

OUTPUT
Input tokens
Output tokens
Appropriate flags
(verbose)

Tokenization breaks input text into linguistically correct tokens and decorates these tokens with a number of flags which will trigger subsequent processes.

1 **AEOWPER**
Attached End of Word Period
AEOWPER marks tokens which were recognized as abbreviations. The period is not removed from these tokens.
Tokens flagged as abbreviations play a crucial role for sentence splitting mechanism.

2 **POSNBRK**
Post-Noun Phrase Break
POSNBRK is used later by the Noun Phase analysis mechanism.

3 **SEOWPER**
Sentence End of Word Period
These periods are removed. SEOWPER is also used by sentence splitting mechanism.

■ **MOBILE COMPUTERS FROM THE IBM THINKPAD™ FAMILY** are marvels of technology. Their high quality was in marked contrast to the poor design of packaging and literature provided to the buyer. Dynamic Diagrams was asked by IBM to analyze this problem and to suggest improvements. ■ First, we recorded the whole process of unpacking the existing box and assembling a computer. Not surprisingly, we found a total lack of order and logic in the way parts were packed, labeled and supported by instructions. An inexperienced user would have a hard time finding which parts hook to which place on the computer, and in what order things should be assembled. With that user in mind, we suggested the addition of a product map to support assembly. ■ The map is a poster-size diagram, abstracting the computer and all its pieces in their proper relationship. Such a map frees the user from the familiar anxiety of making a serious assembly error. Our map suggestion was accepted by IBM and, thanks to the company's enthusiasm, it became part of the larger effort of redefining packaging for mobile computers. Sam Lucente and Debbie Dell of IBM led the project, Tom Hughes of Tom Hughes Design provided the art direction.

MAPPING A PROCESS A poster-size product map (below) was produced to simplify the understanding and assembling of components in an IBM computer. Same-size spaces on the map help the buyer to easily identify, place, and connect each component.

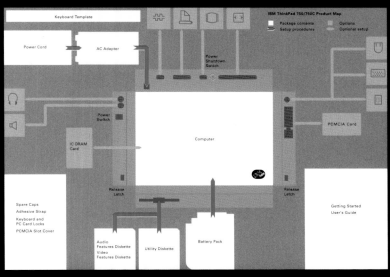

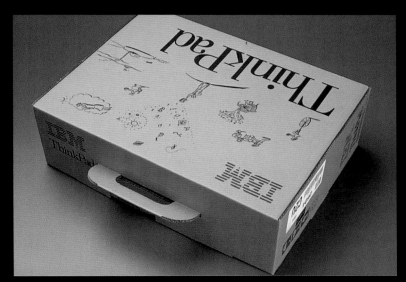

INFORMATION LANDSCAPES It is night. You are dreaming. You float above your house, gently drifting in the night sky. You fly higher, and higher, as fast as thought . . . and you find a space, dense with information. The landscape slowly shifts, some information drifts and fades away, other information comes closer, until it appears in sharp relief. As you look more closely at one part of the picture, new interests come to mind. They appear as constellations on the horizon. With a thought, you can go to any one of them, seeking, discovering. It is truly a flight of fancy, a flight of imagination. ■ The new work at the Visible Language Workshop at MIT recreates this sort of dreamscape where clusters of information objects are scattered throughout the three-dimensional space on a computer. The viewer can fly through this space and encounter the separate intelligent objects and not get lost. The environment provides *context.* For the moment, these objects are discrete groupings of data—small systems that tell us about air traffic control problems, mutual funds, or automatic text layout, for example—each placed in a dynamic new environment. Muriel R. Cooper coined the term *Information Landscape* to describe this new work. In

contrast to an Information Highway which is linear, a landscape is an environment for information. It provides a continuum of paths from one place to another. ■ A landscape reveals itself slowly. Approach a valley and you first make out the shape of the hills, the path of the streams, and fences. At closer range you distinguish a maple from a pine. The journey itself begins to have meaning. Also, multiple scales are constantly available—an individual flower or petal is visible close at hand while distant peaks and the slopes between provide a sense of place. We are building abstract information structures that have these qualities. ■ The information shown (right) is an outline of research in the Media Lab. There are three sections within the lab, identified by color. You are moving into the Information and Entertainment section (in blue). We represented the relationship between professors and their groups by having two planes of information—the primary one in white and in front, the secondary group in color. In the distance, you can see the outline of more detailed information

INVENTING INFORMATION ENVIRONMENTS The future MIT student sits at a computer terminal looking for information about the Institute. First, he sees a broad overview of the school (opposite). Then he "flies" into text at smaller scales to find more details about his specific interests. Permitting smooth travel from one level of detail to another maintains the information's context.

Massachusetts Institute of Technology

Bulletin 1994-95
Courses and Degree Programs Issue

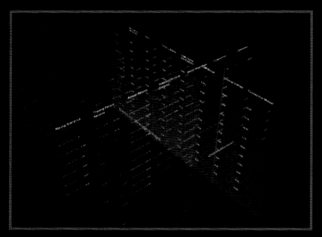

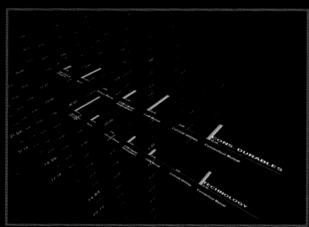

INVENTING INFORMATION PERSPECTIVES In this project, comparative figures for seven mutual funds were organized on grids in space. Several views, or contexts, of the information can be displayed to assess it differently. Translucent planes slice orthogonally through the grids to highlight, for example, seven categories of information for one fund (such as annual returns and sector weightings), or one information category for all seven funds.

about our area, the Visible Language Workshop. The action of zooming to it corresponds to getting more detailed information about a subject. ■ The large piece (previous page) is the cover of the *MIT Bulletin* by David Small and Suguru Ishizaki.

■ **FINANCIAL VIEWPOINTS** By Lisa Strausfeld. An experimental, interactive information space (left and opposite) uses three dimensions to volumetrically represent a sample portfolio of seven separate mutual funds. Giving depth to the user's point of view makes it possible to represent the context and context shifts of the data, allowing many "pictures" of the fund information in a single, continuous environment. ■ *Financial Viewpoints* uses many visual and numerical representations of the funds, including bar charts, graphs, and photographs of the fund managers. Each one of these representations by itself can produce a specific meaning or force a particular interpretation of the information. Using graphical and spatial design techniques to focus attention, such as transparency and dynamic objects, *Financial Viewpoints* allows all of these representations to coexist in one space. The user's ability to move freely through the space and access these representations from many points of view allows him or her to grasp the complexity of the information, much like we grasp the complexity of our physical environment by aggregating a sequence of familiar, simple representations.

■ **GEOSPACE** By Ishantha Lokuge and Suguru Ishizaki. Suppose you want to live in Cambridge. You are new to the city, you want to explore the area around it, and you want to find an apartment. Having heard of the perilous life style in Cambridge itself (let's say), you are interested in relative crime levels and accessibility to hospitals in towns near it. ■ First, you ask the GeoSpace program: *Show me Cambridge.* An area map appears, the label *Cambridge* on the screen grows more opaque and larger. The information related to Cambridge, such as hospitals, highways, colleges and so on, also

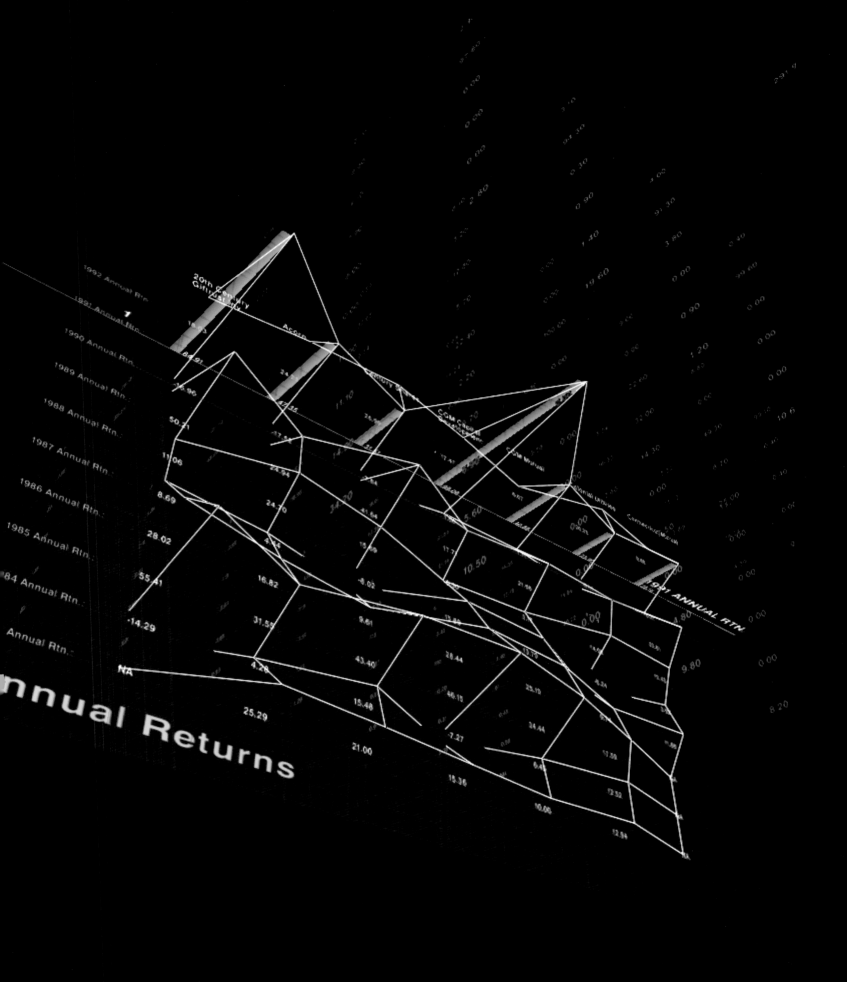

strengthens visually, but to a slightly lesser degree. In effect, the system has begun
to react to your wants, and is ready to emphasize the information you request within the area's visually dense environment.
■ Then you ask: *Show me crime data*. The
system rotates the map, showing a three
dimensional view of relative crime data in
the greater Boston area in the form of rising bars. ■ Looking at the data, you see
that the nearby town of Waltham has a
lower crime rate, and you ask: *Show me
Waltham*. The label *Waltham* and its highways, hospitals and schools now increase
in opacity and size. But while focussing
on Waltham, GeoSpace still maintains the
previous information context by distin-
guishing Cambridge from other regions on
the map with graduations of translucency.

■ Now you ask: *Show me hospitals*. All hospitals near Waltham are promptly shown
using the same visual techniques. But suppose you wanted to see pharmacies too, and
the system did not realize that. You can teach it your explicit wants by saying: *Show*

chelsea
brookline
boston
needham
Elizabeth
walgreens
cvs
93
95
Glover

me pharmacies too. Then the system displays pharmacies as well. Furthermore, it will have learned the relationship you have specified between hospitals and pharmacies. Thus, in any future interactions, it will display both simultaneously. It has learned to respond just as you want it to respond.

■ **NEWS VIEWS** By Yin Yin Wong. Finding your way through the news today is a formidable chore. This project uses multiple viewpoints to filter news stories. A square plane culls stories and organizes them into piles. When the plane is rotated, different sides of it show different story views, such as the headline, source, or an agent's explanation of the story's importance. Tilting the plane flat expands the story for reading.

British Airways ready to buy larger jetliners
U.S. automakers' sales up sharply in January
Chrysler LHS -- evidence of evolution
jetliners
superhighway
Government says airline complaints down
Czech privatization plan triggers Parliament cri
Hungarian deputies seek reinsta
Justice blocks Texas execution
China steps up lunar new year execution spree
Eric Bogosian's new
Clinton administration announces public housing anti-crime effort
Infomercial advertisi
execution
High court injunction
death penalty
Lebanese clan executes killer in line with Islamic law
Richards says high-speed rail franchise should be
Souter denies request for new challenge of abortion
'Hello Again' elevate
Richards says high-speed rail franchise should be
Court order bans Max
revival
South Lake Tahoe bans panhandling Box Score
Legislator seeks state control of Yankees
Clinton offers assistance in evacuation of Sarajevo
Storage unit tenants accuse Caltrans of deception
U.S. supports U.N. request for airstrike authorization
food aid
Mass. jobless rate 7.2 for January
U.N. says 22 million in Africa will need emergency food aid
earthquake
Sen. Kennedy improves behavior image, but will i
L.A. officials offer reassurance in wake of quake
kennedy
O'Connor refuses California request in labor cas
jobless
Delta flight lands safely in Atlanta despite dama

ss Briefs

buy rice from the United States

Jobless rate for 11 selected states

ed up privatization of arms industry

Jobless rate by industry

or David Owen against lifting of Yu... Nielsen monopoly threatened in TV ratings field

tinue aid to Nepal

Fear of earthquake in California mounting

d during morning jog

ht

Poll: New York lawyers think they're tops

remains high in NYC, lower in New Jersey

vinent

ls & howl

Survey: Labor lead over Tories has strong foundation

mbs job growth in January

Broadway

Cruise to lose -- weight that is -- on today's ships

ll musical

Poll: Harding should not skate in Lillehammer

cal season

Few trust British or Chinese rule in Hong Kong

king to the stage Goldberg to host 66th Academy Awards

Poll finds Japan-U.S. relations viewed as good

lifestyle

Actor Joseph... dead at 88 and passenger services delayed

'Angie' a major part of Disney's hopes for '94

'Mrs. Doubtfire' dominates European box office

'Mrs. Doubtfire' now No. 18 on all-time list

s?

'Ace Ventura' finds top spot at nation's box office

academy awards

Sliver, 'Indecent Proposal' favored for Razzies

disney

Masur, relatively speaking

ical rift widens

s visit to Cuba heralds thaw

mes editorial

oblems force NASA to cancel satellite deployment

ty unveils manifesto for South African election

■ **NYNEX SHUTTLE** By Rob Silvers. The new information landscape must accommodate changes in the ways information can be represented, and in the ways you want to see it. For example, as new technologies are developed, the viewer must be able to shift among them, transforming the same data from one representation to another, from an abstract image, to a realistic map, or to a diagram. The NYNEX experimental video conferencing system connects its corporate offices in White Plains, New York, with MIT's Media Lab in Cambridge. Each node represents a person with whom one might confer. The user can shift from a more familiar, two-dimensional representation of the network, to a spatial, three-dimensional view of this "office" structure and its services.

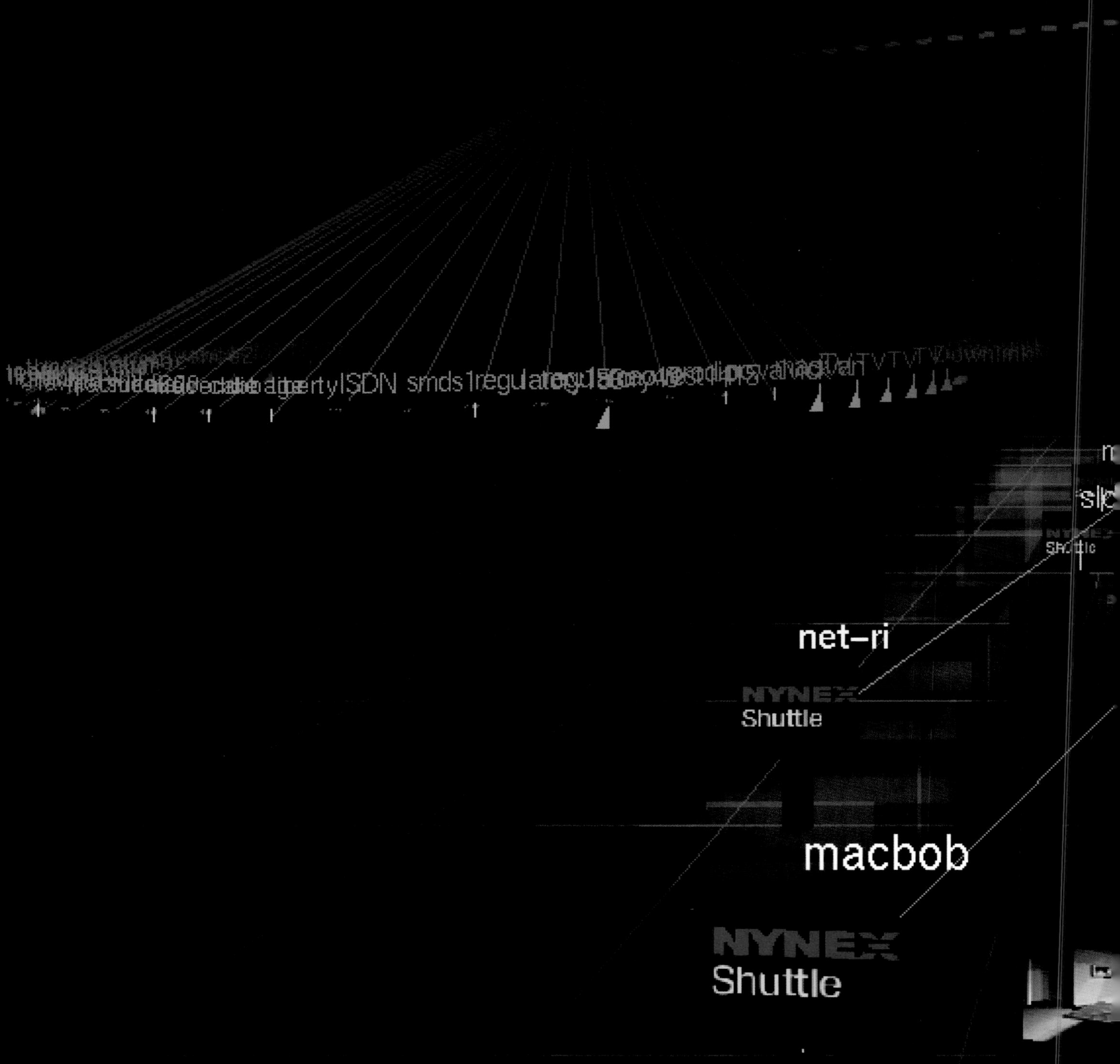

net–ri

NYNEX
Shuttle

macbob

NYNEX
Shuttle

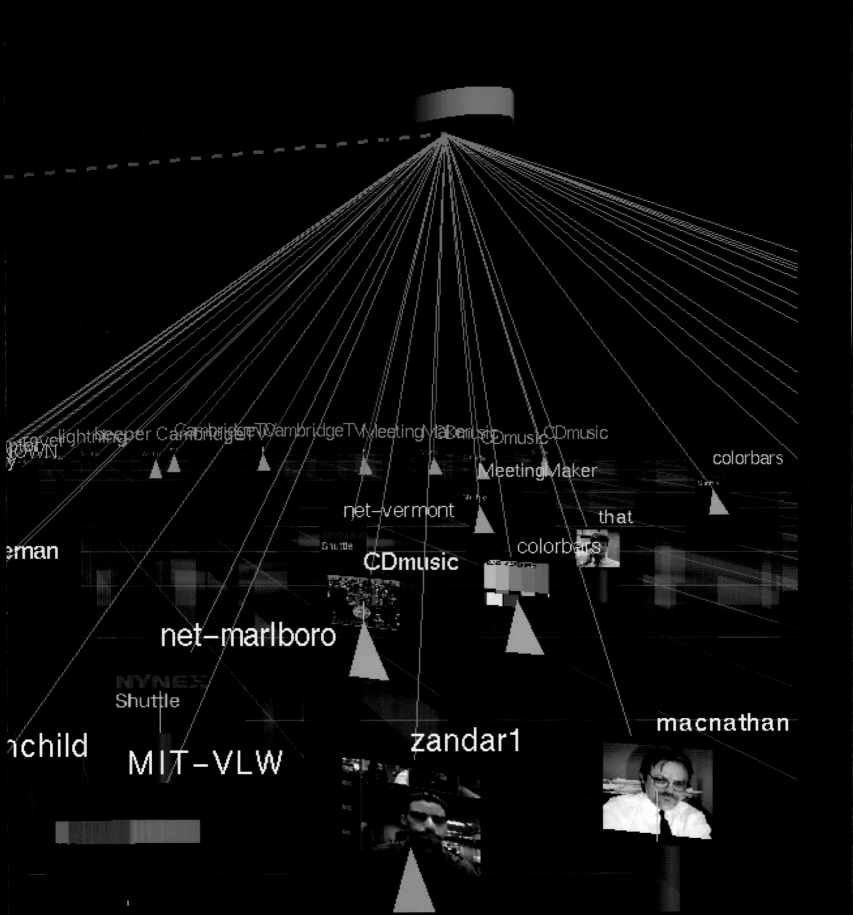

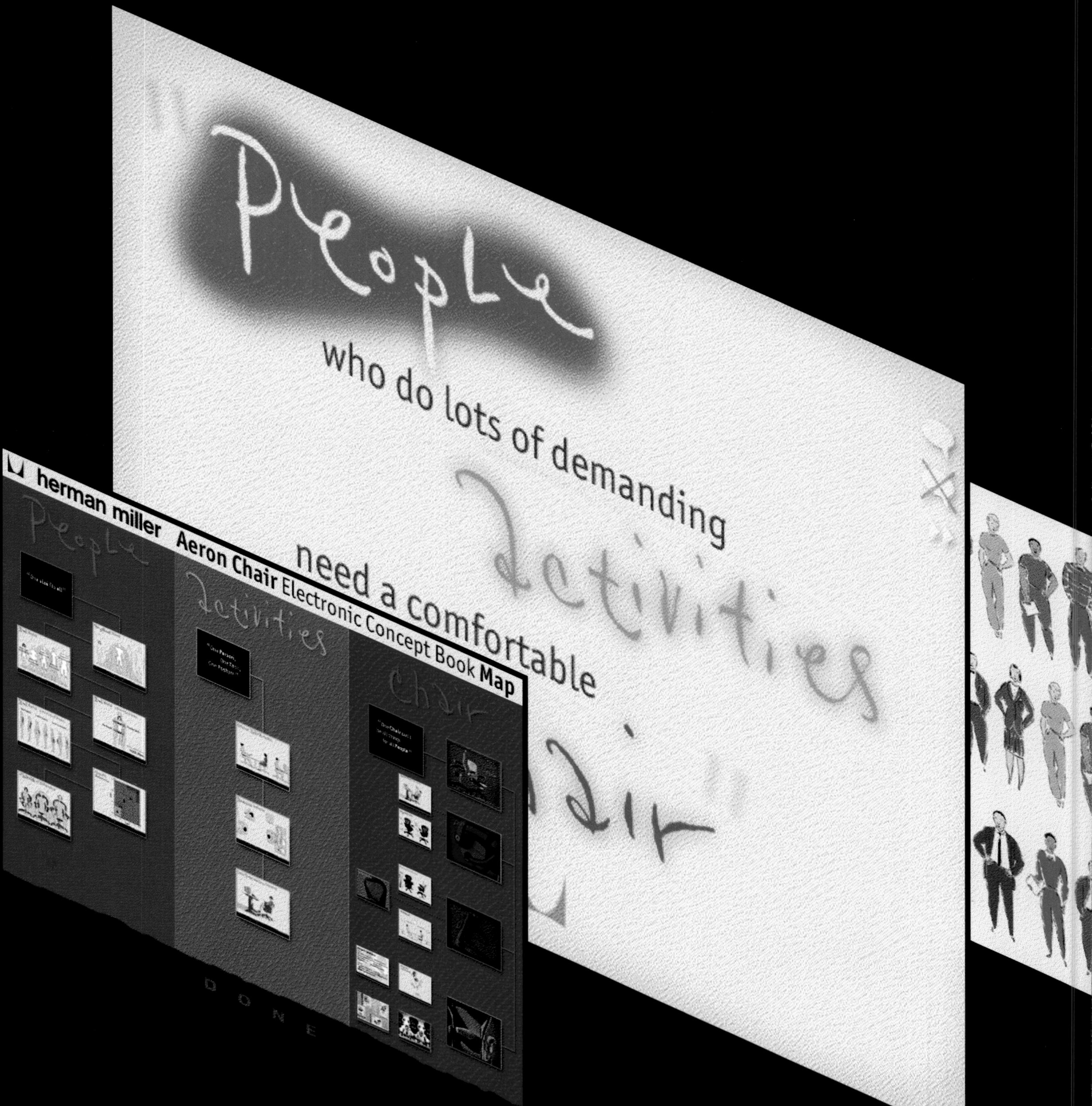

People
who do lots of demanding
Activities
need a comfortable
herman miller Aeron Chair Electronic Concept Book Map
People
Activities
Chair
D O N E

THE AERON CHAIR When introducing the new Aeron chair, Herman Miller had to overcome a rather difficult hurdle: the market's perceptions of what a chair should be. In the industry, the criteria for a well designed chair is often based on its aesthetic form and price. Critical evaluation of its function and ergonomic performance are often overlooked. Compliance to regulations and broad ergonomic standards are marketed as "comfort." One has to sit in an Aeron chair to experience and appreciate how differently this chair behaves. The chair is unquestionably in a category of its own. ■ Throughout a series of interviews with the products development team at Herman Miller, and their prospective customers, we realized the chair's unique attributes were the sum of many innovations—in form, in structural engineering, in applied materials, in manufacturing techniques and

PLANNING INTERACTIVE INFORMATION The new Aeron chair is presented on a CD-ROM, with information divided into three sections: the physical diversity of people, the diversity of their activities while seated, and the ergonomic features of the chair itself. The words *people*, *activities*, and *chair* are used to navigate between sections. Whimsical titles and illustrations create a non-technical personality for this technically advanced product.

processes, and in ergonomic approaches. Our challenge was to present the innovations, and convey the volume of research that went into the development of the chair, without numbing anyone's mind with tech-

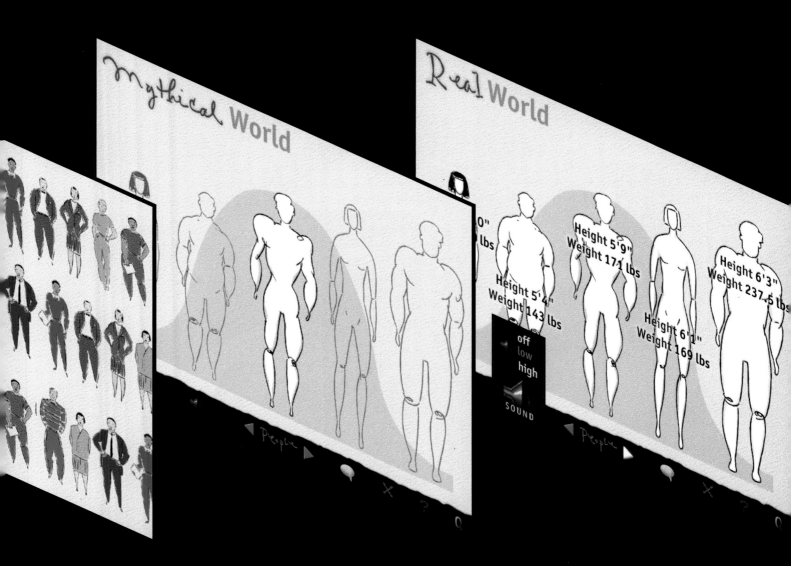

nical features. ■ We developed a computer-based presentation of the chair, with a focus on what one should consider when selecting a chair. What could have been a dry, technical discussion became an engaging look at the diversity of people, the activities

they pursue, and the chair that makes them all more comfortable. The presentation is multi-lingual, delivered on a CD-ROM, and utilizes video interviews, ergonomic simulations, animatics, and a user-controlled navigable movie (right) to provide the viewer multiple perspectives of the product and these interwoven topics. ■ In addition, the movie of the chair was produced to enable Herman Miller sales representatives to "show" the chair to prospective customers without having to crate and transport a real chair to each sales presenta-

ACTIVATING PARTICIPATION The viewer is in the driver's seat when watching the three-dimensional, user-controlled navigable movie of the Aeron chair. This animation was created from 1568 still photos which were taken in five-degree increments around the chair at several distances and angles. It enables the viewer to spin, twirl, and zoom in (sequence below) on specific chair details. This virtual demonstration is the next best thing to a real test drive.

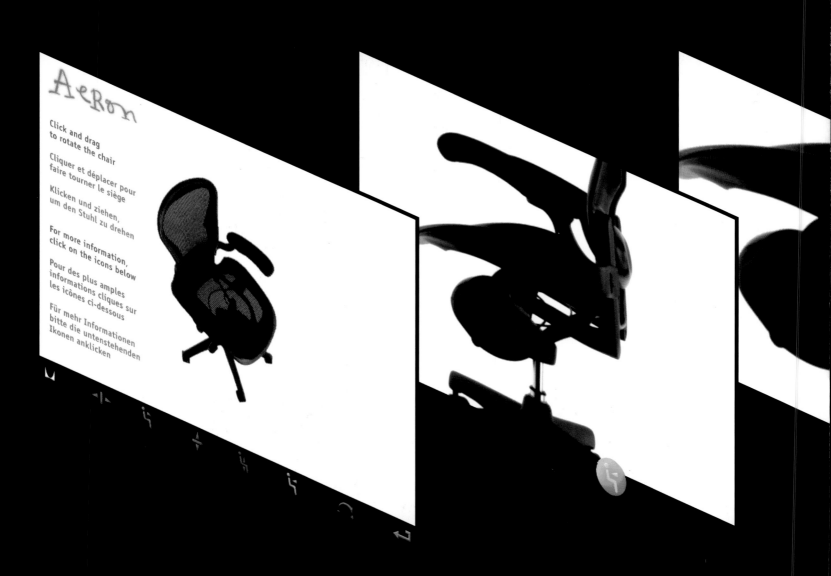

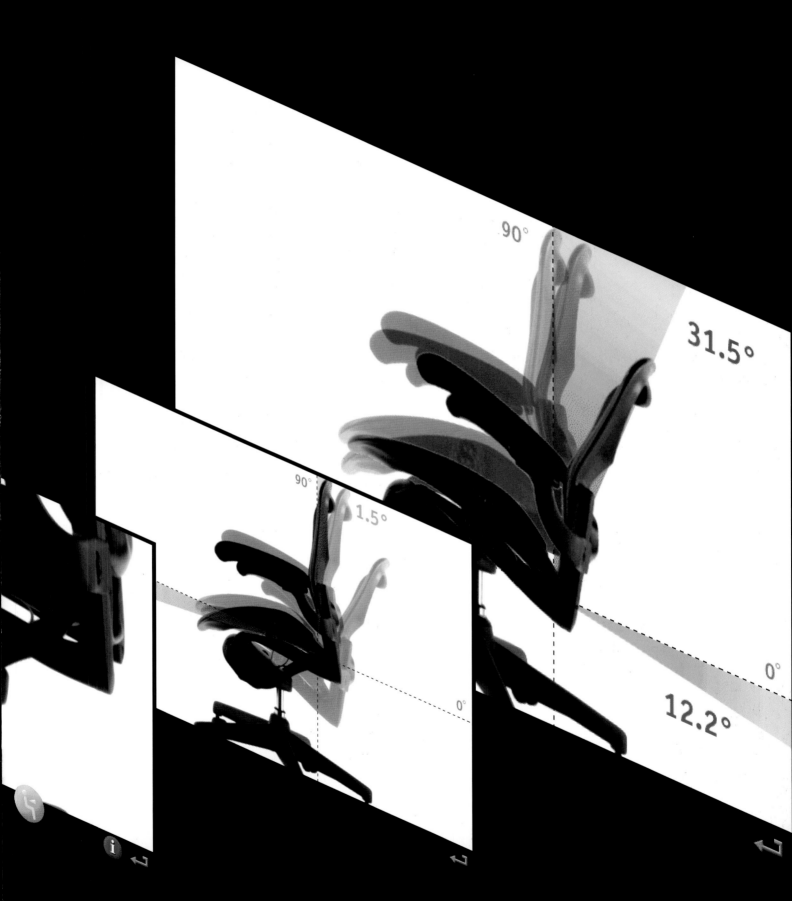

tion. The viewers can examine the chair from any angle they want and view specific details at their own pace. ■ **CREDITS:** Art Director: Claire Barry; Interface Designers: Claire Barry, Paula Meiselman, Blair Beebe; Programmer: Dan O'Sullivan; Photographer: Stan Musilek; Illustrator: Ward Schumaker; Production Artist: David Weissberg.

■ **THE MAYO CLINIC PHARMACIST** The idea of this CD-ROM is to give the inquisitive and health conscious lay person a tool to obtain intelligent medication information, and help them create a reference guide for themselves and their family. ■ The original information source is a three-volume, 1700-page publication containing drug information about patient prescriptions and over-the-counter medicines. Though the books are written in a layman's language, they have several drawbacks. If you want to know everything about any prescribed medicine, you have to flip through all the volumes, as well as the 50-page addendums that come out monthly. While the information is cross-referenced, one has to search thoroughly for specifics, and hope nothing is missed. And, the information does not take into account one's personal medical profile and medication history. ■ The CD-ROM has been designed to help the consumer find informed advice about personal medication. It is NOT a diagnostic tool. The intent is to combine the organizing and processing power of the computer with the technology of interactive multimedia to deliver valuable pharmaceutical information. ■ We did not try to re-format the pharmaceutical database into an alphabetic listing with a spiffy search and retrieval engine. Instead, we customized the information by incorporating the user's own medical profile in all searches and listings. The information found is personally relevant. The user can keep a running record of it, and develop a fairly extensive record of his or her medical history. So, usage became our organizing and access principle, rather than topic categories. One uses the CD to search drugs based on medical conditions, and on drug names, colors, shapes and sizes. ■ **CREDITS:** Creative Directors: Clement Mok, Carl Halverson; Designers: Clement Mok, Carl Halverson; Photography: CMCD Visual Symbol Library; Technical consultation by Bill Falke, M.D.

■ **THE MICROSOFT NETWORK (MSN)** is the centerpiece of Microsoft's first effort to position itself as a provider of on-line information services. CMd was engaged to create the first user interface. The assignment, though apparently simple, required an interdisciplinary approach to define and solve the entire problem. Not only was the user interface to be the navigational system of this service, the interface had to reflect the visual identity and personality of the service. More importantly, the design needed to create a sense of place for the user—a place where people

PLANNING A PERSONAL REFERENCE The pharmaceutical information on this CD-ROM can be organized by users. They can install their personal medical histories and search for relevant medicines based on their own profiles, or search by the name, color, shape, or size of a drug, or by treatment procedures. They also can check for a drug's interactions and its proper application.

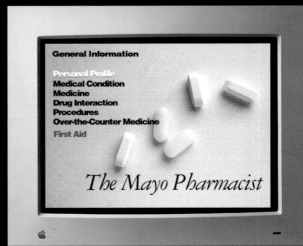

General Information

Personal Profile
Medical Condition
Medicine
Drug Interaction
Procedures
Over-the-Counter Medicine
First Aid

The Mayo Pharmacist

Medicine Search

Search Medicine by Characteristics

Color

Shape

Tablets
Capsules
Liquids

Size   mm
9

General Information · Personal Profile · Drug Interaction · Medicine · Medical Condition · Treatment Procedures · Over-the-Counter Medicine

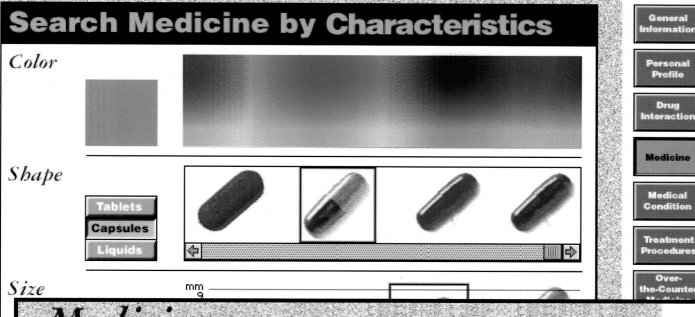

Medicines

Search By Name	USP: Nitroglycerin
Drug Picture	**Nitrobid**

Generic Name
Brand Name

2.5 mg

6.5 mg

9 mg

Brand Name: Nitroglycerine (sublingual)
Strength: 300 mcg
Dosage Form: Tablet   Use: Angina
Refills: 5   Quantity: 100
Instructions: One tablet under tongue

Nitroglycerin Tablets, USP (Sublingual)
Usual adult dose: Antianginal – Sublingual
or buccal, 150 to 600 mcg (0.15 to 0.6 mg)
repeated at five-minute intervals as needed
for reuef of angina attack.
Note: If relief is not otained after a total of
3 tablets used over a fifteen-minute period,
the physician should be contacted or the
patient taken to a hospital.
Note: If relief is not otained after a total of
the physician should be contacted or the

Brand Names	Proper Use
Description	Dosing
Before Using	Precautions
Age Group	Side Effects
Other Therapy	Additional Info

Previous Picture	Next Picture

Search by Name	Search by Characteristic	Drug Interactions

Sidebar buttons: General Information · Personal Profile · Medicines · Medical Conditions · Non-Prescription Medicines · Early Detection · First Aid

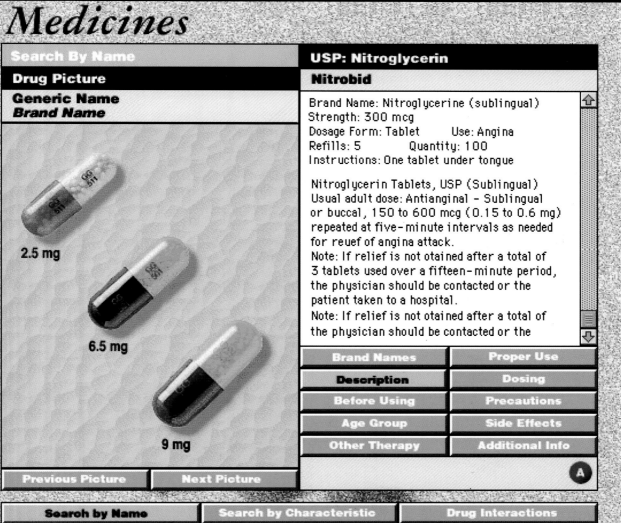

MICROSOFT INVITES YOU TO TRY:

msn.
The Microsoft Network

Just Click OK.

OK

Cancel

msn.

The Microsoft Network

Processor

RAM (MB rounded)   80486

CD-ROM installed   32

Hard disk size (MB rounded)   NO

                                    515

Note: The hard disk described is the drive on which
you are currently running Windows.

Do you want to send this information with your
registration?

<Back   ◆ Yes
Next>   ◇ No

Cancel

crosoft Network

matic Sign-In Next Tim

would want to visit again and again. ■ How do you create a system that accommodates all ages, nationalities and interests? A system that is simple and inviting for home users, while robust and serious enough to engage corporate audiences? In short, with an identity and design that encourages audience plurality as it provides information in depth. We found that photographs best supported such a rich, universal system. Too often, we regard them as elements of style, and not as effective ways to tackle complex information projects. But, properly selected pictures are visual symbols; they are quite adept at communicating tone and meaning. ■ **CREDITS:** Creative Director: Clement Mok; Information design: Lillian Svec; Interface design: Claire Barry; and Production: Paula Meiselman.

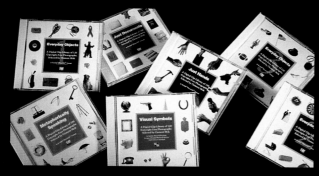

INVENTING ELECTRONIC IDENTITY The Microsoft Network (MSN) wanted to create an attractive screen identity for a new on-line information service that was to accommodate both home and corporate audiences. Photographs were used for their universal appeal, with imagery drawn from the CMCD Visual Symbol Library (above). CMCD, a sister company of CMd, has now published eight titles, each having 120 copyright-free images with clipping paths.

■ **COLLEGE VIEW** produces interactive reference systems that enable high-school students to review the curriculae and entry requirements for every college and university in the United States and Canada. They allow students to search for a college based on their interests, financial situation, religious affiliation, and locale. Students can store lists of choices as they search, or go directly into the interactive catalog of colleges they pick. They can even send an immediate request for application information by e-mail. ■ Structuring this information was an interesting challenge. Selection of a relevant interface model—folders, tabs, notebooks, and pads—was pivotal to the design because it had to accommodate many information organizations in the overview, or macro-level, as well as in the micro-level. The consistency of the model helps manage and update this massive data easily. Knowing a student's attention span may be rather limited, "video agents" are sprinkled throughout to perform help instructions and provide comic relief. ■ **CREDITS:** Art Director: Clement Mok; Designers: Clement Mok, Steve Simula; Illustrations: Steve Simula.

INVENTING ELECTRONIC PERSONALITY An interactive reference was produced to help high-school students review their college options. The introductory and location-search path (below), and the entire architecture of the program (following two pages) show the "video agents" sprinkled throughout to perform help instructions and provide some comic relief. The agents actively move around the screen to point out features of the information.

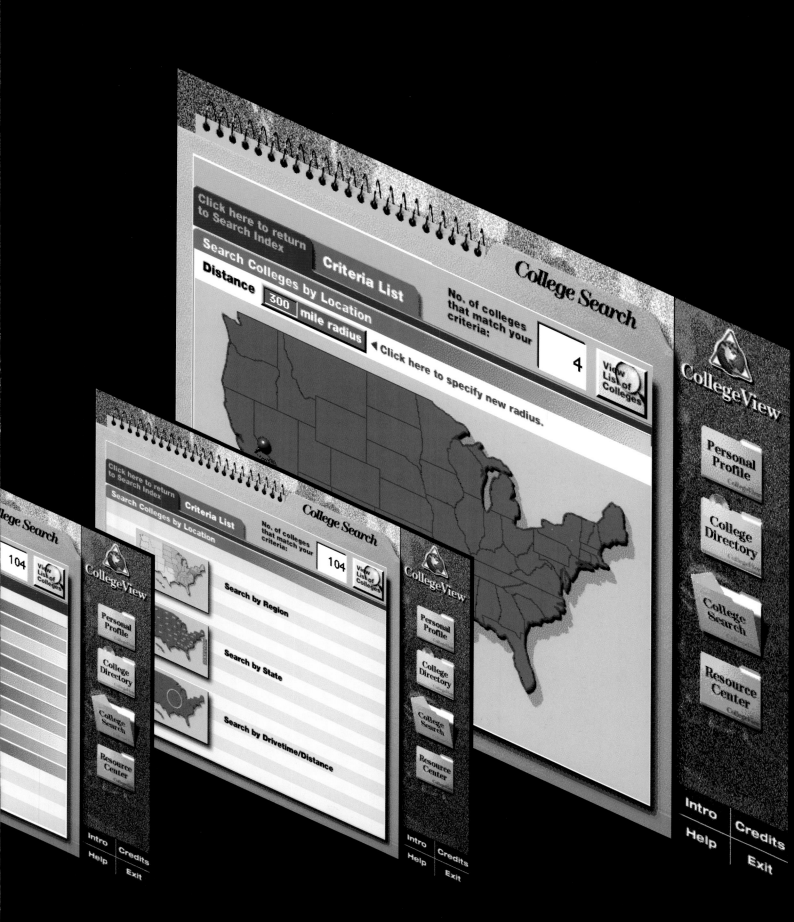

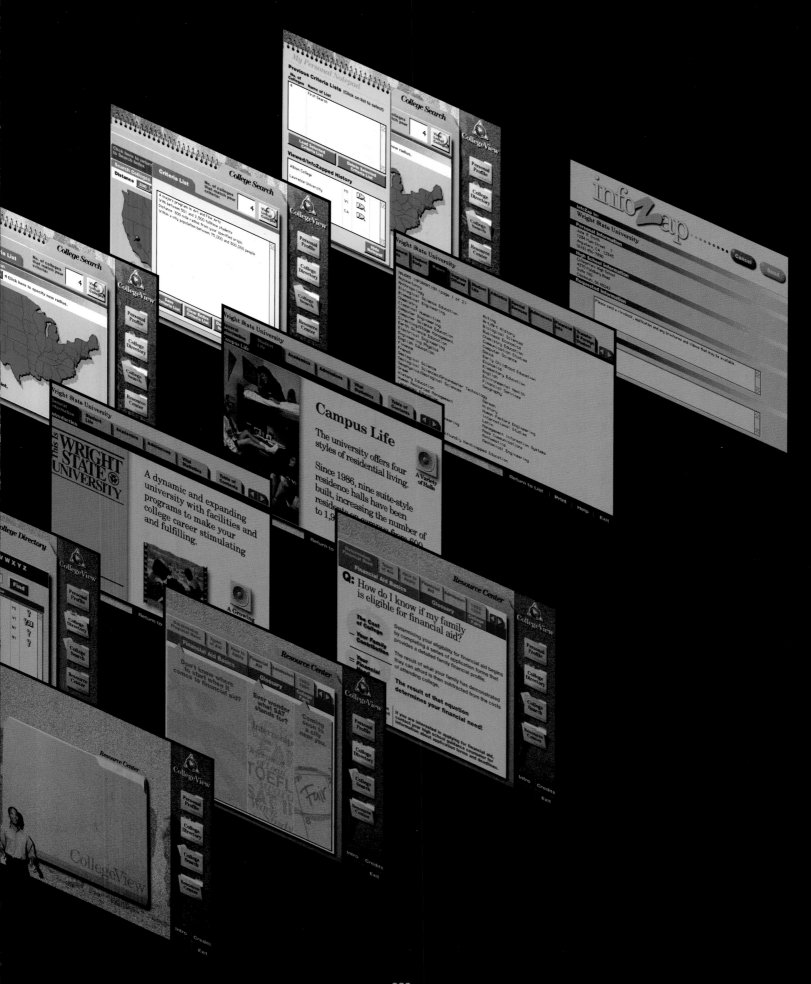

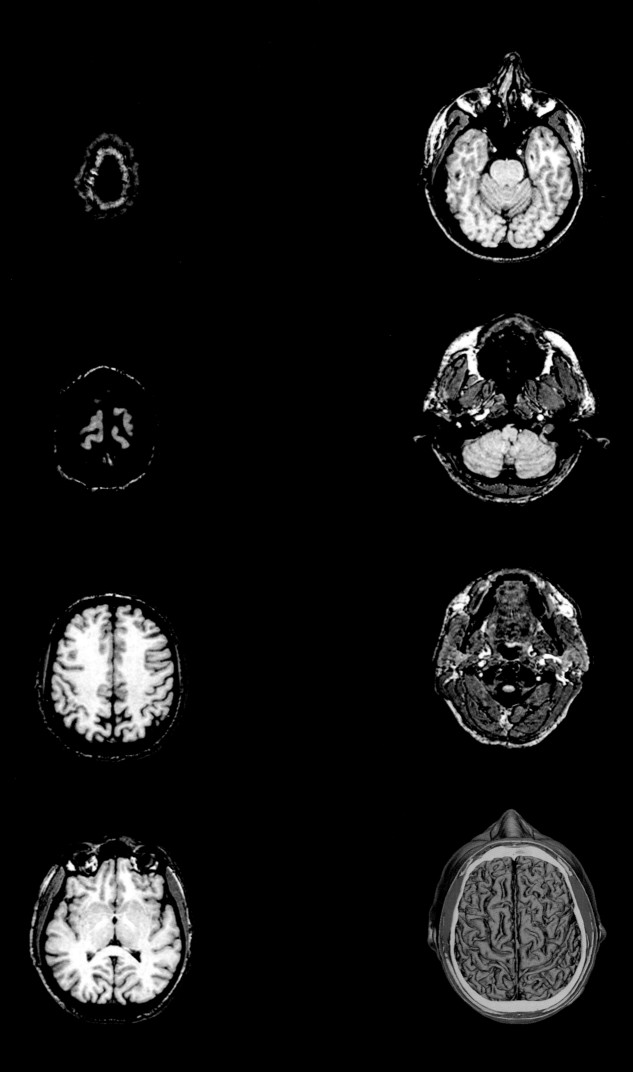

VOLUME RENDERING I relate radiologists to hermetic cubists and abstract expressionists. They are capable of creating or recognizing a whole from a section or a slice. They have the unique vision and educated talent to compile and interpolate in their minds a body part or entire body from a single body slice. ■ Surgeons are totally different creative creatures. I liken them to sculptors. Like sculptors, surgeons love the three-dimensional and the tactile. Therefore, when a radiologist shows a surgeon a complex series of two-dimensional images, he speaks in a language not absolutely familiar to the surgeon. The information should be assembled in three-dimensional images so that the surgeon sees it in a language familiar to his sensitivities and day-to-day work. This is where imaging techniques called volume rendering come in. Views of three-dimensional volumes are created by assembling two-dimensional slices of data. ■ With three-dimensional images, orthopedic surgeons can try different surgical approaches on a patient before entering the operating room. The images offer considerable assistance in repairing joints and bones disabled by

TRANSFORMING MEDICAL DATA Three-dimensional volumes are created from two-dimensional slices of data (opposite). The slices are compiled in order like slices in a loaf of bread. Types of tissue are identified according to density, then computer-enhanced.

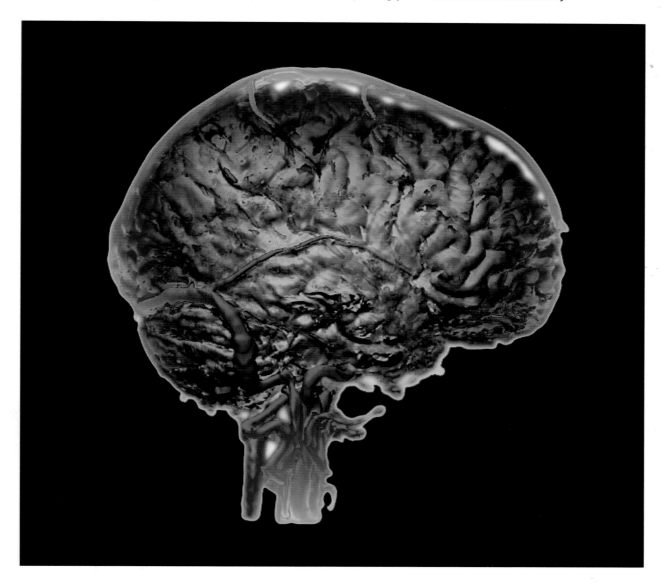

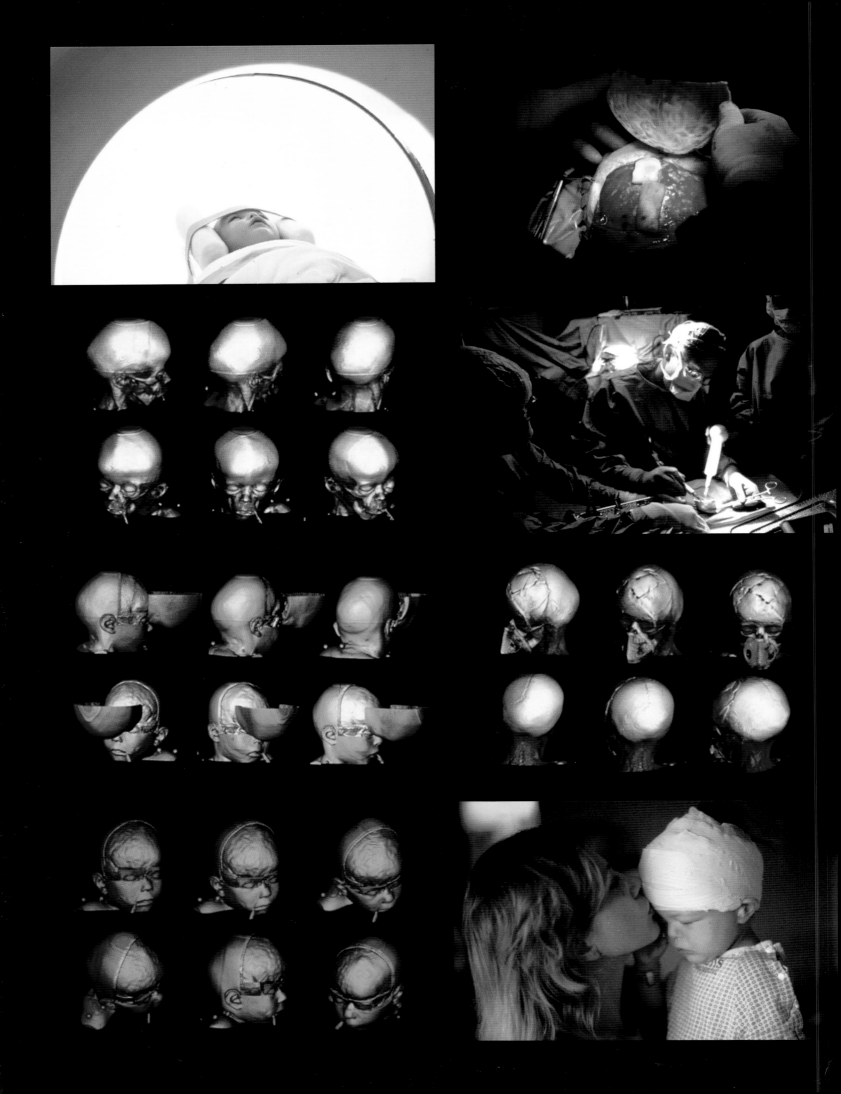

arthritis, injury or cancer, and they have revolutionized the design of artificial bone and prostheses. The image techniques are also extremely precise; they provide an accuracy that was impossible with older imaging methods. When cancer therapists project powerful beams of radiation to destroy tumors, a good aim is critical since healthy tissue can be blitzed as well. Therapists can now determine a tumor's precise shape, location and density, allowing the calculation of exact doses of radiation to penetrate it.

■ **CRANIAL FACIAL OPERATION** Surgeons say that before volume rendering, surgery was like walking into a dark room and feeling your way around the furniture. Now it's like walking into a room, turning on the lights, and seeing exactly where you're going. We use volume rendering techniques on a clinical level, both to simulate an operation and to help perform it. This happened in the case of a little girl whose skull had prematurely stopped developing. She was just short of being totally handicapped by the physical and psychological deformity, and she needed a cranial operation. ■ In all of us before birth, our ears are actually near the base of the shoulders migrating up, and our eyes are on the sides of the head migrating forward. Four plates in our heads shift like the continents. Unfortunately, sometimes the brain will form properly, and the eyes will be perfect, but the cranial facial structure alone stops growing. When it's extreme, you can spot it immediately and operate at birth, but often you can't. In the case of our little girl, one of her plates was sealed and there was no place for her brain to go. She could have become blind in one eye. ■ We wanted to visualize the operation in advance for the surgeon (opposite, left column). Rather than using two-dimensional imagery, we put the girl in a scanner and gave the surgeon a clear view of the muscle and bone in her skull. He could see the pressure on the orb of the eye, the part of the eye that had to be popped back out, and the part of the head that had to be made even again. We extrapolated the skin, segmenting it away from the bone so the surgeon could see where his first critical cuts would be. We provided a number of coordinates to give him the measurements he needed. As you can see the brain is exposed, so a neurosurgeon will be needed to carefully separate the skull from the dura so that the dura isn't penetrated. ■ After the simulation, I followed the surgery as it was performed to see if it was done according to plan (opposite, right column). Very similar to the simulation, the first cuts were made, the skull was lifted and sawed, according to the coordinates. (When the operation is done immediately after birth, the skull is as soft as cardboard and can be cut with scissors. But here, the girl is two years old and the surgery must be done with saws.) ■ It was a severe operation and the planning was crucial. But because of this technology, the time of the operation was cut by half, four hours instead of eight. Now the head is nice and round, once again there's room for the brain to grow. The child didn't have to go to intensive care, she went immediately to her room with her mother. Two weeks later, we put the little girl back into the scanner to make sure the sutures were healing properly. Two months after that, I followed her home to the Ozarks to see

PLANNING AN OPERATION The first column of images (opposite, left) uses CT scans to simulate a cranial operation on a severely handicapped child. The second column follows the performing of the operation and shows the healthy results (see text).

how she was doing. You see she's healing very nicely. Then four months later, I visited her again and she was perfectly healthy.

■ **THE SCIENCE OF RADIATION SCANNING** The visualization of medical data is not very different from the visualization of most datas acquired from energy. In the case of electron microscopy, magnetic fields focus a beam of electrons into a vacuum tube which contains the specimen. In geology, explosions are set off around a geographic area and slices of the earth are recorded from seismographic resonances. ■ In the case of CT scanning (computerized Axial Tomography), the energy of a rotating X-ray beam is used, and the radiation is detected by a receiver on the other side of the body. Theoretically, if the body were transparent (without mass), beams would pass through the body unchanged; in actuality, some rays in the beam are absorbed depending upon the density of the tissue. In the end, whatever radiation passes through is recorded and we have a picture of a single slab of tissue. ■ The process is repeated sequentially so that a series of images of adjacent planes throughout the body is produced. Then they are compiled in a volume like the slices in a loaf of bread. With three-dimensional or Multi-Planar Reconstruction you can travel through the loaf (body), viewing it vertically, horizontally, or obliquely, and use a variety of tools to isolate the seeds (tumors), or see just the crust (skin). ■ The image shown (following page) is a three-dimensional rendering of a spiral CT scan of myself. I've thelshed my softer body parts (removed certain tissue types of a particular density like skin, muscle, and cartilage) to leave only the bone. To enhance the bone I've attenuated the lighting, using ray tracing (light absorbed or reflected by materials) and four light sources to dramatize the image in a chiaroscuro effect. Such a technique is used by orthopedic surgeons to reveal stress fractures to bone, principally in the foot and hand. Such slight lines in the bone are usually very hard to interpret without techniques that highlight the thin fractures. In this specific image, I am concentrating on enhancing the seven bones of the orbs of the eyes. ■ Tissue detail in a CT scan can be manipulated according to its density. The density is calibrated in a measurement system called Hounsfield Units (there are 4000 possible HUs) by putting a water phantom into the CT scanner. Water is calibrated at zero HU and shows up as a darkish gray, while air, not an obstacle to the x-ray's energy, is darkest, or pure black without detail. Teeth show white because they are dense and absorb the greatest amount of light. Computer segmentation tools can automatically remove tissue or body parts of specified densities. Through windowing, a physician can assign any variation of black, gray, and white tones to any portion of the density scale to emphasize tissues of particular interest. ■ **THE SCIENCE OF MAGNETIC FIELD SCANNING** MRI (Magnetic Resonance Imaging) uses magnetic fields and weak pulses of radio waves to detect the distribution of hydrogen atoms in the body. The subject is placed in a very strong magnetic field, causing the proton of each hydrogen atom to line up with other protons in one direction. The effect is similar to the way in which a compass needle aligns with a magnetic field. The protons are exposed to brief pulses of waves. When the radio pulses stop, the protons re-align with the magnetic field, producing energy in the process. In essence, our water is relaxed, the relaxing produces energy, and that energy is picked up by detectors.

REFINING MEDICAL DATA As three-dimensional image techniques grow more sophisticated, more refined tissue detail can be revealed. Our cellular and molecular structures can be explored— perhaps even viruses and deposits in the body that signal cancer.

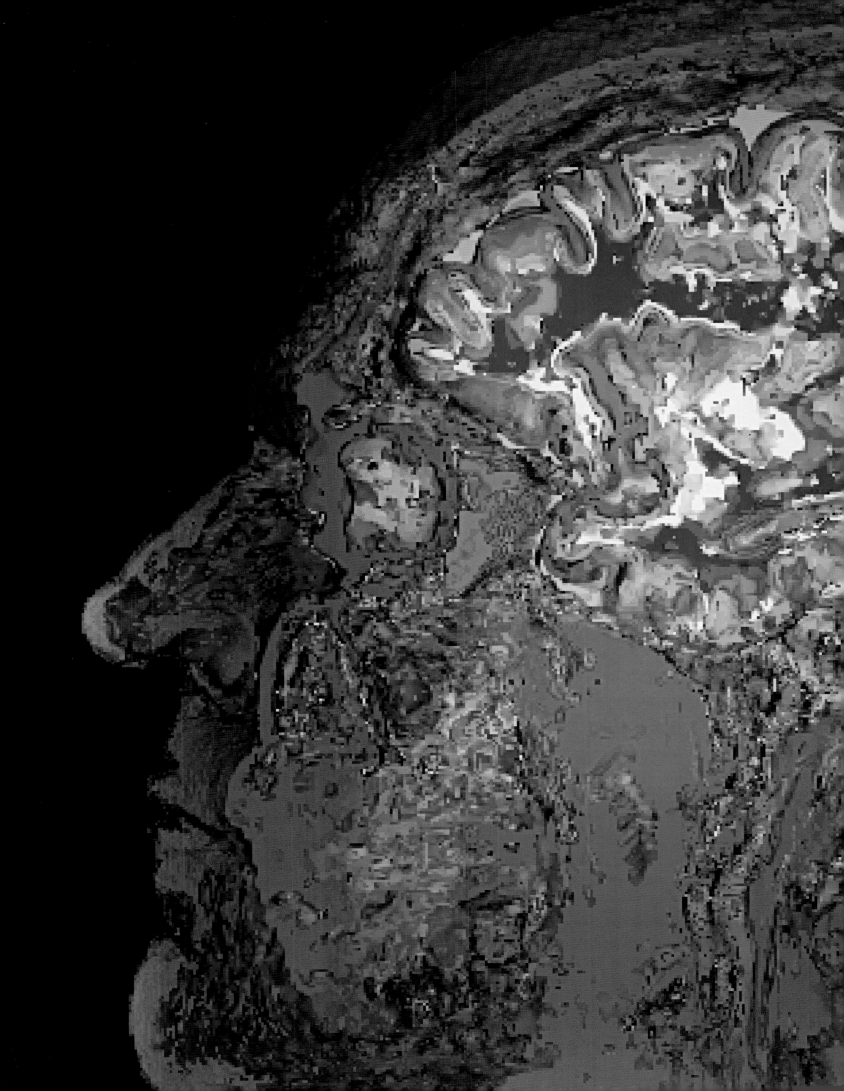

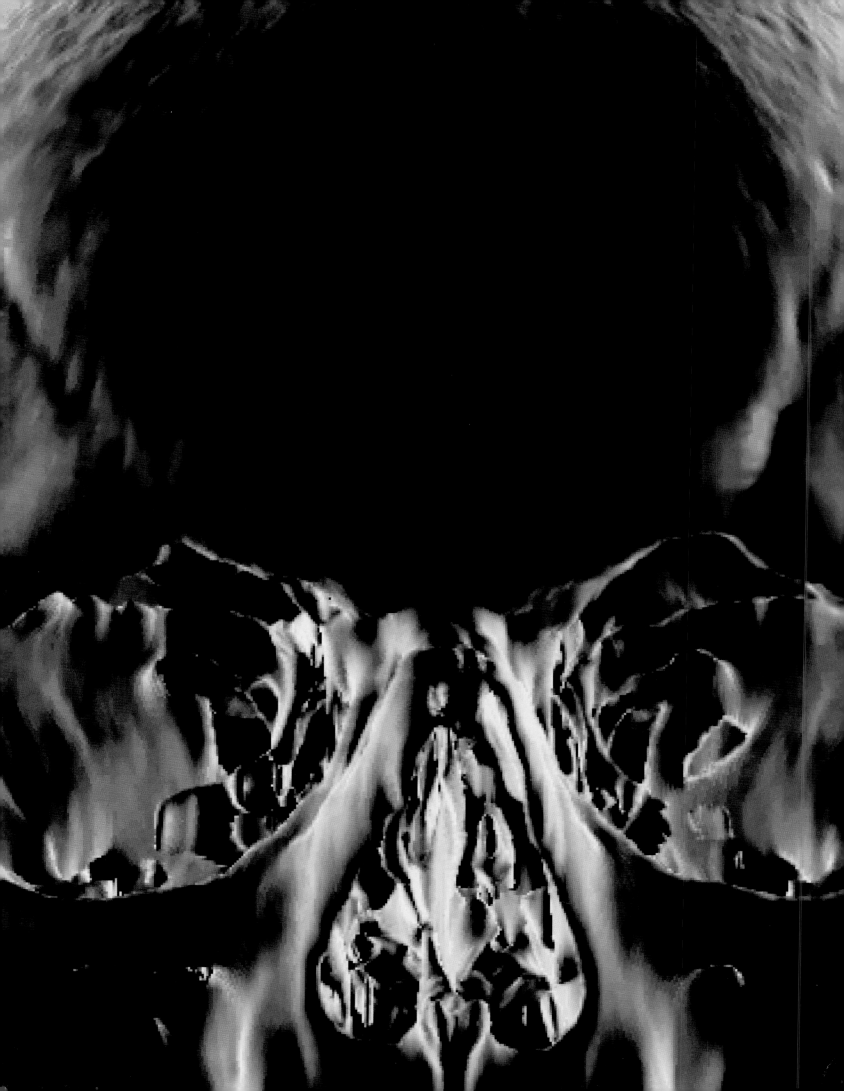

■ **CT VERSUS MRI SCANS**   People are always wondering about the difference between CT and MRI scans, and why one would be used instead of the other. If comparative shopping is important to you, CT scanning is faster and cheaper than MRI. CT offers higher resolution bone-scan detail, especially within the head, neck and spine. MRI is poor to worthless in the imaging of bone, but because of its sensitivity to subtle changes in water content, it more reliably detects soft tissue disease. MRI uses no radiation and is therefore physically non-invasive. Also, In the case of detecting multiple sclerosis, MRI is way ahead with an 80% success rate, while CT has an approximate 20% success rate. In the end, when I want soft tissue I use MRI, and when I want hard tissue, I look for a solid dose of radiation. Um, Umm! I think it's probably best to ask your doctor. ■ **CELLULAR AND MOLECULAR VISUALIZATION**   Three-dimensional visualization is somewhat confined to larger anatomical data like lungs, head and pelvis. But as dramatic as that is, it is well understood that fundamental answers in

SEPARATING MEDICAL DATA To reveal slight fractures in bones, CT scans manipulate and remove soft tissue according to density (opposite). They offer higher resolution bone detail, while MRI scans more reliably detect soft tissue (below, left and right).

medicine will be found in the small cellular, and even the smaller molecular data. For example, it might be possible to apply

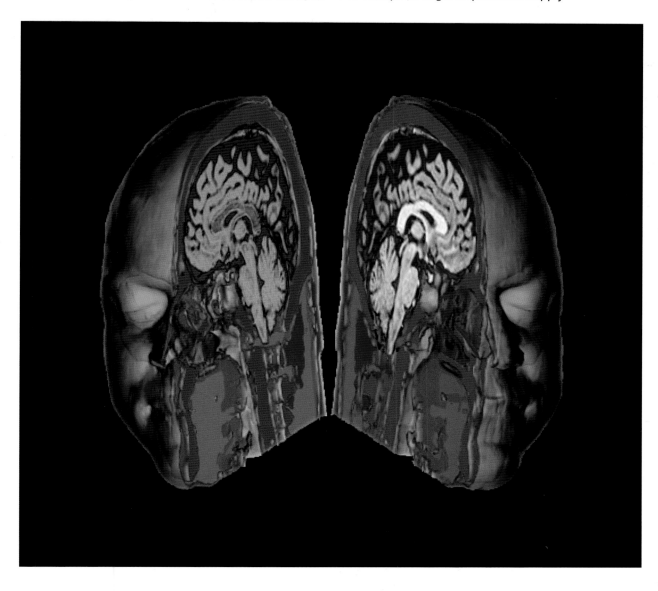

these visualization tools to a single red blood cell of an Olympic marathon runner. It is quite feasible that we can travel through his blood, measure its hemoglobin, and calculate if the runner is a better oxygenator than say, a couch potato. Or, on an even smaller level, we can pass through the ever-mutating molecular structure of an AIDS virus. ■ We can also start introducing more dimensions to investigate data; we can use four, five, or even six dimensions. In gross anatomy, we use x-y-z coordinates for the dimensions of height, width, and depth. The fourth dimension would be time, and the fifth and sixth dimensions would be elements. For example, breast and lung cancer start as calcium deposits imperceptible to the eye. If patients could be scanned for the data, early signs of the disease might be detected. As we become more familiar with norms and irregularities, new algorithms can be written to automatically detect abnormalities and picture even the smallest ones. ■ **BEAUTIFUL SCIENCE** Science visionaries are quite close to art visionaries. But it appears that the twain shall never meet. Although we have a long history of beautiful science and anatomical art by such notables as DaVinci, Dürer, Vesalius, and Rembrandt, the science and art communities remain and see their work as separate. ■ In the case of scientists, I believe that once they have enough visual data to conclude their studies, they pull the plug and stop massaging the data. Of course, this massaging can be more time consuming than the science itself, and is often more costly in terms of software, equipment, and memory. Sometimes scientists don't have the aesthetic touch, sometimes they just don't care. Whatever the reason, their work provides a small community with valuable information, but usually ignores the larger community—the one that would be attracted to and study the information if it was aesthetically presented. ■ Visualized science is often the beginning of an art form. Rembrandt's paintings of surgery and Goya's "Disasters Of War" are two sets of explicit images which would be difficult to view in lesser hands. I firmly believe that if DaVinci were alive today, he would be hummed to sleep each evening by the whirring fans of a workstation. He would embrace the probability that the next generation of great anatomical rendering would be computer-generated. He would ask why there is no compelling scientific imagery when the entertainment industry, using the same algorithms, has produced extraordinary computer graphics. He would then, like myself, study that industry, and proceed to steal as many ideas as possible to claim as his own. ■ Actually, there are ideas to borrow from everywhere. For example, studies show that an object of one color has many different color tones and textures. Paintings by the Impressionists exemplify this. But, when we look at our patients in RGB space in one color, they look as if they are dead. Therefore, we must use tools to enhance color with subtle variations—without unduly influencing the clinical data. Science can be art without sacrificing its critical information. ■ After all the research and number crunching, after having myself irradiated, after thousands of hours in front of a CRT, after reading thousands of pages in science journals—in the end, I probably will be remembered by a single one of my most strange images, which I saw on a van once as it drove by me on its way to a Grateful Dead concert.

TRANSFORMING SCIENCE TO ART Visualizations of medical data can be extraordinarily provocative. Entering the human lung, travelling closer, then entering the enhanced tissue of its walls reveals body landscapes that defy the imagination (following page).

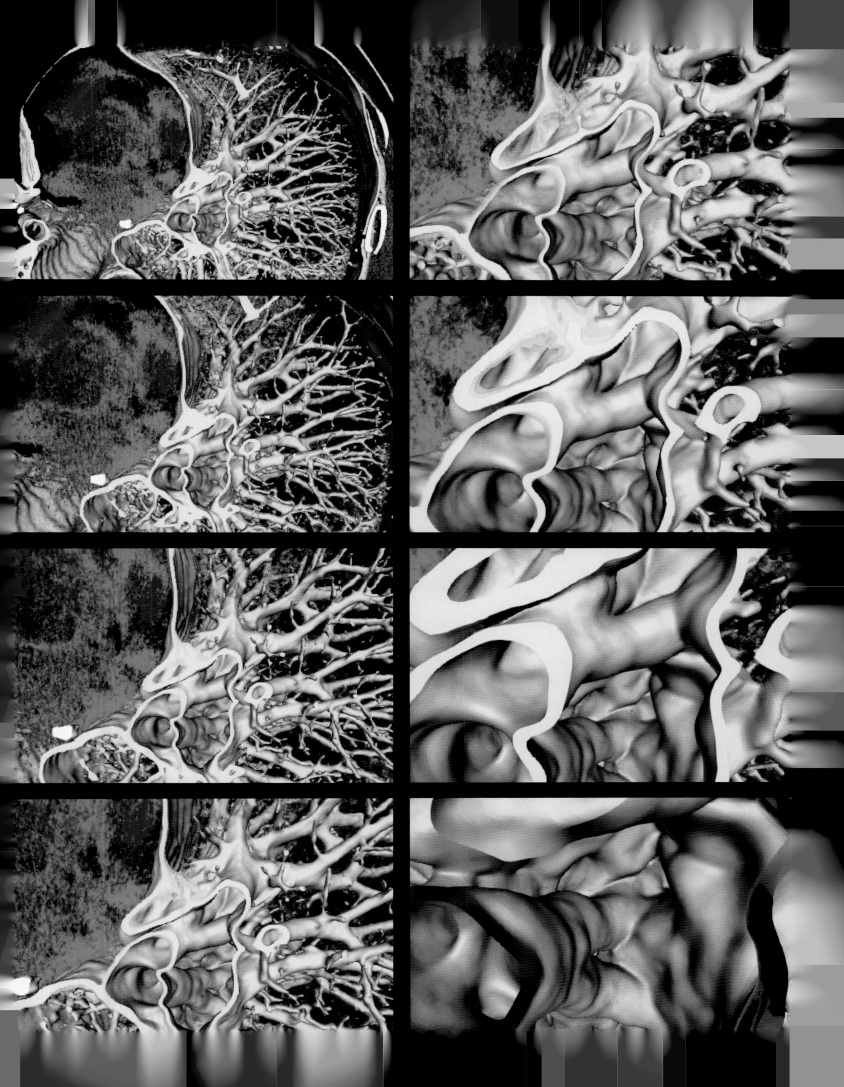

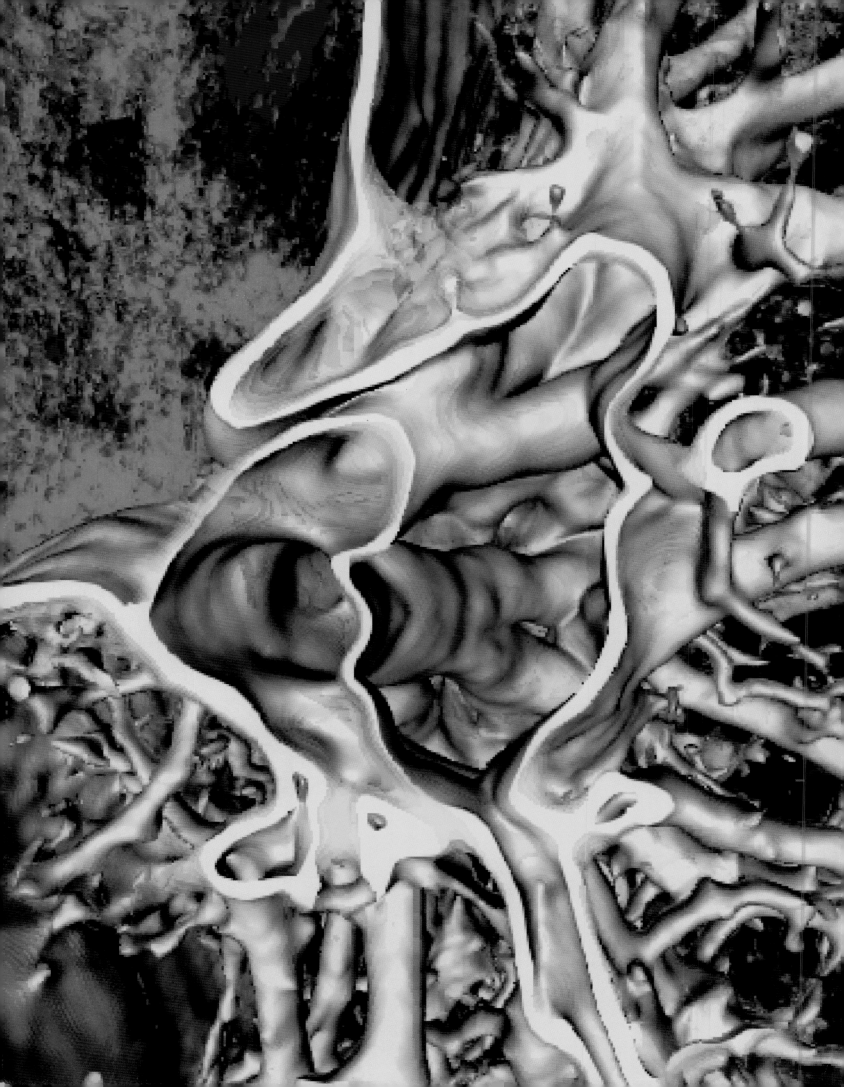

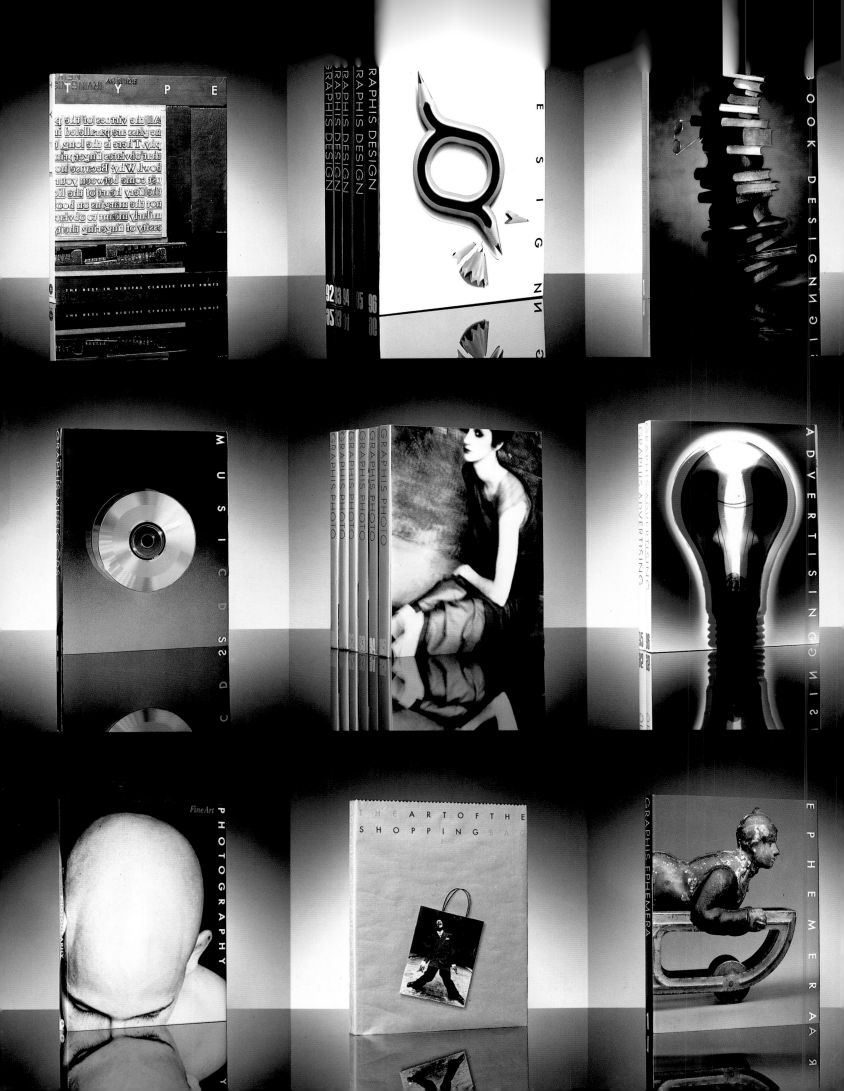

BOOK ORDER FORM: USA, CANADA, SOUTH AMERICA, ASIA, PACIFIC

BOOKS		ALL REGIONS
☐ GRAPHIS ADVERTISING 96	US$	69.95
☐ GRAPHIS ALTERNATIVE PHOTOGRAPHY 95	US$	69.95
☐ GRAPHIS ANNUAL REPORTS 4	US$	69.95
☐ GRAPHIS BOOK DESIGN	US$	75.95
☐ GRAPHIS CORPORATE IDENTITY 2	US$	75.95
☐ GRAPHIS DESIGN 96	US$	69.95
☐ GRAPHIS EPHEMERA	US$	75.95
☐ GRAPHIS FINE ART PHOTOGRAPHY	US$	85.00
☐ GRAPHIS INFORMATION ARCHITECTS	US$	69.95
☐ GRAPHIS MUSIC CDS	US$	75.95
☐ GRAPHIS NUDES	US$	89.95
☐ GRAPHIS PHOTO 95	US$	69.95
☐ GRAPHIS POSTER 95	US$	69.95
☐ GRAPHIS PRODUCTS BY DESIGN	US$	69.95
☐ GRAPHIS SHOPPING BAGS	US$	69.95
☐ GRAPHIS TYPOGRAPHY 1	US$	69.95
☐ GRAPHIS TYPE SPECIMENS	US$	49.95
☐ **GRAPHIS PAPER SPECIFIER SYSTEM (GPS)**	US$	395.00

** ADD $30 SHIPPING/HANDLING FOR GPS; AFTER DEC. 1, 1995, GPS IS $495.00

NOTE! NY RESIDENTS ADD 8.25% SALES TAX

☐ CHECK ENCLOSED (PAYABLE TO GRAPHIS)
  (US$ ONLY, DRAWN ON A BANK IN THE USA)

USE CREDIT CARDS (DEBITED IN US DOLLARS)

☐ AMERICAN EXPRESS   ☐ MASTERCARD   ☐ VISA

CARD NO. _____ EXP. DATE _____

CARDHOLDER NAME _____

SIGNATURE _____

(PLEASE PRINT)

NAME _____

TITLE _____

COMPANY _____

ADDRESS _____

CITY _____

STATE/PROVINCE _____ ZIP CODE ____

COUNTRY _____

SEND ORDER FORM AND MAKE CHECK PAYABLE TO:
GRAPHIS US, INC.,
141 LEXINGTON AVENUE, NEW YORK, NY 10016-8193, USA

BOOK ORDER FORM: EUROPE, AFRICA, MIDDLE EAST

BOOKS	EUROPE/AFRICA MIDDLE EAST	GERMANY	U.K.
☐ GRAPHIS ADVERTISING 96	SFR. 123.–	DM 149,–	£ 52.00
☐ GRAPHIS ALTERNATIVE PHOTO 95	SFR. 123.–	DM 149,–	£ 52.00
☐ GRAPHIS ANNUAL REPORTS 4	SFR. 137.–	DM 162,–	£ 55.00
☐ GRAPHIS BOOK DESIGN	SFR. 137.–	DM 162,–	£ 55.00
☐ GRAPHIS CORPORATE IDENTITY 2	SFR. 137.–	DM 162,–	£ 55.00
☐ GRAPHIS DESIGN 96	SFR. 123.–	DM 149,–	£ 52.00
☐ GRAPHIS EPHEMERA	SFR. 137.–	DM 162,–	£ 55.00
☐ GRAPHIS FINE ART PHOTOGRAPHY	SFR. 128.–	DM 155,–	£ 69.00
☐ GRAPHIS INFORMATION ARCHITECTS	SFR. 123.–	DM 149,–	£ 52.00
☐ GRAPHIS MUSIC CDS	SFR. 137.–	DM 162,–	£ 55.00
☐ GRAPHIS NUDES	SFR. 168.–	DM 168,–	£ 62.00
☐ GRAPHIS PHOTO 95	SFR. 123.–	DM 149,–	£ 52.00
☐ GRAPHIS POSTER 95	SFR. 123.–	DM 149,–	£ 52.00
☐ GRAPHIS PRODUCTS BY DESIGN	SFR. 123.–	DM 149,–	£ 52.00
☐ GRAPHIS SHOPPING BAGS	SFR. 123.–	DM 149,–	£ 52.00
☐ GRAPHIS TYPOGRAPHY 1	SFR. 137.–	DM 162,–	£ 55.00
☐ GRAPHIS TYPE SPECIMENS	SFR. 75.–	DM 89,–	£ 37.00

(FOR ORDERS FROM EC COUNTRIES V.A.T. WILL BE CHARGED IN ADDITION TO ABOVE BOOK PRICES)

FOR CREDIT CARD PAYMENT (DEBITED IN SWISS FRANCS):
☐ AMERICAN EXPRESS   ☐ DINER'S CLUB
☐ VISA/BARCLAYCARD/CARTE BLEUE

CARD NO. _____ EXP. DATE _____

CARDHOLDER NAME _____

SIGNATURE _____

☐ PLEASE BILL ME (ADDITIONAL MAILING COSTS WILL BE CHARGED)

(PLEASE PRINT)

LAST NAME _____ FIRST NAME _____

TITLE _____

COMPANY _____

ADDRESS _____

CITY _____ POSTAL CODE _____

COUNTRY _____

PLEASE SEND ORDER FORM TO:
GRAPHIS PRESS CORP.
DUFOURSTRASSE 107, CH–8008 ZÜRICH, SWITZERLAND

GRAPHIS MAGAZINE

SUBSCRIBE TO GRAPHIS: USA, CANADA, SOUTH AMERICA, ASIA

MAGAZINE	USA	CANADA	SOUTHAMERICA/ ASIA/PACIFIC
☐ ONE YEAR (6 ISSUES)	US$ 89.00	US$ 99.00	US$ 125.00
☐ TWO YEARS (12 ISSUES)	US$ 159.00	US$ 179.00	US$ 235.00
☐ AIRMAIL SURCHARGE (6 ISSUES)	US$ 59.00	US$ 59.00	US$ 59.00

☐ 25% DISCOUNT FOR STUDENTS WITH COPY OF VALID, DATED STUDENT ID AND PAYMENT WITH ORDER

☐ CHECK ENCLOSED

USE CREDIT CARDS (DEBITED IN US DOLLARS)

☐ AMERICAN EXPRESS

☐ MASTERCARD

☐ VISA

CARD NO.   EXP. DATE

CARDHOLDER NAME

SIGNATURE

☐ PLEASE BILL ME

(PLEASE PRINT)

NAME

TITLE

COMPANY

ADDRESS

CITY

STATE/PROVINCE   ZIP CODE

COUNTRY

SEND ORDER FORM AND MAKE CHECK PAYABLE TO:
GRAPHIS US, INC.,
141 LEXINGTON AVENUE,
NEW YORK, NY 10016-8193, USA

SERVICE BEGINS WITH ISSUE THAT IS CURRENT WHEN
ORDER IS PROCESSED.   (C9B0A)

SUBSCRIBE TO GRAPHIS: EUROPE, AFRICA, MIDDLE EAST

MAGAZINE	EUROPE/AFRICA MIDDLE EAST	GERMANY	U.K.
☐ ONE YEAR (6 ISSUES)	SFR. 164.–	DM 190,–	£ 68.00
☐ TWO YEARS (12 ISSUES)	SFR. 295.–	DM 342,–	£ 122.00
☐ AIRMAIL SURCHARGES	SFR 65.–	DM 75,–	£ 30.00
☐ REGISTERED MAIL	SFR 20.–	DM 24,–	£ 9.00

☐ CHECK ENCLOSED (PLEASE MAKE SFR.–CHECK PAYABLE TO A SWISS BANK)

☐ STUDENTS MAY REQUEST A 25% DISCOUNT BY SENDING STUDENT ID

FOR CREDIT CARD PAYMENT (ALL CARDS DEBITED IN SWISS FRANCS):

☐ AMERICAN EXPRESS   ☐ DINER'S CLUB

☐ VISA/BARCLAYCARD/CARTE BLEUE

CARD NO.   EXP. DATE

CARDHOLDER NAME

SIGNATURE

☐ PLEASE BILL ME

(PLEASE PRINT)

LAST NAME

FIRST NAME

TITLE

COMPANY

ADDRESS

CITY   POSTAL CODE

COUNTRY

NOTE TO GERMAN SUBSCRIBERS ONLY:
ICH ERKLÄRE MICH EINVERSTANDEN, DASS MEINE NEUE
ADRESSE DURCH DIE POST AN DEN VERTRIEB WEITERGELEITET
WIRD.

PLEASE SEND ORDER FORM AND MAKE CHECK PAYABLE TO:
GRAPHIS PRESS CORP.
DUFOURSTRASSE 107
CH–8008 ZÜRICH, SWITZERLAND

SERVICE BEGINS WITH ISSUE THAT IS CURRENT WHEN
ORDER IS PROCESSED.   (C9B0A)

INVENTING POINT OF VIEW In *The Amazing Brain*, a book illustrated by David Macaulay (see pages 54 to 61), the brain was imagined as a city museum. Its exterior architecture (early sketch above) and construction are shown, then views of the skull's interior with visitors wandering around and looking at the internal workings.